*Shrubs
in
the
Landscape*

McGraw-Hill Series in
LANDSCAPE AND LANDSCAPE ARCHITECTURE

Albert Fein, Ph.D., A.S.L.A.(hon.)   *Consulting Editor*

Shrubs in the Landscape

Joseph Hudak

McGraw-Hill Book Company

New York St. Louis San Francisco Auckland Bogotá
Hamburg Johannesburg London Madrid
Mexico Montreal New Delhi Panama
Paris São Paulo Singapore
Sydney Tokyo Toronto

Library of Congress Cataloging in Publication Data

Hudak, Joseph.
    Shrubs in the landscape.

    Bibliography: p.
    Includes index.
    1. Ornamental shrubs.   2. Landscape gardening.
3. Landscape architecture.   4. Ornamental shrubs—United
States.   5. Ornamental shrubs—Canada.   I. Title.
SB435.H838 1984   635.9′76   84-4345
ISBN 0-07-030842-X

2 3 4 5 6 7 8 9 0   HAL/HAL   8 9 8 7 6 5

ISBN 0-07-030842-X

*The editors for this book were Joan Zseleczky and Georgia Kornbluth,
the designer was Naomi Auerbach, and the production
supervisor was Thomas G. Kowalczyk. It was set in Caledonia
by University Graphics, Inc.*

Printed and bound by Halliday Lithograph.

This book is dedicated to all who enjoy shrubs and especially to my parents

Contents

Both evergreen and deciduous shrubs contribute important elements
of silhouette, color, and texture to landscape designs.

Preface

This book is primarily concerned with the ornamental attractions of shrubs in the landscape and the proper handling of them for practical and aesthetic satisfaction throughout the United States and the lower part of Canada.

A shrub is classified botanically as a woody perennial with several main stems coming from a common point at ground level and also as being shorter than a tree. Nature does not arrange plants conveniently to tell us this, and many authorities are still debating whether the criterion of size helps or hinders our way of defining plant types. I have chosen a well-liked system to separate trees from shrubs mainly by their natural silhouettes and growth habits. Trees, then, usually are found in nature as single-trunked plants with a potential for great height and spread along with hefty trunks and branches. Shrubs, on the other hand, are considered woody plants with a *multiplicity of equal-sized main stems* coming from a common root system and having a generally meandering habit closer to human eye level. Think of shrubs as similar to the fingers of your hand as they connect with the wrist; picture trees as your arm outstretched above your head with the spread fingers translated to branches at a far higher distance. The silhouette comparison should be readily apparent, and while there are some treelike shrubs and shrublike trees in the world, the majority of plants called shrubs or trees will maintain their essential differences of growth habits.

Although there is no final count of shrubs, the current tally stretches to many tens of thousands and is longer than the list of known tree types. Diversity has always been a hallmark of shrubs, and there is a wide selection of both evergreen and deciduous kinds available worldwide. This broad spectrum of shrubs offers unique advantages: relatively faster growth than trees (since the water-supply roots are closer to the expanding stems and leaves), lowered cost compared with trees of the same age, and perhaps more consistently showy and wider-ranging colorings from the flowers, foliage, and fruit than exist in trees. Selected to act as freestanding specimens or massed in borders for a solid effect, shrubs can contribute admirable design strengths of form, texture, color, fragrance, and multiseason interest while also solving site problems of shade, erosion, screening, wind and sun control, noise, and animal intrusion. That shrubs can be both attractive and functional causes them to rate high in value for any landscape setting.

The motivating objectives of this book were several: to select only shrubs with a large number of desirable features, to include representative examples for all the hardiness zones across the United States and southern Canada, to list the superior types cultivated today in commercial nurseries, and to identify those shrubs with a relative freedom from important diseases and insect pests that makes them especially low in maintenance needs. Thus, this book highlights shrubs which have wide appeal, adaptability, and availability. Some shrubs with good qualities and easy growth have been omitted because of their narrow geographic range for successful cultivation or because their availability to nurseries from seeds or tiny rooted cuttings is limited.

The selections in this book represent the author's personal experience with shrubs over a 30-year span of design practice in many parts of the United States and Canada, in addition to the expressed satisfaction of clients and growers with particular shrubs. Both the professionally trained landscape designer and the amateur will find this book usefully reliable and comprehensive enough for many planting decisions that involve shrubs.

Joseph Hudak

P lants expand from a complex and remarkable interaction of their roots, stems, and leaves. No part is more important than any other, but damage to one can lead to a loss of vigor or function in the other two. Although plants certainly produce flowers as well, these specialized parts are unique and serve a separate reproductive function not directly related to the needs of the other growth elements. Any plant can develop effectively before flowering, but a plant cannot maintain its full health after any severe loss of roots, stems, or leaves during its active growing season.

Roots

Roots are usually hidden in the earth and have several important life functions: absorbing dissolved minerals and water from the soil, anchoring the plant against the stress and strain of wind thrusts, storing essential nutrients for later use, and serving as a possible reproduction mechanism of the plant. Contrary to a long-held belief, plant roots do not often penetrate very deep since there is little of the essential oxygen or water available for growth beyond the first 5 feet of soil depth. While there are a few exceptions to this generalization, most plants keep their major roots in the favorable upper soil layer, thereby making digging them up for transplanting both economically feasible and horticulturally safe.

The two main root types are *tap* and *fibrous*. Occasionally you will find plants with a combination of deep-searching taproots and a thin mat of fibrous rooting; these are called *semitaprooted*. A true taprooted plant has a deep, downward-reaching, and thick set of main roots with only a few lateral branchings close to the surface (mainly for anchoring). The pursuit of water in lower soil levels provides these plants with a substantial edge in times of drought, but such shrubs are usually difficult to transplant easily except when quite young since almost 100 percent of the taprooting must be collected if the plant is to survive. Of necessity, the dug root ball is a narrowly tapered one. Because there is less root volume than on

Shrubs can adjust well to growing near deep-rooted trees since most have shallow surface rooting.

a fibrous-rooted shrub, recovery after transplanting is often sluggish, and overwatering can become a hazard.

Fortunately, the majority of shrubs have crisscrossing layers of shallow, fibrous roots and will transplant much more simply and easily. Here the dense network of roots generally is set in a regular pattern about the stems and extends at least to the tip spread of the branches and twigs. However, the roots can stretch well beyond this area to a point called the *drip line,* where rainfall sheds abundantly from the foliage and branch ends to the concentrated root system beneath. These horizontal, much divided, finely elongated roots are normally found within the first foot or so of the surface in the humus-filled, loose part of the upper soil, allowing the plant to gain the most water accumulation from rain or irrigation quickly. Below them develop the heavier anchor roots.

These surface feeding roots can be hampered severely in their important functions by soil compaction created when heavy equipment or concentrated foot traffic consistently passes over them. Because they are geared to collecting oxygen from air in the soil, they also react poorly to having deep fill suddenly deposited on them, especially clay or silt types that retain great quantities of surface water and drain poorly, making themselves and the soil beneath oxygen-deficient. Roots have to roam freely in search of food and water and must maintain a free interchange of oxygen with the soil or they will be severely handicapped. For these reasons roots do not enjoy being replanted at a depth lower than that at which they were originally growing or being installed in waterlogged, contaminated, or hardpan soils.

It may be surprising to learn that only the minute, growing tip of a root absorbs water and nutrients from the soil and that the older root structures act mainly as food and water conductors as well as underground supports for the stems and branches. This amazing system of absorption at the root tip is handled by a vast number of microscopic *root hairs* with a capacity to increase the water intake of a root many hundreds of times. Root hairs have only brief life spans, but they are replenished constantly as the entire root system expands during the growing season. This replacement factor answers the question of how shrubs in active growth can take up all the water they need; it also shows how they manage to repair the shock damage of severed roots as a result of either transplanting or invasive construction activity in their root zone.

Roots continue to expand in temperature climates as long as the soil—not the air—temperature remains above freezing. When the earth does freeze for a prolonged time, all root activity slows appreciably and the shrub enters a period of rest called *dormancy,* which is also a reliable time for safe transplanting if the weather allows. In temperate zones this dormant season usually arrives by late autumn and continues until early spring. With many needled evergreens, however, the start of dormancy often occurs in late summer, allowing a longer period for transplanting activities. Whether late autumn or early spring is the better moving time for shrubs varies with the locale and with personal experience, including that of nurseries and contractors. Foliage damage to deciduous plants is obviously less of a bother in autumn as leaves begin to drop, but springtime is often a hectic, unreliable time in terms of consistently rising temperatures or ground thaw. In any event, the plant will attempt cooperation with any transplanting schedule.

Subtropical and tropical plants also pause, but their resting cycle is far shorter, and moving them is often best accomplished when it coincides with the start of the normal rainy season, both to gain the extra moisture and to shield the foliage and stems from excessive, bright sunlight while they adjust. Even in temperate areas, full-foliaged deciduous shrubs can be transplanted during summer with reasonable success by competent professionals, but this abnormal scheduling is not

Transplanting is better handled during either early spring or late autumn dormancy in temperate growing areas.

Nurseries today offer either plastic-containerized or balled-and-burlapped plants.

preferred since known chemical changes can occur in many plant types if the aftercare maintenance should be mishandled during that time. For your investment and peace of mind, using dormant planting times is still the recommended approach.

Since exposure to air, wind, and bright sunlight dries out dug roots quickly, always avoid delays in completing the transplanting work and always shield the fragile, exposed roots adequately with moist coverings while they are out of the ground. Although young deciduous shrubs can often be dug and handled as *bare-rooted* plants, none of the evergreens accept such treatment. These must be dug instead with a firm ball of earth around the roots, a process known as *balled and burlapped*—or perhaps *balled and plasticized* is a more appropriate term today since synthetic wrapping fibers are not only less costly but more durable in handling than the natural burlap product. Small shrubs also are available now as *containerized* material enclosed in plastic, metal, or molded fiber pots which allow planting schedule flexibility throughout most of the year; larger plants normally are handled at all times with the balled-and-burlapped technique. If restrained too long, containerized shrubs tend to produce girdling, overlapping roots around the sides of the container and then require hand loosening of this root mass (and perhaps some root trimming) when they are removed for planting. Always discard these containers since they are not likely to disintegrate in the soil.

Stems

Stems are the strongly upright, aboveground parts of most plants which support the leaves, flowers, and fruit; on creeping shrubs these stems tend to be prostrate. There are three main types: *columnar* (mostly seen with trees such as the palm), with an unbranched trunk topped by a heavy crown of foliage emerging from one point; *excurrent* (also dominated by tree types such as pine), with a conical outline and a single tapering trunk having horizontally radiating branches arranged like spokes on a wheel; and *deliquescent* (displayed by many deciduous trees and the majority of both evergreen and deciduous shrubs), with a heavier centralized trunk arrangement, a generally rounded outline, and constantly dividing upper branching that "melts away" to terminate in fine twig ends.

The deliquescent stems of many deciduous trees as well as those of most evergreen and deciduous shrubs end in fine twigs. (*Left*)

Shrubs usually are classified as having many equal-sized stems arising from a common ground point, as with this *Ilex verticillata*. (*Right*)

A *shrub* is defined here as a woody perennial with a multitude of mostly equal-sized stems arising from a common ground-level point. A tree, on the other hand, is usually seen as a woody perennial with one main stem rising upright from the ground to lofty heights and with a wide-spreading set of heavy branches. Although some authorities define a shrub as also having a certain arbitrary height (it varies), there never can be a precise separation in terms of height alone. Whether a plant is considered a tall shrub or a short tree is a semantic matter, and since this book is about the pleasurable aspects of shrubs, some types included here could well be covered by either main definition. It seems foolish to eliminate them because of a still faulty classification system.

Another main function of stems is to act as conduits for transferring water and dissolved minerals to all living parts of the plant in a special mix called *sap*. With cone-bearing shrubs there is also an extra ingredient called *resin*, a gummy substance with an attractively pungent odor; this modified sap has the unusual quality of acting as a natural antiseptic on the cut surfaces of pruned or damaged branches in order to curtail the inroads of insect pests or diseases that would take advantage of these openings to reach the soft inner tissues of the plant and do damage. It is unnecessary to bother painting such wounds since paint will not long stick to resin.

Living stems are always full of water both in winter and in summer, but in the dormant stage the water remains static where it is. There is no truth to the myth that sap moves down a plant stem in autumn and up again in spring; sap is always handy in all stems. Its constant presence, however, does suggest caution in scheduling wintertime or early spring pruning since the pressurized sap then can bleed out profusely from the cuts. Midsummer, when dormancy in shrubs is starting, is a preferred pruning time, but there are exceptions, as noted under "Pruning Adjustments."

Woody plants have a thin layer of dead cells called *bark* surrounding the outer portion of older stems as protection from drying winds, intense sunlight, debilitating cold, and insect invasions. Just beneath the bark is an extremely shallow but vital ring of very thin, moist cells called the *cambium layer*. Cambium alone forms the new stem tissues of lateral expansion, and any serious damage to it will cause deformity or even the total loss of existing branches and new twigs. When functioning properly, cambium creates *xylem* tubes for moving sap upward in the plant and *phloem* tubes for returning sap and by-products to the roots. The marvel—and it is not yet fully explained why this system works so efficiently—is how the delicate and intricate process continues without letup over great stem lengths

Pruning flowering shrubs to remove overgrowth and to create more shapeliness is managed better immediately after completion of the blooming period.

and on such a regular basis. But mysterious or not, the protection from abuse provided by cambium is important in the life of a stem.

If a cut is made *horizontally* into the cambium in a circle around the entire stem, all growth above the cut will shortly wither and die, but if a *vertical* slash should occur (such as one makes when pruning off a branch), the plant will continue to function satisfactorily as it slowly repairs the wound with new tissues. One disheartening fact about plant health is that the quick kill of large branches often results from the horizontal girdling habits of some insect pests solely interested in the tiny layer of stem cambium beneath the bark.

This annual expansion of the cambium produces a layer of woody stem enlargement called *sapwood* (most noticeable in trees), which occurs as a two-season spurt in the spring and again in late summer. The rapid need for springtime sap in the upward and outward growth of a plant brings about the development of mostly thin-walled cells. Once this surge of expansion is over for the growing season (usually by midsummer), bud development for next year's stems, leaves, and flowers starts, and by late summer or early autumn the older stems expand *laterally*. This change in stem girth exerts pressure on the inflexible outer bark, causing it to crack, peel, and furrow in a characteristic pattern that often is useful for identification. Inside the stem, the conclusion of the yearly expansion, known as the *annual ring*, is marked by dark-colored cells. Counting these rings on a felled stem or its stump gives the age of the plant. While all this activity is going on above ground, the main roots also thicken in the same rhythm. There is always a balance in nature.

Every plant has on its stems tiny breathing pores called *lenticels* that are generously spread from ground level to the topmost twigs. These act as natural vents for the needed exchange of gases in and out of the plant. On some plants they are either raised noticeably or colored differently from the main stem, and thus they become a decorative addition in the landscape. Exactly where lenticels begin at ground level—that hazy zone dividing root structure from stem—is unclear, and it is therefore unwise to pile anything, even temporarily, against a stem since this may soon cause some degree of suffocation in the plant.

Many shrubs carry stiff *thorns* (which are only modified and elongated xylem structures from the cambium) along their stems in single or multiple configurations

Stiff thorns on *Rosa rugosa* are natural barriers to casual trespassing.

as protection against inroads from animal feeding or as a deterrent to other abuse. Some shrubs have twig ends which terminate in sharp points, while others have softer, less menacing deterrents called *prickles*. Any of these obstacles can become somewhat dangerous to humans and should be evaluated carefully when shrubs are considered for public spaces or for areas where children are likely to play.

Leaves

Often the most noticeable part of a shrub is its foliage, since it is usually in place longer than both flowers and fruit. With evergreens, of course, the leaves are noticeable year-round. Each young stem always develops its leaf and stem *buds* in the previous summer—not, as many still believe, in the spring—and these dual-use buds are found nestled at the axils where the existing leaf joins the stem. Any topmost bud is called *terminal* because of its position, and it is likely to be larger than the others in the axils since it usually contains the embryo of a flower along with the rudiments of new leaf and stem forms yet to come. Buds regularly given a secondary position on the stem—and from their axil location—are called *axillary* or *secondary* buds; they act as replacement growth if anything fully damaging should happen to the terminal bud. Some of these remain unused after a year's time and then slowly become covered by the expanding stem tissue as it turns into bark. While these axillary buds are hidden, they are not dead but only dormant. If older stems and branches are accidentally scarred importantly, these buds, which are now called *adventitious*, spring into active growth around the wound. Such bud stimulation also occurs when heavy pruning is done, and it is one of nature's ways of quickly shielding bark from exposure to too much strong wind or sunlight. When such odd stem growth comes from the root area, the new growth is called *suckering;* when it appears in the upper stem portion, it is named *water growth*, and here the initial leaves are usually oversized.

All leaves are importantly involved with a mystifyingly complex process called *photosynthesis*, in which sunlight and carbon dioxide unite to create both the energy for growth and the carbohydrates for plant enlargement. Since leaves get their basic stimulus to emerge from dormant budding through the increased pres-

Noticeable terminal budding on this *Rhododendron catawbiense* foretells showy flowering during late spring.

Leaf blades are held to stems by petioles obvious on this waxy-leaved *Prunus laurocerasus,* while the adjacent needled evergreen, *Taxus cuspidata,* has sessile ones. (*Left*)

The simple leaves of *Codiaeum variegatum pictum* often are mottled in various colorings. (*Right*)

sure from spring sap flow, they also must shed at some point—even on evergreens—or else they would pump the roots dry. Annual leaf drop is normal for *all* woody plants and generally comes at the end of the growing season; the degree of shedding varies, of course, from total shedding on deciduous shrubs to limited removal of the older leaves on evergreens. Any leaf loss in summer, while abnormal, often functions as a safety mechanism for the plant during prolonged drought, since there is then insufficient moisture available to maintain the entire foliage head; again, it is usually the older leaves which drop first.

The largest part of a total leaf (however small in size) is the *blade,* a flattened broad surface jutting away from the stem. It is secured in place by a flexible, sap-carrying stalk called a *petiole* which has the unique ability to twist and turn to bring the blade—the factory for photosynthesis—to meet the greatest concentration of available light. Some leaves, called *sessile,* have only a fragment of petiole and appear to rest directly on the stem; this is a common arrangement with many needled evergreens that produces their densely solid appearance.

Because the petiole moves the leaf blade to the light, large shrubs in city locations shaded by tall buildings may develop lopsided stems as a result of the major shift in foliage weight toward the brighter side of the space. This condition holds true as well for shrubs crowded by taller plants and those heavily shaded by nearby trees. Symmetrical plant shapes can occur only where there is equalized light intensity on all sides of the plant, and in natural woodlots, most plants, especially those in the shaded interior, tend to grow very slender as they stretch their stems constantly upward to find the sun.

The two main leaf types are defined by their own persistence on the plant: *deciduous* and *evergreen.* Deciduous foliage sheds entirely at the conclusion of the annual growth season and then is often aided by rapidly cooling nighttime temperatures in autumn, while an evergreen maintains its verdant foliage even after consistent frost. Evergreens are further divided into two main forms in accordance with the shape of their leaves: *broadleaf* and *needle.* This does not mean that unfrosted tropical plants never drop their foliage. Such leaves eventually lose their resiliency with age and then draw less and less sap to keep them fully pliant. Soon their sagging weight ruptures the sap tubes entirely, and then the leaf withers and finally drops away.

Leaf outlines are either *simple* or *compound* in makeup. A simple leaf is one that retains its entire outline—no matter how wavy its margin or how indented its lobes—when it drops in autumn. A compound leaf, on the other hand, is made of

The bipinnately compound leaves of *Nandina domestica* offer fine texture on a large scale. (*Left*)

New leaves of *Pittosporum tobira* are glossy from a coating of cutin. (*Right*)

several (or many) *leaflets* cojoined during the growing season for mutual benefit. When this type of leaf drops, the various independent members separate cleanly so that in a month's time you can hardly imagine what size or shape the compound leaf originally had. The basic divisions of compound leaves are *palmate* forms, where all the individual leaflets fan out from a common attachment point on the petiole (just as fingers radiate from the human palm), and *pinnate* forms, where the elongated petiole (now renamed a *rachis*) carries matched sets of leaflets in ladder fashion, placed either directly *opposite* each other or zigzagged in *alternate* patterns. Occasionally, pinnate foliage offers double divisions of itself (palmate never does) to become *bipinnate*. The total dimensions of some bipinnate leaves are sizable and create a fascinating display for landscape use.

Leaves are usually fitted to the stems in either opposite or alternate patterns, yet the bounty of nature has also provided a variation called a *whorl*, in which more than the normal two leaves sprout from a common junction around the twig. Every fallen leaf leaves behind a scar on the stem where it was formerly attached beneath the dormant budding; the arrangement, size, and shape of this *leaf scar* can aid in identifying dormant deciduous plants. Evergreen plants of course are always ready for leaf identification.

Leaves provide needed shading for tender, emerging stems and also cool the surrounding air in summer by expelling oxygen and water vapor in a process called *transpiration*. These gases discharge from myriad microscopic openings called *stomata*, which are located mostly on the undersurface of the leaf so that dust and other pollutants have less chance of clogging this essential mechanism. Many plants gain an additional aid for shedding dust with their production of a thin, waxy coating named *cutin* on the top side of the leaf, which slides dirt away readily with every heavy rainfall. Such glossy foliage has long been valued as a landscape bonus, whether evergreen or deciduous.

Because a large plant (usually a tree) can disperse up to 60 gallons of water vapor from its leaves *per day* during the growing season, the ready availability of replacement soil moisture has a vital influence on the continued vigor and health of a plant. In times of excessive heat, wind, or dryness—and especially when all three conditions combine—leaves tend to lose more water than they can have replaced and then show less than normal *turgidity*, or stiffness, becoming limp in a process called *wilting*. This flaccid condition is also common with newly transplanted material, especially in brightly sunny, warm weather, but here the wilting is tied to the lack of a completely adjusted root system and its reduced water-carrying capacity. (You can anticipate that first-year foliage and stem length on transplanted shrubs will be smaller in size and thickness than normal because of the time needed for root repair.)

To reduce wilting under these circumstances, schedule the planting work for cool and overcast days, which are common at either end of the dormancy cycle. Wilting also can be combated by artificial watering, but only deep and thorough penetration of this rescue moisture will prove truly helpful since any shallow irrigation tends to bring the feeder roots closer to the surface. Because very dry soil takes longer to absorb water, it is good practice to maintain a consistently moist soil condition by irrigation around all established shrubs that dislike dryness well before an expected drought occurs. Just as a moist sponge takes up water more quickly than a dry one, rainfall is less likely to roll away unused if the ground is already moistened well.

Living foliage usually contains a high percentage of green coloring matter called *chlorophyll*, but when leaves turn unnaturally yellowish during the growing season, they are said to be suffering from *chlorosis*, or insufficient chlorophyll. There appears to be no single cause for this deficiency, and it can result from inadequate rain, a superabundance of moisture, infertility of the soil composition (especially trace elements), inroads by insects or diseases, soil contamination from chemicals, compaction of the root zone, accidental spray poisoning from weed killers, or a combination of several of these elements at once. Always investigate the probable cause before applying any remedies since a sick plant can be made worse by random treatment of its ills.

In addition to the dominant green pigment in both evergreen and deciduous leaves, there are smaller percentages of yellow and red pigments, which generally

An occasional *Nerium oleander* cultivar sports conspicuously margined leaves. (*Top left*)

Several cultivars of the deciduous forms of *Ligustrum* offer brightly contrasted foliage. (*Top middle*)

This gray-needled dwarf *Abies* provides year-round color value. (*Top right*)

Subtle coloring is a feature of *Pittosporum tobira* cv. 'Variegata' leaves. (*Bottom left*)

Cultivars of *Euonymus japonica* with bright yellow markings are popular accent shrubs. (*Bottom right*)

remain hidden until the leaf is ready to drop off. When the production of new chlorophyll diminishes through aging, the sudden emergence of these other colorings, alone or in combination, produces the brilliant display of autumnal foliage on most deciduous plants. Some novelty foliages, however, emerge differently colored from the start and appear during the entire growing season with leaves that are bronze, yellow, gray, or plum throughout or that are margined or streaked with pink, cream, or white; for the most part these plants do not change color further before they fall. Shed leaves of any plant eventually dry out completely on the ground and become brown-toned. Browned leaves on a plant during the growing season, however, signify that some damage has been done to the stem or petiole supplying the sap; special remedial treatment may be needed, and the condition at least requires prompt investigation.

Flowers

The specialized reproductive mechanism of plants is found primarily in their flowers. After the successful fertilizing of the female, or *pistillate*, member by the male, or *staminate*, partner, either by wind action or by insect nudging, the final stage of a plant is formed: fruit. Without flowers there can be no fruiting. Because the blossoms are both fragile and short-lived, any interruption to their normal development from frost, drought, insect and disease nuisances, high winds, or drenching downpours can destroy the full value of a plant as a landscape ornament with fruit, since the plant will be barren.

Embryo flowers are located in buds, and the largest usually are found in the terminal buds. Other, smaller flowers are stored in axillary buds and may appear after the terminal bud has produced the main bloom and foliage becomes more full; a select few wait to flower until midsummer to late summer in a special statement that has little to do with previous budding. Because there is so much diversity and complexity in the size, shape, position, coloring, and schedule of flowers, they deserve a book to themselves; unfortunately, there is little space available here to explore these wondrous details in depth. By any standard, their true beauty and landscape worth are unique attributes fully capable of producing grand showiness,

Spectacular flowering is a main attraction with *Paeonia suffruticosa* cultivars.

Generous spring bloom on *Viburnum dilatatum* generally assures abundant fruiting by late summer. (*Top left*)

Cultivars of *Rhododendron catawbiense* enliven shady locations attractively. (*Top right*)

Durable from summer into autumn, the sterile blossoms of *Hydrangea paniculate cv.* 'Grandiflora' develop generously even on young plants. (*Bottom right*)

Colorful *Rhododendron obtusum* cultivars highlight the spring season. (*Bottom left*)

vibrant colorings, heady fragrances, and dramatic if brief sparkle in the annual parade of ornamental effects. Life would be dull without flowers.

Flowers are botanically *perfect* if they have both male and female reproductive parts close together in one blossom, allowing easy fertilizing. When these sexual partners are placed separately from each other but still appear on the *same* plant, the plant is called *monoecious* ("one house"), a condition that is seen with cone bearers such as spruce. But if, in an unusual twist, the male and female parts are produced on entirely *different* plants (as in holly), the plant is labeled *dioecious* ("two houses"). Obviously, dioecious plants require more space to accommodate their separated diversity, but records prove at least that one male plant can supply sufficient fertilizing power to satisfy a number of close-at-hand females of the same type.

Cone bearers like *Pinus mugo mugo* are monoecious and carry conspicuous male flowers high on the stems. (*Left*)

Flowers are held to the stems by peduncles which later become the attachments for the fruit, as shown on this *Pieris japonica*. (*Right*)

Flowers, like leaves, have flexible supports that attach them to the stem. These photosensitive, movable parts are called *peduncles* and appear beneath the blossom. Most elongate somewhat after successful flower fertilization in order to support the added weight from fruit production. Both deciduous and evergreen plants carry flowering and peduncles of some sort, and here too peduncles can be abbreviated almost to nonexistence to become sessile, just as with leaf petioles. Occasionally, these peduncles develop striking colorings of their own that contrast effectively with the fruit formation, and some peduncles persist on the twigs even if fruiting is not forthcoming or has already dropped.

While some stems and leaves have scent only when deliberately crushed or bruised, flowers usually produce some strength of perfume—not always likable to people—without any extra handling effort. The odor evolves from a liquid called *nectar* and is used by the flower to attract pollinating insects. This is accomplished not by the fragrance itself, which is an aspect completely unfathomed by the insect, but by an increase in the air density around the blossom that somehow becomes comprehensible to an insect and then acts as the insect's navigational guide to the waiting flower. Flowers with little or no odor generally are pollinated through wind action, and such plants usually show only bland flower colorings. This lack of noticeable color is apparent with most of the nut-producing plants. The majority of shrubs, however, carry brightly reflective blossoms that radiate a wealth of visual attractions for passing insects—and for people.

Plants displaying minute, odorless, and pallid flowers also may create a special helpmeet from adjacent leaves by a device called a *bract*, which is a leaf modified to color differently and more brightly in order to induce insects to inspect the expanded light intensity near the tiny blossom and in so doing fertilize it in passing. Poinsettia and tree dogwood have these unusually cooperative leaf changes, and what some people admire as flowers are in truth only altered leaves.

The appearance of flowers on any plant is arranged by nature according to age, not plant size. Most shrubs wait several years until their surge of initial growth is well established before moving into the complexity of flower production (and its subsequent seed production in fruit) on any showy scale. Maturity has advantages, and while there is no precise age when bountiful flowering begins in every plant, this is not usually a juvenile trait. Once it starts, moreover, flowering does not always occur annually. The nutrient storehouse involved with flower production may be temporarily exhausted (leaf production usually remains constant), with the result that after a bumper display year, a plant may rest and recuperate for a season. Such plants are known as *alternate bearers*, and this omissive behavior is not influenced importantly by the external effects of either winter cold or summer drought; it is simply an exhibition of the natural rhythm of such a plant. Fortunately, only a few shrubs follow this schedule.

The classification of plants into botanic families is done primarily by using the flowers (and later the fruiting) for unified identification characteristics. For landscape purposes, knowing this primary relationship may seem only remotely useful, but a simple understanding of the system can provide some clues to growing plants more successfully. For example, all members of the rose family, which is one of the giants in the plant kingdom, are known to prefer the greatest amount of sunshine to fulfill their flower and fruiting promise; no major shrub in this group really wants shading to any marked degree. Learning family associations for each individual in the conglomerate can help you place them properly from the beginning. Further assistance can come from the observation that if one member of a family thrives in your locale, other, similarly hardy ones also should do well. The easy growing adaptability of lilac, privet, and forsythia—all from the *Oleaceae* (olive) family—in so many landscapes throughout this country provides a useful illustration of the value of knowing something about plant families.

Fruit

Fruit can be produced only when fertilization of the flowers has occurred successfully. Botanically, fruit is the most valued plant part since it guarantees the future by means of the potential production of fertile or *viable* seed within it. For decorative purposes, however, the size, color, shape, grouping, time of appearance, and persistence of fruit are of most interest. Generous and showy fruiting can add a late summer or autumn bonus that earlier flowering displays cannot quite match for durability since some fruit crops persist into winter. However, such noticeability may be only of short duration as fruit attractive to people also may be the staple food in the diet of birds or other wildlife; then the fruit may disappear far earlier, especially if other rations for these animals are in short supply. On the other hand, birds can be deliberately attracted to a setting by planting the fruiting shrubs they want.

Fleshy fruit called a pome is shown on this *Aronia* species.

Fruits are categorized as being *fleshy* or *dry* in the mature stage. The many subdivisions in each category are basically separated in terms of how the seeds are released from the protective coverings. When the seed jacket splits open neatly along a *suture* or seam, the fruit is called *dehiscent;* when it cracks irregularly or not at all, it is known as *indehiscent.* All the fleshy fruits are indehiscent, and the location or quantity of seeds in such fruits is divided botanically into *pome* (rose hip), *drupe* ("stone" fruit such as a cherry), *berry* (blueberry), *aggregate* (strawberry), and *multiple* (blackberry).

The dry fruits are either dehiscent or indehiscent as well, but there are far too many botanic subdivisions to recount here. A dry, dehiscent type generously represented the world over is the *legume*, whose characteristic pod with its central seam is easily recognized on a wide array of plants. A well-known dry, indehiscent fruit is the acorn fruit of oak.

Fruit can be small or large, clustered or individually set, persistent or fast-withering, brightly colored or dull, a nuisance or a boon, and occasionally poisonous to

Drupe fruiting is identified with *Myrica pensylvanica* and other species.

Drupe fruiting is identified with *Ilex verticillata* and other species.

Drupe fruiting is identified with *Ligustrum vulgare* and other species.

Drupe fruiting is identified with *Viburnum setigerum* and other species.

Drupe fruiting is identified with *Callicarpa japonica* and other species.

Conifers bear woody, dry fruit called *cones;* round cones appear on *Juniperus virginiana cv.* 'Grey Owl' and other species.

Conifers bear woody, dry fruit called *cones;* elongated cones appear on *Pinus mugo mugo.*

humans (white fruits should be avoided); like its forerunner, the flower, fruit can have fascinating appeal for landscape use. Of course, the superabundance of some fruit crops and their subsequent seeds can present an expensive maintenance cost resulting from litter, volunteer seedlings, and general decay odors; any designer can benefit from investigating such details—which this book makes some attempt to do for you—before endorsing any fruiting shrub for general landscape distribution. There is still wisdom in the adage "By their fruits you shall know them."

The Botanic Naming of Plants

Official labels for plants are organized botanically into a system of *scientific* names formulated by the International Union of Biological Sciences and issued through their publication *International Code for Cultivated Plants*. This scientific congress meets with irregular frequency to revise and update plant names as additional, specific information about their true histories is uncovered and documented. There is no formal code in existence for the *common* names of plants, but the current botanic preference in writing them is to use only lowercase letters throughout, except for geographic locations and personal names—but even this standard is changing.

The system is based on the formula evolved by the celebrated eighteenth-century Swedish botanist-taxonomist Carl Linnaeus, whose *Species Plantarum*, published in 1753 (together with his *Genera Plantarum* of 1754), has generally been accepted internationally as the starting point for the stabilization of modern plant names. His achievement rests on a keen observation of the *sexual* interrelationships of flowers and their fruits, and the number and placement of these related sexual characteristics has brought unsuspected unity to the enormous quantities of plants throughout the world. Today, over 600,000 different plants are properly identified and cataloged by his system; even when naming revisions are endorsed, this system is still used.

Linnaeus used Latin or Latin-formed words for his own descriptions of plants—not because he wanted to be obscure or difficult but because use of Latin ensured accuracy, since Latin was the language of scholars in his day and was also a tongue no longer in common usage and therefore not subject to further change. In setting out to stabilize confusion, one benefits from using a stable language. Greek words (Greek is another language not subject to many adjustments) also were used by later generations of botanists, but to a much lesser degree.

A major link between plants of broadly similar nature is represented in the *family*, which is identified by its scientific *-aceae* ending, as in *Rosaceae* (rose family), containing such diverse but sexually related shrubs as pyracantha, cotoneaster,

The widely distributed and popular *Rosaceae* family includes the genus *Aronia*.

The widely distributed and popular *Rosaceae* family includes the genus *Cotoneaster*.

The widely distributed and popular *Rosaceae* family includes the genus *Rosa*. (*Left*)

The widely distributed and popular *Rosaceae* family includes the genus *Pyracantha*. (*Above*)

The widely distributed and popular *Rosaceae* family includes the genus *Chaenomeles*.

quince, and spirea. To use the more obvious plant foliage as a primary guide for establishing a family relationship would soon prove chaotic, as many botanists before Linnaeus discovered, since leaves vary from evergreen to deciduous, from simple to compound, from having entire leaf margins to being deeply lobed, and from tiny to sizable—all without an obvious interrelationship that would lead to a true grouping of plants. Flowers and their fruit, on the other hand, remain noticeably consistent in construction and general appearance from plant to plant within an established group. Linnaeus's system has stood the test of time well.

Each plant within a family is provided first with a *genus* name, and its first letter is always capitalized, as in *Taxus* (yew). These *genera* (the plural of "genus") are major divisions with deep-seated flower and fruit similarities, such as having the same number of petals plus fruit with the same number of seeds, yet they do not have *identical* representations of these characteristics from genus to genus.

Since nature is always abundant with variations, there are also subdivisions within any of the genera, and these special differences are categorized as *species* (plural, *species*), a series of noticeable but *secondary* attributes shared by plants of the genus such as distinct changes in leaf shape, flower color, fruit size, or natural geographic location. For example, the genus *Rosa* contains a wealth of interrelated shrubs such as *Rosa hugonis* (Father Hugo rose) which has pale yellow, single flowers in midspring and dark *red* fruit, contrasting with *Rosa spinosissima* (Scots rose) which has deeper yellow, single flowers in midspring and *black* fruit.

Species names are properly written with all lowercase lettering, and the former practice of capitalizing the first letter when the species is derived from names of people and places in no longer recommended by botanic authorities and therefore is not used in this book. Common names, similarly, are currently written without any capitalizing at all, but it will take some time for the general public to accept this change willingly. I have capitalized names sparingly.

A final category of naming is the *variety*, indicating a plant identical in major botanic aspects to the parent species—with at least one definitive exception. The deviation may be differently colored foliage, double flowers instead of single, or larger fruit. It also may involve a silhouette that is weeping instead of erect, or perhaps a dwarfed size. A true variety can be found growing naturally somewhere in the wild and will reproduce accurately from seed.

Becoming more common in usage today is the coined word *cultivar* (from "cultivated variety"), which is used to represent plants with noteworthy horticultural appeal and extensive nursery planting that thus offer a superior form, color, rate of growth (slow or fast), or other factor of landscape interest on an assured basis. These plants are propagated *asexually* by cuttings taken from the parent plant to guarantee exact duplication, since seed from such plants is unreliable for reproduction on an exact basis each time. Cultivars represent a deliberate standardization technique of growing plants; their names normally are set apart by *single* quotation marks and can be given in any modern-day language. A true variety usually is listed in Latin only, without quotes.

The scientific names of *hybrid* plants, those hoped-for improvements created by the deliberate intervention of people in the fertilizing of flowers between members of the same family, are preceded by the multiplication sign—✕—which is not pronounced in conversation. The presence of an ✕ can tell either of two stories about the new plant. If the ✕ comes *before* the genus, the hybrid came about through the pollination of two separate *genera* within the family; if the ✕ *follows* the genus, the fertilizing took place between two and perhaps more *species* members of that genus. In talking or writing about such hybrids, the ✕ translates into either "hybrid genus" or "hybrid species."

Using the full scientific name—genus, species, and variety or cultivar—is essential both for clarity and for accuracy as well as for saving time in discussing or ordering plants. Convenient as they may seem, common names alone are wholly unreliable for describing plants beyond social commentary. Common names often vary greatly throughout the world, at times to the point of being almost unrecognizable, and such vagaries open the way for obvious misunderstandings that can prove costly in time and money. Professionals internationally subscribe to and appreciate the practice of using complete scientific names, and everyone should join in this useful pursuit. The full names of plants are no more troublesome to learn than those of our other friends.

The Basic Requirements of Plants

The needs of plants remain constant: light, water, air, nourishment, a fixed temperature range for durability, and soil. Of course, the specific requirements vary for different plants, but none of the basic needs can be omitted entirely or reduced drastically without causing harm to the plant. All plants have preferred growing conditions for optimum response, and only experience with them over many years, plus much time spent reading about and investigating them, can bring you to a full knowledge of all these preferences for all the various locations throughout the world where a plant may grow. We are constantly learning new details of how plants expect to be treated.

Light and Shade

The sun is the source for all natural light and heat and is an essential element in photosynthesis, where leaves convert sunlight and carbon dioxide into growth energy for the entire plant. This process stops at nightfall (and is only minimally active during winter dormancy with evergreens), but it can be reactivated in a harmful way by high-intensity artificial lighting nearby which burns throughout the night. This round-the-clock stimulation by light can affect all the mechanisms of plant functions in an abnormal way since the usual daily resting period, and even dormancy, is not allowed. Excess winter damage is known to occur under these trying conditions because the soft plant tissues fail either to ripen or to harden completely before harsh seasonal weather changes suddenly occur. Trees are often the plants most disturbed by this perpetual lighting since they are generally closer to the light source because of their size. Someday soon we shall have to reevaluate whether safety illumination as it is now conceived is worth the impairment of normal plant development.

While the majority of plants enjoy having maximum sunshine throughout the year, some have a decided preference for reduced light—*shade*—during some part of the daylight hours. By its degree of intensity, shade can be divided into *full*, *deep*, *half*, and *light*. Full shade is year-round dimness at ground level as a result of the light-obstructing effect of tall buildings or heavily foliaged large evergreens nearby. Deep shading usually comes from the dense summertime foliage of deciduous trees, but here some stronger light does penetrate to the ground from late autumn until midspring, when these plants are leafless. Half shade is an equalized proportion of full sun and heavy shading, but it is important to note *when* the strong light appears since the heat and brightness most productive for growth come between 10 A.M. and 4 P.M. in summer at the northern latitudes. Light shade, the easiest type to use in landscape planning, is simply filtered light that reduces the intensity and heat of the sun for brief periods.

Normal plant growth and hardiness sometimes are influenced noticeably by an increase of shade. Such affected plants often become less vigorous or develop stems which remain thin and elongated as they push their less dense crowns of leaves farther and farther upward to find more light. Constantly shaded soil is affected too and often remains cold far longer into the spring, may compact more readily because useful aerating animal life in it is less prolific, or may retain surface water (and ice) too long and become soggy and oxygen-deficient, producing a well-known condition called "sour" soil. Such unfavorable situations are likely to be negative for plant growth, leading to lackluster performance all around.

Shade and dryness, however, often go hand in hand since the roots of the competing large trees that cause the main shaded conditions usually are superior in

Deep shade limits plant choices and flowering effects but can be managed effectively nonetheless.

Half shade is suited for a sizable list of plants which accept reduced light.

Light shading is agreeable to most plants and also pleasant for outdoor sitting areas.

water-collecting adverturesomeness and leave localized dryness and lowered fertility in their wake. Introduced planting additions of shrubs or groundcovers not immediately adaptable to such competition will probably soon dwindle to weak, pallid shadows of their former selves. Keen competition is troublesome.

Water

Since water can be made available for plant functions only through the roots, the moisture content of the soil, expecially in the active growing season, is critical for continued good response. A constantly moist—not wet—soil is ideal.

Natural irrigation comes from both rain and winter snows, yet this may need to be supplemented by artificial watering during spring and summer droughts. Only deep water penetration is valuable at such times since shallow irrigation will promote the movement of feeder roots even closer to the surface, creating additional problems.

Streamside plantings benefit from soil moisture and increased humidity all year.

Air

Air is also essential for proper root expansion since root hair development depends on the easy availability of oxygen in the soil. The aboveground parts of the plant are not so strongly influenced because air is readily accessible to them at all times but more so because leaves already produce and release oxygen as part of their normal daily routine. Waterlogged, compacted, or clay hardpan soils are known to be oxygen-poor, and only a few stalwart plants can adapt successfully to such negative growing conditions. Roots generally prefer humusy, loose, well-drained sites because these are also oxygen-rich.

Pollutants in the air have become more common recently, and the damage they do to foliage, flowers, and fruit is more noticeable and widespread. It seems safe to say that if the air humans breathe is not of good quality, plant life also will suffer. Evergreens especially seem to be hampered by pollution of the air, which is perhaps understandable since they retain foliage on a year-round basis. Soot, dust, and chemical residues can build up an appreciable layer of light-denying debris on an evergreen leaf during a year's time, with the end result that the plant

may not only be unhealthy but will *look* unhealthy. Most urban locations, with their current concentrations of noxious gases, are hardly ever graced with thriving evergreen plantings of great size and beauty. Only in city parks with large acreage can evergreens be expected to flourish today with reasonable attractiveness.

Nourishment and Fertilizer

The natural nutrients for plant growth are found only in soil; these are minerals dissolved by constant rainfall or irrigation into the weak salt solutions needed for quick absorption by the root hairs. Some of these nutrients also can come from a layer of decayed vegetable and animal remains atop the soil surface—at least in a natural setting—in a system where life returns to life. This decaying debris also acts as a cooling mulch during summer heat, an insulating blanket to equalize winter cold, and a potential erosion control on slopes and embankments.

When a plant grows consistently well and fulfills all its functions readily it can be assumed to be fully supplied with all its nutrient requirements. But if its behavior shows growth or color deficiencies that are unrelated to physical problems such as soil compaction, vandalism, and the like, the plant may require supplemental fertilizing. (Manure and compost, although useful, are not true fertilizers but *soil conditioners* that bring helpful bacteria to improve the composition of the soil; they have little fertilizer value.)

First, take a soil sample adjacent to the ailing plant and have it analyzed professionally to determine whether the three primary nutrients—*nitrogen, phosphorus,* and *potassium*—are available in sufficient quantities and are in a percentage balance with one another. Nitrogen is used by plants mostly for stem and foliage development, phosphorus is involved with root enlargement and extension, and potassium provides the stimulus for flower and fruit production. Of these three, the nitrogen content in the soil is usually the first to be exhausted, and general fertilizer formulas consistently list nitrogen as the largest ingredient. (Specialty fertilizers, of course, vary this amount of nitrogen or even eliminate it altogether to suit the specific need.) Several major shrub categories—such as rhododendron, azalea, and camellia—also require acid soil conditions for best growth and this requirement is often met by an application of ammonium sulfate, which feeds and acidifies in one application.

Although chemical analysis of soil can provide sufficient information when limited only to these three basic nutrient ingredients, recent investigations of how plants grow also recommend having information about the presence of *trace elements* as well. For reasons that are not yet clear, even minuscule percentages of iron, boron, zinc, copper, and magnesium are somehow essential to sustained growth. If any one is lacking, it can be introduced into the soil by yet another chemical additive, usually one applied in a water solution; it often requires a full growing season before any improvement can be noticed in the plant.

Fertilizers are commonly available in slow-acting, organic natural forms as well as in less-expensive, quick-acting chemical combinations of synthetic ingredients. Even more specialized are the liquid and foliar types of nutrients. Each of these has a valid use somewhat different from the others, but with any of them, always follow the manufacturer's instructions for application implicitly, keeping in mind that if a little is good, a lot may not be welcomed by the plant. Heavy concentrations of applied fertilizer, whether in the dry forms or as liquid solutions, can quickly damage the delicate feeder roots, defeating the whole purpose of the operation, but several light doses spread out over a period of time often prove more effective. It is beneficial either to apply a fertilizer just before rain is expected or to flush it into the soil by artificial watering immediately afterward to disperse any concentration of it in one spot. Also, dry fertilizers are water-absorptive and can take moisture away from roots you are attempting to help.

In general, woody plants like shrubs are best fertilized as they start growing in the spring, but in some cold-climate areas, autumn applications appear to work just as well. It is known that sandy soils drain away water quickly, but since nutrients must be in solution for root absorption, rapid drainage can mean that nutrients also will move out of the feeder root zone more quickly. Soils high in sand content often require several applications of fertilizer during the growing season for this reason.

Hardiness Zones

Hardiness in plants is primarily related to a satisfactory adjustment to extended *cold* temperatures, yet a plant's tolerance to both prolonged heat and severe drought has some bearing on its durability as well. While every plant in cultivation is unlikely to face all three extremes together, each of these weather difficulties has some bearing on its growth and development, even if short-lived. Although there are plants throughout the world which are consistently trustworthy for all growing conditions in their zones of hardiness, this list is not extensive, nor are these plants always attractive for landscape purposes. More and more today, international hybridizers and growers are investigating improved plant types with greater landscape appeal and wider durability that are derived from these hardy stalwarts of horticulture. You can verify this easily by reading a current nursery catalog; every year you will learn of "new" and "improved" plant selections in every category. These are welcome bits of news for designers.

Since lengthy periods of cold weather affect a large proportion of the world's populated areas, it is only logical that the tolerance of cold of plants receives a great amount of attention. As useful guides for the geographic range for which a plant has tolerance of cold, authoritative maps (one is given in the Appendix) are readily available today that cover most of the temperature growing areas of the world. These are divided into *zones of hardiness* that range from 1 through 10. The worst weather conditions exist in zone 1, where the wintertime temperatures dip down to $-40°F$ ($-40°C$), while the warmest are in zone 10, where the rare but occasional cold snaps are measured at $+40°F$ ($+5°C$). Generally, plant life is not limited to growing only in one zone of hardiness but will spread across several zones. A listing, for example, of zones 5 to 8 means that the plant satisfactorily

Because of milder climate zone, these Philadelphia-grown shrubs produce more luxuriant and heavier development.

Boston-area rhododendrons perform less vigorously in the colder climate of their hardiness zone.

grows over a sizable territory and is probably much used in landscape developments if it has appeal. The largest number of plant types exist between zones 3 and 8; so does most of the world's population.

Because plants recognized as adaptable to a specific zonal range of hardiness often can be grown commercially in productive quantities over that spread of temperature (soil acidity and rainfall amounts plus mountaintop sites have some influence here, too), nevertheless, plants with the same name still may behave differently at the extreme ends of their zonal limits. Plants which originate in the northerly limits of a zone are known to possess somewhat greater hardiness than their southern counterparts, and southern-grown plants, because of a slightly extended growing season and milder winter temperatures, may fail to adapt well when shipped to the northern side of their range or beyond unless handled when very young. This condition is especially noticeable with some evergreens, whose lush foliage from mostly favorable southern exposures all too quickly fades into a sulk as the plant attempts to adjust to fewer days of heat and more rapid temperature fluctuations in its northern boundary. Plants located close to large bodies of water, however, often benefit from a tempering of both cold and summertime heat to survive better than those planted inland, while plants taken to elevations several thousand feet higher than where they were originally growing will actually be traveling to another hardiness zone (a colder one). While these zone maps have great usefulness, they do not pinpoint the entire layout of the terrain within any of the zone boundaries; one has to contribute a smattering of geography on one's own.

Plants brought south from northern nurseries, however, usually can cross the limits of *two* adjacent zones of hardiness without undue stress, and moving plants from east to west or west to east within a zone appears to be workable as long as the soil type and rainfall amounts wanted by the plant are nearly identical in both locations. At the present time plant materials started in California nurseries have adjusted successfully to Massachusetts nursery plots, and Alabama shrubs are thriving in the far reaches of Oregon. Although this transfer of plant material swells the quantity and variety of plant types available in a commendable way, there is still something to be said for purchasing home-grown material since its behavior is already adapted to local conditions, and it can at least be observed somewhere in large sizes.

Microclimate areas exist in all the hardiness zones, creating those unusual growing conditions which either raise or lower the normal temperature expectations in a zone. The protection given by sheltering buildings, topography changes, fencing barriers, and nearby plants can moderate winter temperatures and wind conditions sufficiently to encourage greater adaptability from plants not normally grown successfully in the vicinity. However, conversely, an exposure to excessive cold and high winds can debilitate plants known to possess reliable hardiness for a zone. Low, enclosed pieces of land often trap frigid air overnight to wither normally dependable plants appreciably. To gain a practical advantage before installing any plant about which you are unsure, review how plantings survive locally on a year-round basis as grown in sheltered private developments or placed openly in nurseries or arboretums. This personalized datum can reward you with information not usually found through any other source.

Even with all these basic hardiness considerations taken into account, there are other factors which influence plant adaptation importantly: pollution of soil, water,

Both fence and building create a microclimate improvement for these shoreline *Ilex glabra.* (*Left*)

Rhododendron catawbiense appear to enjoy this brick-walled courtyard environment. (*Right*)

or air; prolonged dryness or consistent flooding of the land; unsought shading intensity; major alterations in soil alkalinity, acidity, or salt content; changes in the soil water table level; and without a doubt, vandalism. Benevolently, nature has provided us with a selection, however small or large, of plants capable of enduring these abnormal situations. While a goodly number may have limited landscape appeal, they are at least adaptable. It is always wiser to use plants tolerant of the growing conditions than to force others to accept problems they cannot resolve at all well. Understanding the situation to be faced by the plants goes a long way toward gaining horticultural success, and a competent designer knows and uses this lesson constantly. Botanical wisdom grows from attention to important details.

Soil

Soil is the loose layer of the earth in which plants grow; it is composed of varying amounts of minerals, humus, air, water, pieces of decomposed rock, and minute animal life, all mixed harmoniously. The three dominant soil types are *sand, silt,* and *clay;* plant-productive soil is a balanced mix of all three in variations that extend around the world.

Soil is found in natural layers of varying thickness. The uppermost layer, *topsoil,* exists where its name suggests and usually has a dark color because of the decayed animal and vegetable matter it contains, known as *humus.* This layer is remarkably rich in needed plant nutrients, has an open and loose composition, and is generally uniform in quality (at least when it comes from a common source). Where topsoil exists in a reasonable depth, it encourages rapid root and stem development. If excessive—usually beyond 12 inches—it occasionally can produce negative growth effects from its tremendous water-holding abilities; too much of a good thing is not always beneficial. The next soil level down is *subsoil,* a denser, often rock-strewn layer that acts as a dependable reservoir of moisture for plants, especially in times of drought, and as a stockpile of additional nutrients. Its depth very often is measured in feet. Below this level may lie gravel, clay hardpan, pure sand, or even rocky ledge. How quickly and how deeply gravitational water drains through the upper two layers largely determines how far roots finally penetrate and endure.

Sturdy weed crops and a healthy stand of **Rhus typhina** suggest that soil fertility exists here.

This soil water mostly equalizes at a depth of 5 feet, as do most of the roots of a majority of plants, including large trees.

Since soils are often unequal in their texture and nutrient content whenever they exist, they can be improved by both physical and chemical means. Mixing coarse sand with heavier clay soils can help aerate the wet stickiness of the clay enough to improve drainage considerably. There are also some chemical modifiers with the same abilities; both need to be incorporated deeply enough to keep water from pocketing at root levels or they will not be fully useful. Including animal manure, compost, leaf mold, or moistened peat moss in sandy soils can upgrade their poor water-holding nature substantially as well as provide some slight amounts of nutrients. Since soils of any type can be negatively altered in texture by clumsy handling, avoid working either frozen or muddy soils for these changes, especially with heavy equipment. Wait until the soil has thawed or dried out more.

Soils are either *acidic* or *alkaline* in chemical composition, and the degree of either measurement readily determines how well roots adapt after transplanting. Soil acidity is given more notice since most of the world's soils are of that nature. Its presence is measured by testing soil samples in a laboratory or with a commercial kit on the site for the *potential of hydrogen ions*, more commonly known as *pH,* on a scale calibrated from 1 (extremely acid) to 14 (very alkaline), with 7 established as the *neutral balance* between the two extremes. Most plants grow contentedly within a pH range of 4 to 7, yet there are those, such as rhododendrons, which demand a consistently acid soil to survive, and others, such as cotoneaster, which prefer more alkalinity. Because the difference of one full point on this scale means a soil is 10 times as acid or alkaline as the next number, altering a soil's chemical nature is difficult to arrange easily and permanently, although there are ways.

Any reasonable imbalances in pH can be adjusted by applying dry amounts of certain chemicals to the soil (in quantities that may prove astounding at times) and then hand digging, disking, or harrowing these materials thoroughly into the topmost soil layer. To change acid conditions, apply agricultural ground limestone; to alter alkaline soils, use sulphur or iron sulphate. The soil analysis from a laboratory comes in a written form that indicates the quantities of either material to buy and spread. Again, do not work the soil if it is muddy or frozen. Both of these additive materials for changing soil pH are known as *catalysts* and do not enter directly into any chemical reactions but merely *arrange* for these reactions to take place. Because each is independent in terms of how it works, always spread and incorporate pH conditioners well in advance of fertilizer programs.

A curious aspect of dealing with soil pH involves watering. In areas of high soil alkalinity, hose water is undoubtedly alkaline as well, and so irrigating any acid-loving plants grown in such areas is an uncertain procedure. One way around it is to collect rainwater in barrels since this technique at least provides a close-to-neutral pH. Another forgotten detail in northern areas is how much the annual liming of grass lawns can alter the pH of shrub beds next to them; it is often enough to cause anemia in azaleas, rhododendrons, or laurels.

The basic premise of caring intelligently for plants has remained the same from the time horticulture first appeared on the scene thousands of years ago: learn what a plant requires and then provide it. All plants have definite needs for achieving their best growth, and these needs involve site exposure, soil conditions, water requirements, amount of sunlight, and tolerance of cold. Once we gain this knowledge, we can trust that the odds for transplanting and growing any material will improve favorably.

Caring for Existing Shrubs

Any land with shrubs already on it has a visual attractiveness that barren surroundings can never match, no matter how common the plants are. Should these shrubs have an ornamental appeal and value, their care and enhancement should follow as a matter of course. Such shrubs are an investment definitely worth protecting. Yet plants on a natural or predeveloped site are not always set down where they will do the most good for the current design considerations, and when important grading changes or any construction activity must be arranged close to where these shrubs are growing, it is time to consider transplanting them.

A field survey made before any change gets under way is important since you will then know the positioning, size, identification, distribution, and possible uniqueness of the plants involved. Such survey work can be handled by a qualified landscape architect, arborist, or nursery, and the information is very often included in the making of an engineer's topographic mapping. Next, staking out the lines of a roadway or the dimensions of a building, while adding some expense, has the merit of showing the relative proximity of favored plants to the work areas before the bulldozer arrives; at this point there usually is time to make field adjustments to grading or construction in order to avoid disturbing the plants at all. Since new planting is increasingly expensive today, moving plants out of the way for reuse later has economic advantages on most sites.

Grading Influences

Probably earth grading has the most influence on the future health of existing shrubs, since if handled carelessly, both *cut* and *fill* operations create important drawbacks to plant growth. Excessive soil removal near the root spread of a shrub exposes the delicate feeder roots to additional air and sunlight they do not require, and cutting the main support roots can seriously weaken the water intake system as well as affect the sturdiness of the shrub in storms. Deep filling of earth around shrub stems can quickly interrupt the lenticel breathing mechanism there and cause suffocation and stem rot; at the same time this extra weight of soil on the root zone can curtail the exchange of oxygen and water these roots need to stay alive and healthy. Couple the action of grading with the usually heavy equipment used to perform it, and you increase a plant's survival problems severalfold. Not only can this equipment add compaction to the soil, it presents the threat of accidental damage to stem bark and its vital cambium layer, can funnel heat from exhaust pipes into the foliage (this is especially detrimental to evergreens), can contaminate the soil from oil leaks, and may harmfully graze or break branches and twigs as a result of careless handling during its maneuvering. Close supervision of all clearing and grading operations should be made the professional responsibility of the site designer in order to forestall any of these problems.

New grading planned for this slope should promote transplanting of these shrubs beforehand.

Protective Fencing

Protecting shrubs by erecting sturdy fencing barriers around them is worth the added cost, but it is also important that such fencing be located properly. Ideally, such shields ought to be set out at the drip line of the branches since the main feeder roots are also in this zone. Nothing should be nailed or wired to any stem, nor should anything be piled against the stems, even for short periods of time. If the fencing cannot be placed at the drip line but must be moved in closer, special care should be taken to avoid having the fencing rub against any stems during the time the fence is in place.

Soil Cut Procedures

Existing shrubs in areas to be graded lower require hand labor—not mechanical equipment—for removing the soil above the root areas. At best, only a few inches can be taken away safely, and unfortunately, it is the nutrient-rich topsoil that is removed. While it is potentially feasible to induce surface feeder roots to grow deeper and more dense by trenching in a circle at the branch drip line beforehand, this time-consuming operation needs a full growing season to achieve any worthwhile results. Most work schedules hardly allow this much time, and wherever possible, it is wiser in the long run to rearrange the grading layout and not skim off this topsoil. Otherwise, it probably is more sensible to transplant the shrubs elsewhere.

Entirely removing major anchor roots by grading can upset the sap flow balance enough that entire stems on shrubs may quickly wilt and then die. Severed roots of any size should be cleanly cut with sharp pruning tools to encourage faster healing since ragged ends of mangled roots tend to rot. Open trenches through root zones should be backfilled with earth as quickly as possible to reduce the evaporation of soil moisture and the attendant dehydration of the roots themselves. When such backfilling cannot be achieved in short order, arrange for protection of the exposed roots with wet burlap or cloth sheets. While not a wholly endorsed procedure, removal of a portion of the stem growth to compensate for the loss of some roots is often done to maintain a reasonable balance between the reduced root total and the remaining stems and leaves. Thinning out of the secondary, minor twigs and small branches is one place to begin, since this retains the basic plant outline. This is far simpler to achieve with deciduous material than with evergreen because evergreens need greater foliage density to look natural and remain unscalded on their stems.

Soil Fill Procedures

Filling high against the stems of any plant is detrimental in terms of both the closing off of the stem breathing pores and the increased density and weight of soil over the feeder roots. These important surface roots are located where they are by natural necessity, and to place them far deeper upsets the oxygen-water relationship with the soil, possibly resulting in suffocation. Any earth used for fill near plants should be limited in its depth and should be porous, light in composition, and rich in humus. However, it should never be placed so that the plant stems are left in a deep well; such grading will only encourage water to concentrate there at all times, especially in winter, when it will turn to ice and possibly destroy the stems. Grading should be managed so as to drain water away from the main part of the plant comfortably; if it does not, transplanting may be in order.

Dried-out flower buds and mite-infested foliage on this *Pieris japonica* indicate nursery neglect and a weakened plant.

Selecting and Transplanting Shrubs

Shrubs chosen for site development additions usually come from commercial nursery grounds because their planned cultivation allows greater selection and buyer convenience plus some type of stated guarantee of future performance by the nursery owner. Such plants will already have had root pruning, fertilizing, cultivation, irrigation, spraying for insects and diseases, and perhaps some twig shaping. These procedures all are meant to induce compact rooting, uniform growth, and better health than is found in any material simply collected from the wild. Plants dug from nature or even those transplanted from the site carry no guarantee from the digging contractor since their past history and existing root development patterns are unknown.

Choosing the best nursery specimen is a matter of being selective. Always pick shrubs with distinguishing good health, vigor, and a typical silhouette. Be on the lookout for those which are normally dense and bushy with many stems and side branches that indicate strong growing habits. Check also for plump budding when dormant and for full-sized and handsome foliage when in leaf. Verify freedom from insect egg masses and from canker and other diseases since both can disfigure the plant later. Avoid shrubs with shriveled stems, a superabundance of twig dead wood, and off-color leaves or flowers since these often signify previous neglect of watering and fertilizing. Note too the closeness of your selection to other plants in the nursery row since you will want the most complete root ball dug; very crowded plants mean tangled root systems below ground, and you are not then as likely to receive a properly sized or well-dug plant ball.

Of course, there are landscape designers who deliberately choose the offbeat silhouette and the exotic form over standard selections for all the work they handle. Such practitioners bring sly glee to many nurseries that then can unload their malformed flotsam and jetsam at standard prices. Placing such novelties on a site requires serious inventiveness and real courage, yet it is done constantly. I would select a representative plant first and let it become *unrepresentative* later; maybe it will never become nonstandard.

Everyone has prejudices about the ornamental characteristics of various plant types, including shrubs. In choosing which type of shrub best suits your needs and visual pleasures, keep in mind the following checklist of questions and your answers before you make a final decision.

Is it locally hardy?

Does it require special soil?

Does it prefer sun or shade?

Will it tolerate drought and wind satisfactorily?

Is it prone to insect and disease problems?

Is it long-lived?

Does it need extensive pruning attention?

What is its annual growth rate and its ultimate size for your area?

Does it transplant well at any age?

Does it carry injurious thorns?

Will it overseed itself to become a nuisance?

Is any part of it poisonous to humans?

Can it offer several seasons of interest?

Does it carry a pleasant fragrance in the flowers?

Do the leaf and the twig textures blend with the intended site?

Are its colorings compatible with the proposed surroundings?

What does it cost in the required size?

Once you compile a tally of enough positive answers for your intentions, you ought to feel a high degree of confidence that the plant is suitable. If not, look for an alternative.

Site Placement

The majority of site locations for plants present no special difficulties, yet some placement problems often are overlooked in the rush of accomplishment. Crowd-

Proper setback from auto bumpers averts later stem damage to these *Juniperus chinensis cv.* 'Seagreen'.

Potential snow and ice from this slate roof influenced the choice of low plants.

ing, unless deliberately organized for a hedge, is one of the pitfalls; install shrubs only where they can develop normally and fully. Provide enough distance from building walls for years of future growth to keep the plants shapely without continual pruning maintenance. Remember to take into account the normal vigor of some creeping and spreading shrubs by initially placing them far enough away from walks and steps they would soon overrun if spaced otherwise. Avoid planting beneath deep roof overhangs since these remain dry soil areas that rainfall rarely penetrates effectively. Even with an automatic sprinkler system installed here, the year-long moisture content of the soil will be lower, especially in cold areas where the sprinkler system is inoperative during winter. In locales where snow and ice are common, note where icicles and snow slides fall and keep easily damaged shrubs out of those zones. Observe the soil rules for acid-loving plants by positioning them away from close proximity to limed lawn areas; avoid using them near limestone foundations altogether to avoid yellowed foliage and weak growth. While this list is hardly complete, it shows that using a little forethought about site placement can bring all the intended advantages from shrubs and fewer nuisances later.

Spacing Shrubs

There is no foolproof guide for spacing shrubs that fits all growing situations; too many variables exist. Nevertheless, both the ultimate size and the annual rate of upward and outward growth *in your vicinity* have prime importance, along with the purchase size. While pruning techniques to maintain certain personal dimensions of height and width are always available to control growth, reliance on them exclusively entails eternal, expensive, and exhausting maintenance. It is much more profitable in time and effort to select plants which expand at a modest rate and attractively fit the proportions of the design layout when mature. Since most plants are located where we place them, we have only ourselves to criticize if they overrun their sites in too short a time. Their normal exuberance ought not to be punished by constant shearing because of our lack of understanding beforehand of their normal growth pattern. The outcome too often is a collection of shapeless blobs most landscapes can well do without.

Initial spacing of shrubs is determined by the local climate and growth rate.

If a shrub is small-sized when you buy it, do not be fooled into believing it will stay small even with pruning. The youngest seedling of a giant-sized shrub will one day reach its ultimate size, and it will certainly try to get there faster if the growing conditions are to its liking. We have no influence on a plant's built-in energies for expansion, but we can rely somewhat on local climate to tell us more about proper spacing and site location. A shrub growing in a mild-season area will expand more in one season than the same plant installed in a colder climate. The length of the growing season, the number of hot summer days, and the amount of rainfall or irrigation provided can speed up or delay annual growth; take these factors into account as you space for planting.

Natural vigor in plants is no secret, and local growth rates are discoverable by personal observation in nursery grounds, arboretums, and neighborhood installations, as well as from written records in horticultural publications and library reference books. Information about plant growth is so well documented and distributed today that it is puzzling why so many people still are misinformed about what they are shoveling into the ground. *Learn about what will happen next* is the best guide I can offer for the correct spacing of shrubs. You can best learn by looking.

Digging Operations

The majority of field-grown nursery shrubs are handled *balled and burlapped,* but some deciduous shrubs (and just-rooted cuttings of evergreens) are traded as *bare-rooted (BR)* when sent through the mails and then only as small plants. Dormant roses are most often handled by the bare-rooted method and can be shipped surprisingly well in this condition. Digging bare-rooted is also the first step in creating *containerized* deciduous shrubs for sale, too.

The balled-and-burlapped plant is dug with its full ball of earth kept firmly about the roots and is then wrapped either with burlap cloth (which will disintegrate in the soil since it is made of natural fibers) or with durable plastic sheeting (which does not disintegrate and must be fully removed before installing the plant) and then tied securely with rope or pinned with balling nails for delivery to the job site. Very large shrubs often require sturdy wood platforms lashed to the bottom of the ball—or even full crating—for safe handling and transport since any plant dug or moved with a loose ball will have problems later in adjusting to the new site. Bare-rooted shrubs are generally washed clean of any field soil, packed in moistened sphagnum moss or wetted excelsior, and tied loosely about the stems with soft cord either singly or in bundles before being boxed for shipment. Bundled packets of bare-rooted shrubs are often placed in cold storage at some nurseries to reduce stem and root evaporation if the order is predug at a time different from the delivery date.

More and more shrubs, however, are now appearing in nurseries and garden centers in metal, plastic, or paper fiber containers since they are more easily transported and handled this way. Using them means you can delay the planting schedule longer than with balled-and-burlapped or bare-rooted shrubs because their roots are more thoroughly protected from the beginning by the container. Of course, they need watering attention on a regular basis while out of the ground, the same as with any other dug plant, plus protection from wind and harsh sunlight. Metal containers often need to be sliced open on two sides with a special scissoring device so as not to disturb the root ball by simply yanking it free of the pot. It is usually best to have the nursery cut the container beforehand, although tin snips on the job site can do the work, too. These cut edges are very sharp and require more than average caution in handling.

Having the correct depth and width of a plant ball is important for gaining the maximum number of feeder roots. Skimpy balls are a mistake; the shrub will take much longer to recover from transplanting if most of its roots are left in the nursery grounds, and it may collapse entirely. Shrubs dug with broken or loose balls are also suspect since their condition indicates that the soil is not clinging properly to the roots and also that air now is reaching them unnecessarily. All root balls should arrive with the soil in which they grew; do not accept a "manufactured" ball, particularly with evergreens, since these are plants dug more or less bare-rooted, put on a wrapping cloth, and then filled around with loose earth. They generally show a ball with a slumped outline that feels mushy and loose when poked; the plant probably will jiggle around easily, too. Such shrubs have only a limited life span and should be avoided.

Landscape industry standards for proper digging in all the forms used today have long been established by the American Association of Nurserymen, a national organization headquartered in Washington, D.C., to which the majority of nurseries in the United States belong and which they help support. This group regularly publishes information about growing and handling plants. Its 1973 handbook, *American Standard for Nursery Stock*, available to the general public for a small fee.

Once the plants are out of the ground, they require regular and thorough watering to keep them in good condition. At some nurseries these dug shrubs are placed under a special *constant mist* system of overhead watering—out of wind and bright sun for the most part—if the plants have begun to grow at that time. This technique is used to reduce wilting of the new stems and leaves; it is called *hardening off*. It supplements the normal root-ball watering that also is required, and this top-growth misting can be continued at the job site with a hose.

Transport to the Site

Handling large shrubs often requires a truck with a heavy-duty winch or power-driven tailgate both for collecting the material at the nursery and for depositing it conveniently on the site. While in transit, all plants in open trucks should be covered with canvas or other wind-deflective shielding to avoid dehydration and scorching of the foliage. After arrival on the site, skids and rollers are also useful transfer equipment for moving the plants to their locations, along with, of course, the usual bucket-loader vehicles. Make certain, however, that the metal bucket is cushioned along the edges with layers of burlap or other blanketing before loading and be sure that all plant parts are kept away from the potentially searing heat of the exhaust pipe or the motor housing during the transfer. Under no circumstances should any balled plant be tossed from a truck to land unassisted, since this clumsy handling surely will damage the ball. Nor should a plant be lifted by its branches alone; instead, hoist the ball. Like all living entities, shrubs deserve coddling.

Large balled-and-burlapped shrubs are often wheeled by dolly to the planting area.

Using Collected Shrubs

Another method of finding shrubs for a site is to search out and collect them from the wild, but while this may appear to offer sizable cost advantages compared with nursery stock prices, the drawbacks to using *collected material* cannot be overlooked. In the first place, the major roots of wild plants probably have meandered all over in search of water or nutrients and present no assurance they have moved in a regular pattern from the stems. The roots may be entangled with other nearby growth, or they may be arranged lopsidedly to avoid underground obstructions. Second, the possibility always exists that the plant is resting atop a large boulder or a sand layer or hardpan, and this can mean that the depth of the dug ball will prove inadequate to support the weight of top growth in the new location. Collecting shrubs from nature presents risks all the way, and the cost for each digging attempt is borne by the owner even if the experiment fails to produce a usable ball. At no point, however, should shrubs be scooped up with a bulldozer bucket to save time and effort; the proven success rate from this method is generally dismal.

Some prior preparation of natural material can be arranged, however, if you have the time for it. First, encircle the intended root-ball area with a hand-dug trench, roughly 18 to 24 inches deep and wide as a minimum, and then backfill this open circle with a prepared mix of topsoil combined with moistened peat moss, compost, rotted manure, or leaf mold. The intention is to encourage rapid and dense new rooting in the trench for safer and easier digging later, but this technique usually needs a full growing season to create any worthwhile results. Even then it is dependent on adequate rainfall or artificial watering throughout this time to prove effective. Even with this type of handling, there is still no contractor's guarantee attached to these transplanting efforts from the wild.

Occasionally, oversized shrubs are available for sale from private grounds. Since these plants already have had some maintenance and also some root pruning just to reach their present location, digging them offers much less risk than is the case with shrubs taken from nature. Transplanting costs nevertheless may be high because access to the plant on private grounds is very often restricted, handling may be limited entirely to hand labor, and the excavation hole often must be backfilled; also, repairs of damage to lawn areas where hauling equipment crossed may be part of the expense.

Transplanting Timetables

Precisely when any plant is best moved is still hotly debated by many people, and it probably never will be resolved to everyone's satisfaction. The time of year, the age and condition of the plant, the weather at the time of digging, the type of plant (deciduous or evergreen), and the new site conditions are all influential on the success of the operation. The constant is that some plants are known to favor one season over another for proper adjustment when transplanted, but even this factor varies sufficiently throughout all the zones of hardiness and is thus inconclusive for generalization. What is considered standard digging procedure in a cold area is not necessarily useful in more southerly locations, even for the same-named plant. Since the livelihood of both nurseries and landscape contractors depends on the successful handling of local planting problems, relying on their judgment and past experiences is a useful idea when you have any doubts.

Too often owners insist that shrub plantings be done when conditions are far from favorable to success. Out-of-season installations, whether in the heat of summer or in the rigors of winter, along with transplanting before the site is fully ready to take the plants, can greatly reduce root adaptation. It should be the responsibility of the designer to evaluate and redirect such mistaken schedules, especially where constant visual annoyance from shabby plants benefits no one's reputation. As a rule, the majority of established nurseries and contractors will refuse to accept such detrimental planting assignments. They should be applauded for their wise stance.

Shrubs are best dug and handled when they are fully dormant since then there is no soft new growth to bruise and their immediate needs for water are far less. Early spring—or at least the end of the plant's normal dormancy—is often the favored time for transplanting, especially if the shrub requires a full growing season to adjust to its new surroundings. However, spring is often troublesome for weather conditions because of gooey mud and sudden high rises in the temperature at both the nursery and the job site. Autumn planting schedules, however, can be thwarted by early freezing of the ground to some depth or even by unexpectedly early and deep snowfalls. Fortunately, most needle evergreens go into dormancy by late summer and can be moved in early autumn; this is not so with many broadleaf evergreens since they often have too little time to adjust before cold weather arrives and then may suffer foliage and stem damage throughout the winter months. In general, most deciduous shrubs can be transplanted in either early spring or midautumn, and their leafless (or nearly so) condition at these times presents far fewer problems from existing weather.

Preparing the Planting Hole

The *planting hole* or *pit* for a new shrub should be made at least 1 foot wider than the ball diameter and about 6 inches deeper. Stockpile the excavated material so that the topsoil is reserved separately and conveniently for use as backfill. All subsoil should be taken off the site or disposed of on the property where it can prove useful. The bottom of the hole should be loosened slightly beyond its final depth to verify what is beneath it. Bare-rooted and containerized plants should have planting pits of these same dimensions.

Extraneous material uncovered in the digging, such as the various types of construction debris, large rocks, clay hardpan, and dead tree roots or branches, should be removed entirely and discarded. When rock ledge or immovable boulders become evident in the pit excavation, the location of the plant should be changed since these are very restrictive to normal root development. Once the hole is fully dug, check the drainage by adding water to a depth of several inches and verifying the time required for complete removal by gravity below the bottom of the pit. Very sluggish drainage presents enough of a risk to the plant's immediate health that the hole should be abandoned. On the other hand, pits with too rapid drainage are also detrimental, but these can usually be adjusted by excavating the pit somewhat deeper and adding water-holding natural materials such as moist peat moss, ground redwood parts, well-rotted manure, or leaf mold mixed well with the earth in the bottom. What matters most is that the plant receive no additional problems in adjusting to its new home.

Before depositing the shrub into the hole, evenly spread several inches of *conditioned* topsoil—a mix, by volume, of half topsoil and half some humus-rich material but *no* fertilizer at this point—over the bottom of the hole. Frozen or very muddy topsoil should be avoided since it probably will trap pockets of air, which roots dislike. Allow for some slight settlement when the root ball is in place by raising the center part of this bottom fill slightly with more conditioned topsoil. The hole is now ready to accept the shrub.

Installing the Shrub

With a balled plant, place the plant so that it will maintain a finish grade equal to the one it had where it was originally growing. More plants are lost to deep installation than to almost any other cause. Set the shrub so that it is also plumb with the ground level or at least makes a satisfactory alignment with your eye since shrubs have a multitude of stems in their silhouettes and not all are conveniently upright in the same manner. (Creeping shrubs present less of a problem here.) Now add some conditioned topsoil lightly packed around the ball to keep it firmly erect while you again check the alignment. At this point cut back or untie the *top* part of the wrapping. If it is burlap, just fold these loose ends back into the hole; if it is plastic wrap, carefully remove it entirely and discard. With containerized shrubs, remove the pot beforehand and follow the procedure for balled plants. Should the shrub be bare-rooted, first inspect the opened roots for breaks or other damage and prune them off cleanly at the junction of the injury. Then place a cone of conditioned topsoil in the center of the pit and carefully spread the roots evenly over it while maintaining the proper ground elevation for the stems and a plumb balance; backfill as described above. (Bare-rooted rose plants seem to benefit from a novel planting technique of dunking the roots into a bucket of thin mud to coat them before placement in the hole; it is possible that other small shrubs can benefit from this, too.)

Now complete the backfilling with more conditioned topsoil laid down in 6-inch layers gently tamped in place; then puddle well with hose water to remove any potential air pockets since roots want contact only with moist earth. Finish the operation by creating an earthen saucer a few inches high around the dimensions of the pit to concentrate rainwater directly toward the root ball; finally, soak the roots thoroughly. (Slope planting especially benefits from having these water collars.) If the plant settles too low or moves out of plumb, immediately reset it correctly or it will continue to grow that way. Since shrubs have many stems of generally light size that distribute the weight of the foliage over a broad area, they generally do not need staking or guying to keep them solidly in place (unlike most trees), nor do their stems require wrapping with paper to prevent sun scald.

Applying Mulch

Shrubs benefit from living in soil that is kept evenly cool in summer and moist during the entire year. These conditions can be advanced by a *mulch* of some loose form of dead organic matter spread evenly over the root area. In a natural setting this mulching material is commonly in place already. For landscape situations the mulch material varies throughout the world, including nuggets of ground bark, cocoa shells, peanut husks, spent licorice, sugarcane stems (bagasse), pine needles, wood chips, rotted leaves, decayed sawdust, and coarse peat moss, among others. Not all are equal in cost, have easy availability, or possess the same durability. Some blow about easily or decay unpleasantly; others, such as wood chips and sawdust, require one application of a nitrogen fertilizer with them since the bacteria in soil that destroy these fibers deplete the upper soil level of this nutrient while they go about their business. Any type of soil mulch is beneficial, though, since it shields the upper soil from baking and drying out in summer heat, forestalls deep frost penetration in winter, helps reduce weed infestations, and eliminates the need for cultivation. One common mulching material should be avoided, however: stone chips. While neat and durable, the stone tends to hold daytime heat well into the night beneath the plant leaves and stems throughout the summer months; if alkaline in composition, these chips can seriously harm any acid-loving shrubs they surround.

A temporary earthen collar assists in focusing water directly to the roots of new planting. (*Top*)

Wood chips surround this *Calluna vulgaris* cultivar to forestall weeds and conserve moisture. (*Bottom*)

Install mulch right after the planting installation and grading work involved with it are completed. Apply it in even depth reflecting your choice of material. Heavy materials such as wood chips and bark should not exceed 3 inches, while lighter ones such as pine needles can be laid down in depths up to 4 inches (they soon mat down from weathering).

Protective Coatings

Thin wax coatings often are sprayed mechanically on some transplanted or marginally hardy broadleaf evergreens to prevent excess dehydration from winter wind and cold; they are known as foliage *antidessicants*. They should be used in late autumn and applied with caution since heavy coatings of the wax can clog the breathing pores of leaves and stems. Normal flexing and weathering action eventually wears down and dislodges the film by spring. These foliage protections also are used on deciduous material transplanted during the heat of summer while in full leaf for the same purpose of reducing water loss; while effective, they occasionally have the odd side effect of gluing the foliage to the stems far longer into the autumn than is normal. When the annual time for leaf drop arrives, such treated plants are often still noticeably foliaged, and only a heavy snowfall or high wind seems to dislodge the tired foliage in early winter.

Shrubs in Containers

Where natural ground-level planting space for shrubs is neither available nor convenient to arrange on a site, a plant container, usually decorative, has wide appeal today. Planters, tubs, pots, or boxes made of various materials singly or in combination and in colorings to suit the surroundings are now widely available for indoor and outdoor uses. They are, unfortunately, still pots for plants, and as such they keep the shrubs dependent largely on people for any kind of good growth and survival. No containerized shrub can flourish as it would in the ground and all such material must eventually be replaced or transplanted elsewhere, even with the finest maintenance.

Street planters of *Carissa grandifolia cv.* 'Nana' appear less vigorous than their in-ground neighbors.

Even a nonvigorous *Pinus mugo mugo* will outgrow its container eventually. (*Left*)

All planter boxes need adequate drainage holes and reasonable root room. (*Right*)

Soil ages badly and dries out much more quickly in containers, and shrub roots eventually exhaust the size limits of even the largest container and then may inhibit themselves with girdling roots in their constant search for more nutrients and moisture. This ever increasing mat of roots also tends to fill all available space to the exclusion of any soil to hold a reserve of water. When roots fill the container, thorough watering of the entire root ball becomes difficult to achieve since roots are slower than open soil to absorb moisture. Many plants in this condition, even when watered daily, actually suffer drought constraints because the irrigation generally flows down the insides of the container and out the drainage holes before it can penetrate the dense root mass. Once a plant reaches this condition, its top growth will slow down and an increase in defoliation may occur; there is not enough moisture to supply the plant's needs. Transplanting to a larger container or discarding are the usual options.

Because elevated containers outdoors have sides that are exposed continually to wind, the roots are brought into more contact with cold and dryness and may suffer increased dehydration from the heat-absorbing pavements on which they rest. The necessary drainage holes in the bottom of the container also contribute to water loss, yet these holes are essential in order to avoid flooding in heavy storms. Any great amounts of reflected heat and light from nearby buildings, while often useful in moderating winter's harshness, also can be debilitating to plants. In summer these factors may increase the rate of transpiration from leaves, adding to the plant's need for watering. Evergreen shrubs noticeably suffer from these arid summer conditions in urban locations, and they also dislike the stagnation and pollution of the air near city street traffic. The more "citified" the site, the less adaptable evergreens are to in-town survival on a long-term basis; deciduous plants are less demanding.

Dwarf Conifers

Within the wide range of shrub choices are several hundred dwarf conifers ("cone bearers") with unique appeal. These needled evergreens are all miniature in the scale of their parts, dwarfed in their ultimate size from the parent (although some can reach moderate proportions), and so slow-growing that on some an inch a year is considered vigorous. These pygmies (mostly) are called *mutants* or *sports*, terms which signify that the plant has departed radically from its parent in some major way and is able to pass on these characteristics to other generations through asexual reproduction by cuttings only, since seed production is either extremely rare or very likely to diversify the odd characteristics once again.

All are troublesome to find growing in any quantity in nature, at least *in* the earth, and it required many years of patient scientific study by the Arnold Arboretum in Boston and others to clarify their origin. It now appears they are mostly airborne since they come from the noticeably deformed twig and branch ends of certain needle evergreens that are high up in the crown. Apparently, the leaf buds were infected with a virus disorder (called *hexenbesen*, or "witches broom") by insect invaders. These compact growths show much of the same silhouette as the parent but in a greatly reduced form and grow only on the tip ends of certain branches. The majority appear on forest trees and are difficult to locate in the wild. Since these growths have no independent roots, exist mostly out of convenient reach for propagators, and produce extremely limited numbers of cones with fully developed or *viable* embryos, they are not in common supply and are usually expensive for their size in nurseries. Cuttings taken for propagation are just as sluggish in growth as the parent.

They do offer a wide appeal in terms of their fascinating diversity of forms and colorings that is unlike anything else grown. Obviously, their very slow growth and relatively easy maintenance provide unusual landscape values, either as featured

Collections of compatible dwarf conifers offer years of pleasure without pruning.

specimens in containers or as collections grouped in a separate bed to display their range of special characteristics. Throughout the world landscape planting of dwarf conifers has grown impressively, even if the plants themselves do not.

Hedges

Historically, a hedge is a centuries-old planting device that is now defined as a man-made property line barrier composed of similar plants *tightly spaced*. Originally it was used as an unsheared, informal defense (the sound of that word almost spells out its meaning) against various intruders, but later it proved more useful as a convenient way to pen livestock while providing some landscape interest with its flowers and fruits. Not surprisingly, these hedging plants were often chosen for their impressive thorniness. Nowadays, whether armed with thorns or not, a hedge still serves as a physical or visual barrier of some sort, but it also contributes various architectural frames for landscape settings far removed from actual boundary locations. Lofty or low in height, a hedge has rightly been called a "living fence."

Since density is one of the prime reasons for having a hedge, close placement of the individual plants is a foregone conclusion. The individual silhouette and specimen character are surrendered to the fabric of the whole by this deliberate crowding to create a green ribbon of continuous and identical uniformity. Because the separate plants for the hedge may vary slightly in shape and size when they arrive, having a trench predug for the arrangement you have in mind is more advantageous than preparing individual plant pits since this allows for easier on-site adjustments of spacing. Having uniformly prepared soil throughout the bed also contributes to quicker and more even growth. Although single-row hedging is the usual standard—especially from the standpoints of cost and available space—a staggered *double* row of plants provides a far denser and more immediate barrier. This placement also should be set into a predug trench and should be installed in the same manner recommended for an individual shrub specimen that was detailed previously.

Almost any shrub can be trained into a satisfactory hedge, but it is important to choose plants with clearly understood growth habits. Those with exuberant natures, with thorns, or with messy fruit need special evaluation when placed next to public walkways or on property lines; they may create social problems, especially if left untrimmed. They ought to be set back sufficiently so that they can grow naturally without inconveniencing others in later years, but even trimmed hedges should be placed so that shearing can be handled entirely on your own property.

Spacing for hedge plants varies with the intended need for the hedge, with the type of plant used for it, and certainly with the purchase size. A well-known rule of thumb for spacing is to have the plants just touching when they are installed, but this does not take into account either the usual rate of annual growth in your vicinity or the ultimate height and spread of the plant. (As mentioned before, find out how the same plants grow in other locations before you space your own plants.) This system also does not provide for root entanglement in later years and the likely reduction of vigor when too many roots are competing for the same moisture and nutrients. Hedge plants primarily need root room if they are to stay valuable as a screen or barrier.

Rapid-growing deciduous shrubs can probably be spaced farther apart initially since they have more energy for new expansion than evergreens of the same age; deciduous plants do not have to support year-round foliage from the same root system, and so their development usually produces more stems and leaves in the same time period. Slowly developing and dwarf shrubs can obviously be placed closer together from the start, whether evergreen or deciduous.

Expect an imposing screen from *Taxus x media cv.* 'Hicksii' hedges with adequate sun and proper maintenance. (*Top*)

Even today, the centuries-old use of *Buxus sempervirens* cultivars for clipped formal hedges continues. (*Middle*)

When pruned early and consistently, *Taxus x media cv.* 'Hatfieldii' produces a crisply dense wall of greenery. (*Bottom*)

Hedges that fall within the root zone of large trees nearby often show a marked lowering of uniform growth next to these roots. This is to be expected since the established tree roots will automatically collect all the available soil water and nutrients first as well as contribute some possible shading toward the hedge at some point in the day. Since the growing conditions are not equalized under these circumstances, a part of the hedge is likely to look uneven for some time. Some of this root competition can be avoided by installing the hedge in a different manner. Instead of digging the shrubs directly into the root zone of the tree, place the hedge line bed above the roots by adding a raised earth platform (about the depth of the root ball) along its entire length; this will allow the shrub roots to anchor themselves before any tree roots invade the soil space and will also permit more uniform growth from the hedge for many years. If convenient, this raised bed can be graded to blend with the surrounding topography, but if your space or inclination dictates a formal approach, a curbed enclosure for this stacked earth can be arranged. None of this should interfere with the feeder roots of the tree since the grade change is limited to a narrow line of earth fill.

When shaping a hedge into a formally pruned line, one should take into account that sun needs to reach the lowest branches as much as possible if they are to remain dense. You can accomplish this by tapering the shape to provide a base that is wider than the top. Whether you square off or round the top line is a matter of personal choice, although the domed finish has some advantage in snow country since the weight of ice and snow does not accumulate quite so heavily as it does on a perfectly flat surface. Untrimmed shrub hedges offer no special advantages or disadvantages in these wintertime situations; they will simply be rearranged even more informally.

This shearing program should wait until the new plantings have had a full season of adjustment growth behind them and then should be done when the next season's growth has stretched at least 6 inches. The technique is to remove terminal growth and stimulate axillary or side bud development for greater and faster density. In the simplest terms you remove one (the terminal) to gain two (the axillaries). Thereafter, your trimming schedule should be determined by the growth rate in your locale, the amount of neatness you desire seasonally, and the cost factors involved. In some mild climate areas four trimmings a year are not considered excessive, but the usual schedule is to plan for at least two shearings in every growing season. The first shearing is often set to restore the hedge after winter's rigors; the second is usually organized to control summertime growth. With most flowering shrubs used as hedges, the first trimming is best done right after flowering is completed since any later pruning would remove the flower buds for the next year;

Ligustrum japonicum accepts tight pruning readily for architectural accents. (*Left*)

Hedges maintain more lower foliage when pruned with a tapered top. (*Right*)

any midsummer pruning attention should be aimed at simple neatness. Plants with inconspicuous flowering, such as most of the needled evergreens, can be shaped at any time which is convenient.

Established hedges of great size that need reduction or a change in outline require some pondering. Aged evergreens rarely take kindly to heavy pruning at any one time since their denser stem wood does not often stimulate repair budding. Also, since the inner bark of evergreens was originally shaded by foliage, removing this sun and wind shield can dehydrate these older stems beyond any hope of new budding. It is perhaps more sensible under these conditions to move slowly and to stagger the pruning schedule over several seasons. With deciduous shrubs, the possibilities for rejuvenation of older plants are greater since such plants replenish their lost stems and foliage much more quickly than evergreens, are not so troubled by drastic pruning methods, and can actually improve their appearance. Not every shrub conveniently fits into these generalized categories, of course, but you have at least learned some insights to guide you in evaluating whether older hedges are worth the effort of rejuvenation. If not, rip out the old and bring in the new.

Pruning Adjustments

All shrubs need some sort of pruning attention during their lifetimes. What kind and how much is determined by the need you have in mind. In general, shrub pruning of newly installed plantings should be delayed until the work is completed since damage can occur in all the stages of transplanting. Of course, dead, weak, or abused branches and twigs ought to be removed as found since they can contribute little to the total picture if left in place. For pruning, always use tools that are sharp and of a proper weight to do the job correctly. Do not leave stub ends but prune as close to the main stem as possible; this allows repair tissue to make a smooth covering that envelopes only live wood, not half-dead stumps. If there are branches that rub each other, one of them should be removed to avoid bark wounds that allow easier insect penetration. In the same category, promptly repair storm damage to channel the plant's energies into the remaining stems for quick repair of the loss; lengthy delay can lead to more problems. If the damage is extensive, you may have to reshape the entire plant silhouette. Full restoration may require several years.

Remove dead or damaged parts cleanly and promptly for better plant health.

Not all pruning is involved with damage repair. Most deciduous shrubs benefit from thinning out of old, nonproductive stems from time to time; this allows more air to flow through the plant and can aid in discouraging some insect and disease problems that thrive in congested foliage. Removing spent flower heads is yet another type of pruning; it encourages greater bud production for the next season since seed development from the faded blossoming does take energy from the plant. This procedure is especially helpful with rhododendrons. Shrubs with colorful stems can be rejuvenated by pruning out the darker, older wood; the new stems will be brightly noticeable. When silhouette reshaping of spring-flowering shrubs is called for, plan your work for the end of the blooming season so that all new bud development will be directed into the adjusted stem arrangement; pruning these shrubs in late summer removes the flower buds.

Topiary pruning refers to the deliberate shaping of plants into solidly sheared architectural or sculptural forms; a clipped hedge is the most common form used today. With some avid practitioners, however, this forceful dominance over plants has extended to every plant on the property, a make-work situation that has no end and leaves nothing of a plant's natural form; hardly any plant looks good disguised as a chicken croquette.

For the most part, pruning ought to be a remedial activity that serves a clear and logical purpose. It should be managed with a deft approach at all times, fully acknowledging both the natural grace and beauty of the plant silhouette and the expected response the shrub will make to the pruning. Growth can, and should, be tamed, but it will provide more visual satisfaction for a longer time when it is allowed to keep its natural dignity and appearance.

After-Planting Maintenance

Once a shrub is growing satisfactorily in its new home (usually a year after installation), it can be given fertilizer on a regular basis. Adding nutrients when the shrub is installed has a potential for harm since the roots severed by the digging are in some disrepair and can be injured further by a sudden contact with any fertilizer compound; the amended soil backfill usually can provide all the nourishment a shrub requires in its first season. Apply the fertilizer according to the package instructions and follow that with a thorough watering to start the action in motion. Also inspect the plant for damaged twigs or dead wood and for insect and disease inroads; then prune and spray as needed. Maintain thorough and regular

Spent flower removal usually results in greater bud production for the next season. (*Left*)

Careful discarding of *Rhododendron* species seed heads soon after bloom ends conserves energy for other growth. (*Right*)

watering in times of drought stress and keep the mulch at a constant depth and neatly arranged about the roots. Prune only for natural shapeliness or to repair storm damage. Providing these simple attentions on a frequent basis should keep maintenance readily manageable and the plant content for many years.

Fertilizing

While fertilizing programs for shrubs should begin after the first year, how long they should be maintained is still an open question. A vigorous, healthy shrub is not a likely candidate for more growth stimulation (regardless of what some advertisements claim), but a weak performer is. Truly ailing plants, on the other hand, rarely benefit from any concentrated feeding since their problems lie elsewhere and should be treated differently. Some *liquid* fertilizer solutions, however, have a commendable record of assisting lackadaisical shrubs on the road to recovery, but these applications should be of mild strength, and you should follow the manufacturer's recommendations implicitly; otherwise you can do more harm than good. Another form of liquid fertilizer is the *foliar* that is applied directly to the leaves and stems (the other type is given directly to the roots) for an immediate growth response; it should be supplemented at least once a year by a granular, solid fertilizer application in the root zone. Be careful in applying foliar feeding in times of high heat and bright sunshine, though, since the fertilizer salt residue may scorch the foliage and deform the stems somewhat under these conditions; applying it on cooler, overcast days is safer. Again, mix foliar stimulants in full accordance with the instructions and avoid overdosing when you apply.

Generally, the dry, granular fertilizer mixes are the mainstays of shrub feeding programs, and these are commonly available as either *fast-acting* chemical compounds or *slow-release* organic mixes. There are also specialized fertilizers created exclusively for acid-loving plant types. Local experience will indicate whether early spring or late autumn is the preferred time for use, and the package will supply the recommended application rate for the various types of shrubs normally found in any landscape. These annual feedings generally are handled simply by broadcasting the material evenly around the shrub base in a widening circle that also extends over the main feeder root zone. Apply the mixture directly to the mulch covering already in place and follow with a hosing that will prevent unwanted concentrations from staying in place while you inaugurate the fertilizer into solution. Applying this fertilizer just before a heavy rain is also a recommended procedure, as it eliminates the need for hosing down. Another, newer fertilizer system involves inserting preformed cylinders of dry fertilizer into shallow drill holes set regularly spaced into the root zone. This method has the merit of being cleaner and easier to handle; it too should be done annually.

Insect and Disease Controls

Insect pests and diseases (which are minute, primitive plants attacking larger, more advanced plants) unfortunately appear to be a normal part of every environment. While there is supposedly a natural predator or antidote for all these ailments, none ever seems to arrive on any salvation schedule of convenience. Drastic leaf destruction or disease disfigurement is a severe shock to a plant's current health and future growth, and it creates a visual disappointment in the landscape. Timely applications of protective sprays are worth both the cost and the effort. No shrub is known to have died simply of old age, but many millions have died because of marauding insects and fungal infections. As with all health aids, follow the manufacturer's instructions for mixing and dosage. All these treatments are often poisonous in

Burrowing insect larvae contorted and weakened this new growth on *Pinus mugo mugo*.

Powdery mildew disfigurement is common to *Rhododendron* 'Knap Hill-Exbury Hybrid' cultivars during humid summertime weather.

some degree for people (and other animals) and should be applied with caution. Some also have the annoying side effect of staining or disrupting painted surfaces and porous construction materials nearby. Read the caveats before you spray.

A wise approach to shrub selection is to choose only shrubs with a minimum of attractions locally for either pests or diseases, yet neglected shrubs, even those with the highest resistance to these nuisances, will always be prone to more problems than well-maintained ones. The influence of both insects and diseases is included in the individual shrub listings in this book, and it also accounts for some of the necessary eliminations made in compiling it.

Watering

Newly installed shrubs benefit from deep and regular watering during the first year and especially in times of drought so as to encourage continual and rapid root expansion. Consistent saturation of the soil either from constant rain or from over-use of your sprinkler system can prove detrimental, however, by leading to root rot and soil compaction. In planted areas either remote from hydrant water or not favored by sufficient rainfall, plan for pumped irrigation from tank trucks on a regular basis. During all drought situations always keep in mind that nearby established plants are also thirsty and will very likely intrude their own root needs into the watering program; under these circumstances more frequent watering of new shrubs may be necessary to accomplish any long-lasting benefit.

At the beginning of the autumn dormancy season, transplanted shrubs, especially evergreens, appear to benefit from generous and regular irrigation, whether it comes from the sky or from the end of a hose, to keep them adequately water-filled during the rigors of winter. This autumn watering does not instill greater bud and stem durability into the plant since that must be established by adequate moisture during the growth time of midsummer or it will not exist at all; what it does is stabilize the entire plant with moisture for *greater resistance* to dormancy problems. For the best results, shrubs should be kept moist in all seasons. This is especially true of containerized plantings because they are artificially isolated from finding water on their own throughout the year.

All in all, regular maintenance of shrubs is unavoidable, but only an attentive approach to such maintenance can keep landscapes of distinction looking that way.

Landscape design is a visual fine art with a long and distinguished history in human affairs. It began when people deliberately planted and cultivated special places for social use and enjoyment beyond the basic agricultural need of food for themselves and their livestock. After thousands of years of refinement, decorative use of plants in the landscape now takes many unique forms and these condensed remarks about the art cannot be much more than a generalized guide about aesthetic compositions. Since people's life-styles are constantly altering and the zeal of plant hybridizers constantly keeps the public dazzled with improved plant choices, there is always some new and stimulating way to combine plants for visual pleasure. Shrubs are no exception.

Design of any sort is a problem-solving *process* which serves functional needs, creates meaningful forms, and conserves economic means. Landscape design in its total summation differs from all other art forms in its broad scope, its unique materials, and the effect time has on its parts. It is the least static art because it largely involves plant growth, and it is the only profession that is particularly concerned with *living* elements and their skillful placement on the land. One of the curiosities of our work is that all landscape designers are restricted by *existing* colors, textures, and shapes of plant types already on hand; we cannot arrange for new plants on demand.

Because landscape design is primarily involved with the creation of usable outdoor space (although some designers also work with interior plantings), the work of the landscape designer often incorporates both planting and architectural devices to define and explain the intended use and function of the layout. It is also a profession concerned with the effects of outdoor light and of the third-dimensional volume of space. While *horticulture* involves growing plants well, *design* is concerned with arranging them well. Combining both elements attractively and enduringly is the sought-after formula for a memorable landscape setting.

Shrubs are a valuable tool for the harmonious and practical resolution of many physical site problems, and, of course, they provide the owner with durable aes-

Skillful placement of both the architectural and the planting elements creates a harmonious design.

thetic satisfaction. Shrubs offer a variety of noticeable effects: screening, cooling, privacy, enhancement of architectural lines, enframement of views, erosion management, sun and wind control, sound deadening, and horticultural focus and emphasis, plus a potential reduction of maintenance costs. They further contribute *sensory* attractions throughout the year by individual or blended colorings; by fragrances; by moving shadow patterns; by seasonal flower, foliage, and fruiting changes; and by stimulating silhouettes and textures. The generous assortment of shrub types available throughout the world allows for a wide range of designer interpretations.

When planted to define boundaries, shrubs act as "outdoor walls." When used as specimens standing dramatically alone, large-scale shrubs can assume important emphasis. When massed, any shrub form can become a background foil for other landscape elements. Both the branching pattern and the foliage textures can provide fine, coarse, or intermediate accents and contrasts, while the *character* of an individual shrub—the sum of all its inherent growth mannerisms coupled with the varying effect site influences have on its matured final appearance—often supplies us with an emotional response that fluctuates from ruggedness to delicacy, from flamboyance to somberness, and from wistfulness to stately elegance.

The natural silhouette *forms* of shrubs generally fall within these categories: columnar to fastigiate, conical to pyramidal, round to oval, vase-shaped to inverted

Water and shrubs should enhance each other. (*Left*)

Used to define boundaries, large flowering shrubs become striking outdoor walls. (*Right*)

Shrubs offer a wide variety of useful forms from columnar to creeping.

pyramid, dense to open-headed, pendulous to weeping, prostrate to creeping, and irregular to distorted. With selective and patient pruning, any shrub can be modified into an architectural (some say "artificial") shape called *topiary* to suit special landscape purposes: *standarding* to create an umbrella head of foliage (and often flowers) supported by a single stem kept clean of twigs and leaves, *espaliering* to create a flattened two-dimensional wall display, and *sculpturing* to create a three-dimensional figure or shape (mostly done with needle evergreens) of any description, size, or fancy. This style of training shrubs proved highly popular for centuries in Europe as estate decoration. Since these pruning techniques are expensive in terms of time and skilled effort, are required on a continuing and regular basis, and fit only a limited number of landscape settings comfortably, today we usually limit ourselves to simple hedge shearing for our topiary exercises.

Because a shrub is an elastic design element with many variations of size, color, and form, the designer has to recognize and define from the start what is to be the ultimate contribution of shrubs in the development. A thorough analysis of the intended *use* of the space, the established *proportions* of the total area under development, and the *form* of the design layout will influence the site enrichment potential of shrubs both when they are first installed and as they reach maturity.

Standarding shrubs often involves grafting, as illustrated by the *Syringa meyeri* head on the stem base of *Syringa reticulata*. (*Top left*)

Fanciful topiary can enliven any blank wall, as this *Taxus* demonstrates. (*Top right*)

Special pruning effort created this espaliered cotoneaster feature. (*Bottom left*)

Sculptural animal forms are popular topiary subjects. (*Bottom right*)

Of course, careful site analysis also has to include what disposition is made of existing items left on the site as well as what amount of influence neighboring uses, soil conditions, air movement, exposure, utility lines, lighting, and concentrations of human users will have on plant development. Only by clarifying and evaluating all this background information can the designer and owner hope to achieve the finest results. Both ought to have a keen sensitivity to the site conditions and to the plants used in the design scheme to achieve fulfillment, but unfortunately, not everyone is born with such attributes. When in doubt, hire a specialist for professional guidance.

Planting compositions have *principles of order:* repetition, sequence, and balance. *Repetition* is the most fundamental and can be achieved easily by duplicating ad infinitum any of the following: color, shape, texture, size, position, or quantity. For increased visual harmony, however, repetition must be accompanied by both sequence and balance since the overuse of repetition soon brings monotony and a dulling of further interest and appreciation of the scene. While *variety* provides relief from monotony, it is not a principle of order but merely a welcome realization that something has changed. The introduction of variety often leads to excess, however, and to a lack of specific focus that soon degenerates into visual chaos. It is common practice with the amateur to have one of each appealing plant scattered about the property, but although variety can be called the spice of life, it was never intended to become the meal. When treated with abandon, variety can disturb rather than calm the spirit.

Sequence involves arranging the diverse attributes of plant material to lead the eye easily and comfortably in one planned direction. It entails a *progressive change* of at least one plant characteristic as it moves along, perhaps involving the shape, color, or size of some plant part. Subtly arranging for a transition of foliage from coarse to fine is one example of sequence, and when well handled, the interconnected rhythm of the planning effort can lift a mundane setting into a memorable experience. Here, variety is not only deliberately used, it is also deliberately controlled.

Since we are more accustomed to recognizing and accepting objects that have equally distributed parts on a vertical axis (the way people are shaped), we refer to this visual satisfaction as *balance*. There are two types. When both sides of an

Repetition is a commonly used principle of order, as shown by these duplicate beds of roses surrounded by hedges of *Buxus microphylla koreana.* (*Top*)

Sequence involves altering at least one plant characteristic; here it is the amount of leaf variegation. (*Above*)

A symmetrical or formal layout is consistently popular as a garden feature.

Contemporary settings often promote an informal or asymmetric design layout.

The fine texture of *Ilex crenata cv.* 'Convexa' easily melts into this background. (*Top*)

Proportion in design is associated with the comfortable distribution of the various forms and textures used. (*Bottom*)

axis are identical or *mirror images* of each other, they are in *symmetry*, a design formula long distinguished by its ever-popular appeal in landscape developments during many changes in styles. It is simple to achieve on almost any size land form and often shows a crisply architectural influence. It is now commonly known as "formal" design. Its opposite form is *asymmetry*, or *occult* balance, which is popularly labeled "informal." Either type can be visually acceptable as long as it well suits the total landscape concept. Throughout history the fads and fancies of landscape design changes have alternated between these two main types of presentations; our contemporary design resolutions seem to favor the informal landscape approach. It will change, though, as a matter of historical record. The *style* of a design is nothing more than a fixed combination of the materials and the arranged form dominantly given them in any one time period. It is often identified with a known world personality, such as *Victorian*, a style identified with the reign of England's Queen Victoria. When durably influential, the expressions from one artistic discipline eventually emerge throughout all the other arts; new painting styles, for example, may soon influence sculpture and even architecture.

All design elements in a landscape have characteristics of both *size* and *scale*. As one might surmise, living plants create some bothersome problems here since they are constantly expanding. People are the guiding scale by which all objects are measured, and the phrase "out of scale" refers to our own expectations of how compared items relate to one another visually and whether we accept the comparison as valid. As the scale of the surroundings changes, so can the relative scale of a plant also change. Thus, a large shrub in an urban garden may be thought "oversized" while the same plant set in a public park may appear "undersized." It is all relative.

Distance and *perspective* alter the outline and true shape of all objects. The uncountable fine leaves of yew, for example, disappear completely as individuals when viewed from far away; only the silhouette and color are helpful for an association of identification. Close-at-hand planting, alternatively, reveals the intricacies of growth but often less of the total outline, and this relationship of placement provides us with a useful way of enlarging or diminishing outdoor space. Fine-textured or light green plants at a distance will seem optically farther away than they are physically, while nearby coarse-textured and dark-toned plants will

Emphasis contrasts two objects or two characteristics of similar objects. (*Left*)

Design accent leads the eye to the main focus of the space. (*Right*)

Landscape unity harmonizes all the elements into a clearly seen use and purpose.

appear even closer. This effect is also applicable with many colors; "cool" ones such as blue and purple recede from the viewer, while the "hot" colors of red and orange seem to advance.

Design *values* are several: proportion, emphasis, accent, and unity. *Proportion* in outdoor design refers to the distribution percentage of any element, and it soon dictates how many different shapes, colors, sizes, textures, or placement positions can be accommodated comfortably before clutter sets in. *Emphasis* is based on uniqueness and is created by a noticeable contrast between two objects or two characteristics of those objects. It should be used sparingly since all people soon tire of constant visual stimulation, especially if it is always dramatically handled. *Accent* is a collection of low-keyed *secondary* objects arranged into a flowing procession toward a final main focus; it has an obvious relationship with the principle of sequence. *Unity* involves the successful harmonizing of all the elements in a design toward a commonly understood statement of purpose. It is the one landscape skill most prized by every designer since it illustrates true landscape artistry.

Because flowering shrubs bloom only for a few weeks at most, having plants with a dual seasonal appeal is a practical assessment for shrub choices in any design layout. Summer foliage variations, attractive and persistent fruiting, good-colored

Contrasting foliage from *Cornus alba cv.* 'Spaethii' agreeably highlights the spruce background.

autumnal leaf changes, and noticeable wintertime bark all add a welcome visual stimulation far beyond the flowering time. The contrast provided by deciduous shrub silhouettes placed against a taller evergreen backdrop adds yet another worthwhile contribution throughout the year, even when the textural and color effects come only from the foliage. Form and habit also add diversity, and it is possible to create landscape effects from a variety of different aspects with shrubs. Although evergreen plants have rightly been called the "aristocrats" of the plant world, nevertheless, designs filled exclusively with them tend in a short time to seem gloomy, dull, and even overpowering. Groupings of all deciduous shrubs, on the other hand, often appear sparse, leggy, or fuzzy-outlined during winter defoliation. The logical way to handle this difficulty is to make an agreeable mix of the two.

Color in the landscape can make the difference between calmness and excitement since color is a strongly felt *motivating* element for personal response to a scene. If you take away all color by reducing light to pitch blackness or add such intense brightness that you dazzle the eye with brilliance, you will disorient the viewer. Color is naturally and intrinsically involved with light, whether artificial or natural, and all objects reflect it somewhat by their own surfaces and their own color pigments. With shrubs, the size and quantity of the leaf, stem, flower, and fruit surfaces dictate how much light we will receive from them at any time during the year, and this controls what color we perceive them to be. Minute blossoms or tiny foliage offer little surface area for light reflection and tend to disappear from view at any distance. These are best massed together for the greatest effect.

We can alter the quality of color in an outdoor site by changing the *intensity* of the source (filter sunlight through foliage), by changing the type of *surface* catching the light (glossy foliage is more reflective than hairy leaves), and by a *contrast* of different colorings (white flowers intermixed with deep-colored ones enliven them). The time of day also influences color intensity; morning light adds a yellowish overtone, the white brilliance of noontime sun on summer days dilutes all but the most intense color values, and the sunset hours bring a reddish or purplish cast to the entire scene. The nearness of similar color values creates "richness" in landscape effects, while monochromatic schemes tend to unite diverse areas of color in a simple but effective way. The repeated consistency of similar foliage on

Filtering light can alter the color value of leaves and flowers.

Euonymus fortunei cv. 'Emerald 'N Gold' has appeal even on an overcast day.

the hedge is one example of how only one coloring and one texture can provide a unifying bonus of visual appeal. Of course, the dominant color of plant material is green, but which green? In spring the emerging foliage of both evergreen and deciduous shrubs is thin-walled and filmy with a fresh, yellow-green coloring. By summer these leaves thicken and become both opaque and deeper-toned. Aging by autumn further modifies the leaf color and also reduces some of the sheen. Every season offers some variation in the green color a plant is said to have.

Stimulating color combinations in the landscape can readily be created by using the *harmony of triads*. These are three related colors assembled in differing proportions to suit both personal preference and the existing site colorings. A reason-

The play of light and shadow provides depth and richness in any landscape design.

able division can be achieved by pairing two for emphasis and retaining the last for a dash of accent interest. Beginning with the primary colors of red, yellow, and blue, consider their landscape tones of russet, citrus, and slate; with the secondary colors of purple, orange, and green, evaluate plum, buff, and sage as cooperative alternatives. White has an admirable quality of agreeably separating adjacent, intense colorings, while gray-toned shrubs provide an attractive foil for increasing the clarity and intensity of other colors.

With all its potentialities, planting design will always offer a paradox: how to see a plant as an individual while finding ways of incorporating its assets into a larger picture. Obviously, there can be no totally fixed rules for using shrubs attractively in the landscape, only options for your experiments with them. It is an interesting challenge.

Since shrubs are woody plants with many ground-originating stems and are closer to our general inspection because of their shorter size—as opposed to the taller-growing trees—their individual parts come under more visual scrutiny as they develop. Shrubs are also more closely noted because their varying textures, silhouettes, and colorings blend so effectively in a landscape setting; the historic mix of different shrub types in a border development is still a well-used feature of their gregarious nature. Shrubs are somehow *expected* to blend together harmoniously in planting schemes.

In the natural system all shrubs have value, but not all shrubs have the distinguished *landscape* merit of resolving site problems attractively. Since the known quantity of shrubs in the temperate growing areas of the world already adds up to many tens of thousands, some logical selection of the more valuable ones had to be made for this book. However, even with the eliminations, a remarkable and sizable selection of worthy shrub choices remains for landscape uses extending from hardiness zone 3 through zone 10. Like all such individualized lists, this one is based on personal evaluation and is focused on a designer's point of view that couples visual distinction with practicality. There seems little point in creating enthusiasm for a handsome shrub that is commercially unavailable from any source, is extraordinarily demanding of time and attention to grow well, or is only marginally able to survive in the major growing areas as a result of soil, moisture, or temperature conditions it finds unfavorable. Distinction in plants has to be coupled with some endurance for a range of locations to make the plants truly worthwhile.

The several hundred shrub genera and species included in this section should supply enough options to satisfy all your landscape needs. Beyond these basics, however, the list expands to include both *varieties* and *cultivars*. Varieties are plants already growing in nature with traits distinctly different from those of the parent species in some category of color, size, form, or habit which will come through when grown from seed. Cultivars—a created word from "cultivated varieties"—are horticultural selections of an improved plant characteristic generally made from commercially grown stock which then can be reproduced efficiently as exact replicas only when handled as asexual cuttings. Because so many plants worldwide are grown intensively in nurseries today, the finding of additional cultivars has become almost an annual expectation. While not every touted addition to a nursery catalog lives up to its promotion, the words "new" and "improved" have real meaning today in reputable catalogs. Shrubs are no exception to this happy circumstance.

This portion of the book is divided into three divisions based on the major leaf types (both simple and compound): *needle evergreens*, *broadleaf evergreens*, and *deciduous shrubs*. Regrettably, space restrictions and the limited warm areas where they thrive eliminated consideration of the dwarf palms, the bamboos, and the tall succulents for this catalog.

All divisions are alphabetically arranged, and each genus entry is introduced by a short commentary about its major characteristics and family association. This is followed by a detailed explanation for each species (again alphabetically organized), using the currently acceptable *scientific* name as published in the new *Hortus Third* of Cornell University (see Bibliography), along with all the normally available varieties and cultivars. If the name has had a recent changeover, the older name (or names) appears in brackets beside it in the heading. Each entry carries the most usual *common* name as well, with the *Hortus Third* preference, where it is supplied, listed first; you will notice a minimum of capitalization in common names, which corresponds with current recommendations of botanic authorities. Accompanying these plant labels are useful aids that provide information about the normal zones of hardiness, the average height range in cultivation, and the native habitat or time and country of introduction into cultivation, plus data about seasonal appearance, growth habit, rate of yearly expansion, cultural preferences, growing difficulties, pest and disease afflictions beyond the norm, and any special hints for the successful raising of the shrub. The text is supplemented by black-and-white and color photographs that show important aspects of the majority of the shrubs when grown naturally and without extensive pruning (except for hedge displays). The aim of this book is to place all the pertinent information about shrubs within convenient reach.

Because the scientific names of many plants here included also apply equally to the tree forms of those genera and species—and these have been categorized already in my book *Trees for Every Purpose* (McGraw-Hill, New York, 1980)—some differentiation in format had to be considered for this book to clarify and pinpoint the information as it applies to shrubs. When a plant is known to be limited exclusively to multistemmed shrub forms, it is listed only with its genus and species labels; but where the genus contains tree forms as well, the scientific and common names are followed in the heading by the term "shrub cultivars and varieties." This system allows you to determine quickly whether the genus is composed of all shrubs or a mix of trees and shrubs, and it also eliminates repetition of shared background data which has already been provided in the introductory remarks for each genus and each species.

One curiosity should be noted: The dwarf forms of many plants do not always produce the same flowering or fruiting aids to their identification that the parent possesses; these must be separated mainly on the basis of differences in foliage. In dwarfs, form, color, rate of growth, ultimate size, and type of leaf are all important characteristics for separating these cultivars and varieties from one another.

As you read about and assess these opportunities for selection, always match the shrub to the site conditions it will receive since it is far wiser to grow a commonplace plant well than to force adaptation on a specimen ill suited for its new surroundings. It is my hope that through the skilled use of this book you will increase the worth of your landscape efforts both aesthetically and horticulturally. Prior knowledge about plant behavior is a beneficial first step toward satisfactory results in the landscape.

Needle
Evergreens

ABIES (fir)　　*Pinaceae* (pine) family

Composed mainly of conical, forest-sized trees which have given rise to only a few shrubby dwarf forms, this monoecious genus has separate male and female flowering on the same plant. There are forty species of fir distributed worldwide throughout the north temperate areas, and all prefer cool, constantly moist, humusy, acid soil with high year-round humidity and full sun. While they are rarely bothered significantly by pests and diseases, they do object to oppressive heat and air pollution and are therefore not always the best choice for inner-city planting.

The fir can be identified as different from its nearest relative, *Picea* (spruce), in several ways: by its rounded, resin-coated buds; by its solitary, blunt ended needles with two white bands beneath; by the flat cross section of its leaf; by the smooth and disk-shaped marks on the twig when foliage drops; and by the egg-shaped female cones of only a season's duration that appear on the *upper* side of a main branch. When crushed, fir foliage has a turpentine odor.

Abies balsamea　　(balsam fir, fir balsam, balm of Gilead) shrub
cultivars and varieties

Zones 3 to 8　　Variable in size　　Sun

Familiar to most of us as the prime source of trees for Christmas decoration, this species was introduced to culture about 1696. It is also the source of Canadian balsam, a yellow-green sticky fluid from the sap which dries into a transparent mass useful as an undistorting medium for mounting material on microscope slides. Native from Labrador to West Virginia and westward to Iowa, it has winter buds that are small and reddish with an almost varnished look. It has hairy new twigs with round-ended and tip-notched, glossy, 1-inch flat needles that are dark green above and show two white lines beneath. These aromatic needles are a prime source for stuffing ornamental pillows. The cones are oblong and 2½ inches high with a violet-purple coloring. It shares the same basic cultural information listed for the genus, except that it should not be planted in any soil with the least hint of lime. The Fraser fir (*A. fraseri*) is its counterpart in the southern United States since it tolerates much more heat, but it is short-lived compared with *A. balsamea*. The following cultivars and varieties exist.

CULTIVAR: 'Hudsonia' was introduced about 1810 and came from the windswept peaks of the White Mountains of New England; this assures its ironclad hardiness. The form is a cushionlike or flattened globe of rich, glossy, deep but bright green short needles with two white or bluish bands on the undersides. Its foliage is set only semiradially around the short ascending twigs so that part of the stem shows. Very slow-growing, it will reach 1 foot in height with an 18-inch spread within 10 years; the ultimate height is 3 feet. Tolerant of more shading when young, it will also accept a limed soil. This is a sterile plant.

CULTIVAR: 'Nana' came from the same mountain area of upper New England and presents a globose, or rounded, flat-topped bushlet form and very short (¼ inch), bright green needles with two white lines beneath. Its needles are radially arranged entirely around the slender twigs, giving a dense appearance. Expanding at only ½ inch yearly, it will reach an eventual size of 3 feet in both height and width after many decades. It has no cones. This cultivar benefits from protection against hot summer sun by shading from a nearby rock or something similar toward its base as well as from an annual topdressing of sharp sand and leaf mold to encourage sturdier growth.

Abies concolor (white fir, Colorade white fir, Colorado fir)
shrub cultivars and varieties

Zones 4 to 8   Variable in size   Sun to semishade

Native to much of the western and southwestern United States, this symmetrical forest giant is liked for its long, soft-to-the-touch, gray-toned foliage and its tolerance for semishade. It withstands summertime heat and dryness better than any other fir. The 2-inch needles are arranged equally about the yellow-green twigs but twist upward as they expand so that all appear to be coming from the top; these leaves are gray-green to blue-green on both surfaces. The cones are from 3 to 5 inches tall and silvery olive-green to purplish in color.

Provide a deep, rich, acid, well-drained loam (but no clay) in either full sun or semishade on a site away from drying summer winds. It is very tolerant of drought but not of polluted air and will grow satisfactorily in the warm, humid conditions of the northeastern and southeastern United States. Occasionally its stems are bothered by inroads of the sawfly larva or the larva of the fir needle miner. Its cultivar shares the same cultural needs.

CULTIVAR: 'Compacta' is a dwarf form brought to cultivation in 1891 from its native habitat in the southwestern United States. It has an upright, irregular outline far different from that of its parent. The silvery gray, thick, stiff needles are about ½ inch long and are either straight or scythe-shaped; they appear on crowded, dense twigs and branches. Some nursery offerings are more blue-toned than others because of the soil and cultural practices where they are grown, and so this cultivar is often listed incorrectly as *A. concolor violacea compacta*. Cones are nonexistent. In a decade this plant becomes 3 feet square.

Abies koreana cv. 'Compact Dwarf'

Abies koreana (Korean fir) shrub cultivars and varieties

Zones 6 to 8   Variable in size   Sun to semishade

More sedate in habit and less imposing in its tree size than other firs, this inhabitant of the mountain slopes of South Korea is also less hardy than its cousins. It has yellowish twigs that carry glossy, ¾-inch, deep green needles that have silvery lines beneath when mature, but they first emerge more noticeably as bright silver-gray. The erect, cylindrical, 2- to 3-inch cones are conspicuous for their violet-purple coloring as well as for appearing on quite young plants. It prefers sun but will accept a fair amount of shading, too. Provide a well-drained, moist, rich soil on a site away from great heat and air pollution. Its cultivar has the same needs.

CULTIVAR: 'Compact Dwarf' is still unknown in terms of where it originated. The outline is squat and flat-topped with much interlacing of the branches and twigs, and there is no central leader. It has never borne cones. A nearly similar dwarf form, 'Prostrate Beauty', from Europe does, however, carry occasional normal-sized leaders that should be removed promptly to maintain its low shape. Both have ½- to ¾-inch grooved, dark green needles with two broad whitened lines beneath that occur on cream-gray twigs. Slow-growing, each can become 4 feet tall and wide over many years. Both are surprisingly tolerant of a high degree of shade.

CEPHELOTAXUS (plum yew)   *Cephelotaxaceae* (plum yew) family

Introduced from the orient in the 1820s, this unusual genus of seven species has some odd members that accept either full sun or dense shade without concern. It differs from *Taxus* (yew) in its broader and longer solitary leaves with two silvery bands beneath as well as in its almond-shaped fruit

entirely encased in a fleshy covering. It has a good tolerance for limed soils and can grow successfully in the competitive root zone of other, larger plants. All types are adaptable only to warm growing areas. None is pest-prone.

Cephalotaxus fortunei (Chinese plum yew)

Zones 7 to 10   30′ high x 10′ wide   Semishade

Brought into cultivation about 1846 in England by the plant explorer Robert Fortune, this glossy-leaved, soft-needled shrub is native to China, Korea, and Japan. It grows best only in the coastal ocean regions of the United States within its hardiness zones; it is not, however, reliable for Gulf of Mexico shorelines. Since it is dioecious, its female fruiting possibilities, however minor they may appear, are difficult to determine beforehand from nursery stock bought in small sizes without sexual identification. For reasons that are not clear, this plant does not appear likely to reach its maximum potential size on any coast in the United States.

Generally a large, round-topped shrub with many erect and spreading stems that become pendulous with age, it is moderate to fast in growth with a potential of between 3 and 6 inches of annual expansion, depending on location, soil, and moisture conditions. The dark green, highly glossy leaves are set either opposite or spirally on slender yellow-green twigs and are up to 3 inches long (the largest of any species) with a tapered downturned appearance and a sharp tip that is surprisingly soft to the touch; the leaf undersides are gray-banded. Female plants have 1-inch egg-shaped fruit requiring 2 years to mature; the color is first blue-green and then olive green, and the fruit is surrounded entirely with a soft, protective covering. This species grows better directly on a coastal location having partial shading to semishading in a cool, humusy, moist, well-drained acid soil. It cannot tolerate hot, dry winds or sudden cold. Easy to transplant, it adjusts faster when installed with generous amounts of organic matter incorporated into the planting hole, and it later benefits from annual feeding with a high-organic fertilizer. Cooperative to shearing, it makes an attractive and dense hedge. Its listed cultivar has similar cultural needs.

CULTIVAR: 'Prostrate Spreader' is less hardy, and this recent English discovery will grow only in zones 8 through 10. Since it originated as a side cutting, it probably will not remain stable as a dwarf in some locations, and any upright growth should be cut out as it appears. Where the plant succeeds, it will become a broad-spreading groundcover a foot or so high with between 2 and 3 inches of annual growth. Its sickle-shaped leaves range between 2½ and 3 inches in length. Plant it where light shading is continuous.

Cephalotaxus harringtonia (Harrington plum yew)

Zones 6 (warm) to 10   30′ high x 10′ wide   Sun to shade

Although not as widely known as *fortunei* in some locations here, this plant's several cultivars are worth investigating for their diversity of forms. Introduced around 1829 from its natural habitat in Japan and northern China, this bushy shrub usually forms a shaggy mound 6 feet tall and wide in 10 years. The silhouette is rounded, irregularly dense, and spreading; the plant can develop into a tree form with age. Its expansion rate is rapid at 6 inches yearly. Foliage varies between 1½ and 2 inches in length and appears either in radials or in pairs on green twigs that change to red-brown with age. The blunt but pointed needles are dark green above with two gray-green lines below and are less glossy than those of *fortunei*. Male plants have noticeable yellow pollen packets in clusters of two to five; female plants develop almond-looking, 1-inch stalked fruit of olive green that matures to purple in 2 years.

Tolerant to a wide range of light exposures from full sun to heavy shade with almost equal growth development, this species is more cold-tolerant than *fortunei* but still prefers placement in an ocean-oriented site. More adaptable to limed soils, it maintains a preference for a humusy, moist, well-drained location, as do its cultivar and variety.

CULTIVAR: 'Fastigiata' was introduced in 1830 from Japan to Belgium and has the general appearance of the columnar Irish yew *(Taxus baccata cv.* 'Fastigiata'). It is hardy in the colder limits of its range, and it carries stiff, straight, erect stems with glossy, dark green foliage arranged only in spirals. Slow-growing, it usually reaches a 12- to 15-foot maximum in 30 years. Just a male form is known.

VARIETY: *drupacea* makes a dense, globe-shaped bush with 1½-inch, light green, slightly curved needles that form a V-shaped trough on the upper side of its green twigs. Originating in the mountains of central Japan, it was introduced to culture in 1829; it is slow readjusting to a new site but later becomes fully compact, with growth maintained down to ground level and an eventual 6-foot height with a 10-foot spread. The fruit is an inch long and egg-shaped. An unusual common name for this variety is cow's tail pine, a curious association.

CHAMAECYPARIS (false cypress, cypress)
Cupressaceae (cypress) family

There are seven species in this large-tree genus, and four provide most of the shrubby, dwarfed, and highly variable forms now in cultivation. All species inhabit high-humidity areas of either Asia or North America and are very hardy; each is monoecious and generally pyramidal in outline with nodding tip shoots. The very minute, opposite leaves are mostly scale-like on slender twigs resembling fern fronds; any juvenile foliage is awl-shaped and somewhat prickly. Many species carry identifying white lines separating the adult scales. The female cones common to all are small, woody, globular, solitary, and short-stalked; they usually ripen in the same year. The native western United States species thrive in Europe but do not grow nearly as handsomely on the eastern seaboard of this country, although the oriental species perform quite well there.

This genus greatly resembles *Thuja* (arborvitae) in most growth aspects but differs in its rounded fruit (*Thuja* has bell-shaped and slender fruiting), nonscented foliage, and the white lines on the rear of its foliage. Not too long ago those *Chamaecyparis* with mainly juvenile pointed leaves were separated from the others and labeled with a new genus *Retinospora*, but this division is no longer valid. All types grow well on average-fertility soils with constant moisture but good drainage, and all are tolerant of either full sun or semishaded conditions. Insects and diseases are not a problem.

Chamaecyparis obtusa (Hinoki cypress, Hinoki false cypress, Japanese false cypress) shrub cultivars and varieties

Zones 4 to 9   Variable in size   Sun to light shade

Perhaps the most liked species of *Chamaecyparis*, the Hinoki cypress carries bright green, glossy, often curled foliage sprays in an appealing fashion. A major forest tree of Japan, *obtusa* has white markings on the reverse side of its leaves that are noticeably prominent (this is not always true on its cultivars), and its cones can lengthen to ⅓ inch. The foliage twigs are fernlike, flattened, and gently pendulous with unequal-sized, thick, blunt, tiny scale leaves. All forms (and there are many tree types) grow well in sun or partial shade and prefer year-round humidity; they thrive in a moist, acid, well-drained soil but will accept reasonable, unprolonged summer dryness. Each grows well in the eastern parts of the United States. Its less hardy cultivars behave the same.

CULTIVAR: 'Kosteri' (zone 5) is a Dutch discovery from 1915 and may look more fascinating in display if some of its overlapping branching is removed occasionally to show the interesting layered effect of its horizontal growth. To some, this may appear a dwarf tree since it normally maintains a single central trunk; nevertheless, it is very slow-growing and reasonably compressed in habit, and thus it is included among the shrubs in this book. The form is pyramidal and loosely compact—even sprawling—with horizontal branching and flattened foliage sprays on twigs that twist in every direction. Its needles are between light and mid-green in summer and often bronzy during winter dormancy. Cone production is not apparent. It dislikes windy sites and can suffer foliage discoloration or twig dieback in severe winters. It appears to enjoy an annual fertilizing in early autumn. The growth rate is very sluggish; a plant 10 years old probably will be only 30 inches wide and tall.

CULTIVAR: 'Lycopodiodes' (zone 5) is unusual in appearance with thick, contorted, cordlike foliage often flattening and bunching together in a coxcomblike head at the stem ends. It came from Japan around 1861. The shrubby, globose to pyramidal initial silhouette later changes to a tall, open, and irregular shape that some may consider gaunt and unattractive. Its needles vary in coloring from glossy dark green to deep blue-green on different plants; some foliage may even appear mosslike. These leaves appear on slender branches covered with irregularly set twigs. It grows slowly at only ½ inch annually to reach a mature size of 6 feet high and wide. Cones are not recorded.

CULTIVAR: 'Lycopodiodes Aurea' (zone 5) has a similar form and habit to 'Lycopodiodes' but shows bright yellow-green, lemon yellow, butter yellow, or even soft pale yellow needles plus a slightly slower growth habit. Such slow growth should be expected from any plant not containing 100 percent chlorophyll in its leaves.

CULTIVAR: 'Nana' (zone 5) has been cultivated in Japan for centuries, especially as a pot plant or *bonsai*, but since it is extremely slow to expand, it may take over a century before it reaches its ultimate size of 5 feet wide and high. Known here in cultivation since 1861, it has created an ongoing public fascination with its richly convoluted and attractively compressed outline. It should not be confused, however, with 'Nana Gracilis', which is similar-looking in habit but much more robust in growth. Dense, low, globular, and reasonably flat-topped, this cultivar has dark—almost black—green flat needles on small cupped sprays of twigs, providing an attractively sculpted look of high decorative value. No cones appear.

CULTIVAR: 'Nana Aurea' (zone 5) is a pyramidal dwarf form introduced in 1875. Its retarded growth produces a plant that is only 1 foot high and 20 inches broad by 10 years. Its golden yellow new foliage changes to yellow-variegated with age. It is coneless. To some it looks like a very dwarfed tree.

CULTIVAR: 'Nana Compacta' (zone 5) is bright green-foliaged and very compactly twiggy with a conical shape; its leaves are gray-toned beneath. When young it is very similar to 'Nana Gracilis', but it has no later tendency to form an upright plant outline. Its annual growth is slow and no cones form. This cultivar also has been known since 1875.

CULTIVAR: 'Nana Gracilis' (zone 5) is the type most often found in nurseries and landscape plantings. Faster-growing than most other cultivars, it develops a mature size of 6 feet in height with an 8-foot spread. The foliage sprays are larger, too, with a lustrous dark green color; the pyramidal silhouette is rugged-looking and picturesque with its attractive density and twisted foliage. Cones are not recorded. It was first written about in 1863.

Chamaecyparis obtusa cv. 'Nana Compacta'

CULTIVAR: 'Nana Lutea' (zone 6) has clear, golden yellow new foliage that fades lighter to present a white and gold effect throughout the whole plant; this coloring is brighter than that of 'Nana Aurea'. Unfortunately, this novelty is new and not readily available at all nurseries yet. Slow to expand, it probably will become a compact bush with a pyramidal habit; it has the good quality of holding its yellow color nicely during winter dormancy. Cones are unknown. This plant originated at a Dutch nursery in the 1960s.

CULTIVAR: 'Nana Pyramidalis' (zone 5) offers a narrowly conical to pyramidal dense silhouette with very small dark green needle scales held in shell-like foliage sprays. It grows very slowly into a 3-foot specimen. Cone production is unrecorded. It was introduced in 1934.

Chamaecyparis obtusa (Cont.)

Chamaecyparis obtusa cv. 'Tetragona Aurea'

CULTIVAR: 'Tetragona Aurea' (zone 6) is distinct from the other cultivars here in terms of its unusual combination of bizarre foliage, habit, and coloring. Introduced from Japan in 1870, it has taken a long time to become popular in nurseries and with the public, perhaps because it is unyielding in its requirement for full sun at all times. If grown in *any* amount of daily shading, it will turn a wishy-washy yellow-green; if placed in full shade, it will even revert to dark blue-green. When placed in the appropriate environment, this is one of the most beautiful dwarf conifers. Its habit is that of a small to medium-sized shrub with an open, irregular, pyramidal outline having strong leading branches without any fully defined single leader. These upward-pointing main and side branches become long with gracefully curved silhouettes and carry tiny congested scales of frondlike or mosslike foliage on secondary twigs that form a tetragonal cross section. It can reach 12 feet in height with a 6-foot spread, but since it expands very slowly, this will require many decades. It has no cones. Because it tends to put its natural energies into mostly forward growth, it often drops some of its older bottom foliage to lose fullness at ground level with age. In times of drought, this cultivar suffers readily, and its leaves may be sun-scorched in summer and may become windburned during winter if its location is too windy.

Chamaecyparis pisifera (Sawara cypress, Sawara false cypress) shrub cultivars and varieties

Zones 5 to 9   Variable in size   Sun to light shade

Chamaecyparis pisifera cv. 'Filifera Nana Aurea'

Chamaecyparis pisifera cv. 'Squarrosa Minima'

Introduced between 1859 and 1861 from Japan, this species also shows treelike proportions for most of its members, but it presents an unusual variation in that four distinct foliage types come under its bannerhead. The *pisifera* mode shows all adult needles, yet they are often prickly to the touch, a condition usually reserved for juvenile leaves here; the 'Filifera' cultivars have long threadlike leaves with noticeable smoothness; the 'Plumosa' groupings are soft and look feathery but are still a bit raspy to touch; and the 'Squarrosa' variants, which are totally juvenile in appearance, become soft and mosslike. Curiously, none of the members of this species bear heavy fruit crops, and all accept considerable shading plus polluted air conditions without harm. However, they dislike being located in dry, limed, or heavy clay soils, especially those which include strong, cold winds, yet they endure better than other species in the eastern portion of the United States. These statements also hold true for the cultivars.

CULTIVAR: 'Aurea Nana' (zone 5) was lost to culture for a while but reappeared in 1891 in a Dutch nursery. Its globular to conical, wide-spreading, and loosely compact silhouette is slow to expand, moving at only 1 inch per year to produce an eventual size of 6 feet wide and 3 feet high. The main stems are upright and lined with many short twigs that support small needle scales tipped with year-round, rich, golden yellow coloring; in some mild growing areas this bonus of color extends deeper into the plant. No cones are reported.

CULTIVAR: 'Filifera Nana' (zone 4) is hardier than many other cultivars (perhaps because of its threadlike foliage); it came from Germany in 1897. It should not be confused with *C. pisifera cv.* 'Filifera', which is a tall-growing tree. The general appearance is that of a broad, dense, pyramidal, and flat-topped bush covered with strings of thin foliage on weeping stems; young plants tend to look straggly. Development is very slow so that after a decade the plant will be only 1 foot tall with a 3-foot spread; the maximum size is about 2½ feet high and 4 feet wide. Its trailing, pendulous, thin twigs carry dark green minute foliage scales in weeping lines. Cones do not exist. This cultivar may revert to a tree form if bud mutation occurs on the plant; quickly prune out any overscaled growth to preserve the true outline.

CULTIVAR: 'Filifera Nana Aurea' (zone 5) probably came into cultivation about 1891 and should not be mistaken for the tree cultivar, 'Filifera Aurea'. This dwarf offers a full complement of weeping golden yellow foliage and needs more sun to maintain its brightest coloring, yet it will sunscald if the light is too intense and the site is windy. The leaves are slightly smaller than those of 'Filifera Nana' and may appear more densely massed on some plants. It too is coneless. This plant is often marketed as the cultivar 'Gold Mop' since it is dense, globular, and flat-topped with an ultimate size of 3 feet.

CULTIVAR: 'Squarrosa Minima' (zone 6) is another tender member of this group and shows a rounded form that spreads into a dense, prostrate mat eventually reaching 3 feet in height with a 4-foot spread; growth is slow at about 2 inches annually. This cultivar was introduced in the 1920s and has a recognized tendency to revert back to a tree form; thus, any odd vertical growth should be trimmed immediately. The main stems are erect with very crowded and short foliage sprays of gray-green, thin, soft juvenile leaves that give the plant a mosslike appearance. Cones are not known. This cultivar is better placed where it can have light shade throughout the year, and may become sunscalded or winter-burned unless given some wind protection. It cannot survive beyond its northerly limit of zone 6.

JUNIPERUS (juniper)   *Cupressaceae* (cypress) family

Junipers offer many desirable landscape forms on an extended basis (none are found south of the equator, however) and run the gamut from large conical trees to billowing or compact shrubs to ground-hugging creepers, all in useful seasonal colorings of green, gray-green, blue-green, blue, yellow-green, and gold. During winter dormancy they deliver even more interest since many types take on purplish or rosy overtones; bountiful and enduring crops of globose fruiting add yet more value. All are simple to transplant and have remarkable hardiness plus the ability to adapt to a wide variety of growing conditions. Over seventy species are known.

The presence of two types of foliage on the same plant distinguishes certain species readily in this diverse mix of monoecious and dioecious plants. The juvenile needles are stiff, sharp, and very prickly with a tendency to appear in groups of three. The adult types are mostly tiny scales and usually come in opposite pairs closely overlapping on the stems; these are generally smooth and soft to the touch. Some selected cultivars may have needles entirely of one sort or another, especially when mature. Red spider mites, aphids, and juniper blight are common problems, but not at all times or on all plant species or cultivars. Well suited to dry, hot locations in full sun, juniper types can adapt well to shading, cold winds, and more moisture (except swampy soils) and will be unfazed by the transfer. Some juniper types—tree, shrub, or groundcover—will grow almost anywhere in the continental United States and lower Canada. These qualities make them the high contender for the title "plant for every purpose."

Juniperus chinensis   (Chinese juniper) shrub cultivars and varieties

Zones 4 to 9   **Variable in Size**   **Sun to light shade**

The Chinese juniper appeared in cultivation during the 1760s and is native to China, Mongolia, and Japan. It normally is seen as an upright, medium-sized dioecious tree with great variation of form and moderate to slow growth, depending on the zone location. There is some botanic debate whether the proper assignment of cultivars should be made to *chinensis* or to a new species name, *x media*. *Hortus Third* says the *former* designation of *x media* was theoretically valid but later proved unworkable and confusing. This special effort was the work of a New York State nurseryman, P. J. Van Melle, who became dissatisfied in 1946 with the definition by Linnaeus that indicated which plants truly belonged in the *chinensis* species; Van Melle proposed that his new species name, *x media*, be adopted instead. His idea met with only limited acceptance, and it was even rejected outright by some botanists throughout the world over the next decades. The validity of his premise is still being discussed since the name change has been used in print by many botanists and nursery owners. At this juncture, *Hortus Third* considers *chinensis* to be the proper category for all *x media* junipers; this book supplies both forms for convenience.

This species has both kinds of *Juniperus* foliage, and the juvenile plants are dark green with a chalky white banding on the *upper* sides; the adult leaves are cordlike and also dark green but plain on both surfaces. Female cones are ⅛ inch and appear in small clusters; their color varies from gray-brown to purple-brown with age. Since the sexes are separated on different plants, you will have to inspect the shrubs beforehand to assure the presence of the rounded fruit cones of the female; many cultivars are entirely male plants without any known mates. Chinese junipers grow best in full sun but are agreeable to consistent light shading on any average soil with good drainage from acid to alkaline. These cultural pointers apply equally to the cultivars.

CULTIVAR: 'Blaauw' (*x media cv.* 'Blaauw') came from Japan via Holland in 1924. It is considered by some to be very similar to 'Globosa Cinerea' when young, but this other cultivar is more vigorous and less formal in appearance as it ages. This shrub has a rugged-looking, dense, upright, dwarfed form that is vase-shaped in its early years but later develops more irregularly. Moderate in growth, it will become 5 feet tall and 4 feet wide at maturity. Its pronounced upright branching turns outward at the tips, producing an open, spiky silhouette with many short twigs covered with scalelike foliage ranging from rich gray-blue to blue-green, and remains unchanged during the winter; new spring growth is noticeably greener. Cones are unknown.

Juniperus chinensis cv. 'Pfitzeriana'

CULTIVAR: 'Gold Coast' was introduced by a California nursery in 1971. It has the general appearance of 'Pfitzeriana' when young but later remains compactly lower in size. The gold-tipped foliage is difficult to separate conclusively from an older cultivar, 'Old Gold', when both are juvenile plants; supposedly, 'Old Gold' has more bronze-gold coloring. Its upright stems carry many horizontal branches with lace-like plumes of scale needles colored a rich golden yellow; on some plants this color deepens more attractively and remains longer than on any other similarly colored juniper. The eventual size is 5 feet in height with an 8-foot spread; growth is moderate to produce an outline 3 feet tall and 5 feet wide in a decade. It has no cones.

CULTIVAR: 'Hetzii' ('Glauca Hetzii') (*x media cv.* 'Hetzii') is very much planted in the United States—some would say overplanted—for its extraordinary vigor, good blue-green color, and great size potential. It is often confused in nurseries with the wider-spreading and even more vigorous 'Pfitzeriana Glauca' when young. Both require ample room for attractive development plus regular pruning attention to maintain shapeliness. This cultivar was discovered in a Pennsylvania nursery in 1937 and makes an irregularly bushy outline with a noticeable upright silhouette and gracefully spreading branches. Fast-growing, it can easily stretch 6 feet in both height and width within 10 years; the ultimate size to be expected is 10 feet tall and at least 15 feet wide. The long vertical branches thrust upward and outward strongly and carry many side shoots heavily foliaged in very dense blue-green adult needle scales that are consistently soft to the touch. It carries no cones.

Juniperus chinensis cv. 'Pfitzeriana Glauca'

CULTIVAR: 'Mint Julep' (*x media cv.* 'Mint Julep') is another well-liked California introduction (1961), a very hardy, vigorous groundcover which grows well almost anywhere and will retain the rich look of its foliage even in light shading. Compact, tidy, flat-topped, and gracefully spreading in outline, it grows moderately fast in full sun to become 30 inches tall and 4 feet wide within 10 years; its eventual size is 3 feet in height with a 7-foot width. The arching and spreading branches have deep, rich mid-green foliage composed of all adult scale leaves. It apparently does not bear cones.

CULTIVAR: 'Pfitzeriana' (*x media cv.* 'Pfitzeriana') is so widely grown today that its habit and great vigor probably need little explanation. Introduced from China by a French missionary in 1866, it is a successful plant for any site that can provide the extensive room it needs. Very hardy and easy to grow, it takes well even to hard pruning. The eventual size is about 5 feet high with a 15-foot spread, but since it is rapid in expansion, it probably will reach half that size within 10 years when placed in full sun. Easily tolerant to semishade (with reduced vigor), it will grow in a variety of soil conditions that might make other needle evergreens blanch. Its habit is dense and broad-spreading, yet it is reasonably compact. The stout stems carry graceful, arching, horizontal shoots arranged in a fountain-spray fashion with mostly adult soft foliage in bright green; a small percentage of prickly juvenile leaves can be found on the inner twigs. Female plants usually have noticeable crops of small, gray-toned, berrylike cones that persist for 2 years as they mature.

Juniperus chinensis cv. 'Pfitzeriana Glauca' cone fruit

CULTIVAR: 'Pfitzeriana Aurea' originated in Illinois during 1923. It is shorter in overall size than 'Pfitzeriana' with branches held at a 30-degree angle. Its bright golden yellow new growth does not persist but fades by midsummer to yellow-green and carries such coloring into winter. The cultivar does not always perform even this well in either California or the New England states for unexplained reasons. Its growth rate is slow to moderate and is influenced by the hardiness zone and the amount of moisture where it is grown.

CULTIVAR: 'Pfitzeriana Compacta' came from a New Jersey nursery in 1930; it represents a much shorter version of 'Pfitzeriana' in all aspects. The stiff, thick branching is filled exclusively with prickly juvenile leaves with a gray-green coloring. It is much slower to expand than 'Pfitzeriana'.

CULTIVAR: 'Pfitzeriana Glauca' was found at a Texas nursery in 1940 and has proved exceptionally hardy and vigorous; it was considered unique to the point of meriting its own plant patent number: 422. The foliage mass is heavier than that on 'Pfitzeriana' and colors an attractive silver-blue in summer and a purplish blue in winter dormancy, but its leaves are all annoyingly sharp. The gray-colored fruiting on female plants is generous, noticeable, and annual, even at a young age. Somewhat faster in growth than 'Pfitzeriana', it eventually will match it with at least an 8-foot height and a 15-foot spread.

CULTIVAR: 'San Jose' is highly popular in California as a dependable groundcover, especially on steep banks; it came from a local nursery there in 1935. Low, spreading, and neatly compact but somewhat irregular in outline, it has prostrate horizontal branching with slightly upturned ends and a mix of both juvenile and adult foliage types in a smoky sage green. Curiously, young plants produce nearly all prickly foliage, whereas mature ones are soft to the touch because of the dominance of adult scale needles at that stage. Its occasional blue-gray fruiting is not significant. Moderately fast in growth, it should become 1 foot tall with a 5-foot spread in 10 years; the ultimate size is about 1½ feet in height and 10 feet across.

CULTIVAR: 'Sea Green' is a recent introduction that has a neat, compact, bushy outline with upright branching and graceful tip ends; it is probably a sport of 'Pfitzeriana'. The juvenile foliage is mixed with adult to give a soft feel to the foliage for the most part; in summer the leaves are mid-green, but in winter dormancy they turn a dull deep green. Modest-growing, it eventually should provide a feathery profile 4 feet tall and 7 feet wide. Fruit is produced sparsely.

VARIETY: *procumbens* until recently was a separate species, but *Hortus Third* now concludes that it belongs with *chinensis*. Originating in the mountains of Japan and introduced to cultivation in 1843, this groundcover juniper is low and irregularly spreading with stiff, twisted branching having characteristically upturned ends; the plant usually mounds in the center as it matures. Slow to establish itself after transplanting, this shrub soon moves quickly to cover a 7-foot area within 10 years; its ultimate spread is 20 feet with about 1 foot of height. The nearly ½-inch, gray-green to bluish green, sharp-pointed juvenile needles come in threes tightly packed along the twigs; in winter it may take on a purplish cast at some locations. Female plants have occasional ⅛-inch dark brown or purplish brown cones covered with bloom.

VARIETY: *procumbens cv.* 'Albovariegata' is similar in form and size but shows white-streaked new growth. This shrub is often listed erroneously as *J. davurica cv.* 'Albovariegata'. Expansion is slightly slower than in its parent.

VARIETY: *procumbens cv.* 'Aureo-variegata' carries yellow-streaked new foliage and is somewhat denser in appearance. It, too, is often labeled mistakenly since it is offered as *J. davurica cv.* 'Aureo-variegata'.

VARIETY: *procumbens cv.* 'Glauca' is a gray-toned sport with the same growth habit and size as its parent.

VARIETY: *procumbens cv.* 'Nana' is often listed as *cv.* 'Bonin Isles' from its discovery in that part of Asia during 1922. This lower-growing cultivar is generally more popular than plain *procumbens* today. It has shorter branching, greater compactness, and a more pronounced foliage density, yet it grows at a fairly modest to fast rate with a height not much above 6 inches. The foliage is gray-green.

VARIETY: *sargentii* is also a true variety of *chinensis* and will reproduce accurately from seed. Native to the northern Japanese and Korean shorelines, it was introduced in 1892 by Professor C. S. Sargent of the Arnold Arboretum. Over the years it has proved very hardy and unusually adaptable as a low groundcover since it is salt-tolerant, blight-free, and easily manageable for growing in poor soil conditions, especially on rocky slopes. It grows best in full sun, and its habit is dense, prostrate, and centrally moundlike with stout branching and erect twigs carrying some proportion of grass green juvenile needles but mostly adult scalelike leaves that are green above with whitened lines beneath. Its fruiting is deep blue without much bloom. Moderate in expansion, it will become 1 foot tall and 5 feet wide in a decade;

Juniperus chinensis cv. 'San Jose'

Juniperus chinensis procumbens

Juniperus chinensis procumbens cv. 'Nana'

Juniperus chinensis procumbens cv. 'Nana' and *Pinus mugo mugo*

the ultimate size (depending on available rainfall and soil depth) is 15 inches of height with at least a 10-foot spread.

VARIETY: *sargentii cv.* 'Compacta' is more densely foliaged and lower with light green juvenile leaves and dark green adult ones that are gray-toned on top. Slower-growing than its parent, it may develop to the same proportions in double the time span. Introduced from California in 1950, it appears to be coneless.

VARIETY: *sargentii cv.* 'Maney' is a tall shrub with a disputed ancestry. Some authorities eliminate the *sargentii* association altogether because there is now some doubt whether the seeds from which this cultivar arose actually came from an upright form of *sargentii* observed in Japan in 1934. This plant was introduced by Professor Maney of Iowa State University in 1948 as a superior blue-gray-foliaged seedling from plants raised there by a cohort. Even if there is some error of species identification involved here, the plant is still attractive as a 4-foot-tall shrub with upturned branching filled with bright blue-green to blue-gray leaves that are especially noticeable in winter. Cones are not described.

VARIETY: *sargentii cv.* 'Viridis' came from a Dutch nursery in 1940. It is a low groundcover (less tall than the parent) with bright green foliage that matures to a lighter green coloring. It apparently carries no cones.

Juniperus communis cv. 'Hornibrookii'

Juniperus communis   (common juniper) shrub cultivars and varieties

Zones 3 to 9   Variable in size   Sun

This dioecious species probably has a wider natural distribution around the world than any other tree or shrub, existing in many areas of North America, the British Isles, Europe, Asia, and Japan. It is, however, highly variable in form and size, including both trees and shrubs with many geographic and climatic alterations that still fit the basic species description for foliage. It is easily distinguished by its leaves from other junipers since all are quite unmistakably sharp and stand out straight from the twigs in threes; they are about an inch long, grooved in the center, and silvered on the top side. They have the unfortunate tendency to turn brown in winter, however, and are prone to repeated attacks of red spider mites. These drawbacks are not always so prominent with the cultivars and varieties. Since the plant is so hardy, sun-loving, and accommodating to almost any soil type, it should be considered useful for many landscape situations.

This species has a notable claim to fame in that it is plain *communis* which supplies the tangy fruit essence that is used to flavor gin. Even the name for gin is derivative since it comes from the French word *genièvre* (still used today in Holland and Belgium for distilled gin), which means "juniper berry." Its fruit is picked green—the time when it has more volatile oil—dried, and then ground for its unique flavoring contribution. The oil also is prescribed therapeutically in Asia and Europe for a variety of ills. The cultivars and varieties supply most of the other interest which this species offers.

CULTIVAR: 'Depressed Star' is slightly less hardy with a range from zone 4 through zone 9; this is a new name for a groundcover plant which started out under the banner of the variety *depressa* but now is considered sufficiently distinctive to become this cultivar. Low, horizontally spreading with a broad reach, but not prostrate, this vase-shaped plant has irregularly outward-stretching stems with few twig divisions. The summertime foliage is bright gray-green that changes to brownish green in winter. Its leaves have the familiar silver banding common to the species, but this effect does not show clearly since many needles turn downward. Cones are not described. Expansion is slow to moderate (depending on its hardiness zone and cultural practices) to produce a plant 15 inches tall with a 4-foot spread in 10 years; the ultimate size is about 18 inches in height with a 6- to 7-foot width.

CULTIVAR: 'Gold Beach' belongs only in mild climates from zone 6 through zone 9. Introduced in 1960 from a California nursery, it is a matlike creeper with dense flat-spreading branches and new growth of dull yellow that converts to all green by summer. There is no fruiting. Its expansion rate is slow to sluggish with only 2 feet of spread and a 6-inch height by 10 years; the eventual size is about twice this. It needs full sun to maintain its yellow coloring.

CULTIVAR: 'Hornibrookii' ('Pendula') ('Prostrata') (*communis saxatilis cv.* 'Hornibrookii') has had a somewhat confused history of identification since it was discovered near Galway, Ireland, in 1923. Its perfect flatness as a groundcover creates appealing interest, and the plant closely adheres to the outline of any object over which it creeps. Less hardy than the parent, it does best in zones 5 through 9. The male form often is preferred for its slower growth and slightly lower profile; it often is listed separately in nursery catalogs as 'Hornibrookii Nana', but this has no current validity. Its very prostrate, dense, neat-looking silhouette has creeping branches that carry irregularly sized foliage sprays with somewhat broadened, tiny, sharp, twisted juvenile leaves that are dull, dark green beneath and show noticeable white banding above; the foliage turns mildly brown-toned in winter. Moderate in growth, it becomes 10 inches tall and 4 feet wide by 10 years; the expected maximum is 1 foot high with a spread of at least 8 feet. Cone production is minimal.

CULTIVAR: 'Repanda' (*communis saxatilis cv.* 'Repanda') came from Ireland in 1934. It behaves as a vigorous but neat groundcover within the hardiness limits of zones 4 through 9. Prostrate, somewhat center-mounded with age, and very densely foliaged, this shrub creates a circular outline on the ground since it has the unusual property of expanding equally in all directions at the same time. Fast-growing, it spreads 6 feet with a 10-inch height within 10 years; it can be expected ultimately to grow only slightly taller but to cover a 9-foot area. The densely set, low, flexible branching has erect middle twigs spread out at all angles; these are heavily set with recurved, ¼-inch, dull mid-green needles showing broad, silvery white banding above. Its flat lateral growth is very regular in shape and length, and the entire plant is surprisingly soft to the touch. Winter brings some slight bronzing to its leaves. Cones are not known.

VARIETY: *depressa* is a commonly found form often seen in great masses in the wild, and it frequently appears on fallow farmland that was overcultivated previously. Native from Labrador across to British Columbia and south to New York and Montana, it is remarkably hardy and highly suitable to troublesome areas in full sun which are dry, sandy, stony, or gravelly. If shaded to any great degree, however, the plant will thin out noticeably. Its irregular horizontal branching has prickly ⅜-inch needles of gray-green on ascending twigs, and this open, sprawling shrub will grow fast to reach a mature size of 3 feet in height with at least a 10-foot spread. The globose ½-inch fruit on females is green and bloomy when young and needs 3 years to develop into its final coloring of deep blue or black.

VARIETY: *depressa cv.* 'Aurea' has gracefully pendant, golden yellow but still prickly new growth later modifying to bronze by summer and to all green on second-year stems. Slow-growing, it will make a low mat about 1 foot tall and 4 feet across in 10 years. Avoid all shading to maintain its coloring.

Juniperus conferta (litoralis) (rigida conferta)
(shore juniper)

Zones 6 to 9   1′ high x 8′ wide   Sun

This is a well-adapted, vigorous dwarf juniper that was found native on the sandy shorelines of Japan and the Sakhalin Islands in 1915. Useful for stabilizing sand dunes, this species now includes a number of colorful variants worth using. Less ruggedly hardy than many other junipers, the species is bushy, dense, and procumbently spreading as a groundcover creeper. Its thick, wide-ranging branches carry yellow-green, erect, and densely set twigs radially crowded with very sharp, ½-inch, deeply grooved juvenile needles arranged in threes. These leaves have a bright, refreshing apple-green color with white banding above. The female cones are dark blue to blue-black with a gray overtone and reach close to ¼-inch in diameter. Fast in growth habit, this plant will make a mat about 10 inches tall and 6 feet wide in 10 years. Best grown in full sun, it prefers a light, gravelly soil—even alkaline—and readily adjusts to growing on open sand dunes. Its foliage suffers damage, however, on inland sites with regular frost during winter. These conditions apply generally to its cultivars.

CULTIVAR: 'Blue Pacific' recently was introduced from a California nursery and seldom grows taller than 6 inches. The handsome blue-green foliage is at its best on cool coastlines and in full sun. When grown inland, some light shading is preferred. Slower-growing than its parent, it eventually will reach similar proportions for spread. Cones are not known.

CULTIVAR: 'Boulevard' is a recent introduction with a very dense and very prostrate habit; the all-horizontal branching creates a totally matlike groundcover effect. Modest in expansion, this cultivar is too new to establish its eventual dimensions. Its color is green.

CULTIVAR: 'Emerald Sea' was found in Japan and brought into cultivation here in 1972 by the U.S. Department of Agriculture. Remarkably salt-tolerant, it forms a low, dense cover useful for stabilizing shifting sand as well as for other landscape purposes. The summer coloration is a striking emerald green that changes to yellow-green in winter. It grows moderately fast and as yet cannot be documented in terms of its eventual size.

Juniperus horizontalis cv. 'Douglasii Wiltonii'

Juniperus horizontalis cv. 'Plumosa'

Juniperus horizontalis (prostrata) (creeping juniper, creeping Savin juniper, creeping cedar)

Zones 3 to 9   1′ tall x 6′ wide   Sun to light shade

Introduced about 1830 and native from Nova Scotia across to Alaska and down to New Jersey, Minnesota, and Montana, this is a mainstay groundcover for securing steep, rough embankments. It is distinguished from the species *sabina* by its lack of any fetid odor when the foliage is crushed. The naturally prostrate form is neatly regular and looks like a deep pile carpet when grown well. Its procumbent stems lie flat and do not root as they move along the ground, and the short ascending twigs appear in a regularly balanced fashion. While some prickly juvenile needles are evident, the majority of its foliage is oppositely placed, scalelike, and blue-green in color during the growing season. The winter tone is mauve, and only wild female plants have the ¼-inch, blue-black, glaucous fruit; cultivated plants rarely carry cones. Annual pruning of the elongated tip growth for the first two or three seasons induces greater compactness. Like other junipers, this plant prefers a hot, dry, sunny location with good drainage, yet it also will tolerate a fair amount of shading. Its many popular cultivars share these cultural expectations.

CULTIVAR: 'Bar Harbor' originated in the vicinity of Bar Harbor, Maine, about 1930 and has maintained a high popularity since because of its low, compact habit, generally no taller than 6 inches. Rapidly growing when established, this groundcover can extend 15 inches yearly to create an eventual mat at least 7 feet across. The flexible horizontal stems closely follow ground contours and low obstacles with steel blue new growth that later changes to grayish green; the winter coloration is silvery plum. Unfortunately, this cultivar is highly susceptible to local blight fungi in some growing areas.

CULTIVAR: 'Blue Chip' was introduced in 1940 from Denmark and behaves in a very compact and slow-growing fashion compared with the parent. Often erect to 8 inches, it comes with bright blue-toned foliage that maintains that coloring throughout the year. It may reach a 3-foot width.

CULTIVAR: 'Douglasii' (*chinensis* cv. 'Douglasii') came from a Waukegan, Illinois, nursery in 1855 and represents a close-growing horizontal form with strong growth after a slow start. Expansion is about 15 inches annually for an eventual size 1 foot tall and 8 feet across. The procumbent stems have steeply ascending and closely placed twigs turned up to give a somewhat V-shaped spray effect. Its leaves vary so that some shoots are entirely juvenile needles while others have mature scalelike leaves that are tightly set. New leaves are grass green but soon become covered with bloom for a summer tone of gray-green; in winter the tips turn a silvery mauve. This is an unusual juniper for its coloring.

CULTIVAR: 'Douglasii Morton Arboretum' is a newly arrived variant from Illinois with faster and heavier growth plus a greater silvery effect during summer. It is too new to predict its eventual dimensions.

CULTIVAR: 'Douglasii Wiltonii' grows only 3 inches tall at most and has a rich blue-gray color all year. It is popularly sold as the "blue rug" juniper. It enlarges rapidly to a solid mat 4 feet across in just 5 years. The plant was found at Vinalhaven, Maine, by a nursery owner from Wilton, Connecticut, about 1914. Some lists carry it erroneously as cv. 'Douglasii Glauca Wiltonii'.

CULTIVAR: 'Plumosa' originated at the Andorra Nurseries near Philadelphia in 1907 and is taller than most of the other cultivars presented here. Compact and flat-topped, it can rise to 18 inches with feathery, outward-reaching stems and twigs that produce a plumelike effect. The creeping stems often root as they travel along, but most branching at ground level is procumbent and spreading at a modest to rapid rate to produce an eventual cover at least 7 feet wide. All leaves are needle-like with few adult scales evident; their color is grayish green in summer and a noticeable rose-violet during winter dormancy. This cultivar recently has been greatly bothered in some locations by weevil damage to its new growth.

CULTIVAR: 'Plumosa Compacta' is more dense in all aspects, and the gray-green summer foliage turns a bronze-purple tone in winter. Growth is less vigorous than with 'Plumosa'.

CULTIVAR: 'Plumosa Youngstown' originated in Ohio. It is similar in habit to 'Plumosa Compacta' but remains much greener during the winter months.

CULTIVAR: 'Plumosa Aunt Jemima' was found in 1957 at an Illinois nursery and is very low (like a pancake, and hence this name) with spreading branches. It maintains the same blue-green coloring all year. Expansion is at a modest rate.

CULTIVAR: 'Plumosa Fountain' also has blue-green color throughout the year, but it grows faster and taller—to 15 inches—than 'Plumosa Aunt Jemima'.

Juniperus sabina (lusitanica)   (Savin juniper)

Zones 3 to 9   Variable in size   Sun

In cultivation since ancient times, this generally procumbent groundcover has been acknowledged in written records since A.D. 812. Very hardy, it originated in the high mountains of central Europe and also is distributed across western Asia and Siberia. This ambivalent plant is either monoecious or dioecious in its representative members and is noticeably separated from the other junipers by the pungent and disagreeable odor released when its foliage is crushed as well as by its bitter taste if one chooses to nibble on a stem. Highly variable in shape and size, the typically found form is a low creeper without erect stems; other types can stretch up to 10 feet. As a spreading shrub it produces trailing branches with upcurved tips and closely bunched twigs. Both the prickly juvenile needles and the scalelike adult leaves exist on the same plant in either green or gray-green coloring, but both needle types appear only in pairs on this species. Female cones are ¼ inch in size and vary from blue-black to brown-blue with a gray bloom. Best placed in full sun, this creeper needs only an average soil with good drainage. Usually the species is not so sought after as its more attractive cultivars.

CULTIVAR: 'Arcadia' was introduced in 1949 as one of several hopefully improved types imported from Russia in 1934 by an Illinois nursery; it has proved very resistant to the blight disease that is prevalent in the midwestern United States. Ruggedly hardy, it grows fast to make a groundcover 20 inches high and 5 feet across in 10 years; its ultimate spread is about twice this. The foliage is all adult needle scales and soft to the touch in a rich grass green color that deepens slightly in winter. Branching is horizontal with feathery tip ends, much like 'Tamariscifolia'. Cones are unrecorded.

CULTIVAR: 'Broadmoor' appeared in cultivation by 1963. It is a male plant similar in habit to 'Arcadia' but with bright green foliage on very short twigs which mound up in the center as it ages. Dwarfed, low, tidy, and slow-growing to reach 1 foot high and 3 feet across by 10 years, this cultivar is noted for its good performance along seashores. It is grayer in winter.

CULTIVAR: 'Buffalo' is a female plant which bears at a comparatively young age the typical ¼-inch fruiting of the species. Brought into cultivation in 1956, it is remarkably hardy, modest in growth, and about 15 inches tall with bright, deep green foliage.

CULTIVAR: 'Hicksii' originated in 1940 and often is called the "blue Pfitzer" juniper because of its gray-blue to dark bluish green foliage, strong growth, and 4-foot height. The branching is at first ascending but later becomes more trailing; the winter coloring is mauve. Cone production is not listed.

CULTIVAR: 'Skandia' is another of the hardy and blight-resistant types imported from Russia along with 'Arcadia'. Its foliage is a deep gray-blue, and all leaves are the sharp juvenile needle type. Very low-growing and dense, it expands modestly. Cones are not apparent.

CULTIVAR: 'Tamariscifolia' is so popular today that its name has been abbreviated to "Tam" in the nursery trade. Very well-liked in California as a groundcover, this cultivar is eager to spread and can become 20 inches high and 5 feet wide in 10 years; in 20 years it may be 12 feet across. Usually neatly mounded and spreading with layered branching of upturned feathery foliage of rich, deep green (or blue-green), it has a distinctive appearance. Poorly nourished plants fade, however, to a dull, unattractive yellow-green. Reasonably resistant to blight except in heavy clay soils, this cultivar is not quite as hardy as many others and perhaps should be limited to zones 5 through 9. Cones are not produced.

Juniperus squamata   (singleseed juniper, scaly-leaved Nepal juniper)

Zones 5 to 10   Variable in size   Sun to light shade

A highly variable species from central Asia that can range all the way from a prostrate shrub to a small tree (because of geographic adaptation), this species came into cultivation in 1824 and grows wild from India and Tibet eastward to Taiwan. The crowded prickly foliage is set in threes, and noticeable dead leaves persist on older stems, somewhat diminishing its landscape value; the name *squamata* translates to "dry, brown scales." Rarely offered today for itself, this species has some interesting cultivars. One curious note about the low, creeping, slow-growing form offered is that it very closely resembles *J. chinensis procumbens*, and some authorities believe that is just what it is. A true *squamata* juniper should have *nodding* tip ends, not upturned ones like those on *chinensis procumbens*.

The species described here is usually ground-hugging with an irregular arching outline of thick main branches and many short and erect twigs tightly lined with ¼-inch juvenile gray-green needles arranged in threes; all tip ends tend to nod downward. Withered, older, brown leaves remain prominently in place for many years on the stems. Its cones are egg-shaped and first red-brown, later altering to purple-black. Each contains only one seed, a novelty for a juniper. They develop best in full sun on an average soil with good drainage, but they also will accept some continuous light shading. The cultivars share these cultural conditions.

CULTIVAR: 'Blue Star' is a slow-growing Dutch shrub introduced in 1950 that one day may become 3 feet tall and 4 feet across. The foliage is dense and steel blue in color with a low, flat silhouette. Not quite as hardy as the parent, it behaves better from zones 6 through 10. It has a close resemblance in color and form to 'Meyeri' but is much smaller. Cones have not been reported.

CULTIVAR: 'Meyeri' is an upright and spreading bush that can stretch to 10 feet at maturity with an almost equal width. Its strikingly blue coloring is not found commonly in plant foliage, and its popular appeal has been continuous since 1914, when the plant was located by F. N. Meyer of the U.S. Department of Agriculture growing as a small tubbed specimen in China. Its main stems are usually strong-growing and luxuriant with tip ends gracefully curled inward; all leaves, however, are juvenile, sharp, and straight. Prone to disfiguring attacks of red spider mites, this cultivar will lose much of its lower foliage naturally to become a leggy eyesore unless it is trimmed back annually to encourage new growth on older stems. Irregular in its growth pattern since many plants expand equally in both width and height while young, this shrub probably will reach 6 feet in spread and height by a decade. Its ¼-inch cones start brown but mature to black.

CULTIVAR: 'Wilsonii' may well be considered a slower-growing version of 'Meyeri' because of its silhouette, but here the needle coloring is silvery gray-green and the tip ends have the typical nodding characteristic of the species. Discovered in China in 1909, it has a more compact habit than 'Meyeri' with ¼-inch awl-shaped needles with two bluish bands that produce the extra silvery dimension of the foliage. This plant varies in behavior from a spreading form to a more erect style, depending on where it was raised, and it will approach 4 feet in height and width by 10 years. To some authorities this shrub is identical with 'Loderi', which is supposed to carry a more definite set of leaders yet has the same outline.

Juniperus virginiana (red cedar, eastern red cedar, pencil cedar) shrub cultivars and varieties

Zones 4 to 9   Variable in size   Sun to light shade

Juniperus virginiana cv. 'Grey Owl'

Dependably hardy and widely distributed, this tall, upright, dense tree species is common in great numbers along the Atlantic seaboard area and into the Great Plains states. Freely self-seeding on almost any soil, this species grows readily and quickly in all but swampy conditions, and it can tolerate a reasonable amount of shading without problems. It has been in cultivation since 1664, and its lumber continues to be used commercially as wood for pencils (because it is light and sharpens well) and as a moth-slaying lining for cupboards and storage chests. Because of its shredding red-toned bark and reddened inner wood, it was named *baton rouge* ("red stick") by early French colonists in Canada, where it also grows well. When other French settlers discovered the same tree growing in their territory of Louisiana, they gave this name to the state capital site.

This species, however, is the intermediate host to the troublesome apple-cedar rust disease, which excludes it from growing near orchard areas. The juniper sports orange-red 1-inch spore cases randomly spread over its growing tips when it carries the disease; the evidence of disease on apples shows up as deformed fruit and leaves that require a precautionary spraying effort to curtail the damage. Since cedars also have been a commercial crop for the pencil wood they contain in many orchard sites, the slogan "Cider or Cedars!" was once a rallying cry for the orchardists. It is difficult to know which group won out since there still are quantities of both trees around.

Closely related to the western species, *scopulorum,* both in general habit and in foliate appearance, it differs by having round, ⅛-inch, blue-gray fruit (often abundant) that ripens in one season plus leaves that turn a dull purple-brown in winter at many locations. It is separated readily from *chinensis* by its alternate, mostly adult, blunt needles on older plants; *chinensis* generally has very prickly, ternate, juvenile needles in abundance (except on some cultivars). The several cultivars of this species all possess the same hardiness and ease of growing.

CULTIVAR: 'Globosa' ('Nana Compacta') ordinarily will grow to 4 feet tall and wide—but slowly—and is undoubtedly one of the most naturally globular conifers known. It came into cultivation in 1887. It presents a ragged but rounded outline when young; later it matures into a dense, very compact, rounded silhouette. Branching is upright and densely crowded with thin twigs carrying rich, bright green, adult scale needles (plus some prickly juvenile ones) in plumclike tip endings, it unfortunately turns brown-toned during winter in cold growing areas. Cones are unreported.

CULTIVAR: 'Grey Owl' originated in 1938 and is thought to be a hybrid cross between the tree form, *virginiana cv.* 'Glauca', and the shrub, *chinensis cv.* 'Pfitzeriana'. Although lower, it does have a strong resemblance to 'Pfitzeriana' in general outline and vigor, but here the foliage is pewter gray in coloring. It probably will expand to a 5-foot spread with an 18-inch height within 10 years; the mature size is about 4½ feet tall with an 8-foot width. Its youthful shape is open and thin (it will benefit ·from annual tip pruning for greater bushiness) with long spreading branches; later it will become compact and more dense. Its thin yellow-toned twigs have threadlike tip leaves of small adpressed scales that vary from soft silvery gray to gray-blue; the tips may turn purplish in winter, but the inner foliage remains gray. Cones are ¼ inch, oval, gray-blue, and sparsely produced. Best grown in full sun for the richest coloring, this cultivar will accept light shading.

CULTIVAR: 'Kosteri' presents a puzzle since it has the odd foliage odor of *sabina* and the growth habit of *chinensis cv.* 'Pfitzeriana'. If it had fruiting to compare, this species alignment would be easier to identify, but since it does not (this holds true for many dwarf cultivars of all sorts), the true placement will have to remain arbitrarily under the species *virginiana*. Low and flat-growing yet broadly bushy, this cultivar has main branching that is procumbently prostrate with nearly erect and spreading secondary stems that end with feathery tips. The summer foliage is gray-blue to grayish green, but during winter dormancy the tip ends often turn purplish. A fast-growing shrub, it will develop a 10-foot spread with a 3-foot height in 10 years; the mature dimensions are at least 4 feet tall and 14 feet wide. Cones are unknown. It accepts light shading.

CULTIVAR: 'Silver Spreader' is similar in appearance to 'Grey Owl' in terms of growth habit, but it carries silver-green needles in a bright tone. Introduced from a California nursery in 1960, it is slightly less hardy (zones 5 to 9) than the parent. Wide-spreading but low in outline, it grows quickly to make a plant 18 inches tall and 6 feet across in 10 years; the ultimate size is 3 feet tall and 10 feet wide. It has no cones.

PICEA (spruce)   *Pinaceae* (pine) family

The name *picea* is an ancient one, derived from the Latin word *pix*, which means "pitch," a stem resin commonly found in this and other conifers. As a genus it contains an important and hardy group of long-lived forest trees of great size that have given us many attractive dwarf forms (mostly derived from branch tip growth or seed infected by the witches-broom disease). All of its species are monoecious in flowering and generally conical in outline, and they carry sizable, *down-hanging*, durable, slender cones (versus the one-season topside cones of its relative *Abies*). The solitary needles are stiff, sharp-tipped, and squared in cross section (one rolls easily between the fingers), and they leave squat pegs (botanically called *pulveni*) on the twigs when the leaves drop, making older spruce stems rough to the touch. Spruce enjoy full sun but are surprisingly tolerant of modest shade without much loss of foliage density. They have a wider adaptability to cold and wind than many other needle evergreens and are usually hardy from zone 3 through zone 8. At least forty-five species have been identified so far, and of these, some eighteen are located in China; the others are native to the cooler areas of the northern hemisphere.

Best located on a well-drained, moist, sandy loam with full sun, spruce do not do well in the parched, compacted soil of many urban locations, nor do they thrive in the high summer heat of the midwestern and southwestern portions of the United States, where rainfall is often minimal. All are prone to some degree of red spider mite infestations on the leaves, while the spruce gall aphids seriously disfigure the regularity of new growth expansion when they build their seasonal homes in the tips. Usually reliable for transplanting at almost any movable size, spruce are rugged, dependable plants with perhaps only their stiff unyielding forms and sharp needles considered possible drawbacks to their landscape appeal.

Picea abies (excelsa) (Norway spruce, common spruce) shrub
cultivars and varieties

Zones 3 to 8   Variable in size   Sun to light shade

Picea abies cv. 'Clanbrassiliana'

With a potential height of 150 feet, the Norway spruce is a majestic tree having rapid growth and widely spreading curved branches that carry at middle age pendant twigs and foliage in an appealing fringelike fashion. Native to cold areas of northern and central Europe, this species bears the longest (up to 7 inches) cones of any spruce and has shiny, dark green, ¾-inch sharp needles with faint white lines on each side. These leaves point both upward and forward along the yellow-brown twigs; older stems are gray-brown. It grows at its best when given full sun but takes modest shading well; the soil should be of average fertility, should be moist but well-drained, and should possess a sandy texture. Seashore locations for this species are often ideal, especially since it is very cold- and wind-tolerant. Currently, eighty cultivars are known and identified (not all are remarkably different from one another, however), and the following abbreviated list includes the more familiar ones.

CULTIVAR: 'Clanbrassiliana' is commonly known as the Barry spruce for some unexplained reason and is the oldest grown dwarf form of this species. It was first planted in 1798 (this well-worn but identifiable specimen still exists) for Lord Clanbrassil of Northern Ireland. The double *s* in the name finally has been established as correct; almost all texts of the immediate past give only one. This dwarf plant is a low, dense, conical to globose spreading bush with foliage growing right to the ground. Slow-growing at only 4 inches of expansion yearly, it should become 7 feet tall and 12 feet across. The winter buds are noticeably red-brown, while the very short and crowded main branches carry thin, bunched twigs that are light gray-brown above and whitened below; the flexible ⅛-inch needles vary by site conditions from bright to dull mid-green. Cones are unknown. Not quite so hardy as the parent, this cultivar is better grown from zones 4 through 7. A slightly different form of this cultivar was once called 'Clanbrassiliana Elegans', but this label no longer has validity.

CULTIVAR: 'Gregoryana' was found at Gregory's Royal Nursery in England around 1850. It provides a dense cushion of green that is so slow to expand that it will be only 18 inches high and 3½ feet wide after 30 years. After another few decades it should mature to a final size 2 feet tall and 6 feet across. The cultivar 'Parsoni' is very similar to it when young, and these two often are confused in the nursery; 'Parsoni' is more open in outline later and carries flatter, longer needles. The cultivar described here has ⅜-inch, slender pale green needles and a neatly moundlike, dense, low silhouette that is always wider than it is tall. Expanding at only an inch or less annually, the sluggish plant has winter budding that is tiny, yellow-green, and shiny on gray-brown to whitened twigs. It does not produce cones. Less hardy than the parent, this cultivar grows best in zone 4, but it will endure into zone 7 if provided with a consistently cool high-humidity site for the whole year.

CULTIVAR: 'Maxwellii' came into being from a witches-broom-infected tree in Geneva, New York, during 1860. Because it is so widely cultivated now both here and abroad, it has given rise to two different growth habits. In Europe it generally is seen flat-topped, compact, and slow-growing, while in the United States it is a faster-growing specimen having a rounded silhouette with crowded branching and more needles per stem. Curiously, plants sent from here to Europe take on the slower-growing characteristics within a short time. The "true" form is now considered to be this European style. Slow to expand, this dwarf will be only 1 foot high with a 3-foot spread in 20 years; the final size is about 2½ feet tall and 5 feet across. The winter budding is dark brown, ovoid, thick, and blunt; the main branches are short and stiff with heavy, truncated yellow-brown twigs. Needles are ½ inch, coarse, stiff, radially set around the twigs, and bright green in color with white lines showing beneath. Cone production is not reported. This cultivar develops best in zones 4 through 7.

CULTIVAR: 'Nidiformis' also is called "nest spruce" since it develops a depressed center of growth that resembles a bird's nest when the plant is enlarging. Cultivated since 1907, it was found in a nursery near Hamburg, Germany, and it prefers cool growing areas only from zones 4 through 7. Dwarfed, dense, broad, and flat-topped in outline, it expands modestly at between 2 and 4 inches yearly when established;

eventually it will reach 6 feet high and 12 feet across. The winter buds are dark brown, and the branches are horizontally set in radiating layers with crowded, thin, yellow-green twigs that grow both forward and slightly downward to produce a clothed-to-the-ground appearance even when young. The crowded, stiff needles are flat, thin, ⅜ inch long, and colored dull mid-green to dark green. It is coneless.

CULTIVAR: 'Ohlendorffii' came from Ohlendorff, Germany, in 1850 and is an irregularly conical dwarf much freer-growing than most of the other cultivars. It matures at a size 7 feet tall and at least 6 feet wide, but it expands slowly at only 2 inches annually. This plant once was thought to be a sport of the species *orientalis* because of the unusual similarity of their foliage, but this assumption later proved invalid. When young it is noticeably globose, compact, dense, and regular in outline, but age alters this to an irregular, broadly conical but still dense shape with twig development poking out in all directions. The winter budding is dark orange-brown, egg-shaped, and noticeably pointed; the stems grow upright with pale brown twigs and ⅛-inch, thin, flat, pale yellow-green needles. It is without cones and belongs in zones 4 through 7.

CULTIVAR: 'Procumbens' ('Prostrata') was discovered in France about 1850 and represents a large-scaled mound of spreading greenery which can stretch to 15 feet while maintaining a low profile that ascends only 3 feet. Vigorous in expansion, it usually will set out 4 inches of new growth yearly. Dense, procumbent, and dome-shaped, it has light orange-brown, conical, sharp-tipped buds and thick, stiff branching tightly covered with flat, forward-spreading, glossy yellowish twigs. The bright green needles are straight, stiffly sharp, and ⅜ inch long. Cones apparently do not form, and this plant too seems to favor zones 4 through 7.

CULTIVAR: 'Remontii' is not one of the most dwarfed of spruces since its mature dimensions are 10 feet tall and 15 feet across; it is one of the more vigorous types since it can expand from 4 to 6 inches in a year. It originated in 1874 from a non-recorded source. Dense, neatly regular, conical, and very wide-spreading, it has conspicuous winter buds of light orange that are cone-shaped and blunt. The thick branching is crowded but uncommonly flexible as a result of the mid-brown twigs that grow narrowly upward. The straight and thin ¼-inch needles are unusual too by being soft to the touch; they are colored a bright mid-green. Cones are unknown.

Picea pungens cv. 'Globosa'

Picea pungens cv. 'Montgomery'

Picea pungens (Colorado spruce, Colorado blue spruce) shrub
cultivars and varieties

Zones 3 to 8   Variable in size   Sun

Native to Wyoming, Utah, Colorado, and New Mexico, this is the only spruce species able to grow successfully in the dry, hot southwestern and midwestern parts of the United States. Densely pyramidal and totally rigid in outline with unbending horizontal branching, it is a sturdy, cold-tolerant forest tree of mountain locales, and it often reaches 100 feet in height. The very sharp-tipped gray to gray-green needles vary from ½ to 1¼ inches (depending on rainfall amounts and location) and remain on the twigs for up to 8 years; this contributes to the inflexibility of its silhouette. The name *pungens* is from the Latin and means "to prick," an apt evaluation of the sharp, unyielding leaves. The 2- to 4-inch cones are oblong and shiny and come in a noticeable light brown color. Growth is thrifty in full sun on a moderately rich, well-drained, gravelly soil, yet this plant does not seem to mind whether the soil is reasonably dry or consistently moist during the year. Very tolerant to shore conditions and arid climates, it is unfortunately plagued by annual attacks from the spruce gall aphid; this distorts its new growth appreciably and unattractively. While the dwarf cultivars are not commonly bothered by this aphid pest, they share the same cultural needs.

CULTIVAR: 'Compacta' is the oldest dwarf spruce cultivar on record here. Seed taken from normal-sized trees atop Pike's Peak in Colorado during 1863 was presented to the Harvard Botanical Garden (now defunct) in Cambridge, Massachusetts. Grafts obtained from a conspicuously dwarfed seedling were later given to the Arnold Arboretum in Boston in 1890, and Professor C. S. Sargent noted that the growth had reached 3 feet in height by 1897. This original plant is still in existence there today and now measures 10 feet tall and 18 feet across. It expands annually at a moderate

rate of 2 to 4 inches. Dense, compact, and a flat-topped pyramid, this dwarf has nearly all horizontal, crowded branching with short, shiny yellow twigs and rigid, bunched needles between ¼ and ¾ inch long. Rigid and sharp-pointed, these leaves are dark green above with white lines beneath to present an overall gray-green appearance. Cones are unreported. Slightly less hardy than its parent, it develops better in zones 4 through 8.

CULTIVAR: 'Globosa' came from seed raised in a Dutch nursery in 1937. Dwarf, globe-shaped, dense, and irregular in outline, this is a slow-growing shrub that will expand to 2 feet in height with a 3-foot spread by 10 years; the maximum size is about 4 feet tall and 5 feet across. Branches are moderately heavy with thin yellow-brown twigs and ⅓-inch, crowded, slightly sickle-shaped blue-gray needles with whitened undersides. It has no reported cone production. It too belongs in zones 4 through 8.

CULTIVAR: 'Hunnewelliana' is somewhat of a misfit since it arrived as seed from the species engelmanii at a Massachusetts nursery in the 1920s. The plant now appears to be botanically distinct from that species, but it does have an awkward tendency to throw out large central leaders from time to time; these should, of course, be pruned away to maintain the normal dwarf form. Pyramidal or conical in outline, this dense shrub is slow-growing with only 2 inches of expansion per year; its eventual size is close to 3 feet in height and 5 feet in width. The erect, thin branches have white-brown, often crowded twigs and ⅓-inch, thin, narrow, sharp-tipped, pale sea green to silvered blue-green needles (depending, as always, on where it originated and the local growing conditions). It is not a cone producer, and it is found within zones 4 through 8.

CULTIVAR: 'Montgomery' has led a confused life, and this confusion extends into today since some authorities insist that it and 'Globosa' are the same. The original plant was purchased by a Connecticut nursery in the 1930s as a seedling of P. pungens glauca compacta globosa, the then current nomenclature, but its growth habit since that time has more or less established 'Montgomery' as a distinct cultivar. It is dwarfed, very compact, neatly dense, and round-topped, and its main branching is reasonably stout with moderate-sized smooth twigs of pale yellow-brown; the very stiff and sharp straight needles vary from ⅓ to ¾ inch and display an attractive and noticeable gray-blue coloring on both sides. Moderate or slow in expansion (depending on site conditions), it often achieves up to 2 inches of annual growth and eventually will become 5 feet tall and 8 feet wide. Cones are unknown.

PINUS (pine)   Pinaceae (pine) family

Unusual for having their needles in bundles, pines are monoecious evergreens with more species—ninety—than any other conifer; they grow from the Arctic Circle to the equator, but only in the northern hemisphere. The majority are tall forest trees famous for their lumber, but a very few dwarfs are listed among their members. Unique to pine is the multiplicity of needle leaves—two, three, or five usually—carried in circular bundles (or *fascicles*) and encased at the bottom in a papery sheath. The curiously distinctive mature plants also have tiny scalelike leaves flattened along the stems, but these soon fall away; seedlings, on the other hand, often carry only solitary needles in the first years of growth. Identification of pine species begins with counting the number of needles in a typical bundle taken from a plant several years old; the individual needle length, shape, and coloring expand the clues for proper categorizing. Female cones are also different from those of other conifers since they generally possess thick scales with noticeable terminal hooks (often prickly) and take several years to mature on the tree; some dried cones actually remain in place for decades.

Pines have a preference for the fullest amount of sun (when shaded, they lose much of their normal fullness), and they grow easily and rapidly on any well-drained soil of average fertility, provided that it is not too alkaline. Shallow-rooted, they transplant with ease and do not require any regular fertilizing to perform well; they do, however, enjoy having their own needle droppings left as mulch at all times to keep these surface roots moist and cool. Hardy and wind-tolerant, pines do not long survive on sites invaded by smoky or polluted air. Common to all pines are repetitive aphid and scale insect infestations, but the five-needled pines are also seriously disfigured by the white pine blister rust, which is a spore disease carried as an intermediate host by wild currants growing nearby (naturally, these should be uprooted and discarded). Another serious affliction comes from the larva of the white pine weevil, which will burrow through the new stem growth of many species, toppling the leader and greatly distorting the plant's silhouette. Some but not all cultivars have such problems, too.

Pinus mugo mugo

Pinus mugo mugo (montana)   (mountain pine, Swiss mountain pine)

Zones 3 to 7   7′ high x 15′ wide   Sun to light shade

Unusually variable in form because of its wide natural distribution throughout the mountain areas of Europe from Spain to the Balkans, this species alters in different locales from a tall, narrow, treelike mound perhaps achieving 30 feet of height to a meandering domed mat only a few feet high. Seed raised in nurseries also produces plants with such irregular silhouettes, and therefore, most of the selected low-growing cultivars are now propagated exclusively by grafting to ensure commercial uniformity. In its usual nursery form this pine is a bun-shaped, prostrate, and compact shrub showing between 2 and 4 inches of expansion yearly. The winter buds are heavily coated with resin, and the main branching is moderately stout, ascending, and lined with light green smooth twigs that splay outward and later change color to brown. The 1½-inch, dark green or yellowish green, stiff needles come in bundles of two and may occasionally be sickle-shaped. Its ovoid cones range between 1 inch and 2 inches in length with a light gray-brown coloring and can appear either singly or in clusters. Tolerant to some light shading, this dwarf is less afflicted by problems than many others; however, scale insects are bothersome where the climate and exposure are both hot and dry. Its few cultivars and varieties include the following.

CULTIVAR: 'Compacta' came from a selection made in the 1920s here. It is a large, dense, globose plant with dark green slender needles about 1¼ inches long. It may grow to reach 6 feet in height with a 4-foot spread. Few cones are produced.

CULTIVAR: 'Gnom' is a popular European type which originated in Holland about 1927. Dense and squatly globose, it has twisted twigs and crowded, 1½-inch, deep green needles. Coneless, it is wide-spreading from modest annual growth for an eventual size approximately 10 feet tall and 14 feet across.

VARIETY: *mugo (mughus)* is the typical form found now in nurseries. It has a rounded, compact outline from annual growth of between 2 and 3 inches. The cones are an inch or so long, are closely attached to the stems, and change from yellow-brown in the first year to cinnamon brown in the second, when they open and disperse the seed.

VARIETY: *pumilo* is a compact and mound-shaped prostrate dwarf of slow growth that has been known since 1791 in the Alps of central Europe. Eventually it will reach a 2-foot height with a 9-foot spread, but this requires several decades of waiting. The twigs are erect without any definite leader formation and carry short, variably sized, rich green needles. Its winter buds are very conspicuously resin-covered, while the small globular cones are purple-toned the first year but mature as brown.

Pinus strobus (white pine, eastern white pine) shrub
cultivars and varieties

Zones 3 to 7   Variable in size   Sun

Pinus strobus cv. 'Nana'

This species is one of the tallest (150 feet) evergreen trees of the eastern part of North America and often exists in huge forest stands. Five-needled, it carries slender, flexible, 5-inch blue-green foliage with faint white lines beneath, and its leaves are mostly concentrated on the outer twigs. Very easy to transplant, it grows well on almost any soil type, but it must have consistent moisture to do the best. Through its remarkably diverse seed it has given rise to such an unbelievable number of dwarf variations that they completely baffle any system for separating the individuals satisfactorily, and so no definitive attempt at differentiation will be attempted here.

The cultivar name 'Nana', for example, has been used worldwide as a loose collective label applying to any number of low, dwarfed cultivar types with usually dense, rounded, or conical shapes that maintain a growing height of about 3 feet. The name is too often freely translated as 'Densa', 'Compacta', or 'Prostrata' by a grower's whim, and since some of these so-called dwarf variants may very well develop later as tree types, the process of evaluation appears futile. Your own checklist of locally grown *strobus* dwarfs is probably as good a guide as anyone else's.

Pinus sylvestris (Scots pine, Scotch pine, Scotch fir) shrub
cultivars and varieties

Zones 3 to 8   Variable in size   Sun

One of the hardiest and most handsome tree pines in existence, this plant is native throughout the British Isles, Europe, and most of Asia since it grows readily on a variety of soil types and is reasonably resistant to air pollution. The stiff, blue-green, twisted, nearly 3-inch needles are clustered in twos. Its obliquely bent cones are about 2½ inches long, have a dull brown-gray color, and often appear turned backward on the twigs toward the central trunk. Suited best to full sunshine, it needs only an average-fertility, well-drained location; however, it does not manage well on dry chalky soil or soil that is both acid and consistently wet. Somewhat less adapted for easy transplanting (because of a less congested root system), it usually moves better when young. It is subject to fewer pests and diseases, however, than other pines. The few cultivars share the same cultural recommendations.

CULTIVAR: 'Beauvronensis' came from Beauvron, France, about 1891 and is a very dwarfed, densely branched, irregularly dome-shaped shrub with much landscape appeal. Winter buds are noticeably mahogany red, and the light brown furrowed twigs carry stiff, 1½ inch, gray-toned needles that point forward. Generally found multistemmed, this cultivar is slow-growing at only 2 inches annually and eventually reaches a 6-foot height (but only after a half century) with a 10-foot spread. Cones are not recorded. Less hardy than the parent, its range is from zone 4 through zone 8.

CULTIVAR: 'Repens' originated in the United States, but its date of introduction has not been authenticated. Varying in vigor throughout the range from zone 4 through zone 8, it develops into a very low mound with a matlike appearance and rarely grows over 8 inches tall. Expansion comes at a slow rate of only an inch or two yearly, and that growth appears irregularly distributed over the plant. The winter buds are dark red-brown, and the slightly twisted, stiff, gray-green needles vary in size from an average of 1 inch. Cones are not present.

PLATYCLADUS (Thuja) (Biota) (arborvitae)
Cupressaceae (cypress) family

Until recently this needled genus of monoecious trees and shrubs was called *Thuja* (and earlier *Biota*), but it is now considered sufficiently different from its close relative *Thuja* to be classified separately. In comparison with *Thuja*, its branchlets of scalelike foliage are held *vertically* upright and curve inward. The leaves also lack the strongly pungent resin odor when crushed or bruised; its odor is only slightly resinous. The 1-inch woody cones are larger than those of *Thuja*, are blue-toned when young, and resolve each of the six scales with a hornlike ending. While the leaves are still held in flat sprays, those of *Platycladus* have the same color value on both sides. *Platycladus* is much less hardy than *Thuja* but will accept far more summer heat and drought satisfactorily; it is, therefore, a commonly used landscape element in the southern parts of the United States. There is only one species, *orientalis*, but a large list of tree types and shrub cultivars.

Platycladus orientalis cones

Platycladus orientalis (Thuja orientalis) (Oriental arborvitae) shrub cultivars and varieties

Zones 6 to 10   Variable in size   Sun to light shade

Native to northern China and Korea, this monoecious species is composed mostly of tree forms, yet there are enough shrub cultivars to be of special interest. The ⅛-inch or less scalelike and triangular grooved leaves are marked on the back with a tiny resin gland which releases a mildly pungent odor when bruised. This foliage appears in densely branched, erect, inward-curving sprays of bright green with the same color value on both sides. Male flower strobiles are not overly conspicuous, but the female woody cones are about an inch long and have six scales, each with a recurved hornlike tip. At first purplish blue in tone, these cones later mature to brown.

Easy to move, these plants thrive when grown in full sun (but not in cold blustery winds) yet are tolerant to light shading as well. Provide a moist, rich soil that is not overly acid and expect good acceptance of high summertime heat and some prolonged drought. These plants occasionally are bothered by red spider mites, but there may be more damage from ice and snow since the plant becomes more brittle in its stems with age. All cultivars share this basic set of requirements.

CULTIVAR: 'Aurea Nana' has been in cultivation since 1804 and has the odd history of being documented as originating in several places. Often called "Berckman's (or even Berkman's) Golden Biota" in the nursery trade, this shrub is maligned since Mr. Berckman is known to have raised only the taller and more slender cultivar 'Conspicua' at his nursery grounds. By whatever name and background, this is a very compact, round-topped, oval shrub between 3 and 4 feet in height with dense foliage that is a rich golden yellow when new but only yellow-green later; it turns somewhat brown-orange during winter dormancy. The coneless thin stems are conspicuously arranged in upthrust parallel planes. It does not favor any amount of shading, and it also should not be placed where dog urine can reach it.

CULTIVAR: 'Bonita' originated in 1932 in the United States and is a dwarfed, broadly conical form with young foliage starting out a glistening golden yellow but later modifying to bright green. Slow-growing, it will mature at 4 feet of height. Cones are not produced.

CULTIVAR: 'Decussatus' is also known in the nursery trade as 'Juniperoides' since it does have a juniperlike foliage appearance as a result of its all-juvenile leaf type, but the name is not botanically valid. This dwarf came into cultivation about 1850 in England and has a columnar silhouette with a rounded top; it will slowly reach 3 feet in height with a 6-foot spread. Its branches are crowded together and filled densely with twigs carrying light gray-green to blue-green, awl-shaped juvenile needles which appear sharp but are suprisingly soft to the touch. This foliage turns a rich purple-gray in winter. Unfortunately, the plant opens up with age and is easily damaged in areas with heavy, wet snowfalls and ice storms. It apparently has no cones.

CULTIVAR: 'Elegantissima' is a large (to 16 feet) shrub of dense, columnar habit with a broad base and stout, erect branching. Cultivated in England since 1858, it carries golden yellow foliage through the summer yet turns an odd but pleasant shade of brown-pink in winter. Cones are not known.

CULTIVAR: 'Flagelliformis' ('Filiformis Erecta') is different from the other cultivars since it has all threadlike sprawling foliage. Originating in Belgium in 1868, it is less hardy than the parent and should never be exposed to cold blustery winds; its range is probably from zone 7 through zone 10. The silhouette is that of an oval bush with a pointed top, and its sluggish growth rate will require many decades to reach the ultimate 5 feet of height. The leaves are yellow-green in summer and greenish brown during winter. Cones are unknown.

CULTIVAR: 'Rosedalis' has been used in France since its origination there in 1923, and it is the chameleon of these cultivars in that it makes three distinct color changes in its foliage during the year. In spring it emerges as canary yellow, but this soon alters by summer into light green; the winter mantle is plum-purple. All of this variation occurs on a compact globular shrub with narrow, prickly-looking juvenile foliage that is soft and yielding to the touch. Slow to expand, it probably will develop to 2 feet tall and 2 feet wide in a decade; the ultimate size is approximately 3 feet tall and about as wide. It is not a cone-producing plant. In some listings this plant is called 'Rosedalis Compacta', but this name is incorrect.

CULTIVAR: 'Semper-aurescens' ('Semperaurea') came from France about 1870 and looks much like a larger version of 'Aurea Nana' since it is also a dense, rounded shrub. Its ultimate height, however, is 10 feet, and it can be expected to reach 5 feet in a 10-year period. The golden yellow coloring holds throughout the year, but the best brightness naturally comes with new spring growth; in some colder areas, nevertheless, its winter coloration may be bronze. The branching is crowded and erect with very tight twig formations. Cones are unrecorded.

TAXUS (yew)   *Taxaceae* (yew) family

Where it will grow well, the yew is an extraordinarily well-liked multi-stemmed plant for landscape use. Millions are raised annually in the United States alone, and it rivals juniper for the diversity of its forms, its general hardiness, and its easy acceptance of many different growing situations, provided that it is *always* given perfect drainage. Waterlogged soils such as clay and silt types cause *chlorosis*, or "yellowing," of the foliage, resulting in the quick or gradual demise of the plant. Native throughout most of the northern hemisphere, all yews transplant easily because of a surface fibrous root system with a ready ability for quick repair after being moved. Equally at home in acid or alkaline soils with rapid drainage qualities, they are well-suited to sunny locations but are often exceptionally adaptable (with some species) to heavy shade. All types tolerate shearing and hard pruning with ease and have deservedly become prime evergreen choices for hedges and special topiary displays. Cultivated in Europe and the British Isles for centuries, they are legendary for having sturdy durability, with some plants now in existence having a documented history of almost 1000 years.

There are eight species of yew scattered around the globe, and each is mainly but not exclusively dioecious in that it has separate male and female plants for flowering. For no discernible reason, an occasional branch (but not the entire shrub) can change its sex; this occurs mainly with males that suddenly produce fruit crops. Female yews have mostly annual late summer fruiting (in dry seasons these crops may be minimal or nonexistent) of conspicuous red-coated seeds strung along the many stems, and these are much in favor with birds and other wildlife. Male plants disperse great clouds of yellow pollen in the spring, to the regret of some asthma sufferers. Since there is no follow-through effort required later in the fruit production, males usually expand much faster than females in terms of foliage growth. However, young transplants of either sex are sluggish to reestablish themselves immediately and may produce only slight expansion in the first year. This female fruit is a bony seed encased by a fleshy red- or yellow-toned cup that is open at the end; not harmful to cold-blooded animals, it is toxic to humans if eaten, as is the foliage when consumed in sizable quantities.

Yew needles are flat and often sickle-shaped, solitary, glossy, and tip-pointed but not sharp. They appear on green new twigs colored dark green above and lighter green beneath; yews are the darkest-toned of all evergreens. This foliage is arranged either spirally or in alternate ranks about the stems, depending on the species or cultivar. The often exposed bark on mature plants is red-brown, thin, and flaky. Few insects or diseases present a serious problem to their generally easy growth habits in all growing areas.

Taxus baccata cv. 'Fowle'

Taxus baccata cv. 'Overeynderi'

Taxus baccata (English yew, common yew)

Zones 7 and 8   60′ high x 25′ wide   Sun to light shade

Native to north Africa, western Asia, Europe, and the British Isles but unsuited to any part of the midwestern and southwestern United States when cultivated, a contentedly growing English yew may reach the gigantic treelike proportions here listed—and some are certainly in existence—but the norm for most landscape sites is closer to 35 feet, and that height is likely to take all of seven decades to be reached. Because of its fine-textured foliage, this species is very popular for precisely outlined hedges and sculptural shaping; it was used commonly during the seventeenth and eighteenth centuries for topiary extravaganzas, especially in royal gardens. As a result of its long history in cultivation and its wide distribution, it has given rise to an amazing number of forms, some of which are much hardier than the parent. All types accept either full sun or light shade.

Definitively upright in silhouette, this species has a broad, rounded crown with spreading side branches. Fast-growing, it can enlarge 8 inches yearly. The closely set, radially two-ranked (placed in two vertical rows side by side), 1- to 1¼-inch narrow leaves taper to an acute point but are soft to feel. The top surface of the needle is a lustrous dark green, while the underside has two pale green lines. Its female ¼-inch fruit is an olive-brown seed enclosed by a red cup. The cultivar selections offer some diverse options.

CULTIVAR: 'Aurea' (zone 6) has been known since 1855. It is a large sun-loving shrub of compact habit with new growth of golden yellow that changes in the second year to green because of its own self-shading of the older leaves (a common condition with all evergreens of density); its winter coloring is yellowish green. Slower than the parent at only 4 inches of expansion yearly, it achieves a rounded outline 5 feet tall and wide by 10 years; the ultimate size is nearly 15 feet in height. Several types, both male and female, are sold commercially under this name, unfortunately.

CULTIVAR: 'Cavendishii' (zone 6) is very similar to 'Repandens' in its low-growing silhouette, but 'Cavendishii' is a female and stays much lower in profile as it ages. Tolerant of heavy shade (but with much diminished fruiting), it has wide-spreading prostrate branches that droop at the tips with 1-inch blue-green needles that curve both outward and inward along the twigs. Topping out at about 3 feet when mature, it will spread approximately 12 feet; a 10-year-old plant should achieve a 15-inch height and a width of 5 feet. It was first described in 1932 but has an unclear history as to its place of origin.

CULTIVAR: 'Cheshuntensis' came from England around 1857 and is reputed to be hardy even in zone 5 if given protection from winter winds. A narrow and columnar female plant halfway in appearance between the species and its cultivar 'Fastigiata', the Irish yew, it is a fast-growing variant with small, blue-green, glossy needles crowded along the twigs. It expands at about 3 inches annually and eventually can reach a 20-foot height with a spread of 12 feet.

CULTIVAR: 'Elegantissima' (zone 6) is probably the most popular of the golden-leaved yews and has been cultivated since 1852. More compact and upright-growing than 'Aurea' but with a more open outline later, it carries new foliage striped pale yellow at the leaf margins and is best grown only in full sun; if shaded heavily, it will become entirely green. Slow to expand at only a few inches annually, this female is handsomely captivating when covered with red fruit by early autumn.

CULTIVAR: 'Erecta' (zone 6) recently has been overshadowed in popularity by 'Overeynderi', perhaps because of the current difficulty of locating 'Erecta' in nurseries. It is an erect-branching, broadly columnar to pyramidal, open-topped female of great size and spread. Known since 1838, this cultivar may develop to 25 feet high with a 30-foot spread in a century, yet it is modest-growing to suit many landscape sites for many years if kept pruned. The blue-green needles are less than an inch in length.

CULTIVAR: 'Fastigiata' ('Stricta') (zone 6) is commonly known as the Irish yew and is undoubtedly the most prominent and distinguished member of this species. It has triple appeal as a densely columnar form, a female with heavy fruiting, and a plant with a richly deep green accent. It originated in 1780 on a mountain farm in Ireland as two chance discoveries that soon were transplanted to cultivated sites. One died 85 years later, but the survivor kept its vigor to reach 20 feet in height and became the sole source for the worldwide distribution of this outstanding plant. Slow-growing and very narrow when young (becoming only 6 feet tall and 15 inches wide in a decade), it has strongly upright main stems with radially set, 1-inch, black-green needles on much crowded twigs; the fruit is oblong in shape and red. There is now a male form with a broader spread in cultivation.

CULTIVAR: 'Fastigiata Aurea' (zone 6) appeared about 1880 and is a slower-growing male variant with deeply golden yellow needles throughout the year on its newest foliage; the interior leaves are green. It needs full sun to maintain this interest, and should reach a mature height of 20 feet.

CULTIVAR: 'Fowle' ('Adpressa Fowle') (zone 5) represents a cold-tolerant form with foliage unlike that of any other yew in common cultivation; its thick, blunt, dark green needles are only ⅛ inch long and appear very crowded and radially set along the slender twigs. It originated in Newburyport, Massachusetts, as a slow-growing female sport of 'Adpressa', and it can grow into a dense pyramid 8 feet high and 15 feet across after 50 years. The initial form is very open and needs some pruning encouragement for later compact bushiness; it also can be top-grafted to create a unique evergreen standard of slow growth, but this shrub is not overly cooperative in terms of blending together when used as an architectural hedge line. The round ⅛-inch fruit is bright red.

CULTIVAR: 'Overeynderi' (zone 6) developed from a Dutch seedling of 'Fastigiata' in 1860 and is naturally shrubby, broad, and dense with an eventual height of 15 feet and a nearly comparable spread. Expanding at about 4 inches annually, it carries ¾-inch needles that are medium green above and dull green beneath. Fruit is unreported.

CULTIVAR: 'Repandens' (zone 5) has been in cultivation since 1887 and resembles 'Cavendishii' in its nearly prostrate horizontal branching and its needle shape; it is, however, a male plant. Known as the hardiest cultivar of the English yew grown in the United States, it is readily adaptable to heavily shaded locations and actually keeps a better color in its deep green needles if provided with some shading no matter where it is located. The ¾-inch, sickle-shaped, dull-surfaced leaves are dispersed on the twigs both upward and outward; the growth pattern is mostly irregular to create a spreading mound with a ragged outline. Usually slow to expand, it can lift to about 4 feet with a spread of 15 feet in 30 years. Avoid locating it in areas where cold, blustery winds are constant.

CULTIVAR: 'Semperaurea' (zone 6) originated about 1908 and offers a very slow-growing, dense, columnar (but eventually wide) male form with yellow foliage on compactly spreading branches that have very short, crowded twigs. The nearly scythe-shaped needles vary from ⅛ to ¾ inch and are aligned to grow both upward and downward on the stems; they keep their golden yellow coloring well into the second year, making this one of the most desirable of all cultivars.

CULTIVAR: 'Standishii' (zone 6) also has been in cultivation since 1908 and is another cultivar with yellow leaves. It may be the showiest columnar yew of all. Narrowly fastigiate, very compact, and extremely sluggish to grow, with only an inch of expansion likely each year, this female has upright, tightly packed branching and twigs that are spirally set with 1-inch rich golden yellow needles. The red fruit is freely produced, creating a striking accent when it appears in late summer.

CULTIVAR: 'Washingtonii' (zone 6) has been known since 1874. While golden yellow in tone, it is not distinctly a yellow plant since only the newest growth achieves this color, and this does not occur on all parts of the plant in equal strength. Also, this color novelty quickly alters to yellow-green by summer, and the winter hue is bronze. A vigorously growing female plant with ascending branches and twigs, it eventually forms a broad-based open shrub about 6 feet high with a 10-foot spread. The 1-inch sickle-shaped needles curve upward.

Taxus cuspidata cv. 'Densa'

Taxus cuspidata cv. 'Nana'

Taxus cuspidata cv. 'Nana Pyramidalis'

Taxus cuspidata (Japanese yew)

Zones 4 to 7   50′ high x 25′ wide   Sun to semishade

Although it is native to Japan, Korea, and Manchuria, this species thrives in most of North America and is the common staple of many nursery offerings in itself or for its many cultivars of distinction. Rapid-growing at all ages, it can reach treelike proportions in some areas; however, it usually is known as a very wide-spreading, heavily multistemmed shrub with dependable annual fruiting. The needles have distinctively bright, yellow-green undersides, and the plant is much hardier than the English yew. The main branching is upright with wide-spreading, arching or horizontal, flexible secondary shoots that create an open, irregular outline. Rapid in its expansion even when young, it can produce at least a foot of new growth annually. The twigs are yellow-green with somewhat leathery, broad, 1¼-inch dull green needles having conspicuous yellow banding beneath; these leaves are arranged alternately along the twigs to form a V-shaped, distinctive trough appearance. The ½-inch red fruit is egg-shaped, while the stem bark is red-brown to gray-brown and flakes off with age. Adaptable to many soil conditions—except those with poor drainage—it grows easily in any average-fertility soil in either full sun or semishade and is tolerant of both drought and cold. While not always as hardy as the parent, the cultivars show consistent durability and landscape interest.

CULTIVAR: 'Aurescens' (zone 5) came into cultivation about 1920 and has new growth with deep yellow needles. Compact but wide-spreading, this male plant grows slowly and eventually forms a 3-foot-high mound with an 8-foot spread. Requiring some wind protection, this cultivar is not as colorful if planted in too much shade.

CULTIVAR: 'Capitata' (zone 4) behaves vigorously and forms an upright conical shrub with a broad base; it tends to lose the lower branches, however, unless pruned consistently for continued new growth after transplanting. Expanding rapidly at a foot per year, it eventually will reach a height of 20 feet with a similar spread. *Hortus Third* calls this the typical form of *cuspidata*. Both male and female types of this cultivar are offered by nurseries.

CULTIVAR: 'Densa' (zone 5) was introduced to the United States from Japan about 1917 as a dense, compact, low, and spreading bush that has proved very useful for hedges. Normally female, this cultivar has crowded erect stems with dark green 1-inch needles. It develops modestly to produce a plant with an eventual height of 4 feet and a spread of 8 feet.

CULTIVAR: 'Nana' (zone 4) is often mislabeled 'Brevifolia' in the nursery trade because it has shorter needles than the parent; nevertheless, the true *brevifolia* is a distinct and separate species native only to the western parts of the United States, and it does not appear to grow well outside its own area. *Brevifolia* also tends to become a very tall (possibly 60-foot) tree under some growing conditions. The male cultivar presented here has been known since 1861 in Japan; it is deservedly popular for its sluggish growth, irregular silhouette, and moundlike nature. The densely arranged, radially set, glossy foliage appears on bunched short twigs; the leaves are flat, broad, blunt-ended, and ¾ inch with a mid-green coloring on the topsides and lighter green banding beneath. Eventually it will reach 20 feet wide and 9 feet tall, but this requires a century of waiting.

CULTIVAR: 'Nana Pyramidalis' (zone 4) is a female that forms a broad, heavy-foliaged, erect pyramid with thick, tufted, dark green needles and has slow growth. It may reach 12 feet with an 8-foot base, but not until 60 years has passed. It sometimes is listed simply as 'Pyramidalis', but this is not correct.

Taxus x media   (Anglojap yew)

Zones 4 to 7   40′ high x 20′ wide   Sun to semishade

Vigorous and spreading to become a medium- to large-sized shrub, this is a hybrid crossing of *baccata* and *cuspidata* that now represents one of the most versatile yew forms imaginable, even if most of the advantages come from its cultivars. This plant originated in 1900 in Massachusetts and shows more of the *cuspidata* trademarks of growth but manages to establish its own distinctions. Its twigs are olive green and do not change to brown in the second year; the glossy leaves are larger and are spaced farther apart. As hardy as *cuspidata*, it adapts well to half shade satisfactorily too. It is not overly popular for itself, but its ruggedly hardy cultivars are worth noticing.

CULTIVAR: 'Brownii' (zone 4) has been in cultivation since 1940 and presents a fine-textured, dense, rounded to conical outline that is suitable for hedge use. A male plant, it can grow 9 feet tall and 12 feet wide in about 15 years, and it carries semierect branching with short, dense, sickle-shaped dark green needles.

CULTIVAR: 'Hatfieldii' (zone 4) by now must surely be one of the most well-liked landscape plants since it easily develops a clothed-to-the-ground, dense, slow-growing pyramid with tight dark green foliage. Originating in Massachusetts during 1923, this male shrub is extensively planted for both natural and sheared hedgings; it expands to 12 feet in height with a 10-foot width after 20 years.

CULTIVAR: 'Hicksii' (zone 4) was discovered on Long Island, New York, in 1924 and is the companion alternative to 'Hatfieldii' for hedge making throughout much of this country. Since it is a female cultivar, the addition of red late summer and autumn fruiting provides a bonus worth investigating if a choice has to be made between them. As a shrub, 'Hicksii' is more open and vigorous in its growth with a more broadly spreading shape and stiff, upright main branching; it also tends to lift its lowest branches from the ground. The 1¼-inch leaves are dark, glossy green needles set radially around the twigs with more spacing between them than exists on 'Hatfieldii' to allow room for fruit production. A specimen plant can become 20 feet tall with an almost equal spread in just 15 years, but this is uncommon.

CULTIVAR: 'Tauntonii' (zone 4) is a dense, low, slow-growing globe usually no more than 2 feet high and 3 feet wide after 10 years of growth. A male cultivar, it needs little or no pruning to hold its compact shape.

CULTIVAR: 'Viridis' (zone 4) is a narrowly columnar form developed in 1948 with very dense foliage and twisted bright green needles. It expands slowly at 1 or 2 inches per year to become 10 feet tall in 20 years; on some sites it may develop much more slowly.

CULTIVAR: 'Wardii' (zone 4) appeared in cultivation by 1950. It is a dense, semi-globular, sprawling, flat-topped shrub that may become 6 feet tall and 20 feet wide after 20 years of growth. It carries dark green needles and presents a finer textural appearance than 'Nana', its closest similar form.

THUJA (arborvitae)   *Cupressaceae* (cypress) family

Thuja and *Platycladus* are closely related tree genera, and both were called *Thuja* until recent times; each is also a cousin to *Chamaecyparis*. All three differ significantly from one another in the shape and size of the cone fruit, and *Thuja* has woody cones less than ½ inch long, light brown to cinnamon brown in color, that open in a bell shape with upturned ends like the roof tips of an oriental pagoda. *Thuja* is a Latin name for a tree with cones; the North American Indians called the plant "Oo-soo-ha-tah," or "feather leaf," from the general appearance of its foliage. The sprays of scalelike needles give off a distinctive and pleasantly aromatic scent when bruised or crushed. The common name, arborvitae, is Latin and translates as "tree of life," but this label probably was assigned by King Louis XII of France in the early sixteenth century for a specific reason; it also helped to introduce the plant into cultivation in Europe. As the story is told, the explorer Jacques Cartier was investigating the St. Lawrence River, and his men came down with scurvy. The Indian guides concocted a potion of evergreen tips for them to drink—most likely some species of *Thuja*, since it grew well in that vicinity—and the crew soon was revived. Because the sap of *Thuja* is known to contain good quantities of vitamin C, the cure of scurvy, this has logic. As a token of gratitude for such helpfulness, Cartier brought seedlings of *Thuja* to the king, who then dubbed it *l'arbre de vie*, or "tree of life," and introduced it to French horticulture.

Six species are located either in North America or in eastern Asia, and all prefer sites with high humidity and cool summer temperatures (unlike *Platycladus*) in full sun or at least dappled light, although the soil must stay consistently moist. Few insects or diseases bother them seriously.

Thuja occidentalis cv. 'Globosa'

Thuja occidentalis (American arborvitae, white cedar) shrub cultivars and varieties

Zones 3 to 8   Variable in size   Sun to light shade

This very hardy species is native as a tree form from Nova Scotia to North Carolina and west to Illinois but usually is found growing at its best only in cool, moist areas within these boundaries that have high year-round humidity; it often is found in great numbers near lakes or the ocean. Greatly disliking dry compacted soil and high summertime heat for prolonged periods, it will accept limestone and heavy clay soils satisfactorily but is adaptable only from zone 6 through zone 8 in the western portions of the United States. It transplants easily and is rarely disturbed by either insect or disease nuisances, although it can be harmed by red spider mites during times of drought. This plant is fast-growing if kept consistently moist.

The narrowly conical and upright silhouette has flat, crowded sprays of dense foliage composed of tiny, scalelike, glossy needles that are dark green above and yellowish green beneath (its closest relation, *Platycladus*, has same-color leaves on both sides) with a resin gland on the reverse side that gives off a pleasantly pungent odor when crushed. The winter coloring, unfortunately, is apt to be either dull green or dirty brown. This monoecious tree has insignificant male flowers and female cones less than a half inch, oblong and light brown in color; these cones open the scales into a bell shape with recurved ends. Its shrub cultivars offer interesting diversity.

CULTIVAR: 'Caespitosa' (zone 4) originated in Ireland about 1923. It is a very slow-growing dwarf with a cushion-shaped rounded hummock of green needles and very thick twigs. Usually wider than it is tall, it carries scalelike foliage that is not flattened but is irregular and congested. It may become 20 inches tall and wide by two decades. Cones are not recorded.

CULTIVAR: 'Ellwangerana Aurea' (zone 5) came from Germany in 1902. It starts out egg-shaped but later modifies to a dense 10-foot pyramid with several distinct cone-like leaders and a wide 13- to 15-foot base. Slow to expand, it may put out 2 inches of new growth yearly. The golden bronze leaves are mostly adult and scalelike; cones are not present. This cultivar often is sold erroneously as 'Rheingold' when small because both look very similar in form and color at that stage. However, 'Rheingold' remains an egg in silhouette later with a maximum height of just 3 feet, but it distinctively carries only awl-shaped juvenile foliage.

CULTIVAR: 'Ericoides' (zone 6) came into cultivation in the United States by 1867 and presents a novel, slow-growing form with heatherlike foliage composed of juvenile leaves (the genus name for heather is *Erica*). Dwarfed, dense, rounded, or cone-shaped in silhouette, this cultivar has flexible, erect, loosely arranged twigs and dull brown-green or yellow-green awl-shaped needles that do not distinguish themselves aesthetically when they turn donkey brown during winter dormancy. Apt to suffer breakage from heavy, wet snowfalls, it is also tender on windy sites. After 5 years a plant may be 3 feet tall and about 20 inches wide. Cones do not appear.

CULTIVAR: 'Globosa' (zone 4) has been known since 1875 and retains its pleasant gray-green coloring all year long, although it may darken in winter. This is a compact, dwarfed, rounded shrub with closely packed sprays of adult foliage and slow growth. It may reach dimensions of 3 feet in height and width after 10 years; the ultimate height is 5 feet. The main branches ascend, but the side twigs develop at random angles, producing a dense look of crowded foliage. It apparently does not produce cones.

CULTIVAR: 'Hoveyii' (zone 4) came into use around 1868 as a globose to egg-shaped dwarf with bright green or yellow-green leaves in flat foliage planes on erect twigs; the plant turns brownish in winter. To its detriment in areas with many snowfalls, these parallel-set stems readily fall apart and distort the silhouette. Generally higher than it is wide as it expands slowly, this cultivar can become 9 feet tall. Cones are unknown.

CULTIVAR: 'Little Champion' (zone 4) came from Canada in 1935 and is very hardy in a variety of difficult growing locations. This globose shrub is fast-growing when young but soon settles down to a more leisurely rate. Its bright, lively green foliage is lacy and soft, but it will shade to bronze in winter. The ultimate size is about 3½ feet tall and wide. Cones are not produced.

CULTIVAR: 'Little Gem' (zone 4) originated in 1891 as a sluggish-growing, flat-topped, dwarfed dense mound of compact foliage. Turning slightly brown-toned in winter, it carries deep green leaves for most of the year in crowded, crimped sprays on twisted horizontal twigs that grow in all directions. After 10 years a plant may have dimensions of only 15 inches in height and spread; its eventual size should approximate 2 feet with a 3-foot width. There are no cones.

CULTIVAR: 'Rheingold' (zone 4) came from Germany in 1902 and maintains a spreading globular form far lower than that of its youthful look-alike 'Ellwangerana Aurea', topping out at close to 3 feet. The leaves are consistently awl-shaped and juvenile on short thin twigs sprouting from stout, conspicuously forked main branches that give rise to several peaks or cones in its silhouette as it matures. The foliage is an unusual pinkish gold color during summer and changes to a bright golden-bronze tone by winter. Slow-growing, it may become 30 inches tall and 4 feet wide after 10 years. Cones are nonexistent.

CULTIVAR: 'Umbraculifera' (zone 4) was cultivated in Germany by 1892 and displays the most noticeable blue-green foliage of any arborvitae. Dwarfed, compact, and neatly hemispherical down to the ground, this globose plant slowly expands to become 30 inches high and 3 feet wide in a decade; the ultimate size is between 3 and 4 feet tall. Regrettably, it does not transplant at all well except when very small. The branches and slightly curled twigs are erect and carry thin adult needle scales that are green beneath a heavy coating of bloom; in wintertime this bluish tone changes to dark bronze-green. It is coneless.

TSUGA (hemlock, hemlock spruce) *Pinaceae* (pine) family

Graceful, shapely, and fine-textured forest trees, the monoecious hemlocks are remarkable for their easy adaptation to both sun and shade as well as their substantial hardiness. Ten species exist throughout the world, and *canadensis* of North America is not only the hardiest of the lot but has contributed the most variations (seventy-five) in dwarf forms; no native hemlock exists in Europe. *Tsuga*, a name of Japanese origin, is composed of the Japanese words for "tree" and "mother"; this has only obscure significance today but may be tied to the easy movement of the slender branching in even gentle wind. The common name, hemlock, is derived from the New York State tribal Indian description of Canada as *Hoe-nadia* ("the land of the hemlock"). In any event, this is not the poisonous hemlock concoction Socrates was forced to drink in ancient Greece; that was another plant entirely. Common names are often misapplied.

All species have blunt-tipped, short solitary needles with whitened banding beneath (it varies in its intensity) plus relatively small cones placed on pendulous forward twigs. These conical trees are best grown on cool, non-windy sites with consistent ground moisture all year, reasonable humidity, and an acid soil. They are not truly successful in polluted urban air or when located near large expanses of heat-reflecting pavement or building walls. They have little tolerance for ice-melting chemicals that drain freely toward the roots, nor can they abide long periods of drought. Serious diseases are rare, but red spider mite infestations (common to many needle evergreens) can discolor the foliage appreciably during dry, hot summers. Easy to transplant at almost any size that equipment can handle, hemlocks often are sold as multistemmed plants because of their extra fullness; however, such forms often become more distorted or damaged during times of heavy, wet snowfalls. If well grown, the shrub forms do not share these problems to any marked degree.

Tsuga canadensis cv. 'Hussii'

Tsuga canadensis (Canada hemlock, eastern hemlock) shrub
cultivars and varieties

Zones 3 to 7   Variable in size   Sun to semishade

Natively inhabiting large areas from Nova Scotia to Alabama and west to Minnesota, this species is a pleasantly graceful, feathery-looking conical tree with upturned flexible branches and divergent drooping twig ends. The ⅛- to ½-inch blunt needles are shiny, dark green with two white lines beneath and appear densely crowded on thin, somewhat hairy yellow-brown twigs; the leaves remain in place up to 4 years, creating a reasonably dense-looking plant at all times. The ¾-inch oval cones form annually and become gray-brown when mature; they usually are produced generously on the nodding tip ends of the branches. Surprisingly, this species adjusts well to both acidic and alkaline soils within its normal growing range, and the plant may even adapt to both zone 8 and zone 9 if given a cool site on a year-round basis. Few insects or diseases are bothersome. Its cultivars enjoy the same culture.

CULTIVAR: 'Aurea' (zone 4) has been cultivated since 1866 and is somewhat rare today. It presents a compact, pyramidal, irregular shape with golden yellow new growth which later turns yellow-green for the season. The main stems are ascending with side twigs that droop in tightly recurved lines; the crowded ⅛-inch needles are broader than those of the parent and fill the stems densely. Cones are unknown. Slow-growing at only an inch or so yearly, this cultivar eventually will reach a 6-foot height with a narrower spread. It colors best when planted in full sun and actually looks its finest during winter dormancy in areas that are continually cold. At times this plant is erroneously labeled 'Everitt's Golden'.

CULTIVAR: 'Cole' ('Cole's Prostrate') (zone 5) originated in the United States in 1929 and is a remarkably prostrate and wide-spreading form with flat foliage sprays and distinctively exposed stems and twigs. It seems to flow over and around rocks in its path while following earth contours as if painted on the ground. The leaves are dark green and come on pendulous stems; cones are not produced. Slow to expand, this creeping shrub will probably be no larger than 1 foot high and 3 feet wide after 10 years. It behaves best when placed in full sun.

CULTIVAR: 'Dawsoniana' (zone 4) was found in Massachusetts during 1927 and grows into a compact bushy plant with two or three main leaders that start out erect and then spread outward. Its very wide leaves are a bright medium green and appear on crowded twigs. Sluggish in expansion at perhaps only an inch annually, it eventually can reach a 4-foot height and spread after many decades. Cones are not recorded.

CULTIVAR: 'Hussii' (zone 5) appeared in 1900 in Connecticut and develops into a medium to large upright shrub of dense but irregular habit characterized by crowded twigs that do not emerge as pronounced leader growth. Growing at about 1 inch yearly, it has ⅛-inch needles of a medium to dark green closely set on the twigs. The maximum size can approach 6 feet with a spread close to 8 feet, but this may require 50 years.

CULTIVAR: 'Jeddeloh' (zone 5) arrived from Germany in 1965 and presents a flattened, rounded, slow-growing form with a depressed center that is similar to *Picea abies cv.* 'Nidiformis', or nest spruce. The weeping branches are covered with bright lime-green foliage. It is too new for its ultimate size and silhouette to be estimated.

CULTIVAR: 'Nana' (zone 5) has been in cultivation since 1855 and expands sluggishly to become only 30 inches tall after 10 years. It develops a chunky, irregular outline with many erect branches but no central leader and carries short, crowded twigs with ¼-inch green foliage. Cones are not apparent. Eventually it will become wider than tall, with a top height of about 4 feet.

Broadleaf
Evergreens

ABELIA (abelia)   *Caprifoliaceae* (honeysuckle) family

The name commemorates Dr. Clarke Abel, an eighteenth-century physician and author who accompanied Lord Amherst of England on an expedition to China in 1817. There are thirty species native to Asia and Mexico, all with opposite, simple, thin foliage that may be either evergreen or deciduous (especially where cold and frost are the rule) in winter. Blooming freely from early summer to autumn, the small, tubular flowers are either white or pink-toned and appear in generous clusters in the leaf axils or terminally. Persistent calyxes (the outer sepal covering for the bud and flower) of spent blossoms tend to become colorful later in their own right. Closely related to the deciduous shrub *Kolkwitzia*, they differ by having nonbristly fruit capsules. All prefer a well-drained, humus-enriched soil with some wind protection and are popular for hedgings or as specimens. Generally, only the species *x grandiflora* and its cultivars are widespread today. Pests and diseases present little risk.

Abelia x grandiflora (glossy abelia)

Zones 6 (warm) to 9   6′ high x 4′ wide   Sun to light shade

Abelia x grandiflora

Abundant flowering in this plant for 5 months (June to October) contributes landscape appeal not easily found in other shrubs. This cross of *chinensis* and *uniflora* is of unknown origin. It is a dense, spreading bush with modest to fast expansion, often reaching 10 feet in zone 9. At 0°F the plant dies to ground level, but its roots survive to regrow. Blooming on current growth only, it has funnel-shaped, ¾-inch, white to pinkish, somewhat fragrant flowers in clusters of one to four at the leaf axils. The thin, shiny, hairless leaves are red-bronze when emerging but turn bright to dark green soon after; they change to bronze again during winter. Stems are slender, arching, red-brown, and slightly fuzzy. Foliage ranges between ¾ inch and 2 inches long and half as wide with both ends rounded or pointed; the margins are slightly toothed. Its fruit is a tiny, smooth capsule with showy pink-tan sepals in a star outline. Pests and disease are not a problem. This species accepts neglect, drought, and heavy pruning well but dislikes harsh, strong winds. The following cultivars are popular.

CULTIVAR: 'Edward Goucher', a selection made about 1910 from the U.S. Department of Agriculture's test grounds at Glen Dale, Maryland, from a cross of *x grandiflora* and *schumanii*, has abundant lavender-pink blossoms and showy red calyxes but is less hardy and thus belongs in zones 7 to 9. Its size and habit are the same as those of *x grandiflora*.

CULTIVAR: 'Prostrata' is a low, creeping form with a 2-foot height that is useful as a groundcover.

CULTIVAR: 'Sherwoodii' carries smaller foliage and flowers on a 3-foot plant.

AUCUBA (spotted laurel, gold dust tree)   *Cornaceae* (dogwood) family

Found in the warmly temperate zones from the Himalayas to Japan, this group of dioecious shrubs (showing male and female flowering on separate plants) may have three to seven species, but only *japonica* is cultivated currently. Leaves are opposite, simple, and entire or toothed; they appear on thick branching along with terminal clusters of purple flowers. The fruit is a berrylike drupe (stone fruit). Growing them well requires only an average, well-drained moist soil in semishade; they have few troublesome demands or pests. This is the most common evergreen shrub in English city gardens and parks since it shrugs off air pollution, neglect, ill treatment, drought, and city grime. All forms make dense screens and are especially adaptable for containers as well. Its name is a modification of the Japanese word *aokiba*.

Aucuba japonica cv. 'Variegata'

Aucuba japonica   (Japanese aucuba, Japanese laurel)

Zones 8 and 9   5′ to 15′ high x 3′ to 5′ wide   Semishade to full shade

The adaptability of this vigorous species to diminished light, neglect, smog, and competition from other roots makes it a highly regarded shrub in many parts of the world. Found in eastern Asia at Himalayan elevations of 9000 feet (but also in lower valleys), it was introduced to culture in 1861 and has maintained popular appeal for hedgings, borders, and containers in combination with other foliages and flowers. Because it roots easily from stem cuttings, even when this is done by novices, it can be found today in many landscape situations within its range of hardiness, and it is particularly valued for its easy tolerance of heavy pruning. Stiffly upright and dense, this spreading shrub performs best in a well-drained, humusy, light, fertile soil that is consistently moist; yet it satisfactorily accepts placement in the dryness and heavy shade of beech, linden, and horse chestnut on some sites.

The lanceolate, leathery, glossy dark green leaves can be up to 7 inches long and almost half as wide with coarse teeth only toward the tips; the foliage is crowded at the twig ends. Blooming in March and April with tiny purplish flowers, the female plants later develop bright scarlet and occasionally white or yellow ½-inch oval fruit by early winter; however, more male plants are raised commercially since they show faster growth, a typical condition in species where sexes are on different plants. At least fifteen cultivars are available currently, and those showing special leaf colorings need a bright location but not full sun to maintain their unusual values. Here is a sampling of some noteworthy types.

CULTIVAR: 'Crotonifolia' is a male with green foliage spotted ivory-white or marbled in yellow; the leaves are thinner and broader than those of 'Variegata'.

CULTIVAR: 'Dentata' has smaller green leaves with only one or two coarse teeth on the margins. (Calling it 'Nondentata' would be more accurate.)

CULTIVAR: 'Fructu Albo' is a female with pale pinkish buff fruiting and slightly silver-variegated leaves.

CULTIVAR: 'Goldieana' carries larger leaves that are mostly yellow with a green margin.

CULTIVAR: 'Longifolia' ('Angustifolia')('Salicifolia') has deep to bright green, narrow sharp-pointed foliage to 5 inches; it is female.

CULTIVAR: 'Macrophylla' has especially broad sea-green foliage.

CULTIVAR: 'Nana' is female with a compact dwarfed habit and small, sharply toothed leaves, but only in the upper portions.

CULTIVAR: 'Picturata' ('Aureo-maculata')('Latimaculata') is a showy female with large brightly golden leaves edged in green.

CULTIVAR: 'Sulphurea' has sea-green stems and is colored the reverse of 'Picturata', with pale yellow margins on green leaves. It needs bright light to maintain this variation.

CULTIVAR: 'Variegata' ('Maculata') has proved to be the most dependable and vigorous cultivar since its introduction from Japan in 1783 (before the fully green form was known). Its dark green foliage is strongly freckled with yellow dots.

AZALEA (RHODODENDRON) (azalea)   *Ericaceae* (heath) family

Until 1834 azaleas were separated from rhododendrons by botanists on the basis of the kinds then known to exist. All azaleas then were considered deciduous, showed slightly hairy foliage, and had five flower stamens. The related rhododendrons of that time were hairless and evergreen and carried ten flower stamens. As more plant discoveries came to light, these distinctions had to be abandoned as unreliable. Now all azaleas are classified as *Rhododendron* in genus, although the common name, azalea, remains intact. The new arrangement, while botanically sound, will surely not gain easy acceptance with the general public for a long time to come.

There are no *constant* differences today that help distinguish these two readily, although azaleas are largely (if not so exclusively any more) deciduous and produce funnel-shaped blossoms. Rhododendrons, on the other hand, are mostly evergreen and have bell-shaped flowers; the stamen count is no longer valid for this generalization. (Check the *Rhododendron* listings in this division and in the "Deciduous Shrubs" division for azaleas recommended for cultivation.)

BERBERIS (barberry)   *Berberidaceae* (barberry) family

The name is a corruption of the Arabic *berberys*, which describes the shiny foliage on some species. At least 500 species and subspecies are known today, both evergreen and deciduous. Most are spiny shrubs of the north temperate zones, and there are more types in South America and eastern Asia than elsewhere. These plants are difficult to identify precisely because they hybridize freely when grown together, and the seedlings rarely come true to type. Simple to raise and fast-growing once they are established, all are troublesome to transplant except when very small since they resent any root disturbance as older specimens. Their roots and inner stems are unique in that they are colored yellow from light to bright. They accept any average, well-drained moist site but vary in their light need from full sun to semishade. Deciduous forms tolerate more dryness, while the evergreen sorts are not consistently hardy in the northernmost sections of the world.

The alternate simple or compound leaves usually color noticeably in autumn on deciduous types; evergreen kinds may or may not vary their hues significantly. Bloom occurs mostly by early May in tones of yellow to red as small bell-shaped flowers held in groups or individually. The often grooved young stems can be red, yellow, or almost black and are often spiny. The fruit is a red, dark purple, yellow, or black berry generally ¼ inch long and often waxy. In the seventeenth century Europeans preserved this fruit in vinegar and enjoyed it as a condiment with fish or meat.

Puccinia graminis, or black stem rust of wheat, oats, barley, and rye, uses barberry as its intermediate host, and thus it is now unlawful in some parts of the United States to raise these shrubs near grain crops. The species *vulgaris* is the worst offender here, and plants usually are destroyed quickly when found near these valuable crop fields. For these plants themselves, few pests or diseases are bothersome. (Consult the "Deciduous Shrubs" division as well.)

Berberis candidula   (no common name)

Zones 6 to 9   3' high x 5' wide   Sun to light shade

Introduced from western China in 1895 by Maurice de Vilmorin, a noted explorer, this dense, dome-shaped, slow-growing species has rigid, arching branches and solitary, vividly yellow, globose, ⅓- to ½-inch flowers in early May. Its narrow, 1-inch, lustrous dark green leaves are conspicuously blue-white beneath with incurved margins; they appear in tufts at the stem joints along with three-parted, pale brown, sharp half-inch spines. The ⅛- to ½-inch globular fruit looks pale gray but is actually blue-black with a waxy overcovering.

Berberis x chenaultii   (Chenault barberry)

Zones 6 to 9   4′ high x 3′ wide   Sun to light shade

A hybrid of *gagnepainii* and *verruculosa,* the dense, vigorous shrub can become a solid hedge in a moderate time span. Yellow, ½-inch, solitary or three-per-cluster flowers unfold in May; any occasional fruiting will be dark blue. The semilustrous foliage is grayish beneath and narrowly oblong with spiny margins between ¾ inch and 1½ inches in length. Stems are slightly black-dotted and arching with three-parted half-inch spines.

Berberis darwinii   (Darwin's barberry)

Zones 8 and 9   5′ to 10′ high x 5′ to 10′ wide   Sun to semishade

Discovered during the journey of *H.M.S. Beagle* by botanist Charles Darwin in 1835, this barberry is one of the most handsome in flower. Generous and showy, it has up to 4-inch clusters of orange-yellow blossoms tinged with red that appear on reddened stalks during early May. Originating in Chile and Argentina, today they grow best in California and the southern United States and often rebloom to some extent in the autumn months. Densely branched, dark brown stems have three- to five-parted spines and hairy new growth with six-sided, hollylike, ¾-inch leaves ending in spiny teeth. This stiff foliage is a rich, glossy green above with pale yellow-green undersides. The abundant, dark purple-blue or plum-red fruit is round, waxy, and about ¼ inch long. Its cultivars offer attractive options.

CULTIVAR: 'Depressa' has orange flower buds and golden yellow flowering on a low, mounded silhouette only 18 inches tall with a 30-inch spread.

CULTIVAR: 'Firefly' displays richly orange-red flowers.

CULTIVAR: 'Nana' carries shorter stem spines and golden yellow blossoms on a dwarfed, compact, slow-growing form that is about a foot tall and twice that width.

Berberis gagnepainii   (black barberry)

Zones 6 (warm) to 9   4′ to 7′ high x 6′ wide   Sun to light shade

Erect, densely branched with three-parted spines, compact, and free-flowering, this plant can easily form an impenetrable and attractive hedge over a wide growing range. The bright yellow flowers in mid-May are ½ inch long in groups of three to seven and produce clusters of bluish black, oval, wax-covered fruit. Its leaves, narrowly lanceolate and up to 4 inches long, are coarsely spined on the margins in middle to dark green with paler undersides. Intoduced during 1904 from western China, it is a parent of *x chenaultii* and has a few varieties of its own.

VARIETY: *lanceifolia* is the most commonly grown type and has narrower foliage.

VARIETY: *praestans* has flat, narrow leaves without spiny margins.

Berberis julianae (wintergreen barberry)

Zones 6 (warm) to 9 7' high x 4' wide Sun to light shade

Berberis julianae

Only semievergreen if grown at its northernmost limit, this erect introduction from central China came into cultivation in 1900 and is a good candidate for a tall hedge or screen. Flowering is generous from axillary clusters of fifteen to twenty light yellow ⅓-inch blossoms in May followed by blue-toned, oblong, ⅓-inch fruit. Rigid three-parted spines appear along the mature yellowish stems and on the new copper-toned growth. Its narrow, leathery, somewhat wrinkled leaves are between 2 and 4 inches long with twelve to twenty short, spiny teeth; they are dark green above and lighter on the undersides. Older foliage often colors bright red before dropping in autumn.

Berberis x mentorensis (no common name)

Zones 6 to 9 3' to 7' high x 2' to 4' wide Sun

Originating in 1924 at Mentor, Ohio, as a vigorous cross between *julianae* and the deciduous *thunbergii*, this shrub often behaves as a semievergreen in cold, frosty climates. It grows especially well in the midwestern parts of the United States since it is very tolerant to both summer dryness and winter cold. On milder sites it behaves more as a broadleaf evergreen should. The ¼-inch yellow flowers that appear in May develop in pairs or are solitary on grooved stems with thorny twigs. The ellipsoidal fruit is dull, dark red and is not a landscape feature. The oval foliage is between ¾ inch and 1 inch long with only a few marginal spines.

Berberis x stenophylla (rosemary barberry)

Zones 7 to 9 8' to 10' high x 6' to 12' wide Sun

Berberis x stenophylla

Cultivated since 1864, this hybrid of *darwinii* and *empetrifolia* is a thick mass of slender, graceful branches with a very free-flowering habit of distinction. Useful as a tall, dense hedge or a thicket cover on an embankment, it may prove only semievergreen at its northerly growing limit. The rich, golden yellow, sweetly fragrant, ⅓-inch flowers unfold in early May as axillary clusters holding seven to fourteen blossoms; its globe-shaped black fruit is ¼ inch wide and covered with a blue and waxy overlay. Very narrow, ⅜-inch to 1-inch entire leaves are glossy, dark green with yellow-green undersides and noticeably roll backward (or curve inward) in bundles of five or six on dark red-brown stems carrying simple undivided spines. There are many cultivars available.

CULTIVAR: 'Coccinea' is a shorter type with a 3-foot height and width, broader foliage, crimson flower buds, orange-toned blossoms, and purple fruit.

CULTIVAR: 'Corallina' has coral-red budding and yellow flowers plus narrower foliage on a shorter, more open plant.

CULTIVAR: 'Corallina Compacta' is a smaller version of *cv.* 'Corallina' with purplish white fruiting.

CULTIVAR: 'Diversifolia' offers a mix of foliage types between narrow and broad, often on the same stems. The flowers are golden yellow.

CULTIVAR: 'Gracilis' creates a low profile and an open silhouette with bright green foliage that is either narrow and smooth-edged or broad and spiny. Blossoms are golden yellow.

CULTIVAR: 'Gracilis Nana' is a dense, dwarfed, slow-growing version of *cv.* 'Gracilis' with new leaves brilliantly orange-red and mature foliage flecked in yellow. The flowers are deep orange-yellow.

Berberis verruculosa   (warty barberry)

Zones 6 to 9   3′ to 6′ high x 3′ wide   Sun to light shade

Slow-growing, stiffly compact, and mounded, the plant has flowering that produces a very sweet yeasty fragrance somewhat like that of fresh-baked bread. These solitary, ½-inch, golden yellow blooms open by mid-May on densely foliaged, cylindrical, warty, and hairy stems that turn yellowish with age; its spines are triparted, slender, and short. The leathery dark green leaves are almost an inch long with two to four spiny teeth on downturned edges, and they usually color bronze in winter. Foliage undersides are noticeably grayish white or gray-green but are rarely noticed because of the stiffly arched twigs that lack flexibility. The occasional fruit is egg-shaped and bluish black.

BUXUS   (box, boxwood)   *Buxaceae*   (box) family

This genus carries an ancient Latin name traceable to the time of Julius Caesar, and the thirty species which it comprises are found scattered in western Europe, the Mediterranean region, temperate eastern Asia, the West Indies, and Central America. These plants are low or dense treelike shrubs with opposite, entire, leathery, small (to 1¼ inches) leaves on four-angled, grooved young stems; in cold areas the foliage often assumes a brownish cast for winter. The inconspicuous but abundant springtime flowering is monoecious and develops terminally or in the leaf axils to produce a strong scent that is alluring to bees. The fruit is a tiny two-horned capsule. While accepting full sun, all do better with light shading on a moist, well-drained, average acid or alkaline soil, making them highly adaptable and popular plants. Some species have longevity records that show endurance for hundreds of years if the growing conditions are continuously suitable.

Ranking high as ornamentals, box are favored worldwide as natural or clipped hedges, screens, sculptural topiary, and even low edgings since most are very slow-growing and accept shearing very well. The wood of some species is prized for its hard boniness in the making of drafting tools, furniture inlays, engraving blocks, and musical instrument parts. Unfortunately, the foliage of the majority of these shrubs is seriously disfigured by spider mites, leaf miners, leaf spot, and rust disease.

Buxus microphylla   (littleleaf box)

Zones 6 to 9   3′ high x 4′ wide   Light to semishade

Introduced to culture in 1860 from Japan, littleleaf box has the odd distinction of never having been found growing wild there. Nursery plants today show either a compact or a prostrate habit (even a very open form is known) and so the shrub cannot always be simply ordered but may have to be selected personally. It prefers more shade than many others to forestall sunscald of the inner stems, especially with the loose forms. Terminal, strong-scented, greenish yellow, tiny flowers open in early May on sharply four-angled, shiny, smooth twigs with narrowly oblong, thin, up to 1-inch leaves ending in a slight tip notch. Its varieties and cultivars are now more widely preferred.

VARIETY: *harlandii* often is mislabeled as a separate species by growers and possibly may be only a form of *sinica*. Considered tender north of Alabama, it produces an inverted pyramid shape with a 5-foot height.

VARIETY: *japonica* represents the most widely cultivated type, with a strong appeal in California. Its silhouette is rounded to a 6-foot height with spreading twiggy branches that carry light to deep green foliage. Its cultivars are as follows.

CULTIVAR: 'Richardii' has a dwarfed, rapidly growing outline with thicker, bright green leaves.

CULTIVAR: 'Rotundifolia' develops broader foliage on a plant similar to the parent.

VARIETY: *koreana* generally grows only 2 feet tall and maintains greater hardiness than any of these others to persist into zone 5. The ½-inch foliage stays yellowish green all year and appears on hairy new stems; in severe winters, however, these leaves may become brown-toned. Flowering is both terminal and axillary.

CULTIVAR: 'Wintergreen' came from Manchuria to Ohio in the 1930s and keeps a year-round bright green appearance with a spread of about 4 feet.

VARIETY: *sinica* came into cultivation from China in 1900. It is taller, broader, and more open in habit than *microphylla*, with somewhat larger foliage on hairy new stems.

Buxus microphylla japonica

Buxus sempervirens (common box)

Zones 6 to 9   6′ to 15′ high x 4′ to 6′ wide   Sun to light shade

Greatly used and appreciated in the southern United States for either clipped or billowy tall hedges, this box is native to Europe, northern Africa, and western Asia. In very mild areas it may approach 30 feet in height, but it normally remains far lower. Densely bushy with crowded branching, this sluggish plant may expand only an inch or so yearly in cool climates. It carries honey-scented axillary clusterings of tiny yellow-green blossoms from April to May. Four-sided stems support lance-shaped, ½- to 1⅜-inch leaves under ½ inch wide that are broader at the middle and carry a slight notch at the tips; this foliage is dark green with lighter undersides. A highly diversified and extensive cultivar list exists, and it is being expanded constantly because of the popularity of the species.

Buxus sempervirens

CULTIVAR: 'Albo-marginatus' has foliage with white edges.

CULTIVAR: 'Angustifolia' carries narrow, oblong leaves.

CULTIVAR: 'Arborescens' is more treelike and taller with darker and larger foliage.

CULTIVAR: 'Argentea' sports leaves either variegated with white or all grayish white yet often has new shoots that are entirely green-leaved (these can be pruned out). It is wide-spreading but tender.

CULTIVAR: 'Argenteo-variegata' has foliage variegated in white with a very slow growth pattern.

CULTIVAR: 'Aurea' produces yellowish foliage throughout the plant.

CULTIVAR: 'Aureo-variegata' is a large shrub with leaves splashed, striped, or mottled in creamy yellow.

CULTIVAR: 'Bullata' displays larger leaves that are puckered or blistered.

CULTIVAR: 'Columnaris' develops an erect columnar form.

CULTIVAR: 'Conica' is upright with a conical silhouette.

CULTIVAR: 'Cronii' shows greater hardiness than the parent as well as more vigor.

CULTIVAR: 'Elegans' has slender foliage variegated in white.

CULTIVAR: 'Elegantissima' is considered the best silver-leaved box because of its irregularly cream-white leaf margins that present a grayish green total appearance for the plant. Dense, compact, and dome-shaped, it grows slowly.

CULTIVAR: 'Fastigiata' is strongly erect and columnar.

CULTIVAR: 'Glauca' has blue-green foliage and a pyramidal outline.

Buxus sempervirens

CULTIVAR: 'Handworthiensis' becomes erect, dense, bushy, and semirounded with larger, thicker, dark green, leathery leaves.

CULTIVAR: 'Longifolia' is a large shrub with dense sprays of narrowly oblong leaves.

CULTIVAR: 'Marginata' has a large-scaled erect silhouette and puckered misshapen leaves irregularly splotched and margined in yellow. Occasionally it produces all-green foliage which can be removed by pruning.

CULTIVAR: 'Myosotidifolia' carries small deep green leaves on a compact erect outline that is very slow to expand.

CULTIVAR: 'Myrtifolia' is another slow-growing type that eventually produces a large-sized plant. Foliage is small and narrow on dense flattened sprays of twigs. It tends to bronze somewhat in winter.

CULTIVAR: 'Pendula' is basically an open shrub with many dark green leaves on weeping branches; it can be trained successfully to a tree form by eliminating most of the main support stems early.

CULTIVAR: 'Prostrata' shows strong growth but has only a medium size; it has noticeably horizontal branching.

CULTIVAR: 'Pyramidata' is an attractive choice for hedges with its naturally erect and pyramidal outline.

CULTIVAR: 'Rosmarinifolia' has unusual features with its distinctly sage-green coloring and small linear foliage rough to the touch. It is neatly dwarfed and resembles *Rosmarinus*, or rosemary.

CULTIVAR: 'Rotundifolia' carries almost round leaves on a slow-growing, small-sized bush.

CULTIVAR: 'Salicifolia' produces long, narrow, willowlike foliage, but some authorities believe this plant is only *cv.* 'Longifolia'.

CULTIVAR: 'Suffruticosa' is known and enjoyed worldwide as the "edging box" because of its extremely slow growth, totally dense outline of small leaves, and bright green appearance. Almost a century of growing is needed to produce a specimen about 5 feet tall and 7 feet wide.

CULTIVAR: 'Vardar Valley' has slow growth, good hardiness derived from its Balkan habitat, and a low, mounded shape rarely in excess of 2 feet in height with a 4-foot width.

CULTIVAR: 'Variegata' produces either white- or yellow-variegated foliage.

CULTIVAR: 'Variifolia' carries light green leaves.

CULTIVAR: 'Welleri' is strong-growing and very hardy.

CALLIANDRA (powderpuff, fairy duster)
Leguminosae (pea) family

The scientific name comes from the Greek *kalos* ("beauty") and *andros* ("stamens"), referring to the showy pompon flower heads conspicuous with prominently protruding stamens. Native to Asia, Madagascar, and the subtropical parts of the Americas, its twice-compounded, pinnate, alternate foliage is light-sensitive and folds up at night. Best grown in full sun, the flowers appear abundantly in long, hot dry spells, yet it develops as a shrub more attractively when given a moist, well-drained, average soil. The fruit is a flat pod with thickened margins. Very free of insect or disease problems, this genus contains 150 species of shrubs and trees. With only the two popular types given here, almost year-long flowering can be achieved.

Calliandra haematocephela (inaequilatera) (red powderpuff, pink powderpuff)

Zones 9 and 10   **16' high x 10' wide**   **Sun to light shade**

Originating in Bolivia, this slow-growing companion species to *tweedii* blooms from autumn into March with rose-colored solitary budding on long stalks that resembles raspberry fruit in the knobby shape. The plant first was located in Java and was thought to be native, but this proved erroneous, since it more likely came as an immigrant from Bolivia with seeds of some rubber plants sent to Java. The brilliant scarlet compound flower heads have about twenty-five stamen filaments and can enlarge to a 3-inch width in a domed shape. Its richly dark green, velvety leaves are twice compounded and made up of between five and eight sets of leaflets that increase in size as they proceed up the stalk; the final leaflet is often pincer-shaped. These leaflets vary from ¾ inch to 3½ inches in length. Thick fruit pods expand to about 5 inches long. Popular as an accent shrub in southern California and southern Florida as well as on Hawaii (where it is called *lehua haole*), it also can be espaliered for wall decoration. Today there are so many variations from seed that a white form often can be located in some nurseries.

Calliandra haematocephela

Calliandra tweedii (Inga pulcherrima) (Mexican flamebush, Trinidad flamebush, Brazilian flamebush)

Zones 9 and 10   **6' high x 6' wide**   **Sun to light shade**

Found originally in Brazil but now widely distributed, this open, spreading, and slow-growing shrub offers puffy crimson heads of flowers up to 3½ inches wide composed entirely of loosely set wiry stamens in late spring and throughout the summer occasionally. Attractive as a colorful screen or accent, it accepts drought well and has slightly more hardiness than *haematocephela;* currently it maintains a popular appeal in Hawaii, southern California, and southern Florida. The multipinnate, dark green foliage is composed of three or four sets of petiole divisions with up to thirty ⅛-inch, slender, slightly hairy leaflets combining together for a lacy appearance. Its fruit pod is 2 inches long but not showy.

CALLISTEMON (bottlebrush)   *Myrtaceae* (myrtle) family

Curiously, this genus name translates from the Greek to "beautiful stamens," the same meaning as *Calliandra,* but here the showy flowers are carried in spikes or cylindrical heads as the stem continues to elongate beyond the flowering portion, leaving durable, buttonlike woody capsule fruiting closely set along the twigs behind the new foliage and new stem growth. Blooming year-long, this Australian genus contains twenty species of shrubs or small trees so closely resembling one another that certain identification is always difficult, especially since new variations constantly occur naturally both in the wild and under cultivation. Foliage is alternate, simple, entire, leathery, and narrowly cylindrical to lanceolate. The showy flowers (actually, they are only long stamens) appear in red or yellow and resemble a brush used for cleaning bottles.

Sun-loving and not overly particular about soil types—although some of the species prefer dryness and others consistent moisture—none transplants well as a large specimen or accepts poor drainage. Heavy pruning every third year induces more flowering. Excessive soil alkalinity causes yellowing of the leaves and weak growth; acid sites are more suitable. At times a flea beetle disturbs the forward growth pattern by rolling up the new leaves into a bundle, but prompt spraying or elimination pruning can correct this nuisance. Few diseases or other pests present an important problem.

Callistemon critrinus

Callistemon citrinus (lanceolatus) (crimson bottlebrush)
Zones 9 and 10   10′ to 25′ high x 15′ wide   Sun

Introduced from Australia to Europe in the late sixteenth century, the crimson bottlebrush continues to be a landscape asset with its profuse midwinter flowering. A rounded, spreading shrub, it can be trained as a handsome tree form for street or garden use as well. Crimson flower cylinders are 4 inches long and showy with 1-inch wiry stamens. New twigs emerge silky-hairy along with somewhat rigid, smooth, lanceolate foliage that is up to 3 inches in length and vividly green when mature; it is aromatic with a faint lemon scent if bruised. The new growth is copper-toned. The smooth and exceptionally hard sets of depressed globular fruit become ⅜ inch wide and surround the stems tightly. Easily tolerant to heat, drought, salt air (but not as dune plantings), wind, neglect, and alkaline soil, this sturdy shrub is a well-liked addition to many landscapes, but it fares better when provided with a light, sandy soil and abundant water until established. Transplant only as a small-sized plant and provide fertilizing twice annually as it matures. Considered valuable as a windbreak, hedge, screen, or espalier, it shows versatile adaptability marred only by occasional problems with spider mites and scales. A few cultivars are available.

CULTIVAR: 'Chico Red' produces a more uniform flowering effect and superior crimson coloring compared with the parent.

CULTIVAR: 'Splendens' is a dense, narrow-leaved form with dazzlingly scarlet flowering tipped in gold. Its name means "gleaming."

CALLUNA (heather, Scotch heather)   *Ericaceae* (heath) family

Only one heather species exists in the world—*vulgaris*—but it is widely distributed in the temperate parts of Europe, the British Isles, and Asia Minor and well distinguished as a desirable groundcover of great hardiness. Considered the floral emblem of the Scots, it grows plentifully over moor and mountain slope in Scotland and is now also well established in the Pacific northwest because of a remarkable similarity of climate and soil. It behaves outstandingly on seashore locations. The name comes from the Greek *kallunein*, meaning "to sweep," and alludes to the common and ancient practice of cutting heather branches for make-do brooms. This plant differs from its relative *Erica* in its foliage type and because it has colored sepals on the urn-shaped flowers. Combining the two in a design can bring almost year-long flowering since *Erica* blooms from late winter well into spring, while *Calluna* blossoms from midsummer through early autumn. White heather is a folk symbol of good luck and still is used in wedding bouquets, although actors consider its presence a sign of imminent doom.

A huge number of cultivars exist today, and all attract bees in quantity. When cut and dried for indoor use, heather stems retain their color and appearance, including the flowers, for long periods. Sun-loving and slow to expand, heather has roots close to the surface and needs no cultivation; mulch annually instead. All enjoy free air circulation and a low-nitrogen soil, called "hungry," which encourages roots to penetrate deeply in search of water and nutrients. Intolerant of lime, these plants like a light, peaty, sandy location and require an acid fertilizer (such as cottonseed meal) for improved growth. Prune harshly with hedge shears just before growth begins each season to encourage more fullness and greater blooming. Few pests and diseases bother them, but they are not candidates for stuffy, dark, out-of-the-way corners.

Ranging in size from 6 to 36 inches in height and between 1 and 3 feet in width (depending on the hardiness zone and the site), heather has terminal spikes of ⅛-inch florets typically colored purple-pink. Opposite, four-ranked (four leaves centered around each stem joint), very slender, up to ½-inch leaves grow on stems that are mostly upright. Today many cultivars provide a bonus of yellow-toned foliage which turns bronze in the cold months. Install only as small containerized plants since older specimens resent being moved.

Calluna vulgaris (heather, Scotch heather, ling)

Zones 4 to 8   6″ to 36″ high x 1′ to 3′ wide   Sun

Basic information about growing this single-species plant is detailed above. Here is a sample of the many available cultivars in current use.

Calluna vulgaris cultivar

CULTIVAR: 'Alba' has white flowers and a 24-inch height.

CULTIVAR: 'Alba Minor' is a dwarfed sort 1 foot high with white flowering.

CULTIVAR: 'Alba Plena' carries double white flowering freely produced on 1-foot-tall plants.

CULTIVAR: 'Alportii' has vigorous, erect growth to 24 inches and has crimson flowers.

CULTIVAR: 'Aurea' ('Aureifolia') is a foot-tall dwarf with scanty purple-toned blossoms and gold-tipped foliage that turns bronze in winter.

CULTIVAR: 'Camla' ('County Wicklow') behaves in a spreading manner. It reaches an 18-inch height and carries dainty, shell pink double flowers.

CULTIVAR: 'Coccinea' has deep red flowering attractively contrasted with gray-green foliage.

CULTIVAR: 'Cuprea' produces pale mauve blossoms and new growth in golden yellow that darkens to coppery red by late autumn.

Calluna vulgaris cv. 'Aurea'

CULTIVAR: 'Foxii' is a dwarfed, compact cushion of deep green leaves well covered with lavender-pink flowering.

CULTIVAR: 'Hammondii' often is used as a vigorous hedge because of its bright green leaves, 30-inch height, and white flowers.

CULTIVAR: 'Hammondii Aureifolia' grows 20 inches high and carries white flowering plus gold-tipped foliage.

CULTIVAR: 'H. E. Beale' has deep green leaves and very long flower spikes with double bright rose-pink florets that are exceptional for cut use. It grows about 2 feet tall.

CULTIVAR: 'Hirsuta' (Tomentosa') produces gray-toned hairy foliage and pink flowering.

CULTIVAR: 'Kupholdii' stays prostrate to about 6 inches high with deep lavender-pink flowers.

CULTIVAR: 'Peter Sparkes' shows deep pink double flowers on long spikes suitable for indoor use. It is an 18-inch plant.

CULTIVAR: 'Robert Chapman' is the chameleon of this group with new growth that is first gold, then orange, and finally red with soft purple flowering on a 20-inch shrub.

CULTIVAR: 'Searlei' contributes an erect, late-blooming form having dark green foliage, a 20-inch height, and long spikes of white blossoms.

CULTIVAR: 'Tib' has double deep red-purple flowering generously produced on 15- to 20-inch plants early in the season.

CAMELLIA (camellia)　　*Theaceae* (tea) family

Along with rhododendrons and roses, camellias are probably the most appreciated woody plant types used in landscape designs today. Eighty species of shrubs and small trees exist, and these are native to the subtropical and tropical parts of Japan, China, and eastern Asia. The Latinized name was provided by Linnaeus to honor a European Jesuit priest, Georg Josef Kamel, whose missionary work in the Philippines during the seventeenth century also encompassed botanic investigation. Camellias have been known to Chinese horticulture since the ninth century, but they have reached such current popularity worldwide that thousands of single- and double-flowered cultivars now crowd the market. Separating them properly is a mind-boggling task even for an expert.

Flowering time varies with the different species, but all generally have showy flowering that is almost stalkless and either clustered or solitary on upright stems that are handsomely clothed with good-sized, leathery, lustrous, simple leaves set alternately. Modest in growth rate and long-lived, a few species of camellias can eventually reach 40 feet in height under ideal conditions; most remain about 15 feet tall at maturity. Blossoms are generally odorless, range between 2 and 5 inches wide with five to twelve large petals, and develop on terminal growth. The flower colorings are typically pink, red, white, yellow, and variegated; they are often contrasted prominently by rings of stamens with gold tips. The fruit has little appeal as a woody, spheroid, or angular capsule. Bud drop is common in very dry weather, and the leaves suffer damage from cold winter winds that come with any consistency. For the most part camellias are localized for outdoor enjoyment mainly in the mild areas of the southeastern and southwestern parts of the United States, although a few types are hardy in the District of Columbia if protected carefully. Current hybridization continues in a search for additional hardiness and attractive fragrance combined in a single plant.

These special shrubs need a well-drained neutral to slightly acid soil rich in organic matter as well as a location in partial shade. Because they are surface-rooting, do not plant them too deeply and mulch them annually to maintain soil coolness; however, keep the mulch material buildup away from the stems to forestall borer attacks. Camellias have fewer insect or mite disturbances when the foliage is sprayed regularly with hose or irrigation water, especially in hot, dry weather, provided that there is good air circulation to dry the leaves and flowers promptly. Disease difficulties on the foliage can be reduced greatly by regular and timely chemical sprays. Camellias are durable, adaptable, and showy shrubs that are worth the effort it takes to grow them well.

Camellia japonica cv. 'Eleanor McCown'

Camellia japonica (common camellia)

Zones 8 and 9　　**15′ to 45′ high x 6′ to 15′ wide**　　**Light to semishade**

Native to the coastal areas of Japan, South Korea, and Taiwan, this winter-blooming camellia is justly popular as a specimen and informal hedge for its single or double 2½- to 4-inch broad blooms composed of five to seven rounded petals on ½-inch stalks. Smooth twigs have broadly oval, 2- to 4-inch, glossy, deep green, shallow-toothed, hairless leaves. Fruit is angular and almost 1½ inches long and ½ inch wide. These shrubs can be moved safely even in bloom, but the preferred dormant planting times vary from spring only in colder areas of its range to both spring and autumn in mild zones; containerized plants adjust faster than field-dug plants for new installations. Keep them mulched sufficiently at all times, but avoid overfertilizing since they quickly react poorly to it. Provide this supplemental feeding only when the ground is moist and water well after applying. Many pests and diseases are bothersome from time to time, and regular spray programs are required for the finest results. Over 2000 cultivars are known; probably the wisest approach for getting the particular blooming time, the coloring, or the flower type wanted is to consult a local grower or review camellia picture books. The list that follows is just a brief overview of some attractive sorts.

CULTIVAR: 'Alba Plena' blossoms early with pure white, double, 3½ inch flowers.

CULTIVAR: 'Betty Sheffield' flowers in midseason as a double or semidouble white blossom edged with either red or pink; it spreads 4 to 5 inches wide.

CULTIVAR: 'Daikagura' performs early with 4-inch double blooms of rosy red splashed with white.

CULTIVAR: 'Debutante' is a vigorous, upright midseason plant carrying light pink, peony-flowered blossoms about 4 inches wide.

CULTIVAR: 'Donckelardii' has a slow growth habit and displays semidouble 5-inch flowers of cherry red blotched in white.

CULTIVAR: 'Drama Girl' is robust with pendulous twigs and 5-inch blooms of rich salmon-pink; it has a lengthy flowering time.

CULTIVAR: 'Dr. Tinsley' shows compact growth and semidouble flowering 3 to 3½ inches broad in pale pink that darkens at the outer edges.

CULTIVAR: 'Elegans' ('Chandleri Elegans') is not quite fully double with blossoming that is rose-pink often spotted with white; it grows to 4 inches wide by midseason.

CULTIVAR: 'Glen 40' is slow, erect, compact, and hardy with either completely double or only semidouble cherry red 4½-inch flowering at midseason.

CULTIVAR: 'Kramer's Supreme' is one of the few fragrant camellias; it blooms at midseason with glowing turkey red to crimson peony-shaped flowers on a vigorous, compact, upright shrub.

CULTIVAR: 'Nobilissima' has 3-inch incompletely double flowers of white with yellow shading toward the center.

CULTIVAR: 'Tricolor Superba' varies on the same plant from solid red to solid white or to pink striped with red. The 4-inch flowers are semidouble.

CULTIVAR: 'White Empress' is a vigorous shrub carrying 4½-inch blossoms that are white with a yellow blush at the innermost sections.

Camellia japonica cv. 'Pink Parade'

Camellia reticulata (netvein camellia)

Zones 8 (warm) and 9   10′ to 35′ high x 6′ to 10′ wide   Light to semishade

Considered by some to be the most beautiful of all the flowering shrubs, this large-flowered camellia was introduced to England in 1820 by Robert Fortune as a semidouble form he named 'Captain Rawes' to honor a member of the East India Trading Company. For 100 years it was the prototype, but in 1924 George Forrest found the single form growing wild in western China. However, the semidouble form remains firmly associated with this species name by historical precedent. Blooming freely from early March through April, this tall shrub is hardy only in mild climates (but it is hardier than any of its current cultivars) and offers a compact form with loose and leggy branching; it normally stays at a 10-foot height. The 2- to 4½-inch, leathery, dull green oval leaves are very conspicuously netted with veining. Stems are first rosy red to maroon and later mature as gray. Its enormous semidouble rose-red flowers can expand to 6½ inches in width and appear near the stem tips in solitary fashion; petals become wavy and attractively fluted. Some of its less hardy cultivars carry blossoms up to an amazing 9 inches across. The list that follows is abbreviated from current offerings.

CULTIVAR: 'Buddha' produces very vigorous, erect, open growth and immense, semidouble rose-pink flowering maturing to orchid pink.

CULTIVAR: 'Butterfly Wings' develops blossoms almost 9 inches wide in rose-pink.

CULTIVAR: 'Crimson Robe' has 5-inch, semidouble, carmine red flowers.

CULTIVAR: 'Lion Head' carries peony-flowered, 5-inch, deep red blooms.

CULTIVAR: 'Robert Fortune' ('Pagoda') is a strong-growing but compact plant with large, bright crimson double flowering in a roselike form.

CULTIVAR: 'Shot Silk' grows rapidly and displays semidouble, brilliantly pink blossoms with loose wavy petals.

CULTIVAR: 'Tali Queen' has heavily crinkled semidouble flowers of deep pink to deep red with noticeable clusters of yellow stamens.

Camellia sasanqua (sasanqua camellia)

Zones 7 (warm) to 9   15′ high x 6′ wide   Light shade

Blooming in wintertime both with and ahead of the *japonica* types, this hardy species forms a loose straggly shrub or small tree and adapts readily to more sunlight and to greater soil variation. All flowering is easily damaged by pelting rain, however. In the wild form the blossoms are white and fragrant with six to eight petals, showy stamen masses, and a flower width no more than 2 inches across. Its narrowly oval leaves are between 1½ and 3½ inches long with rounded teeth on the margins and blunted tip ends. These shiny, thin, leathery leaves appear on reddish, slightly hairy, new stems. The fruit is a globe about ¾ inch in diameter. Far fewer cultivars exist in this species, but there are several with special value.

CULTIVAR: 'Alba' has single white flowering 3 inches wide.

CULTIVAR: 'Cleopatra' carries semidouble rose-pink blossoms.

CULTIVAR: 'Grandiflora Alba' ('Gulf Glory') shows single white flowering almost 4 inches wide.

CULTIVAR: 'Hugh Evans' develops pendulous branching with pink flowering.

CULTIVAR: 'Rosea' shows large, 3½-inch, single flowers of deep rose-pink.

CULTIVAR: 'Rosea Plena' is the double form of *cv.* 'Rosea'.

CULTIVAR: 'Setsugekka' has 3-inch semidouble white blossoms.

CULTIVAR: 'Sparkling Burgundy' produces ruby red flowering.

CULTIVAR: 'Versicolor' ('Tricolor Magnifica') is a single 3-inch type with white-centered flowers that turn pink with age and are margined in lavender.

CULTIVAR: 'Yuletide' displays single, bright, orange-red flowers about 3 inches wide with showy yellow stamens.

CARISSA (carissa)   *Apocynaceae* (dogbane) family

The name comes from an Australian aboriginal word for this plant, which also is native to Africa and the warmer parts of Asia. Easy to grow in any average-fertility soil, especially at the shore, it takes pruning well at any time to make a hedge or screen. Thirty-five species of much branched spiny shrubs and small trees make up its membership, but usually only *grandiflora* (and its cultivars) is grown and used today. Best located in full sun or light shading, carissa has few to many terminal fragrant blossoms in white to pink to purple-pink; these are tubular with five twisted petals making up the broad face. Opposite, entire, and leathery leaves appear on often-thorny stems with milky sap. Its noticeable fruiting is often edible fresh or cooked and consists of a spherical, leathery, tart-tasting berry. Pests and diseases are not generally a problem.

Carissa grandiflora (Natal plum, amatungulu)

Zones 9 and 10   6' to 18' high x 4' to 12' wide   Sun to semishade

Carissa grandiflora cv. 'Nana'

An inhabitant of South Africa that is very tolerant of salt air sites, this shrub is often kept trimmed as a formal hedge because of its dense, slow habit and glossy foliage. It also finds wide use as a border specimen because of its year-long flowering or fruiting effects. The downturned stems have stout, two-pronged, sharp, 1½-inch thorns developing only where the twigs divide. Its lustrous leaves are oval, deep green (new growth is much brighter), and up to 3 inches long with a 2-inch width, and they carry a noticeable spur at the tip. White, squat, very fragrant, pinwheel-shaped flowers are 2 inches wide and ½ inch long; these are usually followed by oval, bright scarlet, 2-inch fruit that is edible and tastes somewhat like a cranberry. Adapting well to enriched soils as well as very dry sites, it benefits from fertilizer two or three times yearly when grown on very sandy soil. Mealy bugs and scale are its chief pests. The cultivar list is composed of only dwarfed forms.

CULTIVAR: 'Horizontalis' is exceptionally compact and prostrate.

CULTIVAR: 'Minima' has no thorns and carries smaller foliage and flowering on a dwarfed silhouette.

CULTIVAR: 'Nana' is also thornless with small-sized leaves but is taller than *cv.* 'Minima' and has a compact outline.

CULTIVAR: 'Prostrata' behaves in a spreading, low fashion and is thornless.

CULTIVAR: 'Tuttlei' serves as a useful barrier groundcover with its dense, spreading, moundlike habit, even though it is not armed with thorns.

CODIAEUM (croton, variegated laurel)   *Euphorbiaceae* (spurge) family

The name is from the Greek *kodeia* and also may be the Malaysian word for this plant; however, since the Greek word translates also as "head," the reference may be to the use of these leaves in wreath making. Although six species of trees and shrubs are known, only *variegatum pictum* is cultivated today; all are native to Malaya and Australia plus the many Pacific islands and provide their finest leaf colorings in full sun. Alternate, simple, leathery, smooth, and petioled foliage becomes highly variable in the arrangement of the many color patterns possible, even to the point of showing different hues from leaf to leaf on the same specimen. Its monoecious, pin-cushion-like, small, creamy flowers develop from the leaf axils in long strings on an occasional basis. Scales, thrips, and mites often present problems.

Codiaeum variegatum pictum (garden croton)

Zones 9 and 10   6' to 8' high x 4' to 6' wide   Sun to semishade

Marvelously diverse in both their brilliant leaf colorings and their leaf outlines on a year-round basis, the crotons from the East Indies offer yellow, green, and red as dominant values with orange, pink, ivory, brown, and gold all possible as secondary colorations in streaks, blotches, lines, and speckles. The main leaf form is broad and lanceolate but easily diverges into scalloped, twisted, lobed, or slenderized forms; this is especially noticeable in the many cultivars. Flowering is not particularly conspicuous from globular, buff-colored or off-white, ¼- to ½-inch florets set openly on drooping spikes that emerge from the leaf axils at odd times during the year. The nonshowy roundish fruit is ⅛ to ¼ inch, dark green, and tightly held to the stringlike

Codiaeum variegatum pictum cv. 'Amabile'

Codiaeum variegatum pictum cv. 'Aucubifolium'

Codiaeum variegatum pictum cultivar

Codiaeum variegatum pictum fruit

Codiaeum variegatum pictum   (Cont.)

peduncles. These plants are modest in growth, dense, and upright with slender stems; they are very simple to grow well on any moist, average, deep, well-drained, slightly acid soil in full sun (for best intensity of color) to semishade. They adapt well to seaside locations if they are not exposed to constant salt spray, and they will benefit from fertilizing three times yearly. Over 100 cultivars have been named, and the following is an incomplete list of the splendid variations available from nurseries and catalogs.

CULTIVAR: 'Amabile' has lancelike foliage variegated with green, cream, pink, and purple.

CULTIVAR: 'Andreanum' carries broad yellow leaves that turn orange-red with age.

CULTIVAR: 'Angustissimum' sports narrow green leaves with yellow margins and ribs.

CULTIVAR: 'Aucubifolium' has broad foliage blotched with either red or yellow spots.

CULTIVAR: 'B. Comte' develops medium-broad leaves splashed in orange-red.

CULTIVAR: 'Bogoriense' shows stubby oblong foliage variegated in yellow.

CULTIVAR: 'Cronstaedii' has spirally twisted narrow leaves with yellow variegations.

CULTIVAR: 'Edmontonense' carries short, narrow, spiraled leaves of brilliant orange and red.

CULTIVAR: 'Ethel Craig' produces medium-sized pointed foliage in yellow and pink.

CULTIVAR: 'General Marshall' has very long leaves first emerging as all yellow but later changing to orange or red.

CULTIVAR: 'Interruptum' is purplish green and often is divided into two sections held together with just the slender red midrib.

CULTIVAR: 'Kentucky' shows large, lobed, bronze leaves variegated with orange and red.

CULTIVAR: 'Monarch' develops large, very long, green leaves which later turn red and carry brighter red spotting.

CULTIVAR: 'Polychrome' exhibits slightly lobed green and cream foliage shaded with pink.

CULTIVAR: 'Reidii' sports large yellow or pinkish yellow leaves with noticeable red veining.

CULTIVAR: 'Spirale' develops spirally twisted red and green leaves.

CULTIVAR: 'Weismannii' has narrow, wavy-edged foliage variegated with yellow on red leaf stalks.

COTONEASTER (cotoneaster)   *Rosaceae* (rose) family

Considered indispensable for landscape use because of their persistent showy fruiting, cotoneasters have evolved to fifty species of tall or low woody plants with either evergreen or deciduous foliage that are native to European and Asian temperate zones. Many are only semievergreen naturally and are listed in the "Deciduous Shrubs" division. The ones considered consistently evergreen appear in this section. All have alternate, entire leaves and about ⅛-inch, white to pink, five-petaled, cup-shaped or flattened blossoms emerging in the leaf axils as solitary or clustered flowers. Red or black (rarely yellow) fruit is a small pome (applelike in construction) similar to its close relative *Crataegus*, or hawthorn, in that it can set seed without being pollinated by wind or insects. This unique process is called *apomixis* and results in complications in the proper identification of these species since minor variations of the typical and expected form often are overlooked as they are propagated. In brief, the "typical" plant of any species is constantly changing subtly.

Its name derives from the Latin *cotoneum*, or "quince," and *aster*, or "star," and may refer to the star-shaped markings often common on the fruit of the rose family, of which the quince is also a member; some interpretations of this name imply that cotoneaster fruit is inferior to quince.

These root names provide a solid clue about how to pronounce the name properly; it is erroneous to call it "cotton easter."

Sun-loving and durable on windy and coastal sites, these shrubs enjoy a well-drained, somewhat dry, average soil more alkaline than not, and all benefit from annual fertilizing in spring. None transplants well when old, and containerized plants adjust better than field-dug ones. The creeping or prostrate forms are unexcelled as groundcovers (and adapt well for espaliers), but none become especially dense on the ground to forestall weed and grass invasions through them; deep mulching, however, can prove helpful. Fire blight disease often destroys plants quickly, while lacebugs and spider mites are prevalent foliage pests; fortunately, none is consistently threatening. Cotoneasters behave as sturdy performers within all their growing areas. (Consult the "Deciduous Shrubs" division for additional choices.)

Cotoneaster dammeri (humifusus) (bearberry cotoneaster)

Zones 6 (warm) to 9   4″ to 6″ high x 5′ to 7′ wide   Sun

Vigorously spreading with long, trailing stems that root as they expand, this prostrate creeper from central China came into cultivation during 1900 and has attributes as an embankment cover or as a groundcover between other sun-loving, taller shrubs. Solitary (occasionally paired), white, ¼-inch late May flowers have widely spread petals and red-toned anthers. The late summer fruiting matures as bright, glossy red, ¼-inch-wide globose pomes. Leaves are smooth, oval, leathery, and ¾ inch to 1 inch long; they emerge hairy when new and later intensify to deep, shiny green with pale green undersides. Some variations exist.

Cotoneaster dammeri

CULTIVAR: 'Skogholm' came from Germany in 1958 and behaves as an 18-inch-tall vigorous spreader covering an 8-foot area; there is less fruit than with the parent.

VARIETY: *radicans* usually carries twin flowering and smaller wrinkled foliage with either blunt or notched tips.

Cotoneaster glaucophyllus (no common name)

Zones 7 to 9   6′ to 8′ high x 5′ to 6′ wide   Sun

Cultivated since 1915 as an import from western China, here the cotoneaster often is described as deciduous by authorities, although *Hortus Third* classifies it as an evergreen form. Highly adaptable for dry sites, it maintains an arching habit with oval 1¼-inch leaves acutely tapered at both ends that are smooth above with a smattering of fine hairs beneath. The dense clusterings of white ¼-inch flowers in July come grouped from six to twenty in the leaf axils and produce bunches of oval orange fruiting about ¼ inch long, coloring fully by midautumn. Its variety *serotinus* has a potential height of 30 feet under ideal growing conditions and carries 1- to 3-inch smooth leaves which first appear heavily coated with gray hairs; these are more leathery, more rounded, and larger than those of the parent. Forty flowers per cluster create masses of showy, orange-red autumnal fruit.

Cotoneaster lacteus (no common name)

Zones 6 (warm) to 9   12′ high × 8′ wide   Sun

Introduced from western China during 1913, the plant is still mistakenly sold as *parneyi* by some growers. Highly adaptable to heat, wind, smog, salt air, dryness, or poor soils, this species is especially valued for its dense fruiting which is useful as indoor decoration at Christmastime. A majestic shrub of broadly arching branches that can be readily trained as a wall espalier, it serves admirably as well for tall screens and hedges. Creamy white flowers appear heavily clustered in groups up to 2½ inches wide during middle to late June; the scarlet, oval, ¼-inch fruit is prolifically set and ripens very late in the year. Reddish stems carry leathery, deep green, widely oval foliage up to 2¼ inches long and about half as wide with prominent veining. Leaf undersides are persistently hairy. Scale and fire blight are the chief afflictions.

Cotoneaster microphyllus (no common name)

Zones 6 (warm) to 9   6″ to 24″ high x 10′ wide   Sun

Robust, wide-spreading, low, and densely branched, this species arrived in cultivation from southwestern China and the Himalayas as early as 1824 and has proved an exceptionally tough and hardy groundcover ever since. Its June-produced, solitary, ⅛-inch white flowers develop in the leaf axils and create ¼-inch, round, bright, rosy red fruiting crowded along the stems. Lustrous, oval, ⁵⁄₁₆-inch, dark green leaves curl downward at the margins and become densely gray-hairy beneath on creeping and rooting slender stems with upright secondary branching. It appears not to be bothered by pests or diseases. Some variations are available.

CULTIVAR: 'Cochleatus' behaves as a slow-growing dwarf more prostrate and compact than the parent, molding its outline to the shape of obstacles or grading in its path. Bright green foliage is broader and shinier with bottom surfaces covered in long white hairs; its fruit is similar to that of the species.

VARIETY: *thymifolius* is even more compact but with stiff, erect branching; it can stretch upward to 2 feet and outward about 15 feet. Two to four flowers cluster at the leaf axils and develop somewhat smaller fruiting. This plant has the smallest foliage of any cotoneaster known with narrow ⅜-inch leaves that show rolled-under margins.

Cotoneaster salicifolius (willowleaf cotoneaster)

Zones 6 (warm) to 9   12′ to 15′ high x 10′ to 15′ wide   Sun

Not much grown today because its varieties are considered superior, this native to western China was introduced in 1908 and has appeal as a result of its graceful, arching branches, wide growth, and generous fruiting. Tiny, white, clustered flowers come by mid-June in hairy groups of nine to fifteen up to 2 inches wide with spreading petals. The light red, globose, ¼-inch fruit presents a conspicuous show in early autumn. Glossy, narrowly lanceolate, sharp-pointed, wrinkled foliage appears on wooly stems and is between 1½ and 3 inches long with a width about ¾ inch; these leaves become purple-toned for winter. Several varieties exist.

VARIETY: *floccosus* has small, narrow, polished leaves with wooly undersides when young that alter to grayish green later. Branching is slender, arching, and fanlike with durable masses of ⅛-inch red fruit.

Cotoneaster salicifolius rugosus flowers

VARIETY: *repens* can reach a foot of height but remains prostrate in form and carries very narrow pointed leaves and small reddish fruit that is not overly conspicuous. It serves as an exceptional wide-spreading groundcover.

VARIETY: *rugosus* is a vigorous and tall plant with broader dull green leaves which are densely hairy beneath. Both flowers and fruit are larger than those of the parent.

DAPHNE (garland flower, spurge laurel, mezereon) *Thymelaeaceae* (mezereum) family

At least fifty species of pleasantly fragrant deciduous and evergreen shrubs are in this genus, and all are inhabitants of the temperate or subtropical areas of Europe and Asia from zone 6 to zone 9. The name is an ancient Greek one indicating the similarity of the foliage to that of the totally unrelated sweet bay *(Laurus).* Deciduous sorts are hardier than the evergreens, and all species have a history of expiring mysteriously and suddenly even while seeming healthy. None transplants easily except when small and containerized; established plants should be left growing as found. The majority thrive when placed in light shade on a light, rich, well-drained, consistently moist, neutral to slightly acid soil. Aphid infestations on soft new growth are the chief nuisance, while honey fungus and cucumber mosaic diseases present occasional problems in some areas.

The scented flowers appear in short terminal or axillary heads with trumpetlike florets on tough, flexible branching. Blossom colorings vary from white to purple or lilac, but on some species they emerge yellow or yellow-green. The foliage is alternate, simple, and entire. Its leathery or fleshy drupelike fruit (similar to the plum) is quickly toxic to people if consumed in any quantity. (Consult the "Deciduous Shrubs" division as well).

Cotoneaster salicifolius rugosus fruit

Daphne cneorum (garland flower, rose daphne)

Zones 5 to 8   6″ to 9″ high x 2′ to 3′ wide   Sun

Growing wild on dry, stony, limestone mountain areas from Spain to Poland and the Ukraine, this is a popular species with a procumbent habit and long, slender, trailing branches that are hairy when new. Its wedge-shaped, 1-inch-long and ¼-inch-wide, lustrous, deep green leaves remain crowded and clustered only at the twig ends and have grayish blue coloring beneath. Highly scented, pink (mainly) to rose-red, ½-inch hairy blossoms develop terminally in flattened dense clusters of six or more florets during early May; rebloom is possible by early autumn. The tiny fruit is first yellow-brown but matures black. Difficult to establish, the shrub is not adaptable to California but does manage well farther up the Pacific coast. In northerly climates it may require winter protection from drying winds through the use of loosely applied evergreen boughs or salt marsh hay. Some interesting variations are available.

Daphne cneorum

CULTIVAR: 'Albo-marginata' has foliage variegated in white but fails to create any noteworthy bonus because of it.

CULTIVAR: 'Eximia' produces larger flowering in deep pink, making it visually superior to 'Major'.

CULTIVAR: 'Major' is a vigorous plant carrying larger foliage and flowering.

CULTIVAR: 'Variegata' sports leaves narrowly edged attractively in white; it is still marketed erroneously as 'Silver Leaf'.

VARIETY: *pygmaea* has a prostrate, compact, slow-growing habit, achieving only a 3-inch height with ⅝-inch leaves. It is very free-flowering.

CULTIVAR: 'Alba' is the rare white-flowered form of *var. pygmaea*.

Daphne x hybrida   (no common name)

Zones 7 to 9   6′ high x 4′ wide   Light shade

A cross between *collina* and *odora*, this shrub has a vigorous upright form, more hardiness than *odora*, and a blooming season from early winter into early spring. It is justifiably popular. The oval, up to 3½-inch-long leaves spread horizontally from the much branched stems which terminate in clusters of six pinkish to purple-lilac hairy flowers with attractive fragrance. Fruiting is not reported.

Daphne odora   (winter daphne)

Zones 7 to 9   4′ to 6′ high x 2′ to 3′ wide   Light shade

Introduced into culture during 1771, winter daphne is native both to China and to Japan; it has an upright leggy outline but makes no special demand for an alkaline soil. However, it lays claim to a series of important dislikes, and so one should avoid transplanting, cultivating, fertilizing, or pruning this plant. Once installed, it should be left to grow in its own fashion. Overpoweringly scented, hairless, white to rosy purple flowers bloom from early winter to early spring as crowded heads ½ inch wide. The blunt-tipped, thick, leathery, smooth, glossy, deep green leaves are tapered at both ends and range from 1½ to 3½ inches long with a width of approximately ⅜ inch. Its cultivar list is of interest.

CULTIVAR: 'Alba' carries pure white flowers.

CULTIVAR: 'Marginata' ('Aureomarginata') produces intensely fragrant reddish flowering of both deep pink and red plus leaves bordered nicely in creamy white. Hardier and stronger-growing than the parent, it does not thrive in the San Francisco area of California. Provide full sun when grown in cool areas but some shading otherwise. Install this shrub slightly high to prevent ground-line collar rot of the stems.

CULTIVAR: 'Rubra' is more tender and has an open, somewhat spreading habit along with wine-red flowering.

CULTIVAR: 'Variegata' develops pink flowers along with leaves bordered in light yellow.

ELAEAGNUS (oleaster, silverberry, lingaro)
Elaeagnaceae (oleaster) family

A genus composed mostly of deciduous fast-growing shrubs and small trees, it also includes a few evergreen but less hardy types among its forty species native to southern Europe, Asia, and North America. Unexcelled as wind barriers, they tolerate exposed sites and salt spray unharmed. Easily transplanted and without problems of consequence from pests or diseases, these sturdy shrubs accept any soil except chalk. The name derives from the Greek *elaia*, meaning "olive," and *agnos*, meaning "chaste tree," a probable reference to the shape and size of the fruit as well as to the silvered or grayish undersides of the foliage. Pleasantly sweet-smelling, white or yellow, small flowers are abundantly evident in the leaf axils by spring; the fruit is a drupe (plumlike) but resembles a berry. Alternate leaves are undivided and covered on both sides with minute dots of brown or silver. (Consult the "Deciduous Shrubs" division for other selections.)

Elaeagnus pungens (thorny elaeagnus)

Zones 7 to 9   15′ high x 15′ wide   Sun to light shade

Elaeagnus pungens cv. 'Maculata'

Popular for its dense, vigorous habit; spiny, arching stems; and late autumn to early winter flowering, this is a reliable and adaptable plant that accepts any amount of heavy pruning successfully for hedges and screens while also serving as an attractive espalier along fences or on walls. Greatly tolerant to drought, it needs only a fast-draining average soil in bright light to thrive. It has a well-earned success record for plantings on highways and in public spaces that receive much abuse. Introduced during 1830, this native of China and Japan blooms from mid-October into January with gardenia-scented, ivory, small clusterings of ⅓-inch bell-shaped flowers dotted with brown which appear in the leaf axils. Edible, red, ½-inch fruit begins brown but later gains a silvery overcast. The light brown twigs are also noticeably punctuated with silver and carry somewhat pointed to blunt leathery leaves between 1½ and 4 inches long with wavy margins; these are shiny green above but dull white beneath with brown dots. There is a generous list of cultivars.

CULTIVAR: 'Aurea' has foliage edged in yellow.

CULTIVAR: 'Fredrici' ('Fredrici Variegata') displays narrower, smaller foliage with pale yellow centers and dark green edges.

CULTIVAR: 'Fruitlandii' is a compact form showing very silvery leaf undersides.

CULTIVAR: 'Maculata' ('Aureo-maculata') produces modest growth and leaves that get a bright effect from large, golden yellow centers; it is very popular.

CULTIVAR: 'Marginata' carries leaves with silvery white margins.

CULTIVAR: 'Nana' is a dwarfed form with normal foliage.

CULTIVAR: 'Reflexa' has leaves without wavy edges and is very brown-dotted beneath.

CULTIVAR: 'Simonii' is an erect form with broader foliage having few brown dots beneath; occasionally these leaves are variegated in yellow or pinkish white.

CULTIVAR: 'Variegata' maintains a vigorous habit with foliage edged in thin, cream-yellow lines.

ERICA (heath, bell heather)   *Ericaceae* (heath) family

While *Calluna*, its close relation, contains only 1 species, this genus has at least 500. These slow-growing shrubs (rarely small trees) are usually much branched and compact with a dislike for wet, cold, clay, or alkaline soils. They require no fertilizing since that promotes shallow rooting and gross foliage production at a loss of flowers. All do best in full sun on a light, sandy, infertile well-drained soil. Ideal for coastal areas with high humidity and constant breezes, many species are native to Europe and the Mediterranean region plus the Atlantic islands, yet the majority are found growing in South Africa (these sorts are not at all hardy in northern climes). Until the middle of the eighteenth century, few species were thought worthwhile to cultivate; now, hundreds of hardy cultivars are commonly available throughout the species and can provide flower effects all year. The English and then the Germans learned early to appreciate the ornamental virtues of these remarkable plants, yet even before this horticultural revolution, cut boughs were used extensively for stuffing mattresses, thatching cottage roofs, and broom making. The roots of *arborea*, a tree form that grows to 20 feet, are still used in the making of smoking pipes we call briar, a corruption of the French *bruyere*, meaning "heath."

Erica itself comes from both the ancient Greek *ereiken*, translating as "to break," and the Latin word *erice* for this particular plant; the Greek association could refer to the late winter flowering as "breaking" the grip of the season. Nodding flowers develop solitary or in terminal and axillary clusters colored white, rose, purple, yellow, or even green on thin stems with needlelike whorled leaves. Its fruit is a four-valved tiny capsule. These blossoms differ from *Calluna*, which has colored sepals, in that they carry colored petals. Pests and diseases are rare.

Erica canaliculata

Erica canaliculata (melanthera)   (Christmas heath)

Zones 9 (warm) and 10   2′ to 6′ high x 2′ to 5′ wide   Sun

Often sold today by florists as potted indoor decoration, this pest-free but tender species is native to South Africa and has been in culture since 1802. Best grown on moist, peaty sites, it endures drought, wind, and sterile soil with aplomb. Erect, long-lived, slow-growing, and distinctive, the plant bears abundant white to pinkish bells of flowering with protruding dark brown stamens from January to March. The dark, shiny, recurved foliage is ¼ inch long and forms in threes on densely hairy twigs. Pruning stalks for indoor decoration assists the shrub to become more dense, but never cut to bare stems since they rarely refoliate. The few cultivars are as follows.

CULTIVAR: 'Boscaweniana' produces conspicuous white flowering.

CULTIVAR: 'Rosea' carries rose-pink blossoms in clusters of three to six and matures at 4 feet high with a similar spread.

Erica carnea cv. 'Springwood White'

Erica carnea (herbacea)   (spring heath, snow heather)

Zones 6 to 8   1′ high x 1′ wide   Sun

Remarkable for its lengthy blooming period of almost 3 months, this sluggish, matlike shrub has prostrate ridged stems with ¼-inch foliage arranged in fours. The ¼-inch, reddish pink, fragrant, urn-shaped flowers have deep red anthers and are arranged on only one side of the 1- to 3-inch spikes. In cold areas they begin blossoming by late winter to early spring, but in milder sections this schedule expands from late autumn into early spring. Conveniently, all members in this country are lime-tolerant. So many choice cultivars exist today in this species that they can be best examined only by consulting growers' catalogs or inspecting plants in the nursery. In these selections you will find not only flowering differences of timing and colorations but foliage hues of stimulating interest as well.

Erica cinerea   (twisted heath, Scotch heath, bell heather)

Zones 6 to 8   2′ high x 2′ wide   Sun

Ranking high as a summer-blooming ornamental, this species is basically native to the boggy areas of western Europe and the British Isles, although it also has recently naturalized itself extensively on Nantucket Island, Massachusetts. Tolerant to being sheared heavily right after flowering, it responds well to an annual topdressing of coarse sand and leaf mold. Rigid but open and much branched, this shrub has wiry stems that are hairy when new as well as deep green, ¼-inch, smooth, shiny leaves arranged in threes with margins strongly rolled under to conceal the undersides totally. Its prolific blossoming stretches from June to September on 1- to 3-inch, terminal, slender spikes with ¼-inch egg-shaped flowers of reddish purple aging into a close approximation of blue and not having protruding anthers. Innumerable cultivars are offered today with various silhouettes and foliage types that carry flower colorings that are dark red, purple, or pink to white. Consult growers' lists for complete descriptions of these intriguing variations.

Erica vagrans   (Cornish heath)

Zones 7 to 9   1′ to 2′ high x 2′ wide   Sun

Native to southwestern Europe and the British Isles and now naturalized on
Nantucket Island, Massachusetts, Cornish heath is attractive for mass planting
with its low, spreading habit and its blooming time that runs from July to
October. The cylindrical spikes of flowers can be 6 inches tall and appear on
new growth with broadly bell-shaped, ¼-inch, purple-pink blossoms set in
pairs that show protruding stamens. Foliage comes in whorls of four of five
bright green, ⅜-inch, smooth, linear leaves with undersides completely
covered by the rolled-over margins. Its cultivar selections offer appeal.

CULTIVAR: 'Alba' produces a compact form up to 20 inches tall with white flowering.

CULTIVAR: 'Cream' is an improved form of *cv.* 'Alba' that has creamy white flowering on long spikes and an 18- to 20-inch height.

CULTIVAR: 'Grandiflora' grows 30 inches tall and sports very long sprays of pale pink
flowers.

CULTIVAR: 'Mrs. D. F. Maxwell' is an eye-catching form with deep cerise blossoming
on an 18-inch plant.

CULTIVAR: 'Pyrenees Pink' grows 18 inches high and projects long spikes of pink
flowers.

CULTIVAR: 'Rubra' grows 15 inches tall with purple-red flowering.

EUONYMUS (spindle tree, strawberry bush)
   Celastraceae (staff tree) family

Occasionally spelled *Euvonymus* in older texts, the name is an ancient
Greek one for this very serviceable group of sun-loving plants with a great
ability for adaptation to a wide set of conditions. One hundred seventy
species of deciduous or evergreen shrubs and trees are known, along with
occasional creepers and vines (not covered in this volume); all are from the
temperate zones of Asia. Adapting well to almost any exposure or soil—
wet, dry, or chalk—the majority also take easily to constant shearing for
screens and hedges. Scale insects are a constant problem with many types
since they contort stems, leaves, and fruit in a short time. The small greenish or purplish flowers are without ornamental value and develop in clusters during late spring at the leaf axils. The fruit capsule, however, is decorative more often than not because the autumnal seed crop is enclosed by
a showy scarlet or orange cap covering (botanically called an *aril*) supported by long pendulous stalks. This fruiting persists well into winter if
birds do not devour it first. (Consult the "Deciduous Shrubs" division for
additional selections.)

Euonymus fortunei   (wintercreeper)

Zones 5 to 9   10′ high x 20′ wide   Sun to semishade

Basically shrubby by nature but occasionally trailing or even climbing by its
aerial rooting, this is a diversified shrub from central and western China with
a commonly assumed habit of flattening out or elongating its upright growth
during heavy winter snowfalls; this gives it the name of wintercreeper. All of
its types can be sheared at any time for hedges, espaliers, or border specimens
and will accept full sun or partial shade on any soil. The inconspicuous cream-
colored flowering during late spring develops into ½-inch spherical capsules
with pink-toned seeds capped by an orange dome. Oval, toothed, up to 2-
inch-long leaves have white veins evident on the undersides on rounded stems
with noticeable warts. This plant is the parent of many evergreen shrub and
vine types having reliable hardiness and good vigor. The popular 'Emerald'

Euonymus fortunei

Euonymus fortunei cv. 'Emerald Gaiety'

Euonymus fortunei cv. 'Emerald Gaiety'

Euonymus fortunei cv. 'Emerald 'N Gold'

strain (all carry plant patent numbers) originated in an Ipswich, Massachusetts, nursery; it presents a series of durable, smog-resistant forms containing desirably variegated foliages. Together, these variations contribute useful landscape accents.

CULTIVAR: 'Carrieri' grows 6 to 8 feet tall and is wide-spreading to 10 feet with 1½- to 2-inch glossy, deep green foliage on nonclimbing stems highlighted by occasional sport branches of foliage with bright creamy variegation. It creates an interesting informal hedge or a clipped formalized edging; it provides only spotty fruiting effects.

CULTIVAR: 'Emerald Charm' develops a narrowly columnar form to 5 feet with deep green foliage year-round. It has no fruit.

CULTIVAR: 'Emerald Cushion' is a dwarfed, compact type with small green leaves and a mounded outline 2 feet tall. It appears to be fruitless.

CULTIVAR: 'Emerald Gaiety' has achieved great popularity for its year-long green and white foliage contrast (even in shade) from 1½- to 2-inch leaves on a sprawling yet often erect silhouette that grows to 4 or 5 feet. Fruit is unknown. A vinelike form, 'Silver Queen', is mistakenly sold under its label.

CULTIVAR: 'Emerald 'N Gold' requires strong light at all times to maintain its unusual bright yellow and chartreuse green summer color mix on the 1-inch leaves. For winter it usually mottles intriguingly into a blend of pink, red, gold, and deeper green. The ultimate height and width is 5 feet after several decades of growing. It produces no fruiting.

CULTIVAR: 'Emerald Pride' is also fruitless but contributes a loose upright outline to 5 feet with green 1½- to 2-inch leaves all year.

CULTIVAR: 'Sarcoxie' ('Pyramidalis') grows stiffly upright to 4 feet and carries glossy, 1- to 1½-inch green foliage throughout the year.

VARIETY: *vegeta (vegetus)* becomes bushy to 4 feet and wide-spreading to 10 feet with nearly rounded, 1- to 1¾-inch, dull, yellow-green leaves. When mature, it produces annual fruiting of some noticeability. If supported and tied in place (it has no aerial root development) when young, it can rise to 15 or so feet to make an interesting wall espalier. Unfortunately, this variety is exceptionally prone to scale insect attacks that quickly eradicate its good qualities.

Euonymus japonica (Japanese spindle tree, evergreen euonymus)

Zones 8 to 10   10' to 15' high x 10' wide   Sun to shade

Widely used in the southern United States because it cooperatively adjusts to high heat and varying light conditions, this native of southern Japan came into cultivation during 1804. It has tolerance for dryness, coolness, salt spray, and either acid or alkaline soils. Densely branched and slow-growing with an erect, shrubby nature, the plant also can be trained as a small tree form. Flowering is typically greenish white, tiny, and inconspicuous during June, but fruiting rarely occurs in cultivation; should it occur, it will show ⅓-inch pink seed capsules covered with orange arils. The narrowly oval 1¼- to 2¾-inch foliage is dark, glossy green with blunt-toothed margins on slightly four-angled stems. While many destructive pests bother this species, mildew is more disfiguring; it can be controlled by placing the shrub on a hot, dry site originally. Avoid planting this shrub where humid air stagnates in summer. Today's cultivar list is impressively varied.

CULTIVAR: 'Albomarginata' is a slow-growing type with narrow white banding on the foliage; it often is erroneously marketed as 'Pearl Edge'.

CULTIVAR: 'Argenteo-variegata' has leaves margined and streaked with white.

CULTIVAR: 'Aurea' produces mostly yellow-toned foliage and grows slowly.

CULTIVAR: 'Aureo-marginata' ('Giltedge') expands sluggishly with leathery leaves edged in golden yellow.

CULTIVAR: 'Aureo-variegata' is undoubtedly the most popular golden form, with foliage importantly blotched in the centers by deep yellow markings. Growers frequently market this as 'Gold Spot', which is an invalid name.

CULTIVAR: 'Fastigiata' creates a columnar form with narrow leaves.

CULTIVAR: 'Grandifolia' ('Gigantea') has exceptionally large, lustrous, deep green leaves and a stiffly upright form.

CULTIVAR: 'Mediopicta' carries foliage with large yellow blotches over the central parts.

CULTIVAR: 'Microphylla' ('Pulchella') is compact, dense, and slow-growing with narrow leaves between ½ and 1 inch long.

CULTIVAR: 'Microphylla Pulchella' becomes the gold-variegated form of cv. 'Microphylla'.

CULTIVAR: 'Picta' stays dwarfed with dark green leaves.

CULTIVAR: 'Pyramidata' is also columnar but is more compact than 'Fastigiata'.

CULTIVAR: 'Viridi-variegata' ('Duc d'Anjou') sports large bright green leaves variegated with yellow and pale green.

Euonymus japonica cv. 'Aureo variegata'

Euonymus japonica cv. 'Microphylla'

Euonymus kiautschovica (patens) (no common name)

Zones 7 and 8   10′ high x 8′ wide   Sun

Native to eastern and central China and introduced in 1860, this is a potential substitute for *japonica* in colder growing areas, but only in the eastern United States. Spreading and open in habit, the shrub carries oval, 2- to 3-inch toothed leaves somewhat thinner than those of *japonica* plus loose clusterings of green-white flowers during late summer. Its capsule fruit becomes spherical to a half inch wide with an orange-red cap. Several cultivars exist.

CULTIVAR: 'Manhattan' displays glossy green foliage up to 2½ inches long. It has slightly more hardiness than the parent since it originated in Manhattan, Kansas.

CULTIVAR: 'Vincifolia' has 1- to 1½-inch narrow, pointed leaves much like those of *Vinca* (periwinkle) on an upright but spreading form.

Euonymus kiautschovica

X FATSHEDERA (fatshedera)   *Araliaceae* (aralia) family

This is an unusual bigeneric creation derived from crossing the shrub *Fatsia japonica* cv. 'Moseri' with the well-known vine *Hedera helix hibernica* in France during 1910. The resultant seed gave rise to this entirely new plant type, which was awarded formal accreditation in 1923. Carrying no aerial rooting characteristics from its *Hedera* parent, it possesses floppy, weak stems that need support as they elongate. Fruit is not possible since this is a sterile, one-sex plant; therefore, only one species exists so far.

x Fatshedera lizei

x Fatshedera lizei (aralia ivy, tree ivy, ivy tree)

Zones 7 to 10   6' to 8' high x 6' to 8' wide   Light to semishade

Popular today as an indoor plant because it accepts dry air and low light levels well, this erect, sprawling shrub is also tolerant outdoors to air pollution, modest drought, neglect, and shore sites. Any average-fertility soil is suitable if consistently moist; insects and diseases have so far not been a problem. Noticeable terminal flowering appears erratically during the growing season as compound clusterings of ball-shaped, ⅜-inch, strong-scented blossoms with greenish or yellowish color. It compellingly attracts continual forays of buzzing bees and flies, a condition often found annoying in some locations. The floppy stems have rust-colored hairs when young but become entirely smooth and tan with age. Glossy, simple, leathery, palmately shaped, richly green leaves are about 8 inches long and 1 foot wide with deep indentations and three to five lobes. Over the intervening decades a cultivar has emerged. 'Variegata' is even weaker-stemmed than the parent but carries leaf margins banded irregularly in cream. It requires semishade to maintain its best appearance and growth.

FATSIA (fatsia)   *Araliaceae* (aralia) family

Only one species of this genus is known. Native to Japan, southern Korea, and the Ryukyu Islands and introduced during 1838, it is grown primarily for its bold 1-foot-wide leaves both outdoors and inside (as a container plant). The current name is derived from the ancient Japanese one for this shrub; previously it was thought to be an *Aralia* species.

Fatsia japonica

Fatsia japonica (Aralia japonica) (Aralia sieboldii)
(Japanese fatsia, Formosa rice tree, paper plant)

Zones 8 to 10   10' to 20' high x 6' to 8' wide   Semishade

Favored today in contemporary architectural layouts for its bold silhouette and dramatic shadow patterns outdoors, this shrub becomes tall and treelike under ideal growing conditions. Thick but weak unbranched stems often require staking since the typical foliage measures between 12 and 16 inches wide. If larger new foliage is preferred, remove the terminal flowering as it appears; this converts the plant's energies into vegetative growth. Enjoying a moderately fertile, slightly acid, well-drained, moist soil in any degree of shading, it will accept full sun only in consistently cool climates within its hardiness range. Poor soil drainage causes stem gummosis, which is an unnatural collection of gummy sap on the stems. Sooty mold, thrips, scales, and mealy bugs are also a problem.

It benefits from light fertilizing every 2 months during its active growing season to produce glossy, dark green, leathery, toothed leaves which show prominent veining and seven to nine deep clefts beyond the middle of each leaf in a finger design. These weighty leaves are supported on the stems by stalks up to a foot long. Young stems are covered in temporary rusty hairs that later drop off to show green, matured stems. Found generally unbranched, the plant sends out new growth only from ground level. Its milk-white, stiff, long-stalked, strong-scented, compound flowering appears in October or November as terminal sprays up to 18 inches which have the nuisance value of attracting large numbers of flies and bees for their nectar. The fruiting is a spherical, ¼-inch black drupe. A few cultivars are known.

CULTIVAR: 'Moseri' is compact but vigorous with yellow-veined leaves that are hairy on the undersides. It is one of the parents of the new genus x *Fatshedera*.

CULTIVAR: 'Variegata' carries foliage with creamy white margins.

GARDENIA (Cape jasmine)   *Rubiaceae* (madder) family

The name honors Dr. Alexander Garden, an eighteenth-century physician of Charleston, South Carolina, who had an extensive correspondence about plants with Linnaeus in Sweden; the name itself, however, was provided for this genus by a fellow American colonist, John Ellis. The plant is native to the warm regions of the Mediterranean. There are 200 species of shrubs or small trees here, and several are highly popular now as conspicuously flowering border plants or as espaliers. The common name is historically misapplied since these plants are not native inhabitants of South Africa's Cape of Good Hope. It may be that Portuguese colonists there during the seventeenth century had brought the plants from home; because they were observed later growing in gardens of the region, they were thought to be natives.

These plants belong in hot, humid areas with acid soil; they enjoy being fertilized often, responding best to fertilizers with high nitrogen content and an acid residue. Provide a loose mulch at all times to cool the roots. Attractive, usually large and fragrant, solitary or paired, terminal or axillary flowering has waxy petals of either white or yellow from May to September. Budding is distinctively twisted. The foliage is mostly oppositely placed but occasionally may appear in whorls of three on some species. The leathery or fleshy fruit is a berry. Insects are not overly troublesome, but canker disease is a serious problem for all species.

Gardenia jasminoides (florida) (grandiflora)
(common gardenia)

Zones 8 to 10   3' to 5' high x 3' to 5' wide   Sun to light shade

Considered a typical shrub today for nostalgia gardens of the southern United States, this compact, spreading plant has closely packed stems and twigs. Native to southern China, it came into cultivation during 1761. The 3-inch-wide, solitary, waxy white flowering in the leaf axils carries heady perfume and appears in late spring and summer along with glossy, thick, leathery, lanceolate foliage of deep green. These short-stalked leaves are close to 4 inches long and show both noticeable veining and leaf margins turned upward. The fleshy, oval, orange fruit is 1½ inches in length and matures as a ribbed capsule. This species sets flower buds only when night temperatures go below 65 degrees Fahrenheit.

Gardenia jasminoides

Provide an acid, fast-draining, fertile, moist soil and do not plant too deeply. Avoid cultivating since the rooting is shallowly set; mulch instead with rotted organic debris. It benefits from a monthly fertilizing with an acid-residue sort such as cottonseed meal during the active growing season; any lack of nutrients quickly shows itself in yellowish new foliage. Intolerant to coastal salt spray, this plant is hampered by many pests and diseases and requires consistent and regular spray programs. Its variations are of interest.

CULTIVAR: 'August Beauty' is a late-blooming type.

CULTIVAR: 'Mystery' behaves as a compact but vigorous sort with larger blossoms.

CULTIVAR: 'Prostrata' ('Radicans') becomes a low-growing groundcover plant about 2 or 3 feet high with a width of approximately 4 feet carrying only 1-inch flowering and 1-inch leaves. It is difficult to establish easily on some sites.

CULTIVAR: 'Variegata' sports leaves edged in white and is also troublesome to grow successfully.

VARIETY: *fortuniana (veitchii)* has larger leaves and flowers along with vividly dark green foliage. Several cultivars of it are known, but none shows more than a slight variation from the parent variety in foliage or habit.

HYPERICUM (St. John's wort)   *Hypericaceae* (hypericum) family

Both pagan practice and Christian celebration have much to do with the name of this plant group since the scientific label comes from the Greek *hyper*, meaning "above," and *eikon*, meaning "picture," which alludes to the ancient use of cut branches from these plants placed above images (or icons) to ward off evil spirits during pagan festivals; at least one of these holidays has been redesignated as Saint John's feast day. The common name, wort, is from the Middle English word *wyrt*, which translates to "plant"; it is also used in association with many ancient plant types. In later centuries pieces of *Hypericum* were worn or strewn about as a magic safeguard against witches, demons, and lightning—not much really changes over the eras. These plants also carried over into folk medicine, especially as a brew of the species *androsanum*, which was considered very effective in treating nervous and mental disorders. In sixteenth-century England this concoction was called *tutsan*, a corruption of the French *toute-sante*, or "heal-all."

Often exceptionally conspicuous when in flower during summer and early autumn, members of this group have five-petaled blossoms which are invariably yellow in every species, and all are dominated by a large collection of wiry stamens. The opposite entire leaves often carry black or translucent dots. The fruit is a conical capsule that is generally red-toned at maturity. Of easy culture, provided that the soil is fertile and well-drained, the 300 species of this genus are composed of annuals, perennials, and evergreen or deciduous shrubs distributed in the temperate and subtropical areas of the northern hemisphere. Tolerant to full sun and complete shade (depending on the species), they generally are unbothered by important pests or diseases. The European and Asiatic types flourish in alkaline soils. (Consult the "Deciduous Shrubs" division for additional choices.)

Hypericum calycinum (grandiflorum)   (Aaron's beard, creeping St. John's wort, gold flower)

Zones 7 to 10   1″ to 2″ high x 4′ to 5′ wide   Semishade

Tending to become a weedy and invasive groundcover if not properly managed, this shade-loving species blooms from July to September. Native to southeastern Europe and western Asia Minor, it came into cultivation by 1676. Shear back heavily every few years before growth starts to keep plants tidy and more floriferous. Accepting dry soil that is well-drained and light-textured, the plant forms a wide-growing, vigorous mat that enlarges by means of stoloniferous (underground) stems. It will succeed attractively beneath large and dense-headed trees where other material would have difficulty even establishing itself. Medium green, nearly oblong, smooth leaves elongate up to 4 inches and have conspicuous veining beneath. Mainly evergreen except at the northern limits of its range, the foliage turns purplish during winter dormancy in cold areas. Showy blossoming comes from terminal, richly golden flowers up to 3 inches wide with centralized massings of reddish stamens.

Hypericum cv. 'Hidcote' (cv. 'Hidcote Gold')
(patulum henryi)

Zones 6 (warm) to 10   2′ to 4′ high x 4′ to 6′ wide   Sun to light shade

Hypericum cv. 'Hidcote'

Of uncertain ancestry, this plant has a current naming identifying Hidcote Manor in England, where it first was raised in the 1920s. Some authorities believe it to be a hybrid of *calycinum* and *forrestii*, while others consider it a *patulum* derivative. In any event, this very hardy, vigorous, mostly evergreen plant will die to the ground in severe winters but usually revives to bloom the following summer from new ground-level shoots. Its leaves are 2 inches long, triangularly lanceolate, and dark green above, and they present noticeable veining on the paler undersides. Carrying the largest flowering of any type, with rich, golden yellow, clustered, fragrant, saucerlike blossoms 3 or more inches wide, the plant freely blooms from July to October. Fruit rarely sets, and pests or diseases are not usually troublesome. Although it presents a landscape difficulty because of its dieback potential, it has wide popular appeal because of its showy flowering.

Hypericum x moseranum   (gold flower)

Zones 6 (warm) to 10   1′ to 1½′ high x 3′ to 4′ wide   Sun to light shade

Hybridized from *patulum* and *calycinum* during 1877 at Moser's nursery in Versailles, France, this is a compact, modest-growing shrub without a stoloniferous habit that produces spreading and arching reddish stems with oval, up to 2-inch dark green leaves that are gray-toned beneath. The foliage is distinctively arranged in a crisply formal stepladder design along the slender shoots, while its bowl-shaped, yellow, up to 2½-inch flowers appear in clusters of five from July to October. Like *cv.* 'Hidcote', this shrub tends to winter-kill to the ground in extreme cold yet still manages to regrow and bloom by midsummer. Its slow-growing cultivar 'Tricolor' has green foliage variegated with white and edged in pink or red, but it is very tender and requires protection from both wind and winter.

ILEX (holly)   *Aquifoliaceae* (holly) family

Long valued horticulturally for their attractive habits, foliages, and berries, the hollies are popular today for most landscape developments because of their wide range of hardiness and adaptability. The European and Asiatic types are indifferent to soil or light conditions, but the North American forms require acid soil. At least 400 species of evergreen or deciduous trees and shrubs are available, and these are native to the temperate and tropical areas of North and South America, Europe, and Asia. Its scientific name is an ancient Latin word for holm oak *(Quercus ilex)* and alludes to the similarity of some types of European holly foliage to this tree's leaves. The word *holly*, on the other hand, may be a corruption of "holy" since the plant's cut branches often were used by the pagan Druids as religious decorations, and the leaves of at least fifty species are still gathered today for making sought after beverages in many parts of the world. Assigning fully appropriate botanic credentials to many currently available holly types continues to be troublesome since a wealth of created hybrids already exist and new cultivars of them are constantly coming into the market, showing that the intense interest in and popularity of hollies is undiminished.

Best grown in full sun, hollies accept light shading (and sometimes semishade) well on any well-drained, moist, fertile, and humusy soil from neutral to acid. Spring installation is still preferred in cold areas, but early autumn can be added to this schedule in milder sections. The majority serve as dense hedges or shapely specimens, and they are usually raised for their persistent, globose, red (infrequently yellow or black) fruit that is on display from early autumn to late winter; birds and other wildlife are particularly fond of them. The axillary, tiny, solitary or grouped, white to greenish, mild-scented flowers appear in May but are inconspicuous and dioecious, although one male can be relied on to pollinate several close-at-hand females of its species and some occasionally cooperate by fertilizing nonrelated species. Their alternate, short-stalked, leathery, often thick (on evergreen sorts) leaves are entire, toothed, or spiny-margined. Many pests and diseases can be disfiguring, but the leaf miner is undoubtedly the most noticeable. (Consult the "Deciduous Shrubs" division for additional choices.)

Ilex cornuta

Ilex cornuta   (Chinese holly, horned holly)

Zones 7 to 10   7' high x 12' wide   Sun to light shade

Slow-growing, densely twiggy, and compact, this is an unorthodox rounded shrub or small tree with short, stout branching and great variability in both the leaf size and the margin spines on any particular plant. Introduced during 1848 by Robert Fortune from one of his many plant expeditions to China, it blooms by May with clusters of yellowish flowers on the previous year's growth. Lustrous, scarlet, globose fruit enlarges to about ⅜ inch wide and develops on long stalks, but not abundantly; full fruit color may differ by 2 months with some specimens, showing another variable facet of its complex nature. Its distinctively quadrangular leaves appear on green twigs and become deeply indented or noticeably concave at the tip with margins frequently turned downward. This foliage is thick, leathery, deep, and glossy green and carries one to three spines at each side; it has a variable length between 1½ and 5 inches (the majority are usually 2 inches long). No other holly presents such shiny foliage. Its cultivar list contains stimulating options.

CULTIVAR: 'Burfordii' is a vigorous, globose, compact, red-fruiting female with leaves that are entire except for a terminal spine; this foliage is a glossy, deep green and shows both margins turned downward. The name honors T. W. Burford, superintendent of Westview Cemetery in Atlanta, Georgia, who received the first plants in 1895 from an undisclosed source and grew them to perfection.

CULTIVAR: 'D'or' originated in Columbus, Georgia, as a form with entire or spiny leaves and ⅜-inch yellow fruit.

CULTIVAR: 'Dwarf Burfordii' ('Burfordii Compacta') ('Burfordii Nana') presents a dense, slow-growing, very compact habit.

CULTIVAR: 'Hume' is an upright female with larger, quadrangular, lustrous, deep green, flat leaves carrying five spines on each margin and purple twigs. It can grow 4 feet tall but spreads only 2½ feet at most.

CULTIVAR: 'Jungle Gardens' came from Avery Island, Louisiana, as a female with large clusters of light yellow fruiting. The leaves and green stems are typical of the parent.

CULTIVAR: 'National' is also female and displays abundant but smaller-sized fruit on compact, upright growth. It was introduced by the National Botanic Garden in Washington, D.C.

CULTIVAR: 'Shangri-La' shows a vigorous, erect silhouette that can quickly become treelike since the plant can grow 5 feet yearly in a favorable location. The oversized, ½-half-inch fruit is red, very persistent, and generally evident from November until the following March. Quadrangular deep green foliage is both glossy and spine-edged.

CULTIVAR: 'Shiu-Ying' originated in Towson, Maryland, as a slow-growing, compact, but treelike form with dark green, lustrous, strongly spined foliage and generous clusters of brilliantly scarlet fruit. The name translates into "elegant plant."

Ilex crenata (Japanese holly, box-leaved holly)

Zones 6 to 10   8′ to 10′ high x 6′ to 8′ wide   Sun to semishade

Much desired for its many forms, Japanese holly disappoints by carrying black fruit but compensates with good hardiness and easy adaptability to partial shading. Almost every sort is favored either for hedge making or as a border specimen. Leathery, shiny, deep green foliage is paler beneath and develops as oblong leaves up to 1¼ inches long with round-toothed margins. Flowering occurs without notice in spring, and the shiny black fruit matures to ¼ inch wide, generally in clusters, but has little display value. The densely branched, upright, compact, and shrubby habit occasionally evolves into a treelike form after many decades. Native to Japan, this shrub came into cultivation about 1864 and has remained popular ever since. The following cultivar list is just an overview illustrating the divergence possible in this much hybridized plant.

CULTIVAR: 'Compacta' becomes a slow-growing compact form with an upright habit.

CULTIVAR: 'Convexa' is rightly called the "hardy box" since it can substitute for *Buxus* in some cool areas with its similar mounded, dense form and spreading habit. The glistening leaves are noticeably convex with downturned margins. Hardier than the parent, it shows almost toothless, glossier foliage, far more fruiting, and an easy adaptability for heavy shearing into hedges. The plant often is marketed erroneously as 'Bullata', which is an outdated name.

CULTIVAR: 'Excelsa' grows noticeably upright with deep green leaves; it is desirable for tall hedgings.

CULTIVAR: 'Helleri' expands very sluggishly as a densely compact, squat, flat-topped form with ¼- to ½-inch leaves. This female is not as hardy as the parent.

CULTIVAR: 'Hetzii' resembles *cv.* 'Convexa' in general appearance but carries slightly larger foliage and shows broader and faster growth

CULTIVAR: 'Latifolia' ('Fortunei') is a vigorous sort with oblong flat leaves about 1 inch long and ⅝ inch wide that show teeth on the edges in a prominent way. Its hardiness is less than that of the parent.

CULTIVAR: 'Mariesii' ('Nummularia') develops a squat, dwarfed, dense silhouette very slowly and carries rounded leaves crowded at the twig ends. The plant is female.

CULTIVAR: 'Microphylla' has oblong foliage to ¾ inch long but only ¼ inch wide with toothed margins on a stiff, spreading form.

CULTIVAR: 'Rotundifolia' is an upright type showing toothed, glossy, deep green, oval leaves up to 1¼ inches in length.

CULTIVAR: 'Stokesii' ('Stokes') becomes a larger version of *cv.* 'Helleri' with its mounded, dense, compact but spreading, faster development and small leaves. This plant is a male.

Ilex crenata

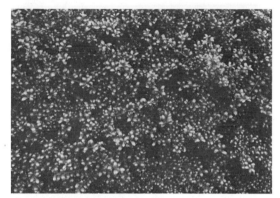

Ilex crenata cv. 'Convexa'

Ilex crenata cv. 'Helleri'

Ilex crenata cv. 'Helleri'

Ilex glabra

Ilex glabra

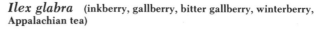

Ilex glabra (inkberry, gallberry, bitter gallberry, winterberry, Appalachian tea)

Zones 4 to 10   6′ to 10′ high x 6′ to 10′ wide   Sun to light shade

This is the hardiest evergreen holly, and it is native to the swampy soils and coastal areas from Nova Scotia to Florida and across to Texas. Introduced during 1759, the plant also is known for the attraction its flowers have to bees. Expanding slowly by underground stems, this stoloniferous shrub develops erect, hairy, and very flexible branching, eventually forming a rounded silhouette. In areas with heavy snowfalls these nonrigid stems often flatten or become disarrayed by the end of winter. Leathery, glossy, flat, light green leaves have yellow-green undersides and range from 1 inch to 2½ inches in length with few marginal teeth. During colonial times here, the ⅜-inch black fruit was crushed to make a durable ink or stain by both the settlers and the local Indians. Several cultivars are available.

CULTIVAR: 'Compacta' fruits heavily and forms a low, compact, dwarfed outline with deep green, somewhat dull-toned foliage.

CULTIVAR: 'Ivory Queen' develops sparse white fruiting.

CULTIVAR: 'Leucocarpa' ('Luteo-carpa') also carries white fruit.

CULTIVAR: 'Nigra' produces dark summertime foliage that becomes purple-green in winter dormancy.

CULTIVAR: 'Viridis' has bright green leaves.

Ilex x meserveae cv. 'Blue Princess'

Ilex x meserveae (blue holly)

Zones 5 to 9   6′ to 8′ high x 6′ to 8′ wide   Sun to light shade

Newly introduced and already uniquely appealing over a wide growing area, this special hybrid of *aquifolium* and *rugosa* shows remarkable hardiness, exceptional foliage, and bright red persistent fruiting clusters even on young females. Irregularly open and slow while juvenile, it soon develops a solid outline—tip-pruning helps—more erect than spreading when in full sun (the reverse type of growth is often the case with more shading). Leathery, oval, deep bluish green, wavy leaves about 2 inches long carry marginal spines and appear on purple-toned new stems; these leaves bear a strong resemblance to those of the *aquifolium* (English holly) parent. Wrinkled-leaved *rugosa* contributed the extra hardiness, but its leaf design is not evident here. Globose, ¼-inch, glossy red fruit comes in groupings that color brightly by late summer. Resistant to cold winter winds with negligible foliage burn, this shrub has an assured future in landscape work as hedges, massings, or specimens. Adapting to semishading satisfactorily, it then produces far less fruit and loses much of its valued bluish leaf tone.

Cultivars of it are appearing more frequently now and are differentiated mainly by sex type and minor foliage or fruiting habits; they are best separated by actual nursery inspection. Available are 'Blue Boy', male; 'Blue Girl', female; 'Blue Maid', female; 'Blue Princess', female; and 'Blue Stallion', male. As with any holly, males tend to grow more rapidly than females since their pollination efforts end by June, while females spend the summer months using their energy to develop fruit. One male can satisfy the needs of several nearby and different cultivars of this plant. Avoid crowding one of each sex into the same planting hole—a practice that is all too common—since each plant will become stunted and the fruiting will of necessity be located only on one portion of the maturing outline. Separate plants deserve separate accommodations.

Ilex pernyi (no common name)
Zones 6 to 9   **24′ high x 10′ wide**   **Sun to light shade**

Behaving either as a tall shrub or a small tree, this is a slow-growing species with the curious history of being introduced here from China several times by the Arnold Arboretum of Boston: originally in 1908, again in 1917, and once more later in cooperation with a university at Nanking. Hairy branches carry almost triangular, short-stalked, leathery, oval, olive green foliage set closely on the twigs. These leaves are about an inch long and half as wide with one to three spines per side, and they end in a slender prickle. Yellowish flowers appear by May, followed by bright scarlet, globose, up to ¼-inch fruiting in pairs. There are several cultivars.

CULTIVAR: 'Compacta' presents a denser form than the parent.

CULTIVAR: 'Veitchi' *(var. bioritensis)* may be only a form of *x aquipernyi* according to some authorities. It carries long leaves to 1½ inches but has the same fruit size.

IXORA (flame of the woods)   *Rubiaceae* (madder) family

Grown primarily for the heads of bright flowers and the desirable foliage, this is a genus with 400 species of shrubs and small trees in its membership. Native to tropical Asia and Africa plus Central America, all prefer light shade and grow easily on an ordinary, well-drained, slightly acid soil that is reasonably moist year-round. The light green entire leaves are opposite or set in whorls of three. Compact domed heads of white, yellow, orange, pink, or red florets are usually terminal, and the fruit develops as a hard but fleshy berry. The scientific name is a Portuguese translation of the Sanskrit word for the Hindu god Siva, and it came into usage on the former Portuguese colony of Malabar during the seventeenth century. Diseases and pests make few inroads.

Ixora coccinea (flame of the woods, jungle flame, jungle geranium)
Zones 9 and 10   **4′ high x 4′ wide**   **Sun**

Greatly used and enjoyed as a hedge plant in Florida, this shrub grows best in hot, humid weather and flowers best in full sun. Tolerant to mild salt air conditions, it enjoys a slightly acid, high-fertility soil with good drainage and benefits from twice-yearly fertilizing. Scale and root rot are occasionally bothersome. The oblong medium green leaves are bronze when new and can reach dimensions of 4 inches, but where soil conditions are alkaline, they generally become noticeably chlorotic or yellowed. Flowering occurs most of the year with large dense clusters of 1¼-inch tubular blossoms of red or yellow (and sometimes orange) tones; the fruit is a small, inconspicuous berry. Its cultivar 'Fraseri' displays brilliantly salmon-red flowers but is sensitive to sudden cold.

Ixora coccinea

Ixora coccinea cv. 'Fraseri'

JASMINUM (jasmine, jessamine)   *Oleaceae* (olive) family

The name is a Latin translation of the Persian word *yasaman* (Arabic *ysmin*) and means "white flower." Natively found in eastern and southern Asia, the Federation of Malaysia, Africa, and Australia, 200 species exist of tropical and subtropical deciduous and evergreen shrubs or vines. All grow easily on an average-fertility moist soil in sun or light shade and carry tubular, white, yellow, or pink mostly terminal clusterings of flowers. Many species have pleasant scents, and shrub forms generally are yellow-blossoming. Pinnately compound, usually alternate foliage shows three to seven leaflets on green stems with the terminal one longer than any of the others. Its small, black berry fruit comes in two lobed sections. Oil of jasmine (from the species *grandiflorum*) still finds extensive use in perfumery, and the shrubs creating it are cultivated intensively near Grasse, France, where 2½ acres of land with 10,000 jasmines can yield about 10,000 pounds of flowers in a season. Jasmine-scented gloves called Jessemy became the social rage for both men and women in seventeenth-century England, and one yellow species is now the official state flower of South Carolina. Diseases and pests are not often a problem. (Consult the "Deciduous Shrubs" division for other choices.)

Jasminum mesnyi (primulinum) (Japanese jasmine, primrose jasmine)

Zones 8 to 10   10′ high x 20′ wide   Sun

This much branched, scrambling, even vinelike shrub from western China is useful in embankment erosion control since rooting occurs wherever its long, thin stems touch the earth. Able to thrive easily in all soil conditions, this rugged plant almost delivers an "install, water, and forget" specification. It flowers from October to June and behaves best in cool winters with its 2-inch, solitary (occasionally paired), faintly scented, bright yellow, showy blooms that have deeper-colored centers. The oblong deep green foliage is up to 3 inches long with only three leaflets. Rarely fruiting, it is bothered only occasionally by spider mites or scales. Named for W. Mesny, the original collector, the plant now exists almost everywhere in northern Florida, both cultivated and wild.

KALMIA (KALMIELLA) (laurel, American laurel)
Ericaceae (heath) family

Exclusively native to North America and Cuba, this shrub genus has only six (or eight, depending on the authority) species. Not related to the true laurel *(Laurus)*, the plants do have foliage that is somewhat similar to it in outline, but the leaves here are poisonous to humans and other animals if eaten in any quantity. The foliage is simple, smooth-edged, leathery, and alternate, opposite, or even whorled; it does not curl during wintertime freezes the way rhododendron, its near relation, does. Floral displays of some species are truly outstanding for their showy terminal clusters of cup-shaped, white, pink to purple flowers with five petals tightly joined together as a pentagonal bud and blossom. When open, these flowers show ten stamens held in tension (two per petal) against the blossom sides; they spring free to trigger pollen toward any foraging insect when they are disturbed. The fruit is clustered as small capsules without landscape interest; removing them, while hardly essential for the plant's needs, is done by many who prefer a tidier appearance from their shrubs. Laurels prefer a humusy, moist, acid soil in sun or light shade; they will accept deeper shading but will flower less. Shade-grown plants usually carry shinier and thinner leaves, often with a pronounced droop. Although pests and diseases are not uncommon, few are exceptionally harmful. The name commemorates Linneaus's assistant Pehr Kalm, who cataloged North American plants during the eighteenth century as a guest of the Virginia Colony, which helps explain why the species name *virginiana* is so frequently found attached to these plant discoveries; it was simple courtesy.

Kalmia latifolia (mountain laurel, calico bush, bush ivy, ivy, spoonwood)

Zones 5 to 8   4′ to 10′ high x 4′ to 8′ wide   Sun to light shade

Kalmia latifolia

Considered the most beautiful and showiest of all, this shrub is unusual since it is the official state flower of both Connecticut and Pennsylvania, where it is widely distributed. Native from Nova Scotia down to northern Florida, the plant was once considered for the national flower, but that program failed, and we are still without a plant selection. An inhabitant of rocky outcrops in ravines with hemlocks or isolated on mountainsides, this laurel has wide appeal when grown in masses as a result of its spectacular June blossoming. Its wood is surprisingly fine-grained and easy to work when freshly cut. North American Indians often used it to make spoons, pipes, or shovel handles, and later colonists followed suit. Curiously, this compact evergreen can receive drastic pruning to 2 inches from ground level in early spring to restore the shape or to reduce the height; it can be expected to restore itself satisfactorily. Pruning for simple neatness should be practiced immediately after flowering, however. Avoid cultivation of the shallow rooting; mulch instead. Fungus leaf spot, flower blight, stem borers (forestall by keeping the mulch material away from the stems), leaf chlorosis, and lace bugs are important problems to combat, but none is consistently troublesome all year.

Kalmia latifolia

The lustrous, 3- to 5-inch, oval, richly dark green foliage is yellow-green beneath and often carries yellow-toned petioles and midveins; these leaves are tapered at both ends and tend to appear creased with upturned margins, especially in full sun. This foliage is poisonous to humans and livestock when consumed in large amounts. Exposed flower budding develops the previous summer as slender, terminal spikes a few inches tall with yellow- or red-toned coloring. The five-sided enlarging buds of spring are oddly knobby from ten stamen sockets inside protruding across the bud; the white, pink, or deep rose bowl-shaped blossoms unfold as compact unscented clusters up to 5 inches wide by June. If ideally grown and fully budded, a plant can obliterate almost all foliage when in bloom, presenting an eye-catching sight rarely matched by any other shrub. The following cultivars are now available, and more can be expected to emerge to satisfy a widespread public interest.

Kalmia latifolia cv. 'Fuscata'

CULTIVAR: 'Alba' carries pure white flowering.

CULTIVAR: 'Fuscata' sports flowers with broad chocolate-purple banding inside.

CULTIVAR: 'Myrtifolia' is a slow, dense, dwarfed form having deep green leaves only 1½ inches long.

CULTIVAR: 'Obtusata' develops compactly and slowly with 2- to 3-inch oval leaves blunted at both ends.

CULTIVAR: 'Polypetala' displays deeply incised flower petals that give it a feathery appearance.

CULTIVAR: "Redbud" carries deep rose budding and pink-toned flowering, but only when grown in full sunlight.

CULTIVAR: 'Rubra' shows deep pink flowering.

LEUCOTHOE (fetterbush, sweetbells)   *Ericaceae* (heath) family

Attractive as a groundcover material and enjoying the same culture as both *Rhododendron* **and** *Kalmia,* **this native of eastern Asia, Madagascar, and North and South America has fifty species of slow-growing, slender-stemmed deciduous or evergreen shrubs in its clan. The name is Greek and identifies Leucothoe, daughter of King Orchamus of Babylon and also the beloved of Apollo, the god who changed her into a shrub when her father, for unclear reasons, buried her alive. All members enjoy moist, peaty, and sandy acid soil that is both deep and humusy in light to semishade. The alternate, simple, glossy, usually sharply fine-toothed foliage may alter to bronze during winter with some species. Its white to pink flowers form themselves erect or drooping from the leaf axils or are terminal in small clusterings similar to those of blueberry** *(Vaccinium),* **its close relation. The nondecorative fruit is a five-valved capsule and develops clustered as well. Pests and diseases are not a problem.**

Leucothoe axillaris (catesbaei) (platyphylla) (Andromeda catesbaei)   (no common name)

Zones 7 to 9   6′ high x 8′ wide   Light shade

The plant has had many improper identifications before reaching its current name, and even today nursery lists are confused. It is very similar to (though less hardy than) *fontanesiana* but differs by its more widely spaced teeth on the leaf margins and by the shorter flowering clusters. It is native to coastal regions from Virginia to Florida and west to Mississippi, and its flattened silhouette carries 3- to 6-inch, pointed, lanceolate, leathery foliage with abruptly pointed teeth on slim green stems. These leaves can change to red-toned for the winter if placed in strong light, but not full sun, which scorches the thin foliage. Creamy white ¼-inch florets appear by May in drooping tassels 2 inches long, originating from the leaf axils. The tan, flattened, spherical capsules are only ⅛ inch long and also develop on pendant strings. It has no problems with diseases or insects.

Leucothoe fontanesiana

Leucothoe fontanesiana (editorum)   (drooping leucothoe, dog hobble, switch ivy, lily of the valley shrub)

Zones 5 to 8   6′ high x 8′ wide   Light shade

This is an elegant, hardy shrub with erect, gracefully arching and spreading slender branches that are reddish and glossy when young; it expands stoloniferously (by underground stems) and eventually covers a broad area. Found wild on the banks of streams from Virginia to Georgia and across to Tennessee, it came into culture during 1793 and performs very well as a large-leaved groundcover. The pointed, lanceolate, leathery, fine-toothed, glossy foliage varies from 3½ to 6 inches in length and turns either bronze or beet red (depending on the strength of daylight reaching it) during winter months. Its ¼-inch exposed budding also reddens then. By May the pendulous, axillary, creamy white flowers elongate in tassellike strings between 1½ and 4 inches long, but the arching stem habit tends to obscure most of the blossoming effect. The fruit is a series of ⅛-inch spherical caps. Except for the flower length and the closely set leaf margin teeth, it is a duplicate of *axillaris,* but with much greater hardiness. Nursery lists still mislabel it as *catesbaei,* which now is considered a former name for *axillaris.*

Chamaecyparis obtusa cv. 'Nana'

Chamaecyparis obtusa cv. 'Tetragona Aurea'

Chamaecyparis pisifera cv. 'Filifera Nana Aurea'

Juniperus chinensis cv. 'Pfitzeriana'

Juniperus chinensis cv. 'Pfitzeriana Compacta'

Juniperus chinensis cv. 'Pfitzeriana Glauca'

Juniperus communis cv. 'Hornibrookii'

Juniperus horizontalis cv. 'Douglasii Wiltonii'

Juniperus horizontalis cv. 'Plumosa'

Juniperus sabina cv. 'Tamariscifolia'

Juniperus squamata cv. 'Blue Star'

Picea pungens cv. 'Montgomery'

Pinus mugo mugo

Platycladus orientalis cv. 'Semper-aurescens'

Taxus baccata cv. 'Fowle'

Taxus baccata cv. 'Repandens'

Taxus baccata topiary

Espaliered *Taxus x media cv.* 'Hicksii'

Thuja occidentalis cv. 'Globosa'

Dwarf conifer collection

PLATE I: NEEDLE EVERGREENS

Abelia x grandiflora

Callistemon citrinum

Calluna vulgaris
cultivars

Camellia japonica
cultivar

Carissa grandiflora

*Codiaeum variegatum
pictum* cultivar

Cotoneaster dammeri
fruit

Daphne cneorum

Elaeagnus pungens cv.
'Maculata'

Erica canaliculata

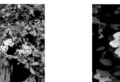

Euonymus fortunei cv.
'Carrieri'

Hypericum cv. 'Hidcote'

Ixora coccinea

Kalmia latifolia cv.
'Redbud'

Mahonia aquifolium

Nerium oleander
cultivar

Pyracantha coccinea cv.
'Lalandei' fruit

*Rhododendron minus
cv.* 'Compacta'

*Rhododendron
catawbiense* cultivars

Viburnum japonicum
fruit

PLATE II: BROADLEAF EVERGREENS

Aesculus parviflora

Buddleia davidii
cultivar

Berberis thunbergii cv.
'Aurea'

Calycanthus floridus

Caragana arborescens

Cotoneaster divaricata
fruit

Cytisus x praecox

Enkianthus
campanulatus

Euonymus europaea cv.
'Aldenhamensis' fruit

Forsythia x intermedia
cv. 'Spring Glory'

Hibiscus syriacus cv.
'Woodbridge'

Hippophae rhamnoides
fruit

Hydrangea macrophylia

Lonicera tatarica cv.
'Rosea'

Paeonia suffruticosa
cultivar

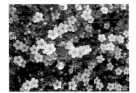

Potentilla cv. 'Primrose
Beauty'

Punica granatum cv.
'Legrellei'

Rhododendron
calendulaceum

Rhododendron x
gandavensis cv.
'Narcissiflora'

Rhododendron yedoense
poukhanense

PLATE III: DECIDUOUS SHRUBS

Rosa hugonis

Rosa rugosa fruit

Rosa virginiana

Spiraea japonica cv. 'Alpina'

Spiraea thunbergii

Stewartia pseudocamellia

Syringa meyeri cv. 'Palabin'

Syringa x persica

Syringa x prestoniae cv. 'Isabella'

Syringa vulgaris

Syringa vulgaris cultivar

Viburnum dilatatum fruit

Viburnum dilatatum cv. 'Xanthocarpum' fruit

Viburnum opulus fruit

Viburnum plicatum tomentosum

Viburnum plicatum tomentosum fruit

Viburnum prunifolium fruit

Viburnum setigerum fruit

Vitex agnus-castus

Weigela florida

PLATE IV: DECIDUOUS SHRUBS

Not a successful urban plant because it dislikes air pollution, it also has no tolerance for strongly windy sites. Provide a moist, peaty, well-drained, acid soil and filtered light. Diseases and pests are of little concern. Some novel cultivars are available.

CULTIVAR: 'Girard's Rainbow' ('Gerrard's Rainbow') carries smaller leaves marbled with pink, creamy yellow, and copper red but requires strong light to hold these special colorings. A tender, slow-growing shrub, it often has winter-burned foliage in colder areas and needs protection there.

CULTIVAR: 'Nana' is only 2 feet tall and has normal green leaves somewhat smaller than those of the parent.

CULTIVAR: 'Trivar' expands slowly and also has less hardiness; its foliage is lightly streaked in cream and pink.

Leucothoe fontanesiana winter foliage color

LIGUSTRUM (privet)   *Oleaceae* (olive) family

At least fifty species of much branched and twiggy deciduous or evergreen shrubs, along with an occasional tree form, exist in this genus; they are found chiefly in eastern Asia and the Federation of Malaysia and there are a few in Europe, Australia, and northern Africa. The name is an ancient Latin word for "privet," which is a corruption of the word "private," alluding to the exceptional screening quality to be had from this plant group. Commonly used today for hedgings because of their fast, neat growth, these are sun-loving and shade-tolerant shrubs that are not particular about soil, not bothered by heat or cold, and not fazed by city pollution. Developing greedy surface rooting as they mature, privets do not allow much other growth to succeed near them. All exhibit their best response in consistently moist soil that is fertilized annually. Few insects except for leaf miners and thrips are bothersome, but honey fungus can kill any plant quickly.

The opposite, entire, often thick, mostly oblong or oval leaves appear on flexible, slender twigs, yet older stems are heavy and sturdy. Its trumpet-shaped small white flowering develops in terminal clusterings by midsummer and emits a strong scent with an enticement for bees. The fruit is a small, black or bluish black, fleshy berry appearing in bunches by autumn and greatly enjoyed by hungry birds. (Consult the "Deciduous Shrubs" division for additional choices.)

Leucothoe fontanesiana cv. 'Girard's Rainbow'

Ligustrum japonicum   (waxleaf privet, Japanese privet)

Zones 7 to 10   6′ to 8′ high x 4′ to 6′ wide   Sun to light shade

Noted for its gleaming foliage (closely akin to the gloss of *Camellia*), this privet accepts drought, dust, smoke, and high heat in stride, but it is not tolerant of shoreline salt spray. Rarely needing fertilizer to grow well, the plant functions well as a screen, border item, hedge, or container specimen. Pest-free except for occasional scale and white fly infestations, this upright and spreading, densely mounded, compact shrub can grow rapidly once it is established. Introduced to cultivation in 1845 by Dr. Siebold, it is native to both Japan and Korea. It carries short-pointed, smooth-edged, thick and leathery, glossy, deep green foliage between 3 and 4 inches long; the leaf margins are sometimes broadly wavy, while the undersurfaces are paler green. White panicles of small flowers appear from July to October and can be up to 6 inches high; these have a pungent smell and may cause pollen allergies. The fruiting is blue-black but sparsely set. When juvenile, this species and *lucidum* very often are mistaken. Some variations exist.

CULTIVAR: 'Variegatum' has foliage variegated with creamy streaks and margins edged in white.

Ligustrum japonicum

VARIETY: *rotundifolium* is slow-growing, compact, and rigid with almost round, black-green leaves that are up to 2½ inches long.

CULTIVAR: 'Suwanne River', a cross between *rotundifolium* and *lucidum*, is a compact, slow-growing, 4-foot-high shrub with leaves somewhat twisted but with few flowers and no fruiting. It is hardier than either parent.

Ligustrum lucidum (glossy privet, Chinese privet, Nepal privet, waxleaf privet, white wax tree)

Zones 8 to 10   10′ to 30′ high x 6′ to 10′ wide   Sun to light shade

Native to China, Korea, and Japan, the plant was introduced in 1794 and is often confused with *japonicum* when young. Tolerant of any soil but intolerant of seaside conditions, this is a fast-growing, dense, compact, and upright shrub that can easily be trained into an attractive tree form. Glossy, smooth-margined, lancelike, pointed-tip foliage is medium green (and lighter-toned than *japonicum*) with a length between 4 and 6 inches. Flowering occurs from July to October from tiny, pleasantly scented white flowers in panicles often 10 inches high; the pollen may produce hay fever attacks. The clusters of blue-black berries are persistent for a long time, unless birds discover them. Because of the similarity between this species and *japonicum*, some cultivars listed here may one day be transferred to *japonicum*.

CULTIVAR: 'Aureo-Marginatum' has leaves edged in yellow.

CULTIVAR: 'Ciliatum' carries smaller foliage.

CULTIVAR: 'Compactum' shows a dense outline with dark, very waxy leaves.

CULTIVAR: 'Excelsum Superbum' has striking leaves variegated and mottled in deep yellow and creamy white with deep yellow margins.

CULTIVAR: 'Gracile' produces a slenderly upright form.

CULTIVAR: 'Macrophyllum' sets larger leaves.

CULTIVAR: 'Microphyllum' has smaller, narrower foliage.

CULTIVAR: 'Nigrifolium' displays very deep green leaves.

CULTIVAR: 'Nobile' is a narrowly upright type that is wider than *cv.* 'Gracile'.

CULTIVAR: 'Pyramidale' contributes a narrowly conical shape.

CULTIVAR: 'Recurvifolium' carries foliage with leaf margins turned downward.

CULTIVAR: 'Repandum' has narrower, twisted foliage.

CULTIVAR: 'Tricolor' carries narrow leaves variegated first in pink and later with yellow.

MAHONIA (Oregon grape, holly grape)   *Berberidaceae* (barberry) family

Although closely related to the thorny *Berberis* genus, especially in its inner yellow stem coloring and flowering, the over 100 species of *Mahonia* remain thornless. The plant is native to Asia, North America, and Central America; its name honors the late-eighteenth-century horticulturist Bernard McMahon of Philadelphia, a close friend of Thomas Jefferson. Like *Berberis*, the group is host to the wheat rust fungus and may be prohibited from such crop areas; however, both *aquifolium* and *bealii* are known to be immune and thus present no such problem. Useful as background, as border items, or as containerized specimens, these slow-growing, upright shrubs have alternate, leathery, pinnately compound foliage on sparse branching; their spine-edged leaflets are very hollylike in appearance. Some species turn reddish or bronze-toned for winter, adding an interesting dimension similar to *Leucothoe*. All enjoy a well-drained, moist, humusy site in light shade (or full sun if kept very moist at all times) on either acid or alkaline soils; they abhor strong winds which can scorch the thin leaves. Flowers are always bright yellow and come in dense clusters by midspring, followed by berry fruit commonly found as dark blue-black and covered with a waxy gray bloom; this fruiting normally develops in grapelike clusters. Plants of the southwestern United States are often called *agarita* or *algarita*, which is the Spanish term for "sour" or "bitter" and refers to the tart taste of this fruit. Pests and diseases are not common.

Mahonia aquifolium (Berberis aquifolium) (Oregon grape, mountain grape, holly mahonia, holly barberry, blue barberry)

Zones 6 to 9   3′ to 6′ high x 2′ to 6′ wide   Light shade

Mahonia aquifolium flowers

Spreading stoloniferously but sluggishly, this species is especially attractive when naturalized as a groundcover with *Rhododendron* and *Kalmia* plantings on a moist woodlot. Native from British Columbia to California and east to Idaho in wind-sheltered areas, this shrub is now the official state flower of Oregon; it was introduced to cultivation during 1823. Slightly wrinkled foliage varies between 4 and 10 inches in length and is composed of five to nine oval leaflets individually up to 3 inches long with six to twelve spines on the margins. Leaves are green on both sides but become highly lustrous above and usually deepen to reddish bronze for winter. New growth is glossy and bronze-purple. The terminal, 3-inch, showy clusters of golden yellow small flowers appear in May, but if cut for decoration, they will quickly shatter. Bunches of spherical, ⅓-inch, black fruit become heavily coated with a waxy violet-gray bloom, making them appear blue when mature; this fruit is edible and can be made into a tasty jelly. Provide a well-drained, average-fertility, moist, humusy site in dappled light for best growth, although the plant is not overly fussy about these details. Older specimens do not transplant well. Several cultivars are known.

Mahonia aquifolium fruit

CULTIVAR: 'Compacta' is dwarfed and more compact-growing.

CULTIVAR: 'Golden Abundance' has great popularity in California because of its vigorous growth habit to 6 feet and its dense foliage with red midribs; it also provides generous flowering and fruiting.

CULTIVAR: 'Moseri' carries lighter green foliage that turns brownish rose for winter.

CULTIVAR: 'Vicarii' becomes broader-spreading with reddish new foliage that turns green for summer and remains green in winter.

Mahonia bealii (no common name)

Zones 7 to 9   12′ high x 6′ wide   Light shade

Stout, upright, and often leggy with age, this species carries oversized pinnate foliage up to 18 inches long. It is often confused with *japonica*, a very similar species having narrower leaflets and larger, *drooping* flowers but reduced landscape appeal; thus, *japonica* is not included in this book. Tolerant of any moist soil, *bealii* produces lemon yellow, fragrant, erect flower clusters about 4 inches tall from March to May; these develop into oval, waxy, blue-black fruit with a gray-toned bloom. The very stiff foliage is a dull gray-green above and a pale yellow-green beneath with five to eight pairs of oval leaflets having three to six spines per side. These stalkless leaflets can each be 4 inches long, and they are spaced widely apart; the terminal leaflet is broader than the others and is stalked.

Mahonia bealii

Mahonia lomariifolia (Chinese holly grape)

Zones 8 to 10   4' to 12' high x 3' to 10' wide   Semishade

Attractively appealing in its foliage, flowering, and fruit, this shrub is tender in any sudden cold and requires filtered afternoon light. A dramatic accent for containers or blank walls with its slender, fernlike, elongated leaves, young plants can be surprisingly gaunt since they usually have only a single unbranched stem to offer. Native to western China and Burma, it came into culture during 1931 and needs a slightly acid, loamy soil that is consistently moist and well-drained. Erect, stout, canelike stems carry little branching as they mature, but they have rigid, leathery, pinnately compound foliage up to 2 feet long as their main attraction. These leaves are composed of twelve to twenty pairs of narrow, oblong, dull gray-green, nearly 3-inch-long leaflets with three to seven spines along each margin. The plant flowers handsomely from February to May with four to eight terminal 6-inch spikes gathered in a cluster; each spike can have up to 250 tiny florets of deep yellow. The oval fruit is black with a blue, waxy coating; it develops in large, noticeable clusterings.

Mahonia repens (creeping holly grape)

Zones 6 (warm) to 9   1' to 3' high x 5' wide   Light shade

Discovered during the Lewis and Clarke expedition of the late eighteenth century, this plant is native from British Columbia south to Colorado and California. A suckering creeper, it creates a valuable and eye-catching low groundcover for open woodlots. Dense, clustered, 3-inch spikes of deep yellow flowers appear by May and are followed by globose, ¼- to ⅛-inch black fruit with a waxy blue covering. The compound leaves are up to 10 inches long with two or three pairs of dull, bluish green, oval leaflets about 3½ inches in length and half as wide. These are wavy-margined and carry between five and nine spiny teeth. The variety *rotundifolia* has few teeth on the margins and shows almost flat foliage; if conditions are favorable, it can grow to a 3-foot height.

MYRICA (CEROTHAMNUS) (MORELLA) (bayberry, wax myrtle, sweet gale)   Myrtaceae (myrtle) family

Widely distributed worldwide in sunny locations in cold, temperate, subtropical, and tropical climes, this genus has fifty species of deciduous and evergreen shrubs or small trees. The name is an ancient Greek one, *myrike*, for some of these fragrant-leaved shrubs. The small dioecious flowers are insignificant, but the drupelike, spherical, gray or purple fruit, which is covered with a heavy coat of wax or resin, has found various uses because of its pleasant scent. Alternate, simple, short-stalked, broadly lanceolate foliage is dotted with resin glands and releases a spicy odor when crushed. Tolerant of dry, sterile soil or acid bogs, the members of this group are often found thriving on sandy shorelines. Some species were used in Europe to flavor beer before hops were grown there, and the berries of the deciduous *pensylvanica* are favored for making holiday candles.

Myrica cerifera (caroliniensis) (Cerothamnus ceriferus) (Morella cerifera) (wax myrtle, waxberry, candleberry)

Zones 7 to 10   35′ tall x 20′ wide   Sun

Introduced in 1669 and native from New Jersey to Florida and west to Texas, this clump-forming shrub is also an inhabitant of the West Indies. Its habit is open, but with patience and applied training, it can be made into a picturesque tree silhouette. The narrowly lanceolate foliage is up to 3 inches long and sharply toothed above the middle with a rusty coloring on both sides. The waxy, gray-green fruit is only ⅛ inch long on females and yields some wax for candle making. Thriving on any moist, peaty or wet, sandy soil, this shrub readily endures shoreside locations. Easily transplanted, it is one of those rugged plants you can install, water, and forget.

Myrica cerifera

MYRTUS (myrtle)   *Myrtaceae* (myrtle) family

Over 100 species were originally credited to this genus, but much of this list has been transferred to other genera, and now only 16 shrub types remain. Favoring hot and dry locations, each is especially welcome in the southwestern United States and at seaside locations. Its history is an ancient one of esteem from both the early Greeks and the Romans; whereas the laurel was the crown of military victors, the myrtle wreath became the accolade of poets, magistrates, playwrights, and athletes. Because the foliage was so much in demand for garlands and crowns, a quarter of the Athens marketplace once was devoted entirely to selling its wares and became popularly known as the *Murrinae*, or myrtle market. Papirius Cursor, who erected the first sundial in Rome, designated myrtle as the symbol of the Roman Empire. Today it often is used in European bridal bouquets as a sign of fertility.

Plants need a well-drained fertile soil on a hot, sunny, fairly dry site, either acid or alkaline. The opposite, simple, toothless foliage becomes spicily aromatic when bruised. White, fragrant, solitary flowers appear in the leaf axils as five-petaled, saucer-shaped blossoms with prominently projecting stamens; the oval or spherical berries are capped with persistent dried sepals. Pests and diseases are infrequent.

Myrtus communis (myrtle, common myrtle, Greek myrtle, Swedish myrtle)

Zones 9 and 10   3′ to 18′ high x 3′ to 8′ wide   Sun

Usually slow-growing, this is a rounded bush with dense foliage that serves commendably as a low hedge or clipped edging. Although intolerant of salt air conditions, it accepts dusty and smoggy sites well and is also drought-tolerant. Native to the entire Mediterranean region and beyond, the plant has been cultivated since A.D. 1500; however, recognizable twigs have recently been identified in Roman tombs known to be almost 2000 years old. The simple, oval, leathery leaves are up to 2 inches long and are tightly placed near the twig ends; when crushed, they emit a strong scent. Soft-haired fluffy blossoms are fragrant and creamy white or pink-toned during June to August (earlier in very mild areas); they vary between ¼ and ¾ inch wide and show many noticeable jutting stamens. The purple-black spherical fruit matures up to ½ inch long and can appear in volume on very fertile sites; birds greatly enjoy them. Red spider mites and scales are the chief pests. A reasonably lengthy cultivar selection exists.

CULTIVAR: 'Albocarpa' has pure white flowering.

CULTIVAR: 'Buxifolia' *(var. buxifolia)* develops elliptical foliage somewhat like that of a box plant *(Buxus).*

CULTIVAR: 'Compacta' is dwarfed and dense with lettuce green new leaves that mature as deep green.

CULTIVAR: 'Flore Plena' is an uncommon sort showing double white flowering.

CULTIVAR: 'Microphylla' produces leaves less than an inch long that overlap along the twigs; it is generally called dwarf myrtle, Polish myrtle, or German myrtle.

CULTIVAR: 'Minima' *(var. minima)* displays a dwarfed habit and much smaller foliage than the parent.

CULTIVAR: 'Variegata' carries leaves margined in creamy white.

NANDINA (heavenly bamboo) *Berberidaceae* (barberry) family

Although this shrub has the general appearance of bamboo because of its stems and foliage, it is unrelated; some authorities, however, now believe it deserves its own family, *Nandinaceae*, because of its uniqueness. Only one species is known to exist. If given sufficient strong light, here is one of the very few temperate zone woody plants which can be raised successfully indoors as a containerized specimen. This plant was introduced during 1804 and is native to India, central China, and Japan. Its name is derived from the Japanese word for it, *nanten*.

Nandina domestica

Nandina domestica (heavenly bamboo, sacred bamboo)

Zones 7 to 10   4′ to 8′ high x 2′ to 6′ wide   Semishade

Alternate, pinnately compound, lacy leaves are divided either twice or three times to create a wide-spreading (to 18 inches across) foliage mass of pale to mid-green in summer, with vivid crimson to purplish tones during winter. New growth emerges bronzy red with some pink overcast, and the multitude of narrow, pointed leaflets are up to 2 inches long. It produces a striking effect. Slow to enlarge, the shrub has erect, canelike, ringed, unbranched, slender stems much resembling bamboo. In June white to slightly pinkish, terminally projecting clusters of tiny flowers appear in 6- to 12-inch pyramidal heads. Even more decorative are the long-lasting groups of oval, glossy, bright red, ¼-inch fruit. Best located in semishade, it will accept full sun if it is kept consistently moist. Provide a fertile, acid, well-drained, porous, humusy soil and install plants in groups to assure cross-pollination for the highly desirable fruiting. Cut back to ground level any leggy stems; they quickly renew. Feed annually in spring with an acid-base organic fertilizer and douse with one of the commercially available acid-producing chelated iron solutions to help rejuvenate any yellow-veined foliage. Generally pest-free, it occasionally is beset by mites and scales.

Attractive in containers and suitable for narrow planting spaces, *Nandina* can be moved successfully even when large. At its northern limits, however, it requires winter protection against strong winds and bright sunlight. When Florida-grown, the plant appears discontent on the sandy soil of the peninsula, but it does behave normally in the upper, Panhandle section. A few cultivars are available.

CULTIVAR: 'Alba' produces white fruiting.

CULTIVAR: 'Nana Purpurea' is compact to 18 inches tall with fewer leaf divisions but larger and thicker foliage; its emerging growth is reddish purple.

NERIUM (oleander, rose bay)   *Apocynaceae* (dogbane) family

Only two species are known, and these are native to the warm subtropical areas from the Mediterranean to Japan. Unexcelled as windbreaks or containerized plants, they are both drought-resistant and salt-tolerant with little need for attention once established. Both types thrive where summers are long and hot and recover quickly from any sudden frost damage. The name *Nerium* is an ancient Greek one for "oleander" and is derived from *neros*, meaning "water"; this alludes to the swampy areas where the plant first was located. Its common name is from the Italian *oleandro*, which translates into "olivelike," reflecting the appearance of the foliage. Unfortunately, all parts of these plants are poisonous to warm-blooded animals if eaten, and both the stems and the flowers can produce body rashes on contact. Even the milky sap is toxic, yet caterpillars, the chief insect pest, devour the leaves quickly and thoroughly without ill effects.

Most floriferous in summer, oleanders bloom continually if sporadically throughout the year with showy, sizable clusters of terminal, much branched, trumpet-shaped flowering. The fruit develops as slender, elongated, paired pods. The stout, straight, erect green stems carry semidrooping branches and mostly whorled leaves in threes. This foliage is narrowly lanceolate and willowlike with pointed, leathery, glossy, entire leaves. These shrubs transplant with ease.

Nerium oleander   (common oleander, rose bay)

Zones 9 and 10   6' to 20' high x 6' to 20' wide   Sun

Nerium oleander

Rivaling *Camellia* for flowering effect, *Nerium* was first cultured in 1596 and arrived in the United States with early settlers from the Mediterranean. It has earned popularity for endurance and conspicuous flowering, even though all its parts are dangerous to people, especially if eaten. In California today over 1200 miles of highway median strips are planted with this shrub, to serve as a headlight barrier of some density as well as for its year-long attractiveness, showing how easily it can adapt to diverse growing conditions. Desirable in containers, massed on embankments for erosion control, at the shore, as informal tall hedges, and even as tree-trained forms, the plant is tolerant of smog, desert, and coastal locations. Flowering develops most fully from June to October, but some bloom is evident all year. Without corrective pruning for shapeliness, these plants become loose, open, and woody; to forestall this condition, cut back by half all older wood which has already flowered. If required, reduce the plants to ground-level stubs; they regrow quickly and easily. Regular watering improves flowering, but curtail irrigation by autumn to allow new stems to become woody before winter dormancy. Pull off—do not cut—any unwanted basal suckering, making certain your hands are protected from the poisonous milky sap.

Rapid-growing and billowy in outline, this much branched shrub needs the fullest sunlight to flower well. The single or double five-petaled, satiny, tubular, occasionally scented blossoming appears conspicuously as terminal clusterings 2 to 3 inches wide in yellow, white, and rose-pink to purplish red as the basic wild forms. Single-flowered types are much preferred since double forms often retain their faded blooms in place. Linear, dark green or gray-green, leathery leaves have prominent midveins and can stretch to 10 inches in length. All grow best in moist, well-drained, humusy soil but are plagued by a host of insect pests and diseases. Its cultivar list is especially large today; listed below is only a brief overview of some popular kinds.

CULTIVAR: 'Alba' has pure white flowering.

CULTIVAR: 'Atropurpureum' carries purple-red blossoms.

CULTIVAR: 'Hawaii' is salmon-pink with a yellow throat.

CULTIVAR: 'Isle of Capri' sports light yellow bloom.

CULTIVAR: 'Jannoch' displays bright red flowers.

CULTIVAR: 'Monsieur Belaguier' performs exceptionally with masses of light pink flowering.

CULTIVAR: 'Mrs. F. Roeding' has abundant double blooms of salmon-orange on a dwarfed, bushy plant.

CULTIVAR: 'Mrs. Swanson' shows double pink flowering.

CULTIVAR: 'Professor Durand' has clear but pale yellow blossoms.

CULTIVAR: 'Professor Martin' produces bright red flowering.

CULTIVAR: 'Sister Agnes' carries larger, pure white blooms.

OSMANTHUS (SIPHONOSMANTHUS) (devilweed, devil wood, sweet olive)   *Oleaceae* (olive) family

Although this genus is mostly native to eastern Asia, a few species exist in New Caledonia, Hawaii, and North America as well. In total, between thirty and forty species of slow-growing but long-lived shrubs and trees make up the membership here; all are easy to grow and accept neglect once established. Long valued for their shapeliness and attractive foliage, these plants are favored for their cut branches as fragrant indoor decoration. Occasionally confused with holly *(Ilex)* by leaf appearance, *Osmanthus* foliage is always set oppositely, while the foliage of holly is consistently alternate. Leaves are either entire or toothed and lanceolate. Attractively fragrant for the most part, the tiny, bell-shaped, four-petaled, white to creamy white (rarely yellow) blossoms are generally clustered at the leaf axils in abundant fashion. Some plants are dioecious (separated sexes), while others are monoecious (separated sexes but on the same plant). The fruit is a blue-toned drupe (like a plum) very similar to a small olive, which is a close relative. Provide a reasonably fertile, well-drained, slightly acid moist soil in full sun to light shading, especially if the soil tends to remain dry) and topdress annually in the spring with decayed compost for improved growth and better flowering. Pests and diseases are only occasionally troublesome.

Osmanthus x fortunei   (no common name)
Zones 8 (warm) to 10   6′ to 30′ high x 6′ to 15′ wide   Light shade

A vigorous and dense male hybrid of *fragrans* and *heterophyllus*, the shrub originated in Japan and was introduced during 1856. It blooms attractively and fragrantly from September to November with axillary clusterings of ¼-inch white flowers on ⅜-inch stalks. No fruit is possible. The broadly oval foliage is 2½ inches long and up to 2 inches wide with ten to twelve sharp teeth on each margin. These leaves are thick and leathery with dark, polished surfaces and conspicuous topside veining. It grows well in acid to neutral soil of any texture but requires consistent moisture. A few cultivars are known.

CULTIVAR: 'Aurea' has yellow-toned leaves.

CULTIVAR: 'San Jose' grows intensively erect and dense to 20 feet with a 10-foot width; the cream to orange flowers develop by October.

Osmanthus fragrans (Olea fragrans) (fragrant olive, sweet olive, tea olive)

Zones 9 and 10   6′ to 30′ high x 6′ to 15′ wide   Light shade

Osmanthus fragrans

Often blooming twice yearly in June and September (but only during the winter months in Florida), this species has creamy white to yellow ¼-inch flowers with an enticing and intense fragrance clustered in the leaf axils. Behaving as either a large shrub or a small tree with a massive trunk, the plant is native to both China and Japan; it came into culture by 1771. In China today, tea leaves are often scented with these dried blossoms to create a special brew. Not tolerant to shoreline salt spray, it has no special need for more than an average moist soil out of bright sunlight. The foliage is entirely restricted to the tip ends of twigs, and these few leaves are oval, deep green, and entire (or just finely toothed); their length can approach 4 inches with half that width, and they show some noticeable veining. Not hampered by many difficulties, this shrub has occasional bouts with scale insects and root rot disease. The variety *aurantiacus* carries less fragrance from yellowish orange bloom, and its foliage is almost toothless.

Osmanthus heterophyllus (aquifolium) (ilicifolium) (Olea aquifolium) (Olea ilicifolia) (holly olive, Chinese holly, false holly)

Zones 7 to 10   6′ to 20′ high x 6′ to 10′ wide   Light shade

Possessing a confused identity for many decades, this species is slow-growing and produces attractively shiny foliage to make interesting hedges. Dense, bushy, and rounded in outline, it is native to Japan and Taiwan and came into cultivation by 1856 through Thomas Lobb, a noted collector. The species name means 'having leaves of diverse forms," and the plant justifies that label with its middle to dark green lustrous oval foliage up to 2½ inches long and about half as wide. These thick leaves vary considerably in size and shape on any one plant and have three to five large spines on each margin, much resembling *Ilex* (holly) in general appearance. The topmost foliage on the plant, however, is generally spineless; the lowest leaves are notably spined, promoting the notion that nature intended a built-in defense against foraging cattle that had an interest in eating the plant. Sweetly scented, pure white, ⅛-inch tubular flowers appear from September to November clustered at the leaf axils in generous displays up to 1 inch wide. Dark blue fruit ½ inch long later develops. Provide a moist, well-drained location in dappled light for good performance. A sizable list of cultivars is available.

CULTIVAR: 'Aureus' carries foliage edged in deep yellow.

CULTIVAR: 'Myrtifolius' has narrow spineless leaves (except at the very tip) between 1 inch and 1¾ inches long. It develops slowly with a compact and spreading habit.

CULTIVAR: 'Gulftide' produces a dense form with strongly spined twisted foliage.

CULTIVAR: 'Purpureus' ('Purpurascens') is hardier than the parent and shows purplish black new foliage that matures green but with a purple-toned cast.

CULTIVAR: 'Rotundifolius' performs slowly to create a compact outline with short, thick, black-green, leathery, spineless leaves between 1 inch and 1½ inches long that are occasionally twisted.

CULTIVAR: 'Variegatus' ('Argenteo-marginatus') has foliage bordered with creamy white.

PHOTINIA (photinia)   *Rosaceae* (rose) family

The name is from the Greek *photeinos*, meaning "shining," which is a standard feature of the young foliage. Related closely to hawthorn *(Crataegus)*, this genus is without thorns. Forty species of deciduous and evergreen shrubs or small trees form the group, and all are native to southern and eastern Asia; however, these are not tropical plants and behave best where the winters are chilly and the soil fertile. Easy to grow well, they require only a deep, average, well-drained site in sun to light shading away from excessive wind. Useful as hedges and screens, they provide more visual accent from their strikingly red or bronze new growth when placed in direct contrast with other foliage types, especially those having gray-green leaves. Alternate, simple, short-petioled, usually toothed shiny leaves emerge noticeably colored and later become deep green. The mostly white to creamy white small flowers are five-petaled and appear during spring in crowded terminal clusters between 4 and 6 inches wide. Round, berrylike pome fruit (similar to an apple in construction) is most often red. Mildew is a constant potential source of foliage disfigurement, but insects are generally not troublesome.

Photinia x fraseri   (no common name)

Zones 8 to 10   20′ high x 10′ wide   Sun to light shade

A stimulating visual accent as a hedge or containerized plant, this shrub may also be espaliered successfully, but not on south or west walls in areas with consistently high summertime temperatures. Vigorous, upright, bushy, and mounded, it can become a small tree naturally or with pruning adjustments. It is more mildew-resistant than other species. The oval, leathery, dark, glossy green, attractive foliage enlarges to about 3 inches, and the new growth is brightly copper-colored. White clustered flowers are bearded inside and bloom in spring. The red fruiting is not overly conspicuous, however; the vividly colorful new foliage is the main attraction. A few cultivars are available.

CULTIVAR: 'Birmingham' originated in Alabama and has abruptly pointed foliage of bright copper-red when new.

CULTIVAR: 'Red Robin' carries sharply toothed, glossy green mature leaves and brilliantly red new growth over long periods in spring; it grows only 7 feet tall.

CULTIVAR: 'Robusta' has thick, leathery foliage, greater hardiness, and vigorous growth to 9 feet. New leaves and stems emerge as vivid copper-red.

Photinia serrulata   (Chinese photinia)

Zones 7 to 10   15′ to 30′ high x 10′ to 15′ wide   Sun

Although it may develop as a treelike form in some warm areas, this plant is generally shrubby with rank, upright growth and heavy twigs that remain bare at the base. Useful as a tall frost-resistant screen or hedge showing coarse foliage, it offers a small bonus when the lower, older leaves turn red before dropping off. Although very tolerant of limed soils, it is intolerant of salt spray locations. Oblong, somewhat leathery, saw-toothed, dark green leaves are yellow-green beneath and can extend to 8 inches in length with a width between 1½ and 3½ inches. The flat clusters of white ¼-inch flowers bloom in May and vary between 4 and 6 inches across; the globose ¼-inch red fruiting is highly desired by birds. Fire blight, mites, scales, and caterpillars are often bothersome, but not at the same time. Its cultivar 'Aculeata' ('Lineata') carries foliage with longer teeth and has new growth of bright coppery red.

PIERIS (AMPELOTHAMNUS) (ARCTERICA) (fetterbush, andromeda)   *Ericaceae* (heath) family

Eight species of dense-growing shrubs or small trees make up this genus; they exist natively in eastern Asia, the Himalayas, and North America. Several have attractive new growth colored in red or copper in the spring. Of interest year-round for their slow, well-mannered habits, these plants are named for the *Pierides* ("muses") of Greek mythology. All enjoy a moist, acid, humusy, well-drained soil out of strong winds and benefit from having a thick mulch over the shallow roots. The alternate (rarely opposite) foliage sometimes develops in whorls with simple, leathery, smooth-edged leaves. The white, terminal or axillary, pitcher-shaped blossoms often provide a heady fragrance. Budding from the previous summer remains exposed and conspicuous in winter months but can frequently suffer damage in the colder areas of its range. The fruit develops as five-valved capsules with little decorative value. While pests and diseases are an infrequent problem, infestations of red spider mites often disfigure new growth in climates with hot, humid, and dry summers. Late frost can curtail emerging growth seriously. Even with these handicaps, *Pieris* remains consistently popular for landscape developments.

Pieris floribunda (Andromeda floribunda) (fetterbush, mountain andromeda, mountain pieris)

Zones 4 to 9   2' to 6' high x 4' to 6' wide   Sun to semishade

Natively found in the Allegheny Mountains from Virginia to Georgia, this is a coarse-textured, slow-growing, mounded shrub that has been in cultivation since 1800. It appears to adapt well only from these mountains toward the coast in the eastern United States and from Vancouver, British Columbia, south to the coastline of mid-California in the western section. Desirable for naturalizing in moist woodlots or as a border specimen, the plant is clothed to the ground with stiff and somewhat brittle stems and carries oblong, pointed, slightly roughened, leathery foliage with dull, deep green leaves up to 3½ inches long. The new growth is bronze-green. Terminal, greenish winter budding is upright and rigid with up to 2 inches of projection; the mid-April flowering develops as waxy, urn-shaped, ¼-inch white florets without much scent on elongated stalks nearly 5 inches long. Provide a consistently moist, acid, peaty, sandy soil in a location where the plant is protected from cold, dry winter winds and can receive full sun or partial shading; it will accept greater shading but at the expense of full flowering. Difficult to establish because of its stringy root system, this shrub suffers no diseases or insect pests of consequence. Fertilizing is rarely needed to maintain satisfactory growth. The cultivar 'Brouwer's Beauty' is a cross between *floribunda* and *japonica* with a dense, compact habit.

Pieris floribunda winter flower buds

Pieris floribunda flowers

Pieris japonica cv. 'Variegata'

Pieris japonica (Andromeda japonica) (Japanese andromeda, lily of the valley bush)

Zones 6 to 9   10′ to 30′ high x 6′ to 8′ wide   Semishade

This plant's foliage is held in tiers on dense clusters of pale green twigs. Slow-growing and upright to a usual height of only 10 feet in the United States, this species dislikes excessive summertime heat and cold winter winds. Desirable as a border item or containerized, it shows conspicuous drooping strings of flower buds that often stay red-toned through the autumn and winter months. These enlarge for bloom by late April into May as ¼-inch, white, waxy florets on up to 6-inch-long panicles that become sweetly scented blooms with the fragrance of ripe grapes; bees are especially fond of the nectar. The narrowly lanceolate, shiny, smooth, dark green foliage can be up to 3 inches long with the margins fringed by bristly hairs; the new leaves are often coppery. Provide a moist, humusy, acid location in partial shading. If kept very moist consistently, this plant will adjust to full sun, but it dislikes great heat and strong winds. Red spider mites are troublesome to new foliage and can quickly discolor the leaves noticeably, distracting from their high landscape value. Many cultivars are currently in nurseries.

CULTIVAR: 'Bert Chandler' is a dwarfed, tender form with striking foliage which emerges salmon-pink, changes to cream and then to white, and finally settles into green for the balance of its year. It requires shading and wind protection.

CULTIVAR: 'Bonsai' has a very dwarfed, compact silhouette.

CULTIVAR: 'Compacta' develops a low, compact shape.

CULTIVAR: 'Crispa' carries leaves with wavy margins.

CULTIVAR: 'Flamingo' sports deep pink flowering.

CULTIVAR: 'Pygmaea' rarely flowers; it has a diminutive, bushy, sluggish nature with tiny leaves and a total appearance very unlike that of any other *Pieris*.

CULTIVAR: 'Scarlet O'Hara' spreads widely and carries new growth in glowing scarlet.

CULTIVAR: 'Variegata' is slow-growing to a 3-foot height but is tender and requires protection. The narrow foliage is flushed in pink when young, and these leaves later become attractively variegated in creamy white. The conspicuous flowering is produced more compactly.

Pieris taiwanensis (no common name)

Zones 7 to 9   4′ to 10′ high x 4′ to 6′ wide   Semishade

Resembling *japonica* in its general form, this is an erect, compact shrub from Taiwan that seldom grows taller than 6 feet in the United States, where it was introduced by Ernest Wilson in 1918. The smooth stems carry oval, dull green leaves up to 5 inches long with teeth in the upper portions. New growth emerges bronze to bronze-red, and the pure white, erect, elongated panicles of ¼-inch nodding flowers appear by late April. It needs an acid, moist, well-drained soil enriched with humus or peat as well as reduced sunlight. The cultivar 'Crispa' has slower growth with curled or wavy leaves plus flowering in very loose clusters developing all over the plant outline; the new growth is coppery.

PITTOSPORUM (pittosporum) *Pittosporaceae*
(pittosporum) family

Native to warm temperature, tropical or subtropical areas from Australia to Hawaii—twenty-six species exist only in New Zealand—as well as to parts of Africa, this genus of 100 trees or shrubs is cultivated for the neat habits and enjoyable foliage, flowers, and fruiting of its members. All genera in this family are dependable at shoreside locations, and some are especially valued as hedges (if kept unsheared and only hand-pruned) or as container specimens. Adapting well to any average, well-drained soil— even a dryish one since these are drought-tolerant plants—they prefer consistent moisture to achieve their best appearance. The simple alternate or occasionally whorled foliage is frequently clustered only at the branch tips. The flowering is dioecious and develops as small five-petaled blooms either solitary or clustered; several species are attractively fragrant. The fruit forms as spherical, yellow-toned, woody or leathery capsules with noticeably sticky seeds. The name is derived from the Greek *pitta*, meaning "pitch," and *spora*, meaning "seeds"; it refers to the resinous coating around the mature seed coats. Aphids, scales, and sooty mold are the chief nuisances.

Pittosporum crasifolium (karo)

Zones 8 to 10   10' to 25' high x 6' to 12' wide   Sun to light shade

Well adapted as a desirable screen or wind shelter at shoreline locations, this tall shrub (or small tree) from New Zealand is indifferent to soil conditions and forms a dense, upright form. The oval, thick, leathery, toothless leaves are up to 3 inches long with rounded tips and color deep green above with russet-felted or white-hairy undersides. When young, both the new stems and the new leaf surfaces are very hairy. The matured bark becomes a smooth dark brown. The dark red to deep purple, sweetly scented, ½-inch-long flowers are up to 2 inches wide and develop in terminal clusterings. Male plants have ten blossoms per cluster, while females carry flowering either singly or in pairs. Globose, gray, hairy fruit is sizable at up to 1½ inches long with black, shiny seeds embedded in a sticky matrix. The slow-growing cultivar 'Variegatum' shows less hardiness and produces foliage nicely margined in creamy white.

Pittosporum tobira (Japanese pittosporum, Australian laurel, mock orange)

Zones 8 to 10   6' to 12' high x 4' to 5' wide   Sun to light shade

A highly adaptable plant accepting heat and drought plus seaside wind and salt spray, this shrub prefers not to be sheared or trimmed mechanically for hedges. Hand-pinch only for greater bushiness or reduced height; obviously, this training has to be started while the plants are still young. Normally a sun lover, it also is amenable to almost dense shade on northern exposures. A dense, broad, and symmetrical shrub or small tree from China and Japan, this slow-growing species came into cultivation by 1804 and is at its best on a fertile, acid, humusy site. Blunt-tipped, oblong, bright green, lustrous leaves are thick and leathery and grow up to 3½ inches long and half as broad with rolled-under edges. This foliage is set in whorls clustered at the twig ends and produces a very disagreeable odor when crushed, making tip pruning an interesting challenge. This leaf disappointment is made up for by the highly satisfactory fragrance of the blossoms, which are white to yellow and ½ inch long; they appear in showy terminal clusters from April into July, depending

Pittosporum tobira cv. 'Variegata'

on the location. The odor is similar to that of orange blossom. The globose, densely hairy, ½-inch-wide fruit first colors green and then matures as brown without much landscape value; it splits to reveal orange seeds, and then the visual impact improves. The popular cultivar 'Variegata' carries gray-green leaves with irregular, creamy white margins and needs more sun than the parent to keep its full coloring value.

PRUNUS (LAUROCERASUS) (no one common name)   Rosaceae (rose) family

This genus name is an ancient Latin one for "plum." The group has major horticultural importance since it now includes all the stone fruits of peach, plum, apricot, cherry, almond, nectarine, and cherry laurel. *Prunus* can designate any of them correctly, but the species name identifies no particular fruiting habit; the common name, of course, proves invaluable. Four hundred species of deciduous and evergreen trees or shrubs are included in this genus, and for our purposes here, only shrubs with persistently evergreen foliage are considered (shrubs that lose their leaves are listed in the "Deciduous Shrubs" division). The leaves are alternate, simple, and mostly toothed. The plants prevail in the temperate climate zones, mostly in the northern hemisphere, and grow well on almost any soil with full sun; they are, however, intolerant of polluted air. While its flowering is similarly colored white or pink, *Prunus* is botanically distinguished from *Malus* (apple, crabapple) and *Pyrus* (pear) by having only one flower pistil to their five. The fruiting also differs by being a drupe with a fleshy outer layer surrounding a hard stone or pit that contains the true seed. Many well-known drupe fruits are edible. The list of diseases and pests afflicting this genus is large (as is often true with rose family members), but not all are prevalent in each growing area, nor are they all totally destructive. Corrective spray programs, however, are recommended on an annual basis for the best results. (Consult the "Deciduous Shrubs" division for additional choices.)

Prunus ilicifolia (Laurocerasus ilicifolia)   (holly-leaved cherry, evergreen cherry, wild cherry, mountain holly, islay)

Zones 8 to 10   3′ to 25′ high x 6′ to 12′ wide   Sun

A slow-growing, dense, compact shrub or small tree, this species suckers continually to create a thicket of stems in a short time and serves admirably as a solid screen or backdrop. Although it accepts drought, alkaline soil, and abuse well, it actually prefers a dry, well-drained, acid soil. Native from California to the northern part of the Baja peninsula of Mexico, this shrub produces shiny, leathery, oval to roundish, coarsely spined, wavy, medium green leaves between 1 and 2 inches long and half as broad. Few to many ¼-inch-wide white flowers appear in terminal spikes up to 2 inches tall from March to May. Its dark red to purple, ovoid, ½-inch fruit ripens in October and is attractively sweet. Diseases and insect nuisances are not overly common.

Prunus laurocerasus (Laurocerasus officinale) (cherry laurel, English laurel)

Zones 7 to 9   8' to 18' high x 10' to 25' wide   Semishade

Prunus laurocerasus cv. 'Schipkaensis'

Vigorous, wide-spreading, and a heavy feeder, this is a tall ground-covering shrub that also can serve as a broad, dense screen. Although hardy into the warm side of zone 6, it very often has winter-burned foliage there and thus loses much of its evergreen appeal. Intolerant of cold, dry winds or shallow and chalky soils, it accepts salt air locations well. The natural preference is for a moist, well-drained, humusy site that is kept dry in late summer to encourage hardening off of the new stems before winter sets in. Twice-yearly fertilizing in both early spring and early summer proves beneficial for its fullest growth and appearance. The oblong, slightly toothed, dark green, leathery, shiny foliage is sharp-pointed and between 2 and 7 inches long on ½-inch green petioles. During the seventeenth century such leaves were dried to add an almond flavor to foods. The May flowering comes as ⅓-inch, creamy white scented flowers held in upright axillary spikes between 2 and 4 inches long; its ½-inch, oval, reddish fruit matures as dark purple. Many cultivars of differing growth habits and leaf shapes abound today, and the following list is just a sampling.

CULTIVAR: 'Angustifolia' has ascending branches and narrower leaves.

CULTIVAR: 'Caucasica' is a vigorous form with an upright habit and very narrow foliage.

CULTIVAR: 'Latifolia' contributes a tall, vigorous, large-leaved outline.

CULTIVAR: 'Magnoliifolia' is the largest-leaved of all with foliage up to 12 inches long and 4 inches wide.

CULTIVAR: 'Reynvaanii' has a slow-growing compact habit and upright branching.

CULTIVAR: 'Rotundifolia' is bushy and makes an attractive hedge with leaves half as broad as they are long.

CULTIVAR: 'Schipkaensis' has proved to be a dependably hardy form since its introduction in 1888. It has narrow leaves and a wide-spreading shape, and it flowers freely.

CULTIVAR: 'Serbica' shows wrinkled foliage and a more upright silhouette than cv. 'Schipkaensis'.

CULTIVAR: 'Zabeliana' makes an exceptional groundcover with its low horizontal form and 2- to 3-inch willowlike leaves; it is also free-flowering.

PYRACANTHA (fire thorn)   Rosaceae (rose) family

Sprawling, rampant, impenetrable as a thorny barrier, and seasonally colorful in its heavy fruiting clusters, the fire thorn is much sought after for landscape purposes, especially as a wall espalier in sun. The alternate, short-stalked, usually toothed leaves have the drawback of often dehydrating partially or fully in the winter winds of cold growing areas, and the plants are not adaptable to high-altitude sites where severe frost is a regular occurrence. Where the foliage remains in good condition, however, these shrubs offer great year-round appeal, especially since they are tolerant to air pollution, to heat (but not dune sites), to neglect, to all exposures, and to reasonably low temperatures. Nevertheless, plants in areas with consistently high humidity or continual fog are subject to many disease problems. None transplants well if large or field grown; containerized small plants are usually the only reliable source for starting new installations, and an average-fertility, well-drained soil is sufficient for their needs. Lace bugs, spider mites, and fire blight are often important afflictions throughout the growing range.

This genus is native to southeastern Europe and Asia. It includes six species of hardy or tender, usually thorny shrubs closely allied to *Cotoneaster* and *Crataegus* (hawthorn); it is seperated either by its thorns or toothed foliage. White five-petaled flowers display twenty stamens along with a strong scent (much like *Crataegus*) by midspring; these flowers are crowded into clusters appearing on second-year wood and usually appear on the short side-spur growth of main stems. The late summer clusterings of fruit are small, showy, and persistent pomes (like an apple in construction) of orange, yellow-orange, or deep red which birds relish. Its name is from the Greek *pyr*, meaning "fire," and *akantha*, meaning "thorn."

Pyracantha atalantiodes (gibbsii)   (no common name)

Zones 7 to 9   15′ high x 15′ wide   Sun

Originally this species was named out of respect for the Honorable Vicary Gibbs, who raised the plant successfully in Aldenham, England; however, the plant later was discovered to have been already identified elsewhere under another name and thus had to be reclassified. A native inhabitant of China, it was first located there in 1880 by General Mesny, but it did not come into cultivation until Ernest Wilson collected it in 1907. Robust, erect, and rigid-stemmed, it is one of the least thorny species. The oval, mostly entire, dark, glossy leaves are between 1 inch and 3 inches long and have only limited evergreen qualities during winter in the northern limits of the hardiness range (remember that plant survival does not assure attractive foliage even if the roots and stems remain alive). The white blossom clusters in mid-May are about 1½ inches across and produce scarlet to bright crimson, ⁵⁄₁₆-inch-wide, oval fruiting that persists much longer in good condition than that of *coccinea*, the popular favorite. Diseases and insect pests are not overly troublesome. Its cultivar 'Aurea' carries richly yellow fruiting, while 'Bakeri' has fruit that is a deeper shade of red.

Pyracantha coccinea cv. 'Lalandei'

Pyracantha coccinea   (scarlet fire thorn)

Zones 6 (warm) to 9   6′ high x 10′ wide   Sun

Abundantly dense with foliage, this is a noteworthy shrub that is probably the best species choice for espaliering on walls, especially its more notable cultivars. Unfortunately, in the cold limits of its growth range, the thin leaves often dry out partially or completely and remain in place unattractively in the last part of the winter months. The foliage is glossy, lanceolate to 1½ inches long, finely toothed, and deep green; it appears on new stems covered in gray hairs. The mid-May, white, ⁵⁄₁₆-inch flowers also have hairy stalks and come in clusters about 1½ inches wide. The fruiting usually develops all along the slender branches as dense bunches of bright scarlet, ¼-inch, berrylike pomes. Its cultivar list is far too extensive to give in detail here, but one of the most enduringly popular ones—'Lalandei'—came from Monsieur Lalande of Angers, France, in 1874 as an erect, vigorous, hardy sort with dark, shiny leaves and somewhat orange-red prolific fruiting. It is still the most sought-after cultivar.

Pyracantha fortuneana (crenato-serrata) (yunnanensis) (no common name)

Zones 7 to 9   12′ high x 12′ wide   Sun

Native to China and introduced here during 1906, this species is similar to *atalantiodes* but differs in having leaves with more teeth and in its increased number of thorns. The foliage develops deep green above with lighter undersides, is broadest above the middle, and can be up to 1½ inches long. White flower clusters appear in mid-May and become masses of ¼-inch, bright coral-red summer fruit that can endure into the following spring if not eaten by birds or other wildlife. The cultivar 'Graberi' shows one of the best hybrid improvements with its strong-growing, graceful branching and 9-foot height; the fruit is richly red. Yellow fruit distinguishes the cultivar 'Knap Hill Yellow'. None of these is especially damaged by diseases or insects on a regular basis.

Pyracantha koidzumii (formosana) (no common name)

Zones 7 to 9   10′ to 12′ high x 8′ to 10′ wide   Sun

Dense and much branched, this native of Taiwan is very popular today in the southeastern United States. It produces reddish and hairy young twigs that later become smooth and purplish. The lanceolate, entire, 1- to 2-inch-long leaves are rounded at the base and come clustered at the ends of twigs. Its flowers come in hairy clusterings during mid-May; the flattened, orange-scarlet, ¼-inch fruit hangs in loose bunches by late summer. The available cultivars fill a long list; here are a few with special merit.

CULTIVAR: 'San Jose' develops wide-spreading branches and carries typical flowers and fruit.

CULTIVAR: 'Santa Cruz' is prostrate to 3 feet tall and shows bright red fruiting.

CULTIVAR: 'Victory' maintains a vigorous habit to a 7-foot height with large deep green foliage and massive clusters of dark red fruiting.

RHODODENDRON (rhododendron, azalea)   *Ericaceae* (heath) family

Here is one of the most important and diverse groups of ornamental plants in existence; its flowering offers far more color value than that of any other plant when massed together. Over 800 species of deciduous, evergreen, and semievergreen shrubs (rarely trees) exist in this complex genus; such a diversity of material is remarkable from only one source. All are native to the temperate zones of the northern hemisphere and grow most abundantly in the Himalayas, southeastern Asia, and the mountains of the Federation of Malaysia; none has been found in either South America or Africa. Expeditions of discovery to these productive areas are pursued continually by many botanists and nurserymen with the end result that even more species are enlarging the total constantly. No color in nature's palette is now omitted from available rhododendron hues, although each sort does not necessarily have worldwide hardiness or even great attractiveness for landscape use. Couple the natural discoveries with the extensive hybridization programs that are now ongoing, and the full extent of rhododendron types will number in the many thousands. Since azalea is now botanically included in this vast grouping, the total popular appeal of the rhododendron genus will remain unchallenged.

The scientific name is derived directly from the Greek words *rhodo*, meaning "rose," and *dendron*, meaning "tree," since these plants were originally seen as tall specimens with deep pink blossoms. All normally have their prime bloom from late spring to early summer and carry simple, alternate, mostly smooth-edged leaves that come crowded toward the ends of the stems by the end of the current annual expansion. Evergreen types tend to curl their foliage inward to ward off dehydration when the air temperature drops below 30 degrees. The flowering appears from large terminal budding set directly above the new stem buds, and each blossom in the cluster has five petals. The fruit is a woody capsule with no decorative value on most forms; though the fruit is often removed after flowering for general neatness, such work is hardly critical to the well-being of the plant. The value of seed removal lies in the redirection of energy into new flower bud formation sooner, but the effort will be wasted if the capsule has already split and the seed dispersed.

Preferring shelter from strong, cold winds as well as shade from continuous hot sunlight, rhododendrons need a moist, fertile, porous, humusy soil for the best performance. Avoid both clay and limestone sites. Remarkably tolerant of air pollution and simple to transplant because of the shallow rooting, they are naturally adapted to the high shade of companion deep-rooted trees and shrubs which also may act as windbreaks. None enjoys competitive, invasive rooting from robustly vigorous adjacent plantings, and few grow readily in the north-central portions of the United States as a result of the sudden weather extremes in summer and winter plus the alkalinity of much of that soil. Pests and diseases generally are manageable.

Correctly separating the many species is highly complex, and because so much already has been published by authorities on this subject, it seems unwarranted to explore the full intricacies here. In general, those we think of as rhododendron types are evergreen with bell-shaped flowering, while the azalea forms are mostly deciduous and carry trumpetlike blossoming. These major types are represented here and in the "Deciduous Shrubs" division.

Rhododendron carolinianum

Rhododendron carolinianum album and *Paeonia suffruticosa*

Rhododendron carolinianum   (Carolina rhododendron)

Zones 6 to 8   6′ high x 7′ wide   Light shade

Compact, thickly branched with a rounded habit, and free-flowering annually, this species from the higher slopes of the Blue Ridge Mountains of North Carolina has colorful blossoming and dependable hardiness. Thought to be only a variety of *minus* until Alfred Rehder reclassified it during 1912, it differs by flowering much earlier and by carrying flat, broader leaves. In cultivation since 1815, the shrub has oval, 1½- to 3-inch, thin, sharp-pointed, semiglossy leaves which are dark green and smooth above with rust-colored scaly undersides. It is the first rhododendron to curl its foliage when the temperature goes below 30 degrees. The pale, rose-purple, funnelform blossoms flower by early May, are 1½ inches wide, and arrive in terminal groups of five to ten. Many times the budding develops in clusters, adding to its showiness. Variations are somewhat complicated to keep clearly separated, but the following list gives the current designations.

CULTIVAR: 'Album' ('White Carolinianum') has white to pinkish flowering and is not identical with the variety *album*.

VARIETY: *album* carries pure white blossoming with a yellow-green blotch and lighter green, more pointed foliage than the parent. It comes naturally true from seed and appears to need slightly more shading to flower well.

Despite the forced brevity in describing the credentials of all evergreen rhododendron here, the following valuable *carolinianum* hybrids deserve mention.

CULTIVAR: 'Dora Amateis' is a semidwarfed form hardy to the warm parts of zone 6 which displays large white blossoming with a noticeable gold blotch in the upper portion of each flower. Slow-growing and moundlike, it dislikes full sun and cold winds, and it blooms by early May. Its narrow, 2-inch, medium green leaves usually have downturned edges. Known since the 1930s, it develops little seed.

CULTIVAR: 'PJM' was named for Peter John Mezitt of Weston Nurseries, Hopkinton, Massachusetts. It carries remarkable hardiness to the lower limits of zone 5, and its richly lavender bloom often appears by mid-April. Its blunt-ended oblong leaves become shiny, bronze, and undamaged by winter. Sun loving and reasonably wind-tolerant, this hardy plant commendably endures summer drought in good condition; it rarely sets seed and therefore can be counted on for profuse annual flowering. Compact and dense, it will accept modest shading, but with a loss of compactness and with less bloom. The height is about 6 feet with a similar spread. Several derivations of it are currently being tested for similar hardiness and quality foliage, especially seedlings with pink-toned flowering.

Rhododendron carolinianum cv. 'Dora Amateis'

Rhododendron carolinianum cv. 'PJM'

Rhododendron catawbiense (Catawba rhododendron, mountain rosebay, purple laurel)

Zones 5 to 8   10′ to 20′ high x 10′ to 15′ wide   Light shade

This large-scaled species is the primary source of hardy cultivars suitable for the northeastern United States. Growing wild in extensive thickets on the mountains of West Virginia and Virginia south to Georgia and Alabama, it came into cultivation during 1809. It is distinguished by vigor, hardiness, wide leaves, and ease of cultivation. The oval, sharp-tipped foliage varies between 3 and 6 inches in length and is half as wide with smooth, shiny, deep green top surfaces and paler undersides. The showy flowering occurs in late May with lilac-purple to pale lilac-rose, broadly bell-shaped (to 2½ inches across) florets in large trusses. The only true variety appears to be *compactum*, but that has given rise to some cultivars as sturdily hardy as the parent; the Catawba name is officially part of the label to identify this direct relationship clearly.

Rhododendron catawbiense cv. 'Catawbiense Album'

VARIETY: *compactum* is dense, slow-growing, and dwarfed, with a 3-foot height and rosy lavender flowering.

CULTIVAR: 'Catawbiense Album' performs vigorously with wide-spreading upright branching; it is hardy to −25 degrees Fahrenheit. Glossy foliage and pale lilac budding that becomes white blossoming distinguish it.

CULTIVAR: 'Catawbiense Boursault' grows upright with rosy lilac flowering. It also is durable to −25 degrees Fahrenheit.

CULTIVAR: 'Catawbiense Grandiflorum' carries semiglossy leaves on a wide, upright silhouette; the flowers are lilac-colored. It does well even at −25 degrees Fahrenheit.

Hybridization of the excellent foliage of *catawbiense* with the clearer flower colorings from other parents resulted in the *Catawbiense hybrids*, an

Rhododendron catawbiense cultivars

Rhododendron catawbiense cv. 'Chionoides'

"ironclad" group of elegant performers continuously in favor for landscape work. The following selections represent only a fraction of the available total.

CULTIVAR: 'Album Elegans' produces white flowering on a tall form in June. It is hardy to −20 degrees Fahrenheit.

CULTIVAR: 'America' develops dark red blossoms on a medium-sized plant in late May with hardiness to −25 degrees Fahrenheit.

CULTIVAR: 'Boule de Neige' blooms pure white in early May on a slow-growing, mounded form hardy to −25 degrees Fahrenheit.

CULTIVAR: 'Caractacus' carries red flowering during early June on a medium-sized plant hardy to −25 degrees Fahrenheit.

CULTIVAR: 'Charles Dickens' flowers in late May in red on a medium-height shrub hardy to −25 degrees Fahrenheit.

CULTIVAR: 'Ignatius Sargent' also has red flowering in late May on a medium-sized plant hardy to −25 degrees Fahrenheit.

CULTIVAR: 'Lady Armstrong' shows pink flowering by late May on a medium-growing form hardy to −20 degrees Fahrenheit.

CULTIVAR: 'Lee's Dark Purple' is highly adaptable to the southwestern United States. It produces purple flowers on a tall plant by late May; hardiness is only to −15 degrees Fahrenheit.

CULTIVAR: 'Mrs. Charles S. Sargent' has rose-colored blossoms in late May on a tall silhouette; it is hardy to −25 degrees Fahrenheit.

CULTIVAR: 'Mrs. P. den Ouden' flowers in early May on a low to medium, compact plant with red blooms; hardiness is to −15 degrees Fahrenheit.

CULTIVAR: 'Nova Zembla' has remarkable adaptability and blooms red during early May on a medium-sized plant hardy to −20 degrees Fahrenheit.

CULTIVAR: 'Parsons Gloriosum' displays pink flowers in late May, with hardiness to −25 degrees Fahrenheit.

CULTIVAR: 'Roseum Elegans' shows lavender-pink blossoming by late May, with hardiness to −25 degrees Fahrenheit.

CULTIVAR: 'Roseum Superbum' also flowers in late May but with a pink bloom; it is less hardy at −20 degrees Fahrenheit.

Rhododendron cv. 'Scintillation'

Rhododendron fortunei (Fortune's rhododendron)

Zones 6 (warm) to 9   12′ high x 12′ wide   Light shade

Most likely the first of the tender Chinese species to become successfully hardy in other parts of the globe, this special plant was found by Robert Fortune in eastern China in 1859. Slightly fragrant, lilac to pink, funnelform to bell-shaped flowers up to 3½ inches wide appear in loose trusses of six to twelve during early June. The oblong, smooth, pointed leaves are light green above and gray-toned beneath; they vary from 4 to 8 inches in length and become up to 2½ inches wide. In general, this species is the parent of many fast-growing cultivars with unusually subtle colorings and oversized flowering that are attractively suitable for the milder growing zones. Extensive hybridization in recent times has introduced a wealth of new variations, and a magnificent display of some 30,000 is open for public viewing during early to mid-June at Heritage Plantation in Sandwich, Massachusetts, to commemorate the painstaking efforts of C. O. Dexter to improve this shrub. One of the most popular cultivars today is 'Scintillation' with its light pink flowering appealingly blotched in gold during middle to late May. Hardy to −10 degrees Fahrenheit, it becomes a rounded, spreading, medium-sized plant carrying lustrous mid-green foliage. Additional, scented, showy, and hardier forms are bound to evolve in the near future.

Rhododendron griffithianum (no common name)

Zones 9 and 10   12′ high x 12′ wide   **Light shade**

Introduced from the Himalayas during 1849, this is a May-blooming, tender sort with slightly fragrant, bell-shaped, enormous individual flowering almost 6 inches wide in loose trusses of three to six colored white with faint green spots. The oblong, smooth foliage is also large and about 1 foot long; these leaves appear on stems with reddish brown peeling bark. In bloom the plant presents a dramatic statement, and further hybridizing of it seems likely.

Rhododendron indicum (Azalea indica) (Azalea macranthum) (Macranthum azalea)

Zones 7 to 9   6′ high x 6′ wide   **Light shade**

Do not confuse this plant with the "Indian Hybrid" azalea, a tender greenhouse form developed primarily for the florists' trade which can survive outdoors only in the very mildest growing areas, such as the warm southerly parts of the United States. This species is not native to India as the name suggests but belongs to southern Japan; it came into culture during 1883. The narrow lanceolate foliage grows up to 1½ inches long and is hairy on both sides with wavy margins; these leaves often convert to crimson or red-purple for winter. Single or paired funnel-shaped flowers are almost 2½ inches broad in red or scarlet by late June. A few cultivars are available.

CULTIVAR: 'Balsaminiflorum' is a dwarfed type with salmon-red double flowering.

CULTIVAR: 'Iveryanum' carries single, white, rose-flecked, showy blooms 3 inches across.

CULTIVAR: 'Laciniatum' sports brick red, deeply incised blossoms.

Rhododendron x laetivirens (wilsoni) (Wilson rhododendron)

Zones 5 to 8   4′ high x 8′ wide   **Light shade**

Neatly low, slow-growing, and mounded, this rhododendron is unusually hardy and differs from many others in that it does not curl its deep green, narrowly lanceolate leaves during cold winters. The foliage is between 2 and 3 inches long, sharp-pointed, and rusty brown on the undersides; these leaves do not lie flat at any time but bend upward along the midrib somewhat like those of *Kalmia*. A cross between *carolinianum* and *ferrugineum*, the plant blooms while the new seasonal growth is already extended, and thus its flowering display is often ineffective. The ½-inch, bell-shaped, deep rose or pale magenta florets appear in small sporadic clusters about 1½ inches wide during late May. Its silhouette and hardy foliage offer appeal for any landscape.

Rhododendron x laetivirens

Rhododendron macrophyllum (west coast rhododendron, California rosebay)

Zones 7 to 9   4' to 12' high x 4' to 12' wide   Light shade

This is the western United States counterpart to the eastern *catawbiense*. When it first was located in the coastal regions of the Pacific northwest, where it is native from British Columbia to central California, it was believed to be *maximum*. Still mislabeled as *californicum*, which now is an invalid name, this stout-stemmed shrub has oblong, smooth leaves between 3 and 8 inches long with deep green top surfaces and either pale green or rusty undersides; the foliage generally is found crowded beneath the flowers. The blossom buds are colored noticeably red, and the June-produced flowers become rose to rose-purple with yellow or brown spotting in a broadly bell-shaped, wavy-edged silhouette about 2½ inches wide. Its trusses are compact and showy with up to twenty blossoms each. It is the official flower of the state of Washington.

Rhododendron maximum

Rhododendron maximum

Rhododendron maximum (rosebay rhododendron, great laurel)

Zones 4 to 8   15' high x 20' wide   Semishade

Valued for its late June to early July flowering and great hardiness, this sizable shrub carries blooms not nearly as large or showy as those of *catawbiense* and only in a limited color range. Native from North Carolina to Georgia and Alabama, it was brought into cultivation by 1736 and shows a decided preference for greater shading than most other types in order to perform well. Serving attractively as a tall screen out of high-wind areas, it nevertheless will endure more weather abuse than almost any other native species. Tolerant to full shade but with reduced flowering, it occasionally can exceed the given height dimensions and stretch to 30 feet under ideal growing conditions. Small plants appear to adjust more quickly than larger, older ones after transplanting. The foliage is slender, oblong, up to 12 inches long, dark and semiglossy above with brown, fuzzy undersides. The blossoms are 1½ inches wide in compact heads about 4 inches across with rose-pink to purple-pink colorings at the edges and broad white centers spotted in olive green to orange-brown. Although they flower after the wide-spreading new growth is advanced, the blossoms still remain conspicuous. A natural white-flowered form and a purple-toned one are often carried by nurseries.

The low-growing, popular cultivar 'Cunninghamii' is a hybrid of *maximum* and *arboreum cinnamomeum* with white blossoms spotted in yellow during late May; the foliage is more olive-green but somewhat dull and shows brownish felt on the undersides. It has a troublesome tendency to bloom far out of sequence in especially warm, rainy autumns, partly ruining the full effect for the following May.

Rhododendron micranthum (Manchurian rhododendron)

Zones 6 to 8   6' high x 6' wide   Light shade

This plant has an interesting and distinct silhouette unlike most others since it is very open, leggy, wide-spreading, and tiny-leaved; it could well be sold as an evergreen *Aronia*, a deciduous shrub with a very similar appearance. Native to northern Korea, China, and Manchuria, it came into culture during 1901. It has narrowly lanceolate, crowded foliage up to 1½ inches long which is a semiglossy deep green in summer and turns slightly brown-toned for winter, showing rusty undersides. The June blossoming is totally unique for rhododendron with its ¼-inch, creamy white, bell-shaped florets set on dense and upright cylinders with noticeable displays of projecting stamens. Bees are especially fond of these flowers.

Rhododendron micranthum

Rhododendron minus (cuthbertii) (punctatum)
(Piedmont rhododendron)

Zones 5 to 8   12' high x 8' wide   Light shade

An inhabitant of the lower mountain elevations of Tennessee and North Carolina, this is the most rapid-growing of the native evergreen rhododendrons. It possesses a loose habit and narrowly oval leaves up to 5 inches long that are tapered at both ends. Deep green above with wavy margins, the foliage is brown-scaly beneath and assumes a brownish tone for winter. The early June flowering presents clustered blossoms with magenta-pink to bright magenta colorings and individual flowers up to 1½ inches wide which may or may not carry yellow spotting and a green throat. A dwarfed cultivar, 'Compacta', creates a lower, more densely foliaged silhouette with light pink June bloom. It often is confused with *carolinianum* when out of flower, but the wavy foliage helps separate them correctly.

Rhododendron mucronatum (ledifolia) (ledifolia alba) (rosmarinifolia) (snow azalea)

Zones 6 (warm) to 9   6' high x 6' wide   Light shade

Although this native of Japan has been cultivated since 1819, it never has been found growing wild; today it is considered a hybrid cross of *ripense* and *linearifolium macrosepalum*. Much branched, spreading, and dome-shaped, it produces fragrant, white, broadly funnelform blossoms up to 2 inches wide during mid-May. The dull, deep green leaves are of two sorts. The spring ones are finely toothed, lanceolate, and about 2¼ inches long, while the summertime ones are oblong, 1½ inches long, and hairy. A fair number of cultivars exist.

Rhododendron mucronatum

CULTIVAR: 'Amethystinum' carries white flowering flushed in lilac with faint spotting. The petals are joined together firmly.

CULTIVAR: 'Lilacinum' has soft purple-lavender flowers with pink blotches.

CULTIVAR: 'Maxwellii Album' shows white blossoms with a faintly greenish throat.

CULTIVAR: 'Narcissiflorum' is a double-flowered white form.

CULTIVAR: 'Noordtianum' displays larger blossoms of white with a noticeably green throat.

CULTIVAR: 'Plenum' has reddish violet double flowering.

CULTIVAR: 'Sekidera' develops white flowering spotted in crimson-rose.

Rhododendron obtusum cv. 'Rosebud'

Rhododendron obtusum (Kirishima azalea, Hiryu azalea)
Zones 7 to 9   3' high x 5' wide   Light shade

These showy plants grow successfully in the warm parts of zone 6 but do not remain reliably evergreen or bud-hardy there. Densely twiggy, dwarfed, wide-spreading, and slow to expand, it is a very free-flowering species with completely hairy new stems. It arrived from Japan by 1844 with Robert Fortune. Long cultivated in China and Japan for the fullness of their foliage-covering bloom during mid-May, these plants often are treated there as topiary specimens in pots or as sheared garden ornaments. The oval, lustrous, deep green foliage is only ⅝ inch long and is produced so prolifically that it obscures all the stems. These leaves develop in two forms. The spring leaves are 1 inch long and oval, but the summertime ones are shorter, more lanceolate, and particularly glossy. The blossoms are bright red, scarlet, or crimson in crowded clusters of one to three funnel-shaped, 1-inch-wide florets. Direct cultivars are few.

CULTIVAR: 'Album' has white flowering.

CULTIVAR: 'Amoenum' came from Japan in 1845 and is considered the hardiest form with a slightly taller, compact, sluggish growth habit. The 1-inch-long flowers are not double but hose-in-hose (one flower stacked inside another) of brilliant magenta or rose-purple with thick, glossy leaves rarely over ¾ inch long. The dense, twiggy form promotes its use for low, colorful hedgings.

CULTIVAR: 'Macrostemon' is low and spreading with single, pale, salmon-orange flowers 1½ inches wide that show conspicuously projecting stamens.

The valuable series called "Kurume Hybrids" are hardy from zone 6 to zone 9 and reach an average size of 2 feet high by 4 feet wide. Many were introduced by Ernest Wilson during the 1920s.

CULTIVAR: 'Benigiri' flowers in bright crimson.

CULTIVAR: 'Blaauw's Pink' has early salmon-pink blooms.

CULTIVAR: 'Hinodegiri' carries richly crimson 1½-inch-wide blooms.

CULTIVAR: 'Hinomayo' is low-growing with clear pink blossoms.

CULTIVAR: 'Hoo' ('Appleblossom') shows greater hardiness; it has pale pink flowers with white throats.

CULTIVAR: 'Ima-shojo' ('Christmas Cheer') carries brilliantly red hose-in-hose flowering.

CULTIVAR: 'Kure-no-yuki' ('Snowflake') is dwarfed with white hose-in-hose (not double) blossoms.

CULTIVAR: 'Rosebud' has a low, slow-spreading habit and blooms late with tiny, rose-pink double flowers.

CULTIVAR: 'Salmon Beauty' sports salmon-red blossoms with darker streaks.

Rhododendron smirnowii (Smirnow rhododendron)
Zones 6 to 8   10' high x 10' wide   Light shade

A compact shrub or even a small tree in some locations, this slow-growing native of the Caucasus Mountains and northeastern Asia Minor came into view during 1886. It is noticeably unique for its white-felted new stems and felt-covered undersides of the foliage, a layer so thick that infestations of lacewing fly (a continual nuisance to rhododendron leaves) never occur. Its leaves are very narrowly lanceolate and up to 6 inches long in deep, dull green with downturned edges. The heavily felted undersides are gray or yellow-gray and become darker with age. The mid-May flowering varies from pale rose to rose-purple with a yellow blotch; individual blossoms are about 3 inches wide and usually carry appealingly wavy margins.

SARCOCOCCA (sweet box)   *Buxaceae* (box) family

A slow-growing, stoloniferous genus native to western China, the Himalayas, and southeastern Asia, these plants remain low and generally act as groundcovers. Fourteen species of monoecious shrubs make up the group, and they are much sought after and used in the southern United States and on the Pacific coast here. Tolerant of drought once established, they need only an acid, well-drained, moist, fertile soil in semishade to perform well. The alternate leaves are lustrous with a close resemblance to those of *Buxus* (box) in size and shape; however, *Buxus* foliage is oppositely set and somewhat dull-toned. Small, white, fragrant flowers appear in axillary clusterings with the male blossom positioned above the female. The fruit is a black or red drupe (like a plum). The name is derived from the Greek *sarkos* ("fleshy") and *kokkos* ("fruit"). Diseases and insects are not a problem.

Sarcococca ruscifolia   (sweet box, fragrant sarcococca)

Zones 8 to 10   3′ to 6′ high x 3′ to 8′ wide   Semishade

Usefully attractive as a groundcover beneath low-branched trees, against shaded walls (where it makes a natural espalier of itself), and as a low hedge, this popular species maintains slow growth and forms a loose mound of much branched, hairy new stems that spread widely. Accepting dryness, cold, and strong wind once established, it performs best on a moist, humusy, well-drained, acid site in semishade to full shading. Inconspicuous but very fragrant blossoms appear during April at the leaf axils and later develop into bright red or scarlet fruiting that matures as black. The thin, leathery, waxy, deep green leaves are about 2 inches long and half as wide, with wavy edges and sharp-pointed tips.

Sarcococca ruscifolia

SKIMMIA (skimmia)   *Rutaceae* (rue) family

Nine species of shrubs exist in this genus that is native to China, Japan, and the Himalayas; all are slow-growing, compact, moundlike, and aromatic. These plants are useful for seaside locations as well as for industrial sites since they accept air pollution well, and they are grown mainly for their persistent and colorful fruit. The leaves are alternate, simple, and lancelike; the flowers either are perfect or have the sexes separated on individual plants (dioecious). Blossoming usually occurs in May from small, white, fragrant, starlike flowers in compact, terminal, egg-shaped clusterings which develop into long-lasting berries. They grow on any fertile, well-drained, acid, humusy site with consistent summertime moisture. Pests and diseases are not important problems.

Skimmia japonica (fragrans)   (no common name)

Zones 7 (warm) to 9   3′ to 5′ high x 5′ to 6′ wide   Light to semishade

In this species the flower sexes are on separate plants. This mounded shrub has smooth stems and oval, shiny, leathery, medium green foliage crowded at the ends of twigs. These leaves are up to 3 inches long. The May flowering is yellowish white and sweetly scented like lily of the valley; it appears in terminal clusters about 3 inches high. The bright red, clustered, globose fruit, which grows up to ¼ inch on females, matures in August and then persists well into the winter. One nearby male plant can service about a dozen females for berry production. A moist, sandy, humusy soil suits it well in

Skimmia japonica female fruit

Skimmia japonica male flowers

varying degrees of shading. Introduced from Japan in 1838, this shrub grows slowly enough for container planting or as a low hedge. The male cultivar 'Fragrans' produces intensely fragrant blossoms and grows more strongly than the parent; it has no fruit, of course.

Skimmia reevesiana (fortunei)   (no common name)

Zones 8 (warm) and 9   2′ high x 3′ wide   Light to semishade

Dwarfed, compact, and mounded, this species has an advantage over *japonica* since its flowers are perfect, and therefore it is not necessary to find space for two separate-sex plants. Native to China, the Philippines, and Taiwan, it came into culture during 1849. It carries narrowly oval, 3- to 4-inch, dull green foliage, usually with pale undersides. The May flowers are white in short terminal clusters and develop into dull, crimson-red, ½-inch fruit with a capacity to remain in good condition through the entire winter. Provide a moist, humusy, sandy, acid soil. The cultivar 'Rubella' is a male form unusual to the species which carries noticeably crimson flower budding.

VACCINIUM   (blueberry, huckleberry, cranberry, bilberry)   *Ericaceae* (heath) family

A genus familiar to most for its edible fruiting, *Vaccinium* contains 150 species of deciduous and evergreen shrubs native generally to the northern hemisphere, with most of them located in North America and eastern Asia; a few are inhabitants of South America. Often enlarging by stoloniferous stem growth, they are very adaptable to excessively acid soil (such as that which is produced after a major forest fire) and accept more soil moisture or shading than the close relative *Erica*, which often coexists in the same growing area. Some species have especially attractive foliage, edible fruiting, or superior hardiness. They abhor limed soils but thrive on peaty or sandy, consistently moist (sometimes wet), acid conditions in sun to light shading. Pests and diseases usually are not difficult to manage, but rabbits have a winter fondness for the entire plant in snowy areas. The alternate foliage is simple, while the small, urn-shaped flowers come either solitary or in spikes and clusterings colored white, greenish, red, or purple. The fruit is a berry that often is edible and tasty. Its name is of an unclear origin and may be derived from the Latin word for "bilberry," an edible fruit of ancient times.

Vaccinium ovatum (California huckleberry, evergreen
huckleberry, shot huckleberry)

Zones 7 to 9   3′ to 10′ high x 6′ wide   Light shade

Native to the coastal areas from British Columbia to Monterey, California,
this shrub was introduced to cultivation by David Douglas, an English plant
explorer of that region, in 1826. It usually is found wild in association with
Gaultheria shallon, a close relation. Much branched and compact with erect
stems, the plant is an important source of florists' greens which are marketed
as "huckleberry" or "leatherleaf." The oval to lanceolate leaves are 1½ inches
long, toothed, shiny, leathery, and dark green; when emerging, the foliage is
bright and coppery red. The mid-May flowers are white to pink with waxy,
bell-shaped, ¼-inch blossoms held in short clusters. The edible ¼ inch fruit is
first red but matures to black with a gray bloom over it.

Vaccinium vitis-idaea   (cowberry, foxberry)

Zones 6 to 8   6″ high x 18″ wide   Semishade

A dwarfed, creeping, sluggishly growing groundcover difficult to establish
(probably because of its reliance on soil microorganisms found only in the
wild), this species has stems with minute black hairs and small, boxlike,
leathery, broad-tipped, notched leaves. This foliage is bright, glossy green
above and paler beneath, with a length up to 1¼ inches. Bell-shaped ¼-inch
flowers that bloom by June are white with a pink cast and come in short,
dense, drooping terminal spikes. The persistent, globular, dark red, ⅛-inch
berries are edible but tart. Native to the mountains of central and southern
Europe as well as northern Asia, this shrub prefers a moist, humusy, acid soil
on consistently half-shaded sites. A few varieties exist.

VARIETY: *majus* has larger leaves and fruiting.

VARIETY: *minus* has been in cultivation since 1825. It has become known over the
years by a lengthy list of common names: mountain cranberry, rock cranberry, ling-
berry, lingen, lingenberry, and lingonberry. The plant is distributed naturally from
Massachusetts across to Alaska and is extremely hardy since it exists in zone 2. Its
silhouette remains dwarfed at only 4 to 8 inches tall to form dense mats at a modest
growth rate. The leaves are up to ¾ inch long, while the pink to red flowers unfold
in June. Its cranberrylike, glossy red, edible fruit is ⅛ inch wide.

VIBURNUM (viburnum)   *Caprifoliaceae* (honeysuckle) family

This genus contains about 225 species of upright deciduous or evergreen
shrubs or occasionally small trees, offering a variety of attractive options
satisfactory for almost every landscape use, need, and desire. Native to
Europe, Asia, and North America, all are easy to grow and prove valuable
as screens, hedges, border accents, or containerized specimens, especially
for the prominent fruiting which is attractive to birds and other wildlife.
The deciduous kinds revel in full sunlight, but the evergreen types perform
somewhat better with some light shading. All species, however, are allergic
to liquid sprays and dusts containing sulfur which are used to combat leaf
spot diseases; such remedies cause quick blackening of the foliage and pre-
mature leaf drop. While the damage is not permanent, it does disturb the
normal rhythm of growth. On hot, dry, very sunny locations, either foliage
type tends to become exhausted within 15 or 20 years; their preference is
for a moist, humusy, well-drained soil with some filtered light.

  The foliage is opposite and simple, while the flowers often carry a pleasant scent and appear as small, tubular, white to pink blossoms in showy,

generally tight terminal panicles or flattened heads. Some species develop large, sterile outer flowering along with the fertile but inconspicuous blooms; occasionally the flower sexes appear on separate plants. The persistent fruit forms as clusterings of small drupes (similar to plums). Insects are not as bothersome as diseases on the stems and foliages. The name is an ancient Latin one for "wayfaring tree," which now is the identification for the species *lantana*, a deciduous member of this group. (Consult the "Deciduous Shrubs" division for additional choices.)

Viburnum x burkwoodii (no common name)

Zones 6 (warm) to 9   6′ high x 8′ wide   Sun to light shade

Vigorous, upright, and spreading with widely spaced foliage, this plant often appears gawky and open while young. Its long straight stems recommend themselves for training as a wall espalier. The plant is a hybrid of *carlesii* and *utile* that was created in England during 1924; it is less likely to contract the discouragingly harmful stem dieback disease that is prevalent with *carlesii*. The oval, slightly toothed, pointed, lustrous leaves are between 1½ and 4 inches long and half that width. These are dark green above and pale, brownish, and hairy beneath; they tend to bronze attractively during cool winters, but in areas of continual frost the foliage is generally semievergreen only. Very gratifyingly fragrant (much like gardenia), the pink-budded flowers open white and waxy in rounded clusters up to 3½ inches across beginning either in January or in early May, depending on the growing zone. The fruit clusters are first red and then mature to black. The popular cultivar 'Chenault' ('Chenaultii') is more compact and earlier to bloom with pale rose budding that becomes white flowering. Its leaves become bronze-brown for winter, but the plant is no more than semievergreen in cold sections.

Viburnum davidii (no common name)

Zones 7 to 9   2′ to 3′ high x 4′ to 5′ wide   Semishade

Performing well as a dense groundcover shrub for partial shade this species grows best either in northern California or in the southeastern and northwestern United States. Mounded, compact, and wide-spreading with a stoloniferous habit, the plant does not favor very cold, consistent winter winds, yet it will adapt to complete shade satisfactorily (with some loss in flowering). The narrowly oval, leathery, slightly toothed foliage varies from 2 to 5½ inches in length and is about half as wide. The glossy leaves are dark green on top and paler beneath, with three noticeably creased, parallel veins in prominent view. Profuse, dull white small flowers appear during June in densely crowded, flattened clusters up to 3 inches broad. Its bright, turquoise blue, shiny, egg-shaped fruiting develops in bunches but will be plentiful only if two or more plants are set near each other for adequate cross-pollination. Pests and diseases are usually not a problem, and any well-drained, average soil is suitable for dependable growth.

Viburnum japonicum (no common name)

Zones 7 to 9   8' high x 6' wide   Sun to semishade

Planted widely as a dense, bushy, screening shrub, this species was introduced from Japan in 1879. It is vigorous with strongly upright stems and a pyramidal outline; young plants tend to be leggy, however. Not particular about soil, it can grow in full sun or complete shade (with reduced blossoming). When juvenile, this plant is often confused with *odoratissimum*, a less hardy, highly fragrant, taller sort with fruiting that turns black at maturity. On this plant the showy and well-scented white bloom appears in June as dense, rounded trusses, but not on young plants. Bright red fruit develops in small quantities later. The firm, somewhat leathery, thick leaves are up to 6 inches long and 4 inches wide with entire margins or are finely toothed only in the upper half. Glossy, medium green above but paler and pitted beneath, this foliage projects noticeably away from the stems on stout petioles which are grooved above. It is not troubled by pests or diseases.

Viburnum odoratissimum (awabuki)   (sweet viburnum)

Zones 7 (warm) to 9   20' high x 12' wide   Light shade

Rivaling rhododendron foliage for appeal, this viburnum has a distinguished appearance but requires ample space since it maintains robust growth to create a dense and wide-spreading outline quickly. Regular—sometimes severe—pruning semiannually is essential to keep it in bounds for most growing areas, but for an attractive, matured appearance and better health, this effort should be started when plants are young since disease spores easily enter large pruning cuts to cause stem decline in a short time. It serves admirably as a screen or tall hedge anywhere it has room, except in the salt spray areas of the coast. Tolerant of many soil conditions, it prefers a deep, moist, well-drained site and can accept full sun on shoreline locations, although it is more attractive when grown there in partial shade. The oval, nearly entire (there are a few shallow teeth in the upper part), thick, leathery leaves are about 6 inches long and half as wide with stout caramel-colored petioles on smooth, green twigs. Its strikingly glossy foliage becomes bright green with a just-varnished look, and older leaves often color richly in autumn before shedding. Since they generally bloom in late April, the flowers are often exposed to damage from late frosts in colder sections. These white blossoms develop in conical, broad clusters up to 4 inches tall and have a fragrance that is pleasing (but not superior to that of many other types). The sparse fruit is first red and then black. Many problems beset this shrub: aphids, white flies, thrips, mites, stem canker, and sooty mold. When young, the plant is often confused with *japonicum* in the nursery.

Viburnum rhytidophyllum

Viburnum rhytidophyllum   (leatherleaf viburnum)

Zones 6 (warm) to 9   10' to 15' high x 10' to 12' wide   Light shade

One of the most cold-hardy evergreen viburnums known, this plant produces a coarse textural effect and is generally grown for its unusual winter-drooping, corrugated foliage; the species name translates as "wrinkled leaves." Robustly vigorous with strongly erect crowded stems, it likes abundant summertime moisture. It is susceptible to dehydration and eventual leaf scorch on very windy sites even with good watering and therefore requires protection in these circumstances. Serving well as a border accent or as a dense *unpruned* screen, it needs to have several plants close at hand to assure pollination for fruiting. The narrow, pointed leaves are up to 7 inches in length, nearly entire, lustrous but greatly wrinkled, and green or bronze-green above with densely fuzzy gray or yellowish undersides. The dull, yellowish white, strongly scented flowers are not particularly showy when they appear in May; they come in stout, flat clusters up to 8 inches wide. Bunches of small bright red fruit mature to black and offer an interesting difference from other species by not ripening all at the same time. Its cultivar 'Roseum' carries buds and flowers of rosy pink. The parent is native to central and western China; it came into culture through Ernest Wilson during 1900.

Viburnum suspensum

Viburnum suspensum   (Sandankwa viburnum)

Zones 8 and 9   6' high x 6' wide   Light to semishade

An inhabitant of southern Japan, the Ryukyu islands, and Taiwan, this shrub came into cultivation by 1850 and has proved adaptable as a modestly tall screen or hedge. Dense, compact, and rounded in outline with many stems and twigs, it enjoys a very humus-laden soil with consistently available moisture. The rounded, leathery, densely toothed (at the tip end), shiny, deep green foliage is lighter beneath and can become 4 inches long; these leaves appear on warty twigs that are rough to the touch. The May flowers are small, rosy pink, and agreeably fragrant; they develop in dense, flat clusters about 1½ inches broad. The globular, bright red fruiting appears only infrequently. Although greatly bothered by aphids, white flies, thrips, mites, and sooty mold, it maintains popularity in the southeastern United States because of its silhouette and scented flowering.

Viburnum tinus

Viburnum tinus   (laurustinus)

Zones 7 to 9   7' to 10' high x 5' to 7' wide   Sun to shade

Considered an indispensable shrub in much of the southern United States, this tall species is probably the most well known and widely cultivated of all. No other viburnum produces such a mass of dense foliage. The name is an ancient one for this plant, which is native to the Mediterranean region as well as to southeastern Europe; it has been grown in England since the late sixteenth century. Highly adaptable to a wide range of acid or alkaline soils, the shrub accepts smog, dust, heat, modest drought, infertility, neglect, and slow drainage. Although it grows well in maritime locations, it dislikes shoreline sites and salt spray. Where humidity is high, the plant adjusts well to full sun, but it favors light to semishade elsewhere. Continuous, very cold wintertime winds are harmful. All in all, this dense, bushy, mounded, fast-paced shrub has sterling qualities that are difficult to overrate. Little wonder it is so popular as a hedge, screen, or specimen over a wide area.

The oval, entire, slightly glossy leaves are up to 3 inches long and 1½ to 4 inches wide in middle to dark green, often with rolled-under margins; they develop on wine-red twigs. The pink budding turns into white, slightly scented flowers in flat clusters between 2 and 3 inches across. Flowering mostly in winter from February into April, in the mildest areas it extends even longer and begins to bloom by late autumn—another valuable quality. The ovoid fruit is first metallic blue and then black, often maturing along with the appearance of the newest flowering at the same time. Thrips, white flies, spider mites, soil aphids, and mildew are troublesome but not continual difficulties. Several interesting cultivars are available.

CULTIVAR: 'Lucidum' is even more vigorous with larger leaves and flowering. It is more resistant to both thrips and spider mites than the parent.

CULTIVAR: 'Robustrum' is taller and less susceptible to mildew.

CULTIVAR: 'Strictum' has a strongly upright habit.

CULTIVAR: 'Variegatum' carries foliage variegated conspicuously in creamy white, but it is tender and needs protection.

*Deciduous
Shrubs*

ABELIOPHYLLUM (abelialeaf)   *Oleaceae* (olive) family

There is only one known species of this genus, whose name comes from
the Greek *phyllon* ("leaf") and from its similarity to the evergreen foliage
of *Abelia*. These simple leaves are opposite, entire, oval, tip-pointed, hairy
on both sides, bluish green, and between ¾ inch and 2 inches long without
prominent autumn color. Botanically, it is closely related to *Forsythia* with
bell-shaped, four-pointed blossoms and squared stems; both bloom in
spring at about the same time. The dry fruit is winged all around and is
about 1 inch wide. Found in central Korea in 1919, it came into cultivation
by 1924. Provide an average, well-drained location protected from cold
north and west winds during dormancy. Even so, the exposed flower buds
on the previous year's stems may, like those of *Forsythia*, be killed or damaged in severe winters. Pests and diseases make few inroads.

Abeliophyllum distichum   (white forsythia, Korean
abelialeaf)

Zones 6 to 8   3′ to 5′ high x 3′ to 4′ wide   Sun to light shade

The budding on this plant is purple-toned but opens white with a pinkish
tinge revealing orange stamens. Conspicuous in mid-April bloom from
generous clusters massed all along the brown stems, these blossoms are
pleasantly almond-scented. Winter-cut branches force easily indoors. Usually
slow to adjust after transplanting, it has upright, slender, arching branches
and a rounded outline which serves as a useful filler between taller, leggy
shrubs. The ground-hugging stems root easily and eventually may form a
thicket.

ACANTHOPANAX (fiveleaf aralia)   *Araliaceae* (aralia
or ginseng) family

About fifty species of mostly deciduous, usually prickly shrubs or small
trees belong in this genus native to eastern Asia, the Malay peninsula, and
the Philippines. However, only *sieboldianus* is commonly cultivated. The
name is derived from the Greek *akantha* ("spine") and *panax* (which is
another genus of this family). All leaves are alternate, palmately compound, and toothed. The inconspicuous dioecious (separate-sex) flowers are
small, clustered, five-petaled, and dull-colored, but they often develop into
large panicles. Any female fruit is a purple or black ¼-inch drupe (similar
to a plum). Pests and diseases are rarely a problem.

*Acanthopanax sieboldianus (pentaphyllus) (Aralia
pentaphylla)*   (fiveleaf aralia, angelica shrub)

Zones 5 to 9   5′ to 9′ high x 5′ to 9′ wide   Sun to shade

Acanthopanax sieboldianus

Easily adaptable to city pollution, heavy shading, and exposed windy sites,
this durable shrub also holds its shiny foliage late into autumn (but with no
color change) and accepts dry, poor soil. It readily serves as a barrier hedge or
screen. Introduced from Japan in 1859, it is native to both Japan and China.
Erect, slender stems develop with gracefully arching end branches as it
matures; when clipped for hedge use, it retains more of an erect and stiff
habit. The leaves are bright green, thin, and glossy, composed of five to seven
narrow leaflets about 1½ inches long with coarse teeth at the tips. These
usually appear clustered on short spurs along the tan new twigs, which also

have small, sharp prickles beneath the leaf stalks. The flowers are greenish white in solitary, flat, 1-inch clusters supported by elongated peduncles up to 4 inches. Readily thriving in a variety of soils and exposures, it is pest- and disease-free. Overgrown plants can be rejuvenated in early spring by pruning them to ground level and then fertilizing. The black fruit on females generally is not found since male plants are not, for some reason, propagated.

AESCULUS (horse chestnut, buckeye)
Hippocastanaceae (horse chestnut) family

There are only two genera in this entire family, and only *Aesculus* receives cultivation. The name is an ancient one for an oak or some other tree producing seed eaten by livestock; this genus identification first was used by Pliny and comes from the Latin word *esca* ("nourishment"). There are thirteen species of deciduous shrubs or trees in this genus, with seven native to North America, five to eastern Asia, and one to southeastern Europe. All are hardy into zone 5, except for the Himalayan and Californian species, and all prefer a reasonably deep, porous, fertile, fairly moist but not wet soil. They transplant readily and enjoy full sun or light shade. The foliage is opposite, palmately compound, and often sizable. The individual flowers have four to five petals and appear in erect, terminal, pyramidal, usually showy panicles of white, yellow, pink, or red followed by either smooth or spiny capsules containing large seeds. Some species are bothered by mealy bugs, Japanese beetles, or tussock moth caterpillars; more often their foliages are made unpresentable by conspicuous leaf scorch during very dry periods in summer.

Aesculus parviflora (parviflorus, grandiflorus, macrostachya, ramosissimus) (dwarf buckeye, bottle brush buckeye, dwarf horse chestnut, white buckeye, spiked buckeye)

Zones 5 to 8   12′ to 15′ high x 20′ to 30′ wide   Sun to semishade

Moundlike and spreading widely by underground suckers, this July-blooming shrub arrived into cultivation during 1781 and is native to the southeastern part of the United States. Probably more of these shrubs grow naturally today in Alabama than are cultivated in the rest of the world. Attractive in bloom at the edges of deciduous woodlots or massed for summer accent, they need room to grow widely and also need a constantly moist and fertile soil enriched with peat or humus. Erect, slender, smooth stems (ungainly in winter since they do not branch much) carry five to seven lancelike, fine-toothed leaflets up to 4 inches long and 1 inch wide that are deep green above and gray-hairy beneath; the autumn color is an attractive yellow. The very decorative and erect terminal blossoming closely resembles a brush for cleaning bottles; it is composed of dense masses of ½-inch white flowers with noticeably protruding pink or red-brown stamens on cylindrical panicles or spikes that are between 8 and 12 inches high. Its sparse 1-inch fruit develops at right angles to these flower stalks and is both egg-shaped and smooth; the seeds are a rich brown. A showy new cultivar, 'Rogers', blooms later, does not sucker, and has flowering spikes up to 30 inches tall. The variety *serotina* has less hairiness on the leaf undersides and flowers about 2 weeks later than the parent. Diseases and insects are not important problems with any type.

ARALIA (devil's walking stick, Hercules' club, angelica
tree, wild saparilla, American spikenard, udo)
  Araliaceae (aralia or ginseng) family

This genus includes at least thirty-five species of deciduous herbs, shrubs,
or slender-trunked trees, and many carry spine-studded branches and
trunks. Usually cultivated for their tropical-looking foliage, they are native
to North America, Asia, the Malay peninsula, and Australia. They have a
preference for full sun to light shade and will grow in any moderately
moist, rich soil. The typically pinnate compound leaves are set alternately
and occasionally are subdivided into thrice-pinnate forms with sizable
expansions on some species. Woody plants here have clustered foliage
appearing near the stem tops only. The individual flowers are small, white
to greenish, five-petaled, and grouped in flat displays; the later fruit is a
drupe. Few diseases or insects are bothersome, but transplanting is sometimes difficult since quite a few species have taproots and are best moved
as very small plants.

Aralia elata (Japanese angelica, Japanese angelica tree)

Zones 4 to 9   20' to 45' high x 10' to 20' wide   Sun to light shade

Developing either as a suckering and wide-spreading shrub or as a sparsely
branched tree form, here is a stiffly erect, prickly novelty that is native to
Manchuria, Korea, Japan, and the Sakhalin Islands. It was introduced about
1830 and carries deep green, glossy, twice-pinnate leaves composed of oval
leaflets varying from five to nine (on each division) which are 4 inches long
and tip-pointed with slightly hairy undersides. This compound foliage can
stretch to 3 feet in length with a 2-foot width. Incorporating this plant into a
design takes some effort since the spine-encrusted stems appear threatening
(actually they are blunt-tipped), while the silhouette in dormancy is rigidly
stark. In leaf, however, it assumes an intriguingly tropical aspect, and when
blossoming by late summer it is compelling because of its large, pyramidal,
white, terminal racemes up to 18 inches tall. These tiny flowers are favorites
of bees and other nectar seekers and later develop ⅛-inch drupelike fruiting in
profusion; they color initially green, then cream, then pink, and finally black.
By autumn the foliage develops a reddish orange coloration. Diseases and
insect nuisances are not known. Several cultivars are available.

CULTIVAR: 'Aureo-variegata' has yellow-bordered leaflets which become lighter-col-
ored by late summer.

CULTIVAR: 'Pyramidalis' carries smaller leaflets and has a more erect branching
habit.

CULTIVAR: 'Variegata' develops irregularly white-edged foliage, providing a showy
effect all summer.

Aralia spinosa flowers

Aralia spinosa thorns

Aralia spinosa (devil's walking stick, Hercules' club, American angelica tree, prickly ash, toothache tree)

Zones 5 to 9   15′ to 30′ high x 10′ to 15′ wide   Sun to light shade

Similar in general characteristics to *elata*, this species also has twice-pinnate coarse leaves and spiny stems, but its foliage can stretch to a noteworthy 6 feet in length. Native from central Pennsylvania to Florida and west to Texas, it has become naturalized in New York, New Jersey, and Connecticut. This species blooms earlier than *elata* and has pinwheel-shaped, flat, terminal, white flowers in clusters up to 3 feet wide that show the same fruit colorings as *elata*. The plant often self-seeds prodigiously. Its stout tan or gray stems are mostly unbranched and are encrusted with sharp, broadened spines that are scattered, irregularly but thoroughly, along their full length. The leaflets are from 2 to 6 inches long and medium green; they turn purplish red in autumn. Introduced to cultivation during 1688, this vigorous suckering shrub forms clumps or becomes a small tree; it prefers moist to wet locations but accepts drier conditions well. Insects and diseases are not troublesome, but because this species and *elata* have taproots, they are difficult to transplant except when very small; nurseries usually merchandise them only in pots.

ARONIA (chokeberry)   Rosaceae (rose) family

Three species of deciduous shrubs are members of this genus, which is totally native to North America. Considered a subgenus of pear *(Pyrus)* by some authorities, these plants are useful for naturalizing in acid, low ground with full sun or light shade and are showy both in flower and in fruit. The name comes from a modification of *aria*, the former designation for the mountain ash *(Sorbus aria)*, to which it is closely aligned botanically; they differ because *Sorbus* as a genus generally carries pinnately compound or lobed foliage, while *Aronia* is simple and entire. The flowers are small and pink or white with five petals and up to twenty stamens appearing in clusters at the twig ends; the fruit is a berrylike pome (similar to an apple). These plants are usually pest- and disease-free.

Aronia arbutifolia flowers

Aronia arbutifolia (Pyrus arbutifolia) (chokeberry, red chokeberry)

Zones 5 to 9   6′ to 12′ high x 3′ to 5′ wide   Sun to light shade

Cultivated since 1700, the plant is narrowly erect and much branched but open, often leggy, and of a suckering habit which easily but slowly forms large colonies in time. Natively found from Nova Scotia to Ontario and Michigan as well as south to Texas and Florida, it is an easily transplanted, carefree shrub with a mid-May bloom of from two to twenty-five ⅜-inch white to reddish flowers with black, noticeable anthers in terminal, woolly clusters that are up to 2 inches across. The winter-persistent fruit appears as drooping bunches of round or pear-shaped pomes ranging from dull to bright red that grow to about ¼ inch wide. Because these have an astringent taste, birds avoid eating them. The dark green foliage is gray-felted beneath and turns a rich red in autumn. These oval, point-tipped leaves are between 1 inch and 3½ inches long and noticeably hairy when new. Its preference is for a sandy loam with moderate moisture, but it will tolerate some dryness well. A few variations are offered.

CULTIVAR: 'Brilliantissima' displays more abundant and glossier fruiting along with showier autumn foliage color.

VARIETY: *macrocarpa* has larger fruit.

VARIETY: *pumila* is shorter in growth with smaller leaves, but it has more richly colored fruit than the parent.

Aronia arbutifolia fruit

Aronia melanocarpa (nigra) (Pyrus melanocarpa) (black chokeberry)

Zones 5 to 8   1½' to 4' high x 3' to 8' wide   Sun to light shade

Suckering profusely to expand continually with vigor, this native from Newfoundland to Ontario and south to Virginia and Indiana is well adapted to both dry and wet soils, especially as a naturalizing shrub. Similar in flower and in its young form to *arbutifolia,* it has narrower and shinier foliage than that species and is without hairs on the leaf undersides; the autumn color is purple-red. Lustrous, generously set, black to purple-black fruit crops unfortunately drop early and provide no winter interest. The variety *grandifolia* rises to a 10-foot height and is larger in all its parts, while the variety *elata* carries oblong, pointed leaves and both larger blossoms and fruit than the parent.

AZALEA (RHODODENDRON) (azalea)   *Ericaceae* (heath) family

An explanation of this genus appears in the "Broadleaf Evergreens" division. Both deciduous and evergreen azaleas are now considered *Rhododendron* species and are listed under that heading.

BERBERIS (barberry)   *Berberidaceae* (barberry) family

An explanation of this genus appears in the "Broadleaf Evergreens" division.

Berberis koreana   (Korean barberry)

Zones 5 to 9   4' to 6' high x 3' to 4' wide   Sun to light shade

Offering an attractive alternative to the wild *vulgaris* where that plant is legally prohibited from growing, this hardy barberry is also erect, dense, and multistemmed with useful qualities for hedges and massings. Known in cultivation from Korea since 1905, it flowers noticeably in mid-May with vivid yellow, bowl-shaped, ¼-inch blossoms arranged in drooping clusters of ten to twenty blooms. Winter-durable, glossy, scarlet, beadlike fruit appears in loose strings about 2 inches long. The thin, dull, light green oval leaves are up to 2½ inches in length; they are veined in red and carry ten to twenty spiny teeth along the margins. Their showy autumn color varies from orange-red to red-purple. Mature stems are deep red with either leaflike spines or straight ones with three to seven divisions. Tolerant of any soil, this shrub can be cut to the ground in late winter when overgrown; if kept watered thoroughly and fertilized regularly through the following summer, it recovers satisfactorily and gets a new lease on life. New plants are best installed only in the spring.

Berberis thunbergii

Berberis thunbergii fruit

Berberis thunbergii cv. 'Atropurpurea' flowers

Berberis thunbergii   (Japanese barberry)

Zones 5 to 9   2′ to 5′ high x 2′ to 5′ wide   Sun to light shade

Although seen and noted by Carl Pehr Thunberg in Japan as early as 1784, this shrub did not become cultivated until sometime between 1875 and 1883. Commonly used, it is the easiest *Berberis* species to grow and already has been naturalized in some areas of North America. As one of the few barberries which does not cross-fertilize with other species, it usually comes true from seeding. Useful for barrier hedges, it accepts shearing without damage—except to its normally graceful silhouette. Quick rejuvenation of overgrown or straggly plants can be achieved through late winter pruning to ground level. The mature outline is dense, compact, and rounded with somewhat stiff red-brown branching and arching twigs; new stems are green. The flowering appears in mid-May generously set all along the grooved and thorny stems of the previous year; these are yellow, cup-shaped, and ⅓ inch wide, clustered as two to five blossoms shaded red on the outsides. The winter-persistent fruit, which is enjoyed greatly by wildlife, becomes plump, oval, shiny, and red. Foliage is tufted, yellow-green, spoon-shaped, and untoothed with an average length of ¾ inch, showing silvered undersides. The autumn color is usually scarlet. Best either transplanted at a small size in early spring with a ball of earth or containerized (since large plants are difficult to move), it accepts any soil conditions, including dry and poor ones, but responds with greater vigor and fruiting when treated more suitably. Many attractive cultivars are readily available today.

CULTIVAR: 'Argenteo-marginata' develops foliage with white margins.

CULTIVAR: 'Atropurpurea' came from France about 1913 and has full-season dark burgundy foliage. It needs full sun to hold this coloration.

CULTIVAR: 'Aurea' carries citron-yellow leaves when provided with full sun; in any shade the leaves are only greenish yellow.

CULTIVAR: 'Compacta' forms a dense habit.

CULTIVAR: 'Erecta' is also known as the "truehedge barberry" or "truehedge columnberry" because of its strongly upright stems and branches. It can grow 5 feet tall with a 10-foot spread.

CULTIVAR: 'Globe' is ball-shaped and dwarfed with only minor fruiting.

CULTIVAR: 'Golden Ring' is similar to *cv.* 'Atropurpurea' but has leaf margins edged in yellow; it also requires full sun.

CULTIVAR: 'Inermis' ('Thornless') is a green-leaved, mostly thornless form.

CULTIVAR: 'Maximowiczii' has narrower foliage which is reddened above but green-toned beneath.

CULTIVAR: 'Minor' expands sluggishly to reach an eventual 2-foot height.

CULTIVAR: 'Nana' forms a dwarfed, compact mound with green foliage.

CULTIVAR: 'Pluriflora' shows increased flowering with five to twelve blossoms in each cluster.

CULTIVAR: 'Red Bird' develops with more compactness and deeper color than *cv.* 'Atropurpurea'. It also needs full sun.

CULTIVAR: 'Rose Glow' produces purple leaves lavishly streaked with pink and white but has a tendency on some vigorous shoots to revert to green; these should be cut away as found. Provide full sun for the best color.

BUDDLEIA (butterfly bush, summer lilac)   *Loganiaceae* (logania) family

Some 100 species native to the tropics or subtropics make up this attractive genus of large deciduous or evergreen shrubs (occasionally small trees). The name was established in the late seventeenth century by Dr. William Houston (1660–1715) to honor his contemporary, the Reverend Adam Buddle, who wrote a botanic treatise arranged according to Houston's newly devised system for plant classification. Unfortunately, even Linnaeus corrupted the spelling to *Buddleja* and *Budleja* in his classification work, and later taxonomists confused matters further by labeling it *Budlaea* and *Buddleya*. Such mix-ups were not uncommon in the early periods of botany and identification.

Natively found in North America, eastern Asia, and southern Africa, the tropical forms are evergreen with a variable blooming period, while the deciduous ones from Asia and this country usually flower in late summer; however, in both southern Florida and southern California they bloom by midwinter. All are easy to grow and are cultivated mainly for the profusion of their fragrant, showy blossoming with special appeal in some species for attracting butterflies. The tiny, four-petaled blooms appear in rounded heads, fluffy panicles, or spikes that somewhat resemble lilacs. Most species cross-hybridize readily—notably *davidii* and *alternifolia*—and self-seed frequently, creating mild botanic confusion about the exact nature of each species' form and color. Leaves are generally oppositely set (*alternifolia* is an obvious exception), lancelike, and woolly on angled or winged stems; they provide no autumn coloration. The fruit is either a capsule or a berry, but neither has any landscape merit. A major defect of all types is the retention of faded flowers even into dormancy plus the tendency of the deciduous sorts (because they bloom so late for the most part and have an abundance of soft growth) to lose whole stems to ground level in areas of sustained cold. This awkward trait can leave large gaps in a border or screen during much of springtime since these plants are also late to leaf out.

Any average-fertility, well-drained site is suitable as long as it provides full sun and good air drainage. During the blooming period these shrubs prefer copious water and regular fertilizing. Insect pests are not numerous, but the cucumber mosaic virus can mottle and distort the foliage unattractively. Even with their peculiarities, these are highly popular plants offering attractive and often late flowering.

Berberis thunbergii cv. 'Aurea'

Buddleia alternifolia   (fountain butterfly bush, fountain buddleia)

Zones 5 to 10   8′ to 20′ high x 8′ to 15′ wide   Sun

One of the hardiest species, this form does not attract many butterflies for the simple reason that it normally blooms in late May, before butterflies hatch. Requiring ample room for development, it offers a somewhat ungainly silhouette from its gracefully arching branches that spill irregularly toward the ground. It can be trained by regular pruning into a small tree form or a wall espalier. Thinning out old wood every few years produces better growth and flowering. Considered drought-resistant, it prefers a well-drained, gravelly or sandy soil enriched with compost or peat and generous water when blooming; too rich a soil, however, discourages the fullest flowering. Its delicately fragrant, elegant-looking, soft lilac-purple flowers are between ¼ and ¾ inch long and appear in dense and elongated clusters tightly placed all along the stems of the previous year. The toothless leaves somewhat resemble those of willow; they are 4 inches long, about ½ inch wide, and light to deep green above but gray-hairy and sandpapery in feel below. They remain late

late in autumn without any color change. Discovered in 1875 by the Russian botanist Pavel Piastetski, this shrub did not become cultivated until it was introduced by Reginald Farrar in 1915. The cultivar 'Argentea' is a form that is not grown commonly; it has silky hairs on both leaf surfaces, creating an attractive silvery effect.

Buddleia davidii cultivar

Buddleia davidii (variabilis) (summer lilac, orange-eye butterfly bush)

Zones 5 to 10   6′ to 15′ high x 6′ to 15′ wide   Sun

Ideally suited for seaside locations, this colorful, scented, easy-to-grow species achieves rapid and rampant growth in any average-fertility soil, but it unfortunately dies to ground level yearly in the coldest part of its growing range. While the plant does regrow well to bloom again the following summer, this dieback creates a sizable disruption to the appearance of any border for a long time in the spring. Originally from China, it has naturalized itself now in parts of California from its prolific annual crop of seeds. Best purchased as a small containerized plant because of its taproots, the plant requires spring installation only in order to allow the roots to reestablish themselves adequately. From zone 8 to zone 10 any planting season is workable, but in Florida the plant fails to develop properly except in the western, panhandle section. This species was collected in 1887 by Dr. Augustine Henry, who found it at an altitude of 9000 feet near Ichang, China; he named it for the Jesuit missionary Pere Armand David, an earlier explorer of China who first described the plant. It is seldom seen today for itself; the more colorful cultivars provide greater attraction.

Its showy terminal flowering begins by mid-July and continues until frost (in the north) with 6- to 12-inch dense spikes of lilac to purple tiny florets with deep orange-yellow throats (or eyes) and a honeylike scent. The opposite, finely toothed, lanceolate leaves range from 6 to 10 inches long and about 2½ inches wide in deep green above and silvery white beneath. Its cultivar and varietal selections are impressive, but not all show the contrasting "eye" of the original.

CULTIVAR: 'Black Knight' displays very deep purple flowering.

CULTIVAR: 'Burgundy' carries rich wine-red blossoms.

CULTIVAR: 'Charming' originated in Pennsylvania in 1935 and is considered the best pink form yet; it has long spikes of lavender-pink florets.

CULTIVAR: 'Dubonnet' has striking, massive, deep purple blooms and shows great vigor; it came from an Ohio grower in 1939.

CULTIVAR: 'Empire Blue' also originated in Ohio (1941) and produces short spikes of rich violet or dark blue flowers with noticeable orange eyes.

CULTIVAR: 'Fascinating' ('Fascination') shows vivid orchid-pink blossoming; it was introduced in 1942 from an Ohio nursery.

CULTIVAR: 'Fortune' grows only 5 feet tall with long plumes of soft lilac florets punctuated with orange eyes.

CULTIVAR: 'Ile de France' was introduced in 1931 from a French nursery; it carries long, elegant spikes of deep purple or rich violet.

CULTIVAR: 'Opera' develops magnificent flowering of crimson-purple.

CULTIVAR: 'Peace' is pure white with spikes ranging from 10 to 22 inches long.

CULTIVAR: 'Pink Pearl' carries dense plumes of lilac-pink blossoms with soft yellow eyes.

CULTIVAR: 'Purple Prince' has extra-wide spikes of royal purple.

CULTIVAR: 'Royal Red' is a long-time favorite from 1940 with its huge plumes of wine-red carrying purple overtones.

CULTIVAR: 'White Bouquet' originated in Louisiana during 1942. It is a seedling of *cv.* 'Ile de France' with noticeable fragrance and white plumes accented by yellow eyes.

CULTIVAR: 'White Cloud' is considered by many to be the finest white-flowered form with its dense, pure-color spikes.

CULTIVAR: 'White Profusion' is a dwarfed to a 3-foot height but contributes abundant blossoming from many side-shoot spikes. (Unfortunately, white-flowered cultivars tend to look haggard as the blooms age since the spent flowers turn brown and persist in place.)

VARIETY: *magnifica* is late-blooming and carries very large spikes densely covered with violet-purple florets showing inturned petals and deep orange eyes.

VARIETY: *superba* is similar to *magnifica* but develops even larger blossoms.

VARIETY: *nanhoensis* blooms over a lengthy period with a profusion of bluish lilac flowers accented with orange eyes; it has a graceful silhouette and a 4- to 6-foot height.

VARIETY: *veitchiana* blooms earlier than the parent; it has dense spikes of mauve showing orange eyes.

VARIETY: *wilsoni* has rose-lilac drooping spikes and orange eyes; these often elongate to 2 feet, producing a conspicuous display.

CALYCANTHUS (sweet shrub, allspice, sweet-scented shrub)   *Calycanthaceae* (calycanthus) family

Only four species belong to this genus that is native entirely to North America. These plants all are simple to cultivate and need no special pruning attention. The name is derived from an old reference to the structure of the blossom and combines the Greek *kalyx* ("calyx" or group of flower sepals) and *anther* ("flower"). They prefer fertile, well-drained, moist soil in a location out of strong wind with either full sun or some light shade. When bruised, the opposite, entire leaves are aromatic with either a camphor or a spicy smell. The unusual flowers are solitary, red-brown, and noticeably fragrant; they are composed of a variable combination of sepal and petal parts. The many-winged fruit seeds are enclosed by an expanded, capsulelike flower tube, giving the appearance of a dried fig. Diseases and insect pests are not a serious problem.

Calycanthus floridus (Carolina allspice, pineapple shrub, strawberry shrub, sweet bubbie, peat shrub, sweet betsy)

Zones 5 to 9   6' to 10' high x 6' to 10' wide   Sun to light shade

Introduced to cultivation in 1726, this easily transplanted shrub is native from Virginia to Florida in moist mountain woodlots. During the eighteenth and nineteenth centuries it was a popular dooryard attraction because of both its scented leaves and blossoms, and the dried flowers were collected and used in sachets for linen closets. Its silhouette varies from dense to open, depending on soil and moisture conditions, but it is basically an upright, bushy, and slow-growing plant. Attractive as a border specimen, it also naturalizes well when massed at the edges of deciduous woods. Unfortunately, today few nursery cuttings are deliberately chosen from the mostly highly scented selections in propagation; as a result the intriguing smell is often greatly diminished or even lost, which may account for the lessened popularity of this special shrub nowadays. (Also possible is a nursery mix-up with the similar but less fragrant species *fertilis*, a native from Pennsylvania to Georgia, which can be separated by the lack of hairiness on the undersides of its leaves.) In severe winters much of the branching may die to the ground, yet the plant usually regrows satisfactorily.

Calycanthus floridus flower

Calycanthus floridus (Cont.)

Calycanthus floridus fruit

Solitary 2-inch-wide flowers appear in the leaf axils from late May to July in a dull, dark red-brown coloring with many straplike sepals which give the appearance of petals; these develop an odor resembling that of a spicy strawberry or a ripe and pungent pineapple. When dried, they retain this fragrance for many months. The shiny, 2- to 5-inch, oval leaves are a leathery dark green above and densely hairy beneath on stems which emit a camphor odor when bruised; they turn a clear yellow in the autumn. Its 2½-inch, brown, thick-skinned fruit develops only every few years (for unclear reasons) and looks very much like a dried fig or pear. The cultivar 'Purpureus' has purple-toned foliage.

CARAGANA (pea tree, pea shrub)   *Leguminosae* (pea) family

The name comes from a Mongolian one for this plant. All sixty species are hardy deciduous shrubs (occasionally small trees) native to temperate central Asia; some also carry small prickles. Sun-loving, they are easily grown, and the cultivated types are raised for their showy flowering, tolerance to prolonged drought, hardiness, and durability. They resent transplanting when old, and so it is a wiser procedure to install small plants in a permanent location, preferably one with a light, sandy soil. The early summer flowering is mostly yellow and is composed of solitary or few-flowered clusters which are clawlike in appearance. The leaves are compound, alternate, evenly pinnate, and spine- or bristle-tipped with entire, small leaflets. Any fruit is a slender, straight pod with no landscape significance. Diseases and insect nuisances are uncommon.

Caragana arborescens cv. 'Lorbergii'

Caragana arborescens (Siberian pea shrub)

Zones 2 to 7   10′ to 20′ high x 5′ to 10′ wide   Sun

Erect and narrow in outline but slow-growing, this is one of the hardiest and most accommodating of all plants, succeeding in the most exposed locations on all soil types. Satisfactory as a hedge or a short windbreak, it is very popular in the northern plains of both western Canada and the United States, where the soil is normally dry and alkaline. As a landscape element, however, it has less value than some other choices—except in its variations listed below—since it presents a coarse look out of flower and possesses no autumn coloring. The plant blooms all along the second-year wood during mid-May in clusters of one to four yellow, pea-shaped, somewhat scented blossoms about an inch long; these carry slim, spiny appendages which are the minute stipules of the flower. Its fruit develops as small, slender, brownish pods which burst open forcefully when ripe. The bright green, hairy, oval leaflets expand to about 1 inch in three to six pairs on yellow-green twigs; the entire leaf measures between 2 and 3½ inches long. Several alternative forms are available.

CULTIVAR: 'Lorbergii' was introduced in 1906. It has a graceful nature and fernlike, finely narrow leaflets about an inch in length with a shredded appearance. It rarely flowers well and sets little fruit, but it offers distinctive foliage.

VARIETY: *crasseaculeata* spreads wider to a 7-foot dimension.

VARIETY: *nana* is dwarfed with contorted branching; it can be useful in containers and in rock gardens.

VARIETY: *pendula* has strongly weeping but stiff branching; it often is grafted high on a typical plant and then kept pruned into a final tree shape.

CHAENOMELES (flowering quince, Japanese quince) *Rosaceae* (rose) family

Only three species make up this genus of deciduous or semievergreen shrubs native to eastern Asia. They have been cultivated for almost 500 years in the orient and for at least 150 years in other parts of the northern hemisphere. Many old-time gardeners labeled them as "japonicas," the name normally seen in catalogs of the time, or as "burning bushes" for the fiery colorings of the most popular types. The name comes from the Greek *chainein* ("to split or gape") and *melea* ("apple") on the mistaken assumption that the fruit splits into five parts. The quince with the fruit used in making a well-known preserve now is called *Cydonia japonica*. This genus differs from it by not cross-fertilizing with *Cydonia*, *Malus* (apple), *Pyrus* (pear), or any other close relation to them, although all these are family members and have similarly shaped flowers. The showy, waxy blooms come from winter-naked buds and appear either solitary or in clusters before the leaves emerge with five overlapping petals in red, orange, and white on the previous year's wood. Branches cut in winter force easily for indoor use. Densely branched and usually thorny, these plants make attractive specimens, hedges, or espaliers for walls and fences in bright sun or light shading. The occasional fruit is a large, hard pome (like an apple) rich in vitamin C that is snugly attached to the slender stems. These sometimes are used in making jelly and for perfuming a small room when fully ripe. The deep green foliage is alternate, toothed, and often bronze-toned when unfolding; it provides no autumn color. It is easy to grow in acid or alkaline, dry or moist soils, but mature plants resent transplanting and recover only slowly if at all. Scale insects are sometimes a problem, and fireblight disease can cause severe dieback and shriveled flowers.

Chaenomeles japonica (lesser flowering quince, Japanese flowering quince)

Zones 5 to 9   2' to 3' high x 4' to 6' wide   Sun to light shade

While not as distinguished in flower as *speciosa*, this shrub has merit as a low groundcover or border accent with early spring bulbs since it blooms during early to mid-April. Native to Japan, it was discovered in 1784 by Carl Pehr Thunberg on Mount Hakone there, but he named it *Pyrus japonica*. It was not until 1869 that this species was put into cultivation, but by then the more showy *speciosa* already had overtaken it in flower appeal. Slow-growing and wide-spreading with short, prickly spines, it has bright salmon to orange-red single blossoms that are 1 inch across. The fruit is only 1½ inches in diameter and is slightly sticky; when ripe it resembles a small, gnarled apple. Its smooth, spatula-shaped, deep green leaves are up to 2 inches long and ¾ inch wide with coarse, rounded teeth. A reasonable number of variations are available.

CULTIVAR: 'Dorothy Rowe' has white flowers tinted both pale yellow and pink.

CULTIVAR: 'Maulei' grows taller with salmon-pink to orange flowering.

CULTIVAR: 'Sargentii' is dwarfed and has a salmon-pink to orange bloom.

CULTIVAR: 'Zoge' ('Alba') carries creamy white flowers.

VARIETY: *alpina* has a dwarfed habit with ascending twigs and almost round, tiny leaves; the flowers are bright orange.

VARIETY: *pigmaea* is also dwarfed with almost spineless stems.

VARIETY: *tricolor* carries variegated foliage in pink and white on a dwarfed outline.

Chaenomeles speciosa cultivar

Chaenomeles speciosa fruit

Chaenomeles speciosa (lagenaria) (Japanese quince, flowering quince)

Zones 5 to 9   6′ to 10′ high x 8′ to 12′ wide   Sun to light shade

Native to China, Tibet, and Burma, the plant was brought to Japan in the sixteenth century and has been cultivated there so enthusiastically that it has naturalized itself in some areas. Sir Joseph Banks brought it from Shantung, China, to Europe in 1796, and it has remained popular as a showy-flowering plant ever since. Blooming in early May (but not as generously in constantly mild climates), this dense shrub has many slenderly erect and spreading, thorny branches which are covered (before the leaves) with 1½- to 2-inch-wide cupped flowers in red, white, or pink. Its yellowish fruit is globe- to pear-shaped, fragrant when ripe, and between 2 and 2½ inches long; it is tightly attached to the stems of the second-year growth. The oblong, smooth, sharply toothed, glossy, dark green leaves range from 1½ to 3½ inches in length; they do not color in autumn. Its cultivar list is extensive.

CULTIVAR: 'Apple Blossom' first opens white and then alters to a pink-tinted yellow flower in a mix of single and semidouble blooms.

CULTIVAR: 'Atrococcinea' is single-flowered with deep crimson blossoms.

CULTIVAR: 'Baltzii' has single rose-colored flowering.

CULTIVAR: 'Candida' carries pure white single blossoms.

CULTIVAR: 'Candidissima' ('Alba') is also single-flowered and has pink-tinged white bloom.

CULTIVAR: 'Cardinalis' displays bright red single or semidouble flowers.

CULTIVAR: 'Contorta' has twisted branching and pink-toned white blossoming.

CULTIVAR: 'Grandiflora' shows larger white flowers tinted with both pink and lemon-yellow; these are mostly single.

CULTIVAR: 'Kermesina' has a single carmine-red bloom.

CULTIVAR: 'Kermesina Semiplena' carries semidouble scarlet flowers.

CULTIVAR: 'Macrocarpa' develops spineless stems and single rose-red flowering.

CULTIVAR: 'Marmorata' is taller growing than most others in this group and produces single blossoms marbled in white and pink.

CULTIVAR: 'Moerloosei' has profuse flowering of single white blooms striped in pink.

CULTIVAR: 'Nivalis' is a low-growing type with large, single, pure white flowers.

CULTIVAR: 'Rosea Plena' varies from pink to coral-pink with both semidouble and fully double flowering.

CULTIVAR: 'Rubra Grandiflora' shows enormous single to semidouble blossoming of deep crimson on a low-growing plant.

CULTIVAR: 'Sanguinea Plena' has semidouble to fully double rosy-red blooms.

CULTIVAR: 'Simonii' displays a flattened, dwarfed habit with small, blood-red, semidouble to double flowers.

CULTIVAR: 'Umbilicata' is a tall plant carrying single rose-red to salmon-pink flowers and large fruit.

CULTIVAR: 'Umbilicata Nana' has almost thornless stems and a low outline with orange-red single blooms.

CULTIVAR: 'Versicolor' shows single flowers in white intermixed with two shades of pink.

Chaenomeles x superba (hybrid flowering quince)

Zones 5 to 9   4′ to 6′ high x 4′ to 6′ wide   Sun to light shade

This new group blooms in early May. It is a cross between *japonica* and *speciosa* producing small to medium-sized shrubs of vigorous habits with free-flowering natures that more closely resemble the form of *japonica* than that of *speciosa*. Both the flower size and the leaf length vary—at times conspicuously—between the various cultivars of this collection, but more importantly, these shrubs are *not* equally hardy throughout the growing range listed. Some trial-and-error plantings will be necessary before this important cultural detail is fully workable for all areas. The following are the current offerings.

CULTIVAR: 'Cameo' is spineless with a low habit and double yellowish pink flowering.

CULTIVAR: 'Charming' has single reddish orange or deep yellowish pink blossoms.

CULTIVAR: 'Columbia' ('Semperflorens') carries single pink to rosy-red flowers.

CULTIVAR: 'Corallina' has intense orange-red blossoms.

CULTIVAR: 'Crimson and Gold' is low-growing with single deep red flowering and noticeable centers of gold stamens.

CULTIVAR: 'Crimson Beauty' is single and deep red.

CULTIVAR: 'Glowing Ember' has single reddish orange flowers.

CULTIVAR: 'Knap Hill Scarlet' carries extended flowering into late May on a low plant with yellowish pink to orange-scarlet single blossoms.

CULTIVAR: 'Red Chief' has double, large, bright red flowering.

CULTIVAR: 'Rowallane' displays large, brilliant red single blossoms.

CULTIVAR: 'Texas Scarlet' is low in habit and almost thornless; it has watermelon-red flowers.

CHIONANTHUS (fringe tree)   *Oleaceae* (olive) family

Botanists are uncertain how many species exist in this genus, two or four. All are large, deciduous, dioecious shrubs or small trees native to either North America or eastern Asia with great hardiness and long life; they are useful as sun-loving specimens or screen hedges. The name comes from the Greek *chion* ("snow") and *anthos* ("flower"), referring to the abundant, white springtime bloom. Tolerant of many soils, they prefer a moist, sandy loam with adequate space to expand. The flowers of both male and female plants are attractively fragrant and appear on somewhat squared stems in showy panicles composed of many white, very narrow, lacy blossoms. Young plants do not bloom readily. Late to leaf out, the foliage is opposite, entire, very long, thick, and leathery; the autumn color is yellow. Female plants produce summertime clusters of dark blue, egg-shaped fruit called drupes. Pests and diseases are not a frequent problem.

Chionanthus retusus (Chinese fringe tree)

Zones 6 to 8   10′ to 20′ high x 10′ to 20′ wide   Sun to light shade

While these modest-growing plants appear coarse in leaf design, their June bloom has striking showiness and fragrance. Brought into cultivation by 1845, they are native to China and Korea. The terminal clusters of white, shredded-looking, small blossoms develop on short spur growth all along the expanding new stems. Females later produce clusterings of ½-inch, egglike, deep blue fruit usually hidden by the lengthy oval foliage. These leaves are between 1 and 4 inches long and about 2 inches wide with downy undersides. The autumn color is yellow. This shrub has been difficult to locate in nurseries.

Chionanthus virginicus flowers

Chionanthus virginicus   (fringe tree, old-man's-beard, grandfather graybeard)

Zones 5 to 9   15′ to 30′ high x 15′ to 30′ wide   Sun to light shade

Found native from lower Pennsylvania and lower New Jersey to Florida and west to Texas, the plant does not endure in central or southern Florida but shows remarkable vigor elsewhere. Introduced to culture during 1736, this decorative, stout-stemmed shrub blooms in late May with moplike, drooping, 6- to 8-inch clusters of lacy, greenish white, 1-inch, nicely scented flowers appearing on the previous year's stems. Since the sexes are separated, only the females can produce the ¾-inch, dark blue, bloomy clusterings of summer fruit, which birds enjoy fully. The heavy twigs are downy when new and somewhat four-angled (a common trait with some members of this family) and carry oblong, tip-pointed, lustrous, deep green to bluish green, thick foliage between 3 and 8 inches long; the autumn coloring is often bright yellow. These plants are late to leaf and occasionally may be bothered by summertime spider mites on the foliage. Because they have fleshy roots that are easily damaged during transplanting when older, small plants are a wiser initial choice for a permanent location that provides a well-drained, average to sandy, deep, and moist soil. Water new plantings regularly and deeply until they are established.

CLETHRA   (white alder, summer-sweet, sweet pepperbush)   *Clethraceae* (white alder) family

This family is unique in that only one genus is credited to it, but there is some discrepancy about how many species belong here. Thirty appears to be the average, but one authority estimates that 100 are growing somewhere in the world. Native to eastern Asia, eastern North America, and the island of Madeira, these are deciduous and evergreen shrubs or small trees which are easy to grow—but only in acid soils—and need little pruning. The name is an ancient Greek one for the alder because of some leaf resemblance. This group has alternate foliage which is simple, oblong, and sharp-toothed. By late summer fragrant, white, terminal flowering appears in dense spikes from the leaf axils. The later fruit is a durable, spherical capsule with no landscape merit, but the woody spikes persist noticeably through winter dormancy. Pests and diseases are inconsequential.

Clethra alnifolia

Clethra alnifolia   (sweet pepperbush, summer-sweet)

Zones 4 to 9   3′ to 10′ high x 4′ to 8′ wide   Sun to semishade

This very hardy shrub was brought into cultivation during 1731 and is easily naturalized; it offers more visual effect when massed. Native from Maine to Florida and west to Texas, it blooms in late July with an attractively sweet scent, a noteworthy feature at a time when most shrubs have finished flowering for the season. Clump forming from its suckering habit, it slowly develops a dense oval silhouette. Although intolerant of prolonged drought, it accepts the sandy soil and salt air conditions of the shore readily; however, it prefers fertile, moist woodlots and some shading from the hot afternoon sun of summer. New plantings should be watered thoroughly and regularly until established. The foliage is wedge-shaped, sharply toothed toward the tip ends, deep green, and between 2 and 4 inches long; the autumn coloring is clear yellow. Terminal spikes 2 to 8 inches tall carry masses of tiny white florets with prominently protruding stamens. Occasionally the summer foliage becomes yellowish from spider mite attacks, especially if the soil and air are consistently dry. When in full flower, these plants are of constant interest to bees. The cultivar 'Rosea' has glossier foliage and blooms slightly later with pink budding and flowers; it usually grows only 6 feet tall. It soon may be surpassed by the recent 'Pinkspire', which has deeper pink blossoms. The variety *paniculata* has greater vigor and heavier, showier terminal flowering; it is considered superior to the parent.

Clethra alnifolia

CORNUS (dogwood, cornel)   Cornaceae (dogwood) family

About forty-five species are included in this genus of mostly deciduous (rarely evergreen) shrubs and small trees. Current botanists, however, prefer to transpose some of the more popular species—*alba*, *sanguinea*, and *stolonifera*—to a new genus, *Thelycrania*, on the strength of differences in the flower and fruit arrangements. However, since *Hortus Third* does not, these transfers are not made here. Reliably hardy, the plants of this genus have been known since antiquity and are mentioned in the writings of Homer, Virgil, and Theophrastus. Its name is from the Latin *cornu* ("horn") because the wood of the species *mas*, one of the first to be known, resembles the polished horns of an ox. The common name is a corruption of an old one, "dagwood" or "daggerwood," since daggers for skewering meat were made from some of the *Cornus* species (perhaps *mas*), and the name then was transferred to them all. Mostly these plants are native to North America, Europe, and Asia, but one species exists in Chile and another in Mexico. The shrub forms usually are ornamental in several ways with colorful bark and showy fruiting plus leaf colorings; their flowers are generally nondescript. The shrubs are less troubled by serious pests and diseases than the tree forms, but all grow easily and well in a variety of soil and exposure conditions, including city pollution.

The star-shaped "true" flowers of *Cornus* (some, such as the species *florida* and *kousa*, have very conspicuous leaf bracts to gain the attention of pollinating insects) are centered as a collection of tiny terminal clusterings on the previous year's growth in white, greenish white, or yellow colorings. The small fruit is a drupe much favored by birds and squirrels. Foliage is simple, entire, usually opposite, and distinguished by many lateral veins running parallel to the leaf margins. The autumn color varies among red, purple, and bronze, making a distinguished genus with many attractions.

Cornus alba (Tartarian dogwood, Tatarian dogwood, Siberian dogwood, red-stemmed dogwood)

Zones 3 to 9   5' to 10' high x 5' to 10' wide   Sun to light shade

Native to Siberia, northern China, and northern Korea, this very hardy shrub came into culture during 1741. It offers slender, blood-red stems that give it winter interest along with rapid growth as a mass for screening or naturalizing. Erect stems later arch and quickly form thickets if provided with a fertile, moist location. The late May flowers appear in 2-inch clusters with white or bluish coloring. By late summer groups of blue-tinged white fruit the size of a small pea develop but are not overly conspicuous. The thin, oval, medium to dark green leaves range from 1½ to 5 inches long and are tip-pointed; by autumn they change to purplish red. Pests and diseases are of little concern. The cultivar list contains plants with more colorful effects.

Cornus alba flowers and fruit

Cornus alba (Cont.)

Cornus alba cv. 'Argenteo-marginatus'

Cornus alba cv. 'Argenteo-marginatus'

Cornus alba cv. 'Spaethii'

CULTIVAR: 'Argenteo-marginatus' ('Elegantissima Variegata', 'Sibirica Variegata', 'Variegata') has leaves attractively edged and mottled in white, making an effective accent with an evergreen backdrop; it is tolerant of semishade.

CULTIVAR: 'Atrosanguinea' is a dwarfed form with brilliantly crimson stems.

CULTIVAR: 'Gouchaultii' has foliage variegated or streaked with yellow-white and pink.

CULTIVAR: 'Kesselringii' develops stems of black-purple with reddish foliage when first emerging.

CULTIVAR: 'Rosenthalii' has leaves broadly margined in yellow or gold, but only when grown in full sun.

CULTIVAR: 'Sibirica' ('Splendens', *var. sibirica, C. sibirica*) grows more slowly than the parent and has bright coral-red stems; it is the most noticeable cultivar in terms of winter branch interest in the group. Some authorities believe this may be identical with *cv.* 'Coral Beauty', a catalog name.

CULTIVAR: 'Spaethii' ('Aurea') has foliage more broadly edged with yellow or yellow-green than *cv.* 'Rosenthalii'; this plant also needs full sun to color at its best.

Cornus mas winter flower buds

Cornus mas (cornelian cherry, sorbet)

Zones 5 to 8   15′ to 20′ high x 20′ to 30′ wide   Sun to light shade

Densely branched to the ground when mature, heavily multistemmed, and wide-spreading, this native of central and southern Europe plus western Asia makes an impressive specimen or barrier screen. It grows readily in any soil condition, even wet. The tiny winter-exposed buds enlarge by the beginning of April (earlier in its southern limits), exposing ⅛-inch bright yellow blossoms in ¾-inch domed clusters all along the stems of the previous year. These later develop into bright to dark red, semitranslucent, edible cornels (fruit shaped like a bolster pillow with flattened ends to the cylinders); these are obscured in late summer by the foliage and have little ornamental value at that time. The shiny, oval, deep green leaves can enlarge to about 4½ inches with pointed tips; they turn reddish purple or bronze in autumn. Diseases and insects are rarely bothersome. When pruned regularly, this shrub can be trained into a small tree of some distinction, but the effort has to begin when the plant is young. Wood of this species is very hard and is still used today for furniture inlays, toys, and scientific instruments. The cultivar list contains some interesting variations.

CULTIVAR: 'Alba' ('Albacarpa') is a rare form with white flowers.

CULTIVAR: 'Aurea' develops into an even larger plant with leaves mottled in yellow.

CULTIVAR: 'Aureo-Elegantissima' ('Elegantissima') is a less rapid sort carrying large leaves edged in gold and flushed with carmine when they mature for the season; it benefits from some afternoon shading in summer.

CULTIVAR: 'Flava' ('Macrocarpa', 'Xanthocarpa') produces yellow fruiting.

CULTIVAR: 'Nana' forms a compact, rounded bush.

CULTIVAR: 'Variegata' has leaves bordered noticeably and handsomely in white.

CULTIVAR: 'Violacea' is another rare type; it develops violet-blue fruit.

Cornus mas flowers

Cornus mas fruit

Cornus sericea (stolonifera) (red osier dogwood, American dogwood)

Zones 2 to 8   7′ to 10′ high x 7′ to 10′ wide   Sun to light shade

In general appearance this is the North American counterpart to *alba;* it is native to wet areas from Newfoundland to Manitoba and south to Nebraska, Kentucky, and Virginia. Both have red stems, but this species expands vigorously by suckering as well as rooting where the arching stems touch ground, thus creating an unexcelled embankment cover or wide screen in a relatively short period. In cultivation since 1656 and reliably hardy over a vast area, this thicket-forming shrub has bark that once was used by American Indians to make *kinnikinnik,* which they smoked for pleasure. Adapting to all soils, especially consistently moist or even waterlogged ones, it is not bothered by pests or diseases. In late May loosely set 3-inch-wide clusters of dull to creamy white blooms occur, followed by white to blue-toned small fruit that is quickly consumed by birds and other wildlife. Bright to deep red stems support oval to oblong deep green leaves that are whitened beneath and are up to 5 inches long with pointed tips; their autumn color is purplish red. Several cultivars are known.

CULTIVAR: 'Flaviramea' ('Aurea', 'Lutea') grows somewhat shorter than the parent with bright yellow or yellow-green stems, but it is susceptible to disfiguring canker and twig blight diseases.

CULTIVAR: 'Kelseyi' ('Nana') was discovered by Dr. Spaeth (for whom an *alba* cultivar is named) in 1899. It is a dense, low-growing form with great twigginess and heavy foliage.

CULTIVAR: 'Nitida' has green stems.

COTINUS (smoke tree, smokebush)   *Anacardiaceae* (cashew) family

Three species are represented here, one each for North America, southwest China, and southern Europe. Its name is not entirely verified in terms of the association, but it seems to have some reference to the ancient Greek word for the wild olive, since both have yellow inner wood and strong-smelling sap. All *Cotinus* adapt well to dry, poor soil with good drainage and have an affinity for full sun; in fact, they grow too lushly and then flower sparsely when provided with richer soil. Once established, they need very little attention and persist for a long life. The alternate, simple, toothless leaves are supported by long slender stalks and produce rich autumnal tints. The flowers behave oddly and are of themselves not importantly noticeable, but at maturity they become showy and persistent; this is the novel feature of this shrub. Large, loose terminal panicles appear in middle to late spring of very tiny, yellowish or greenish, nondescript blossoms composed of both fertile and sterile florets. The fertile ones mature as minuscule, compressed, sparsely produced drupes, but the flower *stalks* of the sterile ones continue to elongate appreciably with expanded silky hairs and eventually create delicately fluffy masses that cast a "smoky" appearance over much of the plant. These are not flowers in the normal sense but only elongated flower parts which persist throughout the season. Although generally trouble-free, these shrubs occasionally are pestered by powdery mildew and verticillium wilt on the leaves and new stems. At one time these intriguing plants were assigned to the *Rhus* genus, which is sumac.

Cotinus coggyria

Cotinus coggyria (Rhus cotinus) (smoke tree, smokebush, smoke plant, Venetian sumac, wig tree)

Zones 5 to 9   10′ to 15′ high x 15′ to 20′ wide   Sun

Bushy, broad-spreading, and dense, the smoke tree creates a novel summer accent when in fruit with its smoky haze of expanded and fluffy flower parts. It was introduced to cultivation in 1656. The wood yields a yellow dye called "young fustic," and the foliage contains high amounts of tannin, which is used in the leather industry. Crushed leaves and twigs give off a strong, aromatic scent. The plant can be moved easily and adapts well to dry conditions; however, new plants require generous and regular watering to become fully established. The foliage is bluish green, oval, smooth, and up to 3 inches long with slim, ½-inch to 1½-inch petioles, providing a total outline much resembling a tennis racket; the autumnal colors range from yellow to orange-yellow. The tiny greenish flowers emerge by mid-June as much branched clusterings; fertile ones produce ⅛-inch kidney-shaped fruit which are enmeshed in the masses of the more showy, wiry, and hairy flower stalks of the sterile blossoms. These fluffy heads are fawn-colored or pink-toned, may extend to 8 inches in height, and remain persistent into late autumn. When matured, these flower parts provide a decorative haze over much of the silhouette. Several cultivars are known.

CULTIVAR: 'Pendulus' *(var. pendulus)* carries drooping outer branches.

CULTIVAR: 'Purpureus' *(var. purpureus, var. rubrifolius)* has purplish green foliage and flower panicles with dark purple hairs; this color variation often fades with the approach of autumn. Several selected cultivars with deeper and showier foliage color are often listed in catalogs, but they do not perform well consistently in all growing areas; however, the cultivar 'Velvet Cloak' offers the most constancy in its coloring.

COTONEASTER (cotoneaster)   *Rosaceae* (rose) family

An explanation of this genus appears in the "Broadleaf Evergreens" division.

Cotoneaster adpressus   (creeping cotoneaster)

Zones 5 to 9   6″ to 10″ high x 3′ to 4′ wide   Sun to light shade

Prostrate, compact, and slow-growing are the identifying characteristics of this groundcover shrub which often roots where it touches earth. It also tends to take on the configuration of its immediate grading form or the shape of any adjacent boulder; it differs from the similar habit of *horizontalis* in its wavy-edged leaves and lack of a "fishbone" twig pattern. The roots are both sparse and stringy, limiting transplanting possibilities to small containerized plants. Flowers develop by early June as stalkless tiny blossoms in white with pinkish tips set either solitary or in twos at the leaf axils. These become very ornamental, berrylike pomes that are ¼ inch wide in bright red. The dull green, broadly oval, ¼- to ½-inch leaves carry undulating margins and turn reddish in the autumn. Cultivated since 1896, it is a native of western China with a preference for a well-drained, loamy soil. The popular and robust variety *praecox* was discovered in 1905; it sometimes is known as the Nanshan or early cotoneaster for its quick production of fruit. This plant evolves into a domed or mounded form about 2 feet high with arching branches and leaves up to 1 inch long. Its blooms are pink and produce large orange-red fruit sooner than the parent; these usually persist into late November.

Cotoneaster adpressus praecox fruit

Cotoneaster apiculatus   (cranberry cotoneaster)

Zones 5 to 9   2′ to 3′ high x 3′ to 6′ wide   Sun to light shade

This species is also similar to *horizontalis* in form but develops more irregular branching and larger-sized fruit. It is very popular in the midwestern parts of the United States and tends to remain semievergreen in the southern portions of its growing range. The habit is low and creeping with some tendency to stand erect where it comes into contact with a wall, illustrating its potential usefulness as an attractive espalier when trained. Nurseries often treat it as a top-grafted standard to display its pendulous branching, but this special form is difficult to maintain where heavy, wet snow or constant ice is a problem. Normally this shrub is well considered as an embankment cover; draping it over the backs of high walls will highlight its dense branching and showy fruit. Because of its stiff mass of twigs, however, it tends to trap air-blown debris readily. The early June blossoms are mostly solitary and ¼ inch wide in rose-pink. The fruit somewhat resembles a cranberry in size and shape with its ⅜-inch diameter and shining, scarlet color. It often lasts well into November if chipmunks do not eat it first. The leaves are glossy, dark green, nearly oval, thin, sharply top-pointed, and up to ½ inch wide; they turn bronze-red to purple-red by autumn.

Cotoneaster apiculatus

Cotoneaster dielsiana fruit

Cotoneaster dielsiana (applantus) (Diel's cotoneaster)
Zones 6 to 9   5′ to 7′ high x 6′ to 9′ wide   Sun to light shade

Native to central and western China and introduced by 1900, here is a gracefully mounded shrub with slender, arching branches and generous fruiting clusters much enjoyed by pheasants and other wildlife. Rapid-growing, it serves well as an informal hedge or border specimen; it may be semievergreen in mild and protected growing areas. The flowers are pink or white with a red tinge; they appear early in June as groups of three to seven at the leaf axils. Its bright red, ¼-inch, round to pear-shaped fruit becomes even more striking when the foliage turns orange and red in the autumn. The almost oval leaves are about an inch long and have felted hairy undersides which become brown-toned in late summer; the new stem growth is also hairy. A few varieties are known.

VARIETY: *elegans* tends to remain semievergreen with smaller and more rounded foliage; the pendulous fruit is orange-red and somewhat fuzzy in appearance.

VARIETY: *major* carries thinner but longer leaves up to 1½ inches.

Cotoneaster divaricatus flowers

Cotoneaster divaricatus (spreading cotoneaster)
Zones 5 to 9   5′ to 6′ high x 6′ to 8′ wide   Sun to light shade

One of the best cotoneasters for reliable annual fruiting and autumn color, this rapidly growing, fine-textured shrub from western and central China came into cultivation by 1904 and has remained popular for hedges, masses, and specimens. It blends well with other shrub forms, and although its outline is not quite as graceful as that of *dielsiana*, it presents an attractively rounded shape with its interlacing branches. Adapting well to both windy and seashore conditions, it also grows acceptably on dry, rocky sites, although its preference is for a moist, fertile, well-drained soil. Pests and diseases are less of a problem than with many other species. The number of late May blooms varies from two to four; they are produced mostly in threes of light, purplish pink color about ⅛ inch wide. Its bright to dark red, ellipsoid, ¼-inch fruiting is abundantly set and is favored by wildlife; however, the plant tends to self-seed freely. The shiny, dark green foliage is acutely tapered at both ends and lengthens to almost 1 inch with a width of ½ inch. One of the last shrubs to drop its leaves, this plant ends the season in a color blend of orange and red.

Cotoneaster horizontalis

Cotoneaster horizontalis (davidiana) (rock cotoneaster, rockspray cotoneaster, quinceberry, plumed cotoneaster)
Zones 5 to 9   1½′ to 3′ high x 5′ to 6′ wide   Sun to light shade

This is probably the best known and most widely planted of all the *Cotoneaster* species. Native to western China and cultivated since 1870, it offers horizontally spreading branches with "fishbone" outlines, producing an unusual textural effect, especially when handled as an espalier. Slow-growing, it often takes the shape of large adjacent rocks or irregular grading. Like other low-growing cotoneasters, it makes an admirable groundcover, but it also tends to trap debris because of its stiff and heavy branching. Mostly deciduous except in mild climates, the plant has dark, glossy, roundish leaves between ¼ and ½ inch long showing flat edges; its autumn color is rich crimson where it is not semievergreen. The flowers open by mid-June in pink-white to white with one or two set in the leaf axils. Its bright red but small (³⁄₁₆-inch) fruit is more plentiful and conspicuous at the southern end of its growing range.

Cotoneaster lucidus   (hedge cotoneaster)

Zones 4 to 9   6′ to 10′ high x 6′ to 10′ wide   Sun to light shade

Native to Siberia and northern Asia, this vigorous, large-scaled, glossy-leaved shrub has been in cultivation since 1840. It carries generous crops of fruiting, but they are black. One of the hardier species, the plant serves well for screening and for hedge making with its erect, dense, and bushy habit. Blossoming arrives by early June in large clusters of three to eight small white flowers with pink overtones. The oval, ⅓-inch-wide, black fruit is conspicuous only for its large quantity. More noticeable are the sizable, up to 2-inch-long leaves with their shiny top surfaces and heavy concentrations along the slender, spreading stems; these become vivid yellow and red in the autumn. Webworms are important defoliating pests in some growing areas. This species is often mistakenly sold as *acutifolius*, the Peking cotoneaster, which is similar in habit but is hardier (zone 3) with less flower production and carries foliage showing somewhat hairy surfaces.

Cotoneaster racemiflorus   (no common name)

Zones 5 to 9   6′ to 8′ high x 8′ to 10′ wide   Sun to light shade

Especially attractive for its fruit, here is a graceful species native from northern Africa to western Asia with slender, arching branches seldom found erect. Cultivated since 1829, it blooms during early June with white, ¼-inch, generous flower clusters holding three to twelve blossoms. The brick-red fruit is round and ¼ inch wide; it presents a showy display in summer, especially when contrasted against the glossy leaves with their gray or whitened undersides. This foliage is pear-shaped and up to 1⅛ inches long but does not color appreciably in the autumn. New growth shows noticeable hairiness in either gray or reddish brown. Several varieties are available.

VARIETY: *nummularius* has broader foliage and only two to seven flowers in a cluster.

VARIETY: *royaleanus* is a dwarfed form with smaller leaves and sketchy flowering.

VARIETY: *soongoricus (C. soongoricus)* is hardy into zone 4 and carries gray-green leaves plus larger pink to red fruit; it is the most attractive variety in this group.

VARIETY: *veitchii* develops leaves that are acutely tapered at both ends and large, dark red fruiting.

CYTISUS (broom)   *Leguminosae* (pea) family

Fifty species of spiny or thornless deciduous and evergreen shrubs belong in this genus; however, some botanists relegate some to other genera now, especially to *Genista*. All are showy in bloom and generally achieve heights between 4 and 6 feet. Most live natively in the Mediterranean region or on the Canary Islands. The name may be derived from one of two sources: the Greek *kytisos* (a kind of clover), which would refer to the leaf shape, or *Kythnus*, an island of the Greek archipelago where it may

have grown. They are easy to cultivate provided that they are given full sun and a soil that is well drained, not overly rich, and neutral in balance. While tolerant of lime, they dislike very acid conditions. All are remarkably free of pests and diseases. Cut branches have been bound together and used for centuries as household brooms, and the wood is unique since it does not readily catch fire, even when thoroughly dried. Its cured and roasted seeds have served adequately as a coffee substitute, while the immature flower buds have sometimes been soaked in vinegar and used as a salad topping; they have a caperlike flavor.

Difficult to transplant except when young (preferably containerized), all are best moved only in spring, and to permanent locations. Any serves attractively as a groundcover, especially in erosion control, as a border specimen, or as an espalier for a wall or fence. In pruning for shape, avoid cutting into the hard older wood since this has a negative effect on future growth. While most of its flowering is yellow, plants with cream, white, crimson, purple, and bronze blossoming are not rare. The tiny foliage is alternate, compound with three leaflets (cloverlike), generally not over an inch long, and supported by very slender—almost wiry—green twigs and young stems. The small, flat, podlike fruit is dull-colored and offers no landscape value. Where they thrive, brooms offer special attractions of form, color, and texture.

Cytisus x kewensis (Genista kewensis) (Kew broom)
Zones 6 to 9   6″ to 12″ high x 4′ to 6′ wide   Sun

This is a chance seedling of *ardoini* and *multiflorus* that was found at the Royal Botanic Garden of Kew, England, in 1891. Procumbent and mat-forming with slender green stems, it is very attractive and showy when in bloom and serves admirably as a small accent or rock garden plant. Pale sulfur-yellow to creamy white ½-inch flowers appear by mid-May in groups of two or three generously placed along the stems of the previous season. Some leaves are simple and tiny, while most are trifoliate with hairy, very narrow shapes.

Cytisus nigricans (Lembotropis nigricans)
(spike broom)
Zones 5 to 9   3′ to 6′ high x 2′ to 3′ wide   Sun

Because these flowers turn black when dried, Linnaeus provided the plant with the *nigricans* identification. Otherwise, this is an elegant and unique upright shrub with consistent annual flowering regardless of weather. Native from central and southeastern Europe to central Russia, it has been cultivated since 1730 because of its dependable and lengthy blooming period. Flowering begins by early July and extends into early September with bright, lemon-yellow, ⅜-inch blossoms crowded along slender terminal spikes up to 1 foot tall. Its narrow, slightly hairy pods are almost an inch long and nondecorative. The mid-green, nearly acute leaves appear on downy, cylindrical twigs and are 1 inch long with somewhat hairy undersides. Its variety *elongatus* reblooms in the autumn at the tips of the fruiting stems. Spring-prune both of these to encourage an abundance of new stems for flowering.

Cytisus x praecox (Genista praecox) (Warminster broom)

Zones 6 to 9   6' to 10' high x 4' to 6' wide   Sun

Cytisus x praecox

This plant is a natural cross between *multiflorus* and *purgans* that has been cultivated since 1867. It has a vigorous, dense, rounded habit of arching stems and showy flowering during mid-May. It is often the first species to bloom, and it requires perfect drainage along with poor soil to remain durable. While its pale yellow coloring combines well with early azaleas and spring bulbs, this soil requirement is difficult to meet in combined plantings. The plant resembles *albus* when young and is often mistakenly sold for it but has denser branching and very sparse foliage. Old plants resent any major pruning. The flowers are solitary or paired in the leaf axils and are produced generously. These are ½ inch long with the two upper petals green-yellow and the lower two pale yellow; unfortunately, their odor is offensive. The foliage is oval, gray-green, and silky-hairy; it is composed only of simple ¾-inch leaves skimpily distributed over the green stems. From any distance this plant appears to be leafless. The cultivar 'Albus' carries white flowers, while *cv.* 'Allgold' has arching sprays of deeper yellow blossoms.

Cytisus purpureus (Genista purpurea, Chamaecytisus purpureus) (purple broom)

Zones 6 to 9   1' to 2' high x 3' to 5' wide   Sun

Ideally suited by its creeping habit for groundcover use, this species is unique for its flower coloring. Often featured as a specimen, it has lilac-purple to deep purple ¾-inch flowers clustered in the leaf axils of the previous year's growth. The bloom appears during late May in company with dark green foliage of three leaflets about an inch long. The smooth pod fruit ranges between 1 inch and 1½ inches in length.

Cytisus scoparius (Genista scoparia, Sarothamnus scoparius) (Scotch broom, Scots broom, common broom)

Zones 6 to 9   6' to 10' high x 4' to 6' wide   Sun

Cytisus scoparius cultivar

Abundant in western Europe and the British Isles (where it is the only native broom), this popular shrub has naturalized itself in North America both on the Pacific coast and in the northeastern United States. Introduced here during colonial times, it tends to be prolific as a self-seeder to the point of becoming weedy where it thrives. The extensive cultivar list, however, tends to be more sedate about this detail as a result of its own genetic complexity, and the cultivars today are by far the more popular plants. Although these shrubs are considered mainly trouble-free, gall mites on the stems often can be very destructive. All forms are usually erect with slender, downy, very green stems, and all show generous flowering from middle to late May. The parent plant has rich, bright yellow, mostly solitary, 1-inch flowers at the leaf axils of the previous year's growth. Foliage is mostly oval and only ½ inch long, while the narrowly oblong, hairy fruit can be up to 2 inches in length. All brooms have flowers composed of two parts with differing lengths; the two main, longer sections are referred to as the "standards," while the side, smaller petals are called "wings." The following cultivars are popular.

CULTIVAR: 'Andreanus' *(var. andreanus)* came from Normandy, France, in 1884. It develops yellow standards and wings of dark brownish crimson.

CULTIVAR: 'Burkwoodii' has deep red blossoms.

CULTIVAR: 'Butterfly' carries orange-yellow flowering.

CULTIVAR: 'Cornish Cream' displays cream-colored blossoming.

CULTIVAR: 'Dragonfly' is vigorous with deep yellow standards and rich crimson wings.

CULTIVAR: 'Firefly' has yellow standards and bronze wings.

CULTIVAR: 'Fulgens' is a compact plant with late bloom of bright copper-orange.

CULTIVAR: 'Golden Sunset' has a vigorous spreading habit and cream standards with gold wings.

CULTIVAR: 'Hollandia' is purple-red.

CULTIVAR: 'St. Mary's' is pure white in flower.

CULTIVAR: 'San Francisco' shows rich red coloring.

DAPHNE (garland flower)   *Thymelaeaceae* (mezereum) family

An explanation of this genus appears in the "Broadleaf Evergreens" division.

Daphne x burkwoodi (Burkwood daphne)

Zones 6 to 8   3′ to 4′ high x 3′ to 4′ wide   Light shade

Introduced in 1935 by Allan Burkwood of England, the plant is a cross between *caucasicum* and *cneorum*. Upright and rounded in outline, it is vigorous with a middle to late May, freely produced bloom of creamy white that fades to light pink. The ½-inch, star-shaped, tubular florets are sweetly fragrant and come grouped from six to sixteen in terminal heads that are about 2 inches wide and surrounded by emerging foliage. The fruit is a red berry up to ⅛ inch wide, but it is rarely produced. Foliage remains partly evergreen in many locations; it is bluish green, narrowly lancelike, and about 1½ inches long. This shrub prefers a well-drained, moist, almost neutral soil for its best response; move it only as a small containerized plant. The popular cultivar 'Somerset' came into culture during 1939 and is almost identical to the parent except for somewhat denser branching and a stronger growth habit. Reportedly, it can elevate to 6 feet (probably only in protected, mild-climate areas), but it is also said to possess more hardiness and to grow in some parts of zone 5. In any event, this cultivar should become the preferred choice since it is propagated by nurseries now more than the parent.

Daphne mezereum

Daphne mezereum (February daphne, mezereon, mezereum)

Zones 5 to 9   4′ to 5′ high x 2′ to 3′ wide   Light shade

Daphnes are attractive but mysterious plants, and even with the best of care and placement, this long-cultivated species may die suddenly for no apparent reason. Although one of the most easily grown species, it is workable only when installed as a small containerized plant since large ones resent any transplanting effort. Once established, this is a robust and stiffly erect shrub with a rounded outline. It blooms in April (earlier in southern locations) with ½-inch lilac-purple to magenta or even white flowers carrying an admirable scent; these appear in clusters along the stem growth of the previous year. In cultivation since 1561, the plant is native to Europe, the British Isles, western Asia, and Siberia; it usually is found growing wild on mountain meadows or slopes. All parts are poisonous, especially the egg-shaped, ¼-inch-wide, scarlet or yellow fruit. Avoid having it if children are likely to eat any of its parts. The leaves are alternately placed, thin, colored from dull light green to bright green (depending on culture and soil conditions), and wedge-shaped to 3½ inches long and ¾ inch wide. A recent virus infection causes consistent leaf drop in some growing areas and is as yet incurable. Several cultivars are available.

CULTIVAR: 'Alba' has white earlier flowering and yellow fruit on a more vigorous plant with strongly upright branching.

CULTIVAR: 'Grandiflora' develops to a 6-foot height with larger blossoms which often open in late autumn.

CULTIVAR: 'Rosea' carries clear pink, large flowering.

CULTIVAR: 'Rubra' displays reddish purple blooms.

DEUTZIA (deutzia)   *Saxifragaceae* (saxifrage) family

Between forty and fifty species of deciduous (rarely evergreen) shrubs native to temperate Asia and the mountains of Mexico make up this genus of very hardy plants grown mainly for their flowering effects. They are easily cultivated as a group, and most can be moved bare-rooted when small to adapt to any well-drained fertile soil, especially in full sun. Provide copious water while in bloom and during summertime dryness. The flowers are usually white and unscented and appear in panicles or spikes on stems of the previous season. They have five petals as compared with the four of the close relation *Philadelphus* (mock orange), and the fruit is a nonornamental capsule. Leaves are opposite and toothed and develop on hollow stems with brown peeling bark. Trouble-free, they resist all inroads from insects and diseases but can suffer leaf scorch where the soil becomes too dry. Named by Carl Pehr Thunberg, this genus commemorates his friend Johann van der Deutz, an eighteenth-century Dutch lawyer and patron of botany who financed Thunberg's plant expedition to Japan.

Deutzia gracilis   (slender deutzia, snow flower)

Zones 5 to 8   3′ to 6′ high x 3′ to 4′ wide   Sun to light shade

A popular specimen or hedge plant easy to grow in any good soil, this is the parent of many hybrids; it came into cultivation from Japan in 1840. The habit is compact, dense, mounded, and graceful with wide-spreading and arching branches; its general size is usually only 3 feet throughout much of its growing range. Unfortunately, winter dieback of twigs is common annually in the coldest areas. The blossoming appears by late May as pure white, star-shaped, ¾-inch flowers in loose clusters that are freely produced. The foliage colors dull, pale green with a mild purplish overcast by autumn; these leaves are lancelike to 2½ inches and carry a sandpapery feel on both surfaces. The cultivar 'Aurea' has pale yellow flowering, while the recent *cv.* 'Pink Pompon' develops pale pink blossoms and grows slowly.

Deutzia gracilis

Deutzia scabra cv. 'Plena'

Deutzia scabra (fortunei, sieboldiana) (fuzzy deutzia)

Zones 6 to 9   7' to 10' high x 4' to 8' wide   Sun to light shade

Tall and erect with spreading but stiff branching, this shrub is native to both Japan and China and has been in cultivation since 1822. Attractive as a border accent or a screen, it carries less foliage at the base than many other shrubs and shows no autumnal coloring. Flowers develop from middle to late June in slender, erect panicles between 2 and 4½ inches high with cup-shaped ¾-inch blossom clusters of white which may have pink-toned or purplish exteriors. The leaves vary from oval to oblong and have a potential length up to 3 inches. Both leaf surfaces are covered with star-shaped hairs presenting a gritty feel. Many attractive cultivars are known.

CULTIVAR: 'Candidissima' ('Wellesii') is taller with double pure white flowers.

CULTIVAR: 'Fortunei' has larger blossoms.

CULTIVAR: 'Mirabilis' grows vigorously and develops large flowering.

CULTIVAR: 'Plena' is one of the last cultivars to bloom and displays white double flowers tinged rosy-purple outside in spikes up to 4½ inches.

CULTIVAR: 'Pride of Rochester' is almost identical with *cv.* 'Plena' but blooms slightly earlier.

CULTIVAR: 'Rosea' has rose-tinted flowers.

CULTIVAR: 'Staphyloides' produces very large flowers in drooping clusters.

CULTIVAR: 'Thunbergii' carries white blossoms with orange centers.

CULTIVAR: 'Watereri' shows white flowering tinged carmine outside.

ELAEAGNUS (oleaster, silverberry, lingaro)
Elaeagnaceae (oleaster) family

An explanation of this genus appears in the "Broadleaf Evergreens" division.

Elaeagnus angustifolia (Russian olive, oleaster, wild olive, silverberry, trebizondedate)

Zones 3 to 9   15' to 20' high x 15' to 10' wide   Sun

Cultivated in England since the sixteenth century, this very hardy shrub (it may become a small tree with age) is noted for its silvery foliage (attractive when placed near purple-leaved plants) and its use as a tall screen, hedge, or windbreak, especially at the shore. Native to southern Europe as well as western and central Asia, it requires adequate room to expand and grows easily on almost any soil type. The flowering appears in early June as yellowish white, ¼-inch, noticeably fragrant blossoms set as one to three in the leaf axils. The late summer, ½-inch, olive-shaped fruiting is edible; it is covered with silvery dots or minute scales over a yellow base. Its 1½- to 3½-inch willowlike foliage is distinguished by its silvery undersides, but the tops are a dull gray-green. New stem growth is also silver-colored, and some of its short spur twigs end in a sharpened tip. Trunk development is often very picturesquely crooked and shows brown, flaking, ornamental bark as the plant ages. There is no autumnal color change. Recently, sudden and severe stem loss has plagued this dependable plant; this may be due to verticillium wilt, a disease not readily controlled. The variety *orientalis* carries larger fruit and broader leaves and is usually spine-free, while *spinosa* is just the opposite with spiny twig ends throughout the plant and densely scaly broadened foliage.

Elaeagnus umbellata (autumn elaeagnus)

Zones 4 to 8   10′ to 18′ high x 12′ to 20′ wide   Sun

This is a vigorous, trouble-free, hardy grower with silvery foliage held long into autumn. It has recently become popular for these qualities in highway plantings throughout much of the northeastern United States, among other places, but it self-seeds prodigiously and is now crowding out many other desirable plant types in the vicinity. Such quick dominance by an introduced shrub (it is native to China, Korea, Japan, and the Himalayas) confirms that more careful evaluation needs to be made if we are not to have another weedy shrub on our hands, regardless of its landscape merits. It was first cultivated in 1830 and adjusts well to any well-drained soil. Flowers appear by mid-May as yellow-white, pleasantly scented blossoms of one to three held in the leaf axils. The erect, ¼- to ½-inch-long, scarlet fruit later is covered with silver dots or tiny scales and draws keen interest from birds, which distribute the seeds widely. The elliptic, often crinkle-edged foliage is 1 to 3 inches long and is dark green above and prominently silvered beneath; these leaves persist in reasonable quantities until the beginning of December. New twigs are often spiny and are colored either yellow-brown or silvery brown. (This species is often incorrectly listed in catalogs as *argentea*, which is an outmoded name for the totally different species *commutata*.) The variety *parvifolia (E. parvifolia)* carries silvery branching and silver, pink-toned fruiting.

ENKIANTHUS (enkianthus)   Ericaceae (heath) family

Ten species of deciduous or partly evergreen shrubs make up this genus of tall, durable plants with two seasons of striking landscape interest: spring and autumn. They are native to China, Japan, and the Himalayas. The name comes from the Greek *enkyos* ("swollen") and *anthos* ("flower"), an allusion to the pouched flower of some sorts as viewed in China by the eighteenth-century Portuguese botanist and missionary Juan Loureiro, who published his observations in 1790. Contemporary botanists do not hold to his views, but the name has been established. The Chinese version translates as "hanging bells," a more apt description of the flowering, and at one time boat loads of *Enkianthus* were offered to honor their gods. Recently in Hong Kong the government had to restrict the collection of such huge masses for religious celebrations as being ecologically unsound; it then placed the plants in quarantine under the protection of the law. Enthusiasm for flowers occasionally has its restrictions.

These shrubs thrive in well-drained, acid, moist, peaty soil but are intolerant of drought and alkaline conditions. Protect them from excessive heat and offer shade from intense summer sun. Their narrowly erect silhouette presents an outstandingly unique and neat appearance since the curved branching is arranged in whorls around the central stem much like the spokes of an upside-down umbrella; these decidedly shapely plants require no pruning to look well. The foliage is alternate, simple, crowded toward the ends of twigs, and glowingly colored in the autumn. Flowers appear in the spring as drooping terminal clusters composed of urnlike blossoms much like those of the blueberry, a close relation. Pests and diseases are not likely to cause problems. In sum, these are elegant shrubs worth including wherever they do well.

Elaeagnus umbellata

Elaeagnus umbellata flowers

Elaeagnus umbellata fruit

Enkianthus campanulatus

Enkianthus campanulatus (redvein enkianthus, necklace shrub, bellflower tree)

Zones 5 to 9   15′ to 30′ high x 5′ to 8′ wide   Sun to light shade

Refined in all its parts, this easily grown shrub is native to the mountains of Japan and came into cultivation during 1880. Treat it as you would azalea by providing a moist, acid, well-drained soil and filtered light. It is slow-growing and erect with tiered (whorled) branching and tip-clustered foliage on smooth, red-toned stems. The leaves are narrowly oval, 1½ to 3 inches long, finely toothed, and dull green; they color vividly by autumn in bright red or yellow-red. Its mid-May flowering develops as the foliage emerges in pendulous clusters of cup-shaped, long-lasting blossoms ⅓ to ½ inch long on the previous year's stems; these are yellowish to pale orange with dark red veining on the outsides. The fruit is an inconspicuous tiny brown capsule and appears in clusterings. There are no diseases or insect pests of any importance. This shrub deserves to be more popular than it now is.

Enkianthus perulatus (japonicus) (white enkianthus)

Zones 5 to 9   5′ to 6′ high x 2½′ to 4′ wide   Sun to light shade

Discovered by Sir Rutherford Alcock at Nagasaki, Japan (its native country), in 1859, this species blooms in late May about a week after *campanulatus* and with its new leaves unfurled. Slow in growth, compact, and dense, it carries drooping clusters of green-tinted white flowers that are ⅓ inch long, urn-shaped, and narrowed at the mouths. The top-crowded foliage is wedge-shaped or oval, finely toothed, between ¾ inch and 2 inches long, and bright green on reddened twigs. The normal autumn color is brilliantly red, but occasionally some plants show yellow tones, too. It has no problems from pests or diseases but is bothered by drought and intense sunlight.

EUONYMUS (spindle tree, strawberry bush)
Celastraceae (staff tree) family

An explanation of this genus appears in the "Broadleaf Evergreens" division.

Euonymus alata bark

Euonymus alata (winged spindle tree, winged euonymus, burning bush)

Zones 4 to 7   7′ to 12′ high x 7′ to 12′ wide   Sun to light shade

Here is a popular plant that offers several seasons of interest. It is a dependable, easy to grow, dense shrub with side-spreading stiff branches carrying two to four corky ridges that are prominent along the stems. Serviceable as a specimen, screen, hedge, or small tree (with regular pruning), it grows easily in any soil except wet ones and is immune to the scale insect attacks which greatly damage so many other species. It presents an interesting winter silhouette with its irregular winged branches, but its true prominence in the landscape comes in autumn when the medium to deep green, double-toothed, 2-inch oval leaves turn brilliant crimson or scarlet. Then it appears to be consumed by fire if located in full sun (these leaves turn only purplish red in too much shade). The unnoticed yellowish or greenish tiny flowers develop in late May in clusters of three followed by ⅛-inch purplish capsules which open to reveal an orange aril (or cap) over the seeds. Introduced in 1860, the plant is native to northeastern Asia and central China. A drawback is the dense, fibrous root system near the surface as it matures since this compacted rooting does not allow any other plant to grow around its base for very long. Several variations are known.

CULTIVAR: 'Compacta' is somewhat shorter and slower-growing than the parent with a rounded habit and slender stems that are devoid of any winged growths. (I know this plant can become quite sizable since my own now measures 10 feet high and 20 feet wide after 25 years of growth.)

CULTIVAR: 'Monstrosa' *(E. monstrosa)* develops very vigorously in all its parts.

VARIETY: *aptera* shows either slightly winged or totally wingless stems.

Euonymus europaea (European spindle tree, cardinal's cap)

Zones 3 to 9   12′ to 20′ high x 12′ to 20′ wide   Sun to light shade

Natively found in Europe and western Asia, this shrub has been cultivated for centuries for its handsome fruit crops of autumn; it performs well as a formal or informal hedge. The "spindle" part of its name comes from the commercial use of the wood at one time for making skewers and thread spindles. This is an erect, vigorous, bushy-headed shrub or small tree with four-sided green twigs and dull, dark green, oval to lancelike leaves 1 to 3 inches long with coarse teeth. These offer only a bland yellow or purple-toned color in the autumn, but they last long into the season. During mid-June the yellow-green ⅓-inch flowers appear in groups of three to seven, but they emit a very strong and unpleasant odor. The ½- to ¾-inch fruit varies from red to deep pink and opens to show a vividly orange aril (or cover) atop the seeds; these showy capsules endure for much of the early winter. This species is prone to severe annual attacks of both scale insect and aphid infestations, causing serious disfigurement to leaves and stems unless checked promptly. A goodly number of cultivars exist.

Euonymus europaea **fruit**

Euonymus europaea **scale insect infestation**

CULTIVAR 'Albus' grows only 10 feet high and produces conspicuous white fruiting in the winter.

CULTIVAR: 'Aldenhamensis' is the preferred cultivar with its larger fruit of bright pink on elongated stalks; it expands to about 12 feet in height.

CULTIVAR: 'Burtonii' is a compact form with orange-red fruit.

CULTIVAR: 'Haematocarpa' ('Fructo-Coccineo') has deep red fruiting.

CULTIVAR: 'Pumilus' develops a dwarfed upright silhouette with only a 4-foot height.

CULTIVAR: 'Red Cascade' becomes 10 feet tall with arching branches and heavy crops of rose-red fruit.

VARIETY: *intermedia* has larger foliage and bright red sizable fruiting.

Euonymus sachalinensis (planipes) (Sakhalin spindle tree)

Zones 6 to 9   8′ to 12′ high x 12′ to 16′ wide   Sun to light shade

Attractive in foliage and in fruit, this species is native to northeastern Asia and came into cultivation during 1892. Upright and slow to expand, it matures to a broad specimen that is serviceable for tall hedges and screens. The wedge-shaped, bright green leaves expand up to 5 inches and are top-pointed with rounded teeth; they become an interesting shade of yellow by autumn. The insignificant ⅛-inch flowers appear during early June as yellow-green in loose clusters followed by profuse, pendant, showy, ¾-inch scarlet capsules with an orange aril over the seeds. The plant appears not to be bothered by any major pest or disease.

FORSYTHIA (golden bells)   *Oleaceae* (olive) family

Six or seven species of deciduous, erect or spreading, hardy shrubs make up this genus; most are found in eastern Asia, but one exists in southeastern Europe. All are simple to grow well and transplant readily at any age. They are not particular about soil and exposure, but they are heavy feeders (much like *Euonymus alata*) with extensive root systems. Not tolerant of prolonged drought, they enjoy copious watering in summer, which assists in the formation of more flower budding and greater winter hardiness. Well suited to the rigors of city pollution—if not the occasional dryness— these are some of the most versatile and floriferous shrubs known. For quick rejuvenation when overgrown, cut to ground level in late winter; they will respond readily with generous growth. Winter-cut branches easily force into bloom since these plants have exposed budding. The plant is named for William Forsyth, an eighteenth-century horticulturist to King George II of England and one of the founders of the Royal Horticultural Society there. The first European viewing of this group was in Holland during 1833 as a novelty importation from Japan; they have remained popular since.

The showy, scentless, yellow, bell-like flowers are entire but four-parted at the mouths and bloom generously before the leaves emerge in spring. They form in clusters at the leaf axils during summer, and because they are winter-exposed, they can be readily damaged by severe prolonged cold. The fruit is a small, woody capsule usually covered with warty bumps; it has no landscape merit. Foliage is opposite and simple or tripartly compound on somewhat squared stems. The autumn color is usually bronze-toned or purplish. Pests and diseases are rarely a problem.

Forsythia x intermedia cultivar

Forsythia x intermedia   (border forsythia)

Zones 5 to 9   7' to 10' high x 7' to 10' wide   Sun to light shade

Here is a hybrid cross from Germany made in 1885 between *suspensa* and *viridissima* which has become the source of an extraordinary number of attractive cultivars much preferred to the parent now. Upright, arching, and spreading, the plant blooms from late March to mid-April (earlier in southern locations) with pale to deep yellow flowers about an inch wide. The medium green leaves are oval to lanceolate, toothed, and up to 5 inches long; sometimes three-parted shorter leaves appear on robust shoots. It accepts any soil condition except wetness and has long been valued for border specimens, hedges, screens, and masses, especially the cultivars. The following are the current ones.

CULTIVAR: 'Arnold Dwarf' (1941) has deep green foliage on a low-growing, creeping form that is useful as a sturdy groundcover in difficult situations; its stems root where they touch open earth. The flowering, however, is only intermittent and is of a pallid greenish yellow tone. It is one of many cultivars developed at the Arnold Arboretum in Boston.

CULTIVAR: 'Arnold Giant' (1939) behaves in a stiff, upright manner to 8 feet with thick large leaves and 2-inch deep yellow blossoms.

CULTIVAR: 'Beatrix Farrand' (1944) is derived from *cv*. 'Arnold Giant'. It exhibits great hardiness, an erect habit, dense growth, and vivid yellow 2½-inch-wide flowers.

CULTIVAR: 'Densiflora' (1899) offers a stiffly upright but compact form with profuse pale yellow blossoming.

CULTIVAR: 'Karl Sax' (1944 but named in 1960) is also very hardy and is similar to *cv.* 'Beatrix Farrand', but it develops golden yellow flowering; its buds are hardier in winter than most others and should be preferred in the northern limits of its growing range.

CULTIVAR: 'Lynnwood' ('Lynwood Gold') (1935) originated in Ireland and displays 1¾-inch-wide flowers maturing even wider; these are set more evenly and more generously than usual along the sides of the stems.

CULTIVAR: 'Nana' (1910) is low-growing and sluggish with a late bloom of greenish yellow flowering.

CULTIVAR: 'Primulina' (1910) has pale yellow flowers crowded only at the bases of the yellow-brown twigs.

CULTIVAR: 'Spectabilis' (1906) came from Germany and shows enormously wide, 2-inch, deep yellow blossoms clustered in groups of five to six.

CULTIVAR: 'Spring Glory' (1930) offers clear, pale yellow flowers (deeper-toned than *cv.* 'Primulina') up to 2 inches wide; it is the most popular cultivar planted today.

CULTIVAR: 'Vitellina' (1906) is another German introduction. It develops a strong-growing, erect habit with blossoms that are deep yellow but only up to an inch wide.

Forsythia suspensa (sieboldii) (weeping forsythia)

Zones 5 to 8   6' to 8' high x 10' to 15' wide   Sun to light shade

Both rambling and cascading in form, this species is best planted atop high walls or on embankments; it "bunches up" in a tangled mass of contorted stems when used as a specimen. Although native to China, it was introduced to Holland from a Japanese garden in 1833. Sparsely flowered compared with *x intermedia*, it offers a gracefully slender-stemmed option which similarly accepts any soil but wet. The golden yellow 1½-inch flowers open during mid-April from buds set singly or in small clusters on the very long flowering stems; its petal divisions are narrow and much more widespread from one another than in most other species. The foliage is medium green, oblong to oval, toothed, and between 3 and 4 inches long; occasionally it produces noticeable numbers of tripartite leaves with deep lobes on its normally hollow stems. Several cultivars are known.

Forsythia suspensa

CULTIVAR: 'Atrocarpa' shows a robust habit and dark purple twigs with pale yellow flowers, but this occurs only on older plants since young ones are flowerless for a time.

CULTIVAR: 'Aurea' carries yellow-toned foliage.

CULTIVAR: 'Decipiens' grows vigorously and produces deep yellow solitary flowering held on 1-inch stalks.

CULTIVAR: 'Variegata' has foliage variegated in yellow.

FOTHERGILLA (fothergilla, witch alder)   *Hamamelidaceae* (witch hazel) family

Either four or five species (depending on the authority) of deciduous shrubs belong to this genus. Like *Enkianthus*, these offer two seasons of landscape interest: spring and autumn. They are native to the southeastern United States. Its name honors John Fothergill, an eighteenth-century English physician and friend of both Benjamin Franklin and the botanist John Bartram, who collected native American plants for display in his English garden. Its spring bloom emerges from winter-naked flower buds which expand into 1- to 2-inch-wide terminal spikes or heads of white to cream, scented, feathery-looking masses of fifteen to twenty-four stamens (there are no evident petals) resembling a bottle brush; these appear either when the leaves are just emerging or when they are half developed. The alternate simple foliage is coarsely toothed and carries deep-set veining. The fruit is a beaked, hard capsule of no special landscape merit. Its autumn colorings are a blend of yellow, orange, red, and purplish red distributed throughout the plant; however, the more vivid displays occur only on plants raised in the southern parts of the United States. Provide a cool, moist, acid, well-drained site. These shrubs rarely require pruning attention and are not bothered much by diseases or insect pests. They are not always easy to establish, however.

Fothergilla major

Fothergilla major (large fothergilla)

Zones 6 to 8   6′ to 10′ high x 5′ to 8′ wide   Sun to light shade

Here is the most ornamental species of *Fothergilla*, with more drought tolerance than *gardenii* and a more pyramidal silhouette than *monticola*. Native to the dry and sunny parts of the southern Appalachians, it grows from Virginia to northern Georgia and Alabama. Erect, dense, slow-growing, and stiffly branched, the plant was introduced to culture in 1780 but became lost and was reintroduced during 1902. The creamy white blooms stand 2 inches high and appear during early May with the emerging leaves; these flowers have an attractive fragrance. The dark green, nearly round leaves are 2 to 4 inches in length, are toothed in the upper portion, and are gray-toned beneath. In autumn they will show a bright mix of yellow, orange, and red if the summer was not overly dry. Its fruit is egg-shaped, downy, somewhat woody, and ½ inch long.

Fothergilla monticola (Alabama fothergilla)

Zones 6 to 9   4′ to 6′ high x 6′ to 8′ wide   Sun to light shade

Native from North Carolina to Alabama and introduced during 1899, this species is considered by some authorities to be only a form of *major*. Slow-growing and mounded with spreading branches, it blooms during mid-May with the foliage already developed; these white spikes enlarge to 2½ inches and develop a pleasant odor. The foliage is deep green with lighter green undersides and lengthens to about 4 inches with only slight indentations along the upper margins. In many areas the autumn color is totally scarlet, but in others it becomes a mix of red and orange.

HAMAMELIS (witch hazel)   *Hamamelidaceae* (witch hazel) family

Six species of deciduous shrubs or small trees are found in this genus, which is native to the temperate parts of eastern North America and eastern Asia. All grow easily and rarely require pruning. These hardy plants create appeal with their early spring (occasionally late autumn) flowering and perform satisfactorily as woodlot or border specimens, screening hedges, and small trees (when pruned young for shapeliness); they all generally have an attractive color in the autumn. Provide a cool, moist, fertile, acid, and somewhat sandy soil rich in organic matter for their best performance; each resents drought. Although these plants flower best in full sun, they accept reasonable shading well; only leaf-chewing insects are a problem. Flower buds are usually exposed in the leaf axils whether they bloom in spring or in autumn; they develop as four thin, straplike, wrinkled petals and carry a spicy fragrance. The foliage is simple, alternately set, and coarsely toothed and shows obliquely lopsided bases. The woody capsule fruit explosively discharges the ripe seeds from a coiled, springlike member inside, but only after a full year of development on the stems. This may be nature's way of successfully dispersing the next generation away from the heavy shade and aggressive root growth of the parent.

The genus name comes from the Greek words *hama* ("together") and *mela* ("fruit") and refers to its habit of bearing fruit and flowers at the same time. The "witch hazel" naming is commonly associated with the use of forked branches from this plant to locate underground water in a process called "witching." The name, however, actually may be derived from the Anglo-Saxon word *wice* or *wic*, meaning "weak," an allusion to the plant's more open and looser habit than that of the hazel *(Corylus)*, which often is found in close association with it in the wild. In any event, witch hazels are an attractive landscape asset with their flowering, their screening effect, and their autumn color.

Hamamelis x intermedia (hybrid witch hazel)
Zones 6 to 8   15′ to 20′ high x 10′ to 15′ wide   Sun to light shade

Here is a hybrid cross of *japonica* and *mollis* which produced intermediate qualities of both species, yet this plant is cultivated only rarely since its cultivars are more showy. These cultivars evolved from complex further hybridization performed in Europe, Japan, and the United States over many years, and the differences are so refined that the cultivars are difficult to separate clearly. Perhaps the chief novelty now is the arrangement toward the upward and outward positioning of the blossoms for more noticeability in late winter or early spring. Many begin flowering as early as February (depending on local weather and the growing zone) and show a blossom size between ¾ inch and 1¼ inches across with four long petals folded and crimped; all these cultivars seem to possess only a mild scent. The foliage is variable throughout the group but can be classified only as large, especially on vigorous shoots. The autumn color is generally noticeable. Certainly these cultivars deserve applause for being the showiest in flower of all the witch hazels. The following list provides some of the prominent types now available.

CULTIVAR: 'Arnold Promise' is an American hybrid which grows 20 feet tall in a vase shape and is hardy into zone 5. It carries deep yellow 1½-inch-wide flowering and shows reddish autumn color.

CULTIVAR: 'Carmine Red' came from England. It presents a vigorous, spreading habit with almost round foliage of dark, shiny green. The large pale bronze and copper flowers appear red-toned at a distance. The autumn leaf color is yellow.

CULTIVAR: 'Diane' was developed in Belgium and shows red flowering deeper in value than that of *cv.* 'Ruby Glow'; its autumnal colorings are a mixed blend but are richly presented.

CULTIVAR: 'Jelena' ('Orange Beauty') is another Belgian hybrid. It presents a robust, spreading habit with large, broad, soft-haired foliage. The flowers are oversized and generously set in large, dense clusters; they open yellow with a rich copper overtone that appears orange from a distance.

CULTIVAR: 'Ruby Glow' ('Adonis') has a strong-growing and erect nature with coppery-red flowering and a vibrant mix of autumnal coloring in the leaves.

Hamamelis mollis cv. 'Brevipetala'

Hamamelis mollis   (Chinese witch hazel)

Zones 6 to 8   10′ to 15′ high x 10′ to 15′ wide   Sun to light shade

One of the most popular and showy species, this native of western China came into culture during 1879 and is a parent of the *x intermedia* cultivars. It possesses a neat, rounded habit with ascending branches and soft-hairy, new stems. Depending on the mildness of winter, bloom can start as early as late January, but the norm is usually late February to early March. The richly golden yellow flowers have red bases and ½-inch petals along with a sweet fragrance. Its roundish, oblong, short-pointed leaves are a metallic medium green above and gray-hairy beneath with lengths up to 5 inches; the autumn color is yellow. It has several interesting cultivars.

CULTIVAR: 'Brevipetala' behaves in a vigorous, upright manner with a very free-flowering habit carrying heavily scented ochre-yellow to deep orange blossoms only about ⅜ inch long but with larger foliage than that of the parent. Its autumnal coloring is yellow.

CULTIVAR: 'Pallida' produces large, pale sulfur-yellow flowering in dense clusters and has a noticeably sweet odor; the autumn color is also yellow.

Hamamelis vernalis   (vernal witch hazel, spring witch hazel, Ozark witch hazel)

Zones 6 to 9   6′ to 8′ high x 8′ to 10′ wide   Sun to light shade

Robustly erect and spreading by suckering to form a wide mass, this shrub's form is neat, dense, and rounded; it serves well as a barrier screen, border accent, or naturalized grouping. It is usually the first deciduous shrub of the year to bloom in many areas, and its modest flowering can occur from late winter into early spring; the autumn color is a mix of yellow and orange in clear tones. Blossoming comes from small, dull yellow flowers with ½-inch petals and a pungent fragrance more penetrating than that of most other species. These close on very cold days but reopen on warm ones, extending the blooming period appreciably. The foliage is oval, mostly smooth, and up to 4 inches long with coarse teeth. Very tolerant of overly moist to wet soil conditions, it grows admirably along streams and beside ponds. Native from Missouri to Louisiana and Oklahoma, it came into culture during 1908. The cultivar 'Rubra' ('Carnea') carries petals that are reddened at their bases, while *cv.* 'Tomentella' has foliage with noticeable hairiness beneath.

Hamamelis virginiana   (common witch hazel, American witch hazel)

Zones 5 to 9   15′ to 20′ high x 15′ to 20′ wide   Sun to semishade

The hardiest of all the witch hazels and the last to bear flowers by its late autumn bloom, this is a nonsuckering species with a potential for developing into a small woodlot tree. Robust when young, it naturalizes well and offers great adaptability to a wide range of soil and light conditions. Native to eastern North America from lower Canada to Georgia and west to Nebraska and Arkansas, this tall shrub has been cultivated since 1736. Witch hazel lotion is derived from its bark and dried leaves, while the understock is often used in grafting for the larger-flowered types. The root portions occasionally send up shoots of their own (a common problem with grafted material) when plants are expanding vigorously; these superfluous stems should be cut off promptly below the ground line to forestall possible dominance over the more desirable cultivar part. The small, twisted, golden yellow, sweet-scented flowers appear from November into December with ¾-inch petals expanding just as or just before the foliage drops for the season; the bloom is often obscured by the retained and coloring leaves. Foliage is wedge-shaped, 3 to 6 inches long, coarsely toothed, generally smooth on both surfaces, and mid-green during summer with bright yellow autumn coloring. Its fruit capsules discharge loudly when ripe and hurl the two black seeds a distance of perhaps 20 feet; this device assures greater germination away from the shade and root density of the parent.

HIBISCUS (mallow, rose mallow, giant mallow)
Malvaceae (mallow) family

At least 250 species of annuals, herbaceous perennials, shrubs, and occasionally trees belong to this genus native to the warm temperate and tropical regions of the globe. They thrive in hot weather in full sun and are unusual since their showy blossoms often last only for a day. As a group this genus provides some of the most effective, large-flowering, woody plants known, and they blossom over a long period. The highly attractive evergreen *rosa-sinensis* cultivars, which are at home in the subtropic and tropical areas and are deservedly popular, are not included in this book because they are not reliably hardy very far north; these are usually found summering outdoors in tubs or pots in much of the United States and spend the winters indoors under protection. They are very susceptible to frost damage.

Blossoming in this group is mostly solitary in the leaf axils, and the flowers are bell-shaped with five petals in white, yellow, red, pink, or purple, often with maroon spots at the base. The alternate foliage develops often on hairy shoots. These plants are found in a wide variety of soil conditions from swampy to dry, and while most are ornamentally of interest, some produce commercially valuable crops of food, medicine, or fiber. The species *esculentus*, for example, is commonly known as okra, and its tasty seed capsules have become a valuable cooking ingredient. It originated in Africa and soon moved with early settlers to both the West Indies and the southern parts of the United States, where it is grown as a staple. The genus name is derived from ancient Greek and Latin words for the mallow and may be associated with the ibis, a bird common to many marshy localities where mallows thrive, since the letters are incorporated into the spelling of *Hibiscus*.

Hibiscus syriacus (acerifolius, chinensis) (Althaea frutex,
Althaea syriaca) (rose of Sharon, althaea, shrub althaea)

Zones 5 to 9   6′ to 20′ high x 8′ to 10′ wide   Sun

Not found natively in Syria as its species name suggests, but in China and India, this is a late-blooming shrub with a long history of popularity. The Chinese have cultivated it since the dawn of history and even used the foliage to make an acceptable tea substitute at some point. It has been in culture here since before 1790; the English knew and raised it during the late sixteenth century. As the most adaptable and hardiest *Hibiscus* species of all, the plant thrives from southern Ontario throughout much of the United States, accepting both city pollution and salt-laden shore locations without difficulty. It also is unfazed by frequent trimming and even severe pruning to ground level (which may produce oversized foliage and larger blossoms in the first years of recovery). Perhaps best used for making screen hedges, the plant also

Hibiscus syriacus cv. 'Anemonaeflorus'

has appeal as a border specimen even though it is late to leaf out in spring; with regular pruning it can also be trained into a small tree form. Compact, much branched, and stiffly erect, this shrub is very amenable to many soil types, provided that they are consistently moist, and it responds better if generously fertilized and watered as its blooming time approaches. This is especially important with the double-flowered forms since the single-flowered types accept more dryness and still bloom well. These double-blossoming kinds often fail to expand the flowers completely, however; this is most noticeable when the summer weather remains overcast and wet for prolonged periods, which also promotes important foliage diseases. These are sun-loving shrubs; nevertheless, where summer sun and heat are excessive, they benefit from placement in areas with some afternoon shading. In many areas Japanese beetles disfigure the blossoms, while aphid infestations are constant pests to new stems and leaves unless quickly controlled.

Many forms self-seed generously and annoyingly, and the seedlings rarely come true to type; however, recent cultivars from the National Arboretum in Washington, D.C., are said to be free of this nuisance trait. Spring planting for all is recommended to avoid the winter damage to late-maturing stems that usually results when they are installed in autumn. Large, mature specimens, however, do not relocate easily and may require severe pruning—at an obvious loss of the silhouette—to bring them back into proper growth.

The late July to August flowering extends for a lengthy period up to frost with shallowly bell-shaped, unscented, solitary blossoms in the upper leaf axils of new growth; they persist only a day. These are either single with five petals or double with many petals and are between 1½ and 3 inches long. They are colored white, reddish, purplish, or bluish with a crimson base. Noticeable on the single types is a large central column of fused stamens which projects prominently; it is usually surrounded by foraging bees seeking nectar. The fruit is a five-celled, ¾-inch flared capsule persisting on the twigs through the dormant period in a tan, dried state. The foliage is mostly less than 3 inches long in a triangular to oval shape, deep green to grayish green, deeply cut into three lobes with coarse teeth, and without autumn coloring. Only the cultivar selections are now considered valuable for propagation and planting.

CULTIVAR: 'Admiral Dewey' is double and pure white with 2¼-inch flowers.

CULTIVAR: 'Anemonaeflorus' has double white blooms with deep cerise centers; it is a popular plant.

CULTIVAR: 'Ardens' has been cultivated since the 1870s; it carries large, mostly double flowers of pale rosy-purple with maroon blotches at the bases.

CULTIVAR: 'Banner' is a double white with a red center.

CULTIVAR: 'Blue Bird' is considered the best single "blue" form known; it has 3½-inch-wide blossoms of violet-blue with darker centers.

CULTIVAR: 'Boule de Feu' has been known since 1840; it develops 2½-inch, double, showy flowering of purplish red.

CULTIVAR: 'Celestial Blue' ('Coelestis') is semidouble and 2 inches wide; it produces light violet-blue flowers with reddish bases.

CULTIVAR: 'Duc de Brabant' came into culture about 1870; it shows double deep purplish pink blossoms with paler centers.

CULTIVAR: 'Elegantissimus' has semidouble blooms of white shaded blush-pink with maroon bases.

CULTIVAR: 'Hamabo' carries single, 3-inch, pale blush flowering with crimson centers or perhaps reddish stripes and blotches.

CULTIVAR: 'Jeanne d'Arc' is a compact plant with semidouble white flowers.

CULTIVAR: 'Lady Stanley' ('Lady Alice Stanley') produces semidouble white flowers shaded blush-pink with maroon bases on a tall, narrow plant.

CULTIVAR: 'Lucy' has double blossoms which vary from bright red to bright pink.

CULTIVAR: 'Monstrosus' develops 3½-inch single flowering of white with maroon centers.

CULTIVAR: 'Paeoniflorus' has double pink flowers; it is quite popular.

CULTIVAR: 'Pink Beauty' is well liked for its single pink blossoms.

CULTIVAR: 'Red Heart' has 3½-inch single blooms with red centers.

CULTIVAR: 'Totus Albus' (often incorrectly cataloged lately as 'Snow Storm' or 'Snowdrift') has been known since 1850; it shows single pure white flowers 3½ inches across.

CULTIVAR: 'William R. Smith' produces earlier flowering of single, pure white, 3½-inch blossoms with crinkled petals.

CULTIVAR: 'Woodbridge' is considered the best single red so far produced with its 3-inch vividly rose-pink flowers showing deeper rose bases.

Hibiscus syriacus cv. 'Red Heart'

HIPPOPHAE (sea buckthorn) *Elaeagnaceae* (oleaster) family

Grown especially for their attractive and durable fruiting, the species of this very hardy, spiny genus number either two or three (depending on the authority). All are dioecious with separate male and female plants and develop either as shrubs or as small trees covered with silvery scales on all the parts. They are native to Europe and the temperate zones of Asia; the name is an ancient Greek one for a spiny plant, but not necessarily for this group. All adapt well to windy, seashore, and prairie conditions with a preference for a well-drained, somewhat infertile soil in full sun. They are unfortunately difficult to transplant easily and successfully; use only small containerized plants. The axillary flowers are inconspicuous, tubular in shape without petal development, and yellow; they appear before the leaves. The foliage is alternate, narrowly willowlike, and sage-green or silvery. Its conspicuous fruiting becomes an attractive orange color and is drupelike (similar to plums). Pests and diseases appear to avoid damaging these shrubs.

Hippophae rhamnoides (sallow thorn, sea buckthorn)

Zones 3 to 7   12′ to 30′ high x 12′ to 30′ wide   Sun

Native to the British Isles, Europe, and Asia as far east as northern China, this decorative shrub offers a distinct appeal with its silvery foliage and generous summer fruit crops. Very difficult to establish properly, it prefers sandy, infertile soil and can serve admirably for dune or embankment stabilization. Its habit is rambling with suckering stems (although males often have more erectness) and can perform excellently as an impenetrable barrier maker either massed or treated as a hedge. The tiny, nondescript, yellow-toned blossoms are bunched at the leaf axils and appear during April, followed on females by an abundance of bright, orange-red, egg-shaped, ¼-inch long, tartly edible, and persistent fruit; birds dislike them, however, because of the intensely acrid juice. The tip of the female flower spur evolves into a sharpened point; the male spurs drop off after flowering. Foliage is narrowly linear, between ¾ inch and 2½ inches long, and noticeably and appealingly silvered on both sides. Autumn color is negligible.

HYDRANGEA (hortensia) (hydrangea) *Saxifragaceae* (saxifrage) family

At least twenty-three distinct species of erect or climbing, deciduous or evergreen shrubs from North and South America as well as eastern Asia are known. The differences between them are not great but involve only minor adjustments of flower color or size along with some leaf distinctions. Easy to transplant, they resent constant dryness and prefer a rich, porous, reasonably moist soil ranging from neutral to acid; they turn yellow in very alkaline conditions. Well suited for seashore locations, these shrubs bloom best when given generous watering as they come into flower. The name is from the Greek *hydor* ("water") and *aggeion* ("vessel"), alluding to the pitcherlike shape of the fruit. Flowering is mostly terminal as compound, flat, rounded, or pyramidal clusters carrying both tiny fertile blossoms and showy sterile ones called ray florets. The fruit is a small capsule, but since its sterile florets usually persist into dormancy, the spent blossoms can be gathered for use as indoor dried displays. The foliage is opposite and either entire or toothed. While they enjoy full sun, they prosper and bloom more attractively when given some relief from the hot afternoon summer sun. These are generally trouble-free plants except for aphid infestations which distort the stems and leaves on new growth.

Hydrangea arborescens cv. 'Grandiflora'

Hydrangea arborescens (hills of snow, wild hydrangea, sevenbark)

Zones 4 to 9   3′ to 4′ high x 4′ to 5′ wide   Sun to light shade

Introduced in 1736, this popular shrub is native from New York to Florida and Louisiana as well as west to Illinois and Oklahoma. It has a much branched but gracefully loose habit, and it is easy to grow if provided with an average, well-drained, moist site fortified with peat or compost. Because bloom comes only on new growth, severe annual pruning to ground level does not affect the flowering to any marked degree. Successive blossoms usually appear from early July into September as creamy white, rounded, flattened clusters between 3 and 6 inches wide, but these are almost entirely fertile and have little landscape effect. A few ½-inch sterile florets are usually present but do not add much to the interest; the capsule fruit is also of minor value. It is the cultivars which provide the stimulation of showy bloom. Its oval, toothed, slender-tipped foliage varies from 3 to 6 inches in length and is dark green above and paler beneath; it offers no autumn coloring. The cultivars are very popular.

CULTIVAR: 'Annabelle' is a recent introduction as an improvement of *cv.* 'Grandiflora' with greater compactness and with sterile flower heads up to a foot across that put on a showy display as they fade from creamy white to greenish white to the final brown-tan of the dried remains. It will undoubtedly supplant the old-time favorite *cv.* 'Grandiflora', even though it does not succeed attractively when planted in the southern United States.

CULTIVAR: 'Grandiflora' has a history of appreciation since 1900 for both its substantial hardiness and its 8-inch-wide, all-sterile flowering heads. However, in the future it seems *cv.* 'Annabelle' will outshine it.

Hydrangea macrophylla cultivar

Hydrangea macrophylla (hortensis, japonica, opuloides) (French hydrangea, hortensia)

Zones 6 to 9   5′ to 8′ high x 6′ to 10′ wide   Sun to light shade

This plant is the so-called florist's hydrangea popular at Easter and Mother's Day for its massive heads of sterile, colorful florets. Native to Japan, it has been cultivated in other parts of the world since 1790 and is appealing from late July to September for its long-enduring and conspicuous but unscented flowering. It seems to flourish near the shore. There are two types of flower designs available for landscape use. The better known is a globular, multidivided cluster of 1-inch, mostly *sterile* florets in white, pink, or blue called "hortensia," a name that commemorates Hortense de Nassau, daughter of the Prince of Nassau, a gentleman botanist who accompanied de Bougainville on his botanic world tour of 1766; at one time the genus was called *Hortensia*. The other style, called "lacecap," has a flattened head of mostly *fertile* tiny flowers surrounded by a ring of large, sterile ones also colored in white, pink, or blue; the fertile blooms are similarly tinted. Any fruit is of no consequence on either one. While the attractively glossy foliage of both is considered deciduous, it may be retained very late into winter in very mild growing areas. These leaves are oval, bright green, thick, coarsely toothed, and from 5 to 9 inches long; they are without autumn color. This erect plant expands by suckering and forms a dense and rounded mass. Provide a rich, moist, well-drained, organically fortified site and additional moisture as it comes into flower.

Hydrangea macrophylla cv. 'Blue Lacecap'

This shrub is unusual since its color can be altered by the addition of chemicals. When the plant is grown on acid soils, the flowers will be blue, but they become mauve-toned as the soil becomes closer to neutral in balance; when planted in alkaline soils, the blooms will be pink. Both conditions result from the availability of aluminum in the respective soils. To maintain the "blueness," add solutions of alum, which is short for "aluminum sulphate"; to hold the pink coloration, add ground limestone dug in at the bases of the stems. Because many hydrangeas are placed at the fronts of borders for more showiness, they are often in close contact with the liming treatment of lawns they abut, and this consistent addition of lime often changes the highly favored blue plants to mauve, much to the surprise of the installer. Just repositioning the shrub farther away from grassy spaces is a simple solution to this common dilemma.

Buds for the following season's bloom generally are set at terminal locations on the stems and may be winter-killed in very cold winters, although the roots usually manage to survive. Any tip pruning of stems to create greater shapeliness in early spring also can eliminate flower buds. Excessively organic and rich soils also can be detrimental to flowering since they promote soft, lush growth in summer but lessened bud hardiness for winter. Locations which consistently vary from moist to dry also will promote indifferent blossoming. Since flowering is this plant's chief asset, it pays to observe these rules of growing.

Close to 400 cultivars currently are listed as available because hybridizing (mostly for commercial greenhouse needs) by American, Dutch, French, German, and Swiss breeders takes place constantly. Therefore, no attempt can be made here to offer specific recommendations.

Hydrangea paniculata (panicle hydrangea)

Zones 4 to 9   15' to 30' high x 10' to 20' wide   Sun to light shade

Here is the hardiest and the longest-lived of all the hydrangeas, and it is the only Asiatic species with a pyramidal flower head. Attractive as a late summer landscape accent, its mature flower clusters can be cut and dried successfully for indoor use. To create the largest flower heads, prune in the spring so that only two stem buds remain on each of the previous year's growth; then provide liquid fertilizing during the period of flower budding and expansion. This plant is an upright shrub or small tree that grows to 30 feet with a dense, rounded form and arching branches when heavy with blooms. Native to both China and Japan, it began to be cultivated during 1861. Flowers appear by late July and persist until frost in varying color changes from creamy white when new to rose-tinted by early autumn to tan-brown at the end. The loose, white clusters are terminal, pyramidal, and up to 10 inches long; they have about an equal mix of sterile and fertile blossoms. (This plant is not much

Hydrangea paniculata

Hydrangea paniculata cv. 'Grandiflora'

cultivated today since its popular cultivar 'Grandiflora' has totally sterile, showier blooms.) The oval foliage is light green, toothed, tip-pointed, and between 3 and 6 inches long; it provides no color change of any merit in autumn. Several cultivar selections are known.

CULTIVAR: 'Grandiflora' is the most popularly grown type; it came from Japan in 1867 through Dr. Siebold. In nursery parlance it is called "peegee" for the first two letters of its secondary scientific names. These large, solid, showy, and durable flower heads are almost wholly sterile florets and often become a foot long. Very simple to grow well, it makes a conspicuous specimen or hedge.

CULTIVAR: 'Praecox' is a very hardy, smaller-flowered form with bloom occurring several weeks ahead of the parent.

CULTIVAR: 'Tardiva' is an unusual counterpart to *cv.* 'Praecox' since it flowers only by late August or early September and grows between 6 and 8 feet high.

Hydrangea quercifolia

Hydrangea quercifolia (oakleaf hydrangea)

Zones 6 to 9   5' to 7' high x 8' to 10' wide   Semishade to full shade

Behaving more attractively when grown in mild climates, this unusually striking hydrangea is native from Georgia to Florida and west to Mississippi; it came into cultivation by 1803. Its flaking stem bark, oversized foliage, and appealing flower heads combine to overcome a general impression of textural coarseness. The suckering stems are stiffly upright and stout with other twigs showing peeling cinnamon-colored and tan bark patterns; the new growth is densely hairy. In colder areas of its range it may die to ground level (with the loss of future flower buds) or at least be severely damaged. Since the plant is already slow-growing, it should be protected from cold winds to minimize such problems. Supply a moist, well-drained, fertile, somewhat acid soil and water well as the buds develop if the summer weather is dry. Flowering appears during mid-July as much branched, narrowly pyramidal clusters up to 10 inches tall and 4 inches wide with both fertile and sterile blooms. The sterile blooms are 1¼ inches wide and age from white to purple with deep pink overtones as they age. Its medium green foliage has white-hairy undersides and often enlarges somewhat grotesquely to a foot long with five coarsely toothed lobes (much resembling an oversized oak leaf); the autumn coloring is a mix of orange, purple, pink, green, and bronze, producing a striking effect. Diseases and pests are generally not bothersome, but Japanese beetles favor the foliage in some locales. This plant is highly adaptive for woodlot use since it is very tolerant of shade, but it can also be placed as a border accent in areas where its coarse foliage will be appreciated.

HYPERICUM (St. John's wort)   *Hypericaceae* (hypericum) family

An explanation of this genus appears in the "Broadleaf Evergreens" division.

Hypericum prolificum (broombrush, shrubby St. John's wort)

Zones 5 to 8   3' to 5' high x 2' to 4' wide   Sun to light shade

Noteworthy for its continuous flowering during summer, the plant blooms longer than any other species of *Hypericum*. Compact, densely branched, stiff, and erect, it develops a rounded form with gnarled stems showing brown and gray peeling bark. It thrives in dry, sandy areas and has no problems with insects or diseases. The showy, bright yellow, five-petaled flowers expand to ¾ inch wide in mostly terminal (occasionally axial) clusters that are produced generously. They bloom from late July into perhaps October. The narrowly oblong foliage is medium green above and paler beneath; it varies from ¾ inch to 3 inches long. Native from Ontario to Georgia and west to Minnesota and Louisiana, it came into culture during 1750.

ILEX (holly)   *Aquifoliaceae* (holly) family

An explanation of this genus appears in the "Broadleaf Evergreens" division.

Ilex decidua   (possum haw, deciduous holly)

Zones 5 to 9   7′ to 15′ high x 7′ to 15′ wide   Sun to light shade

One of the best deciduous hollies for the longevity of its fruit, this shrub has slender ascending branches with spreading twigs and may grow to a tree form 30 feet high in some circumstances. Natively found from Illinois to Florida and Texas, it came into culture during 1760. As with all hollies, male and female plants are separate with inconspicuous flowering during late May. Its glossy, orange to scarlet fruit persists attractively until late winter as rounded ¼-inch berries. The toothed foliage is light to medium green, semiglossy, moderately thick, lancelike or oval, and from 1½ to 3 inches long with rounded tips; these leaves often are found clustered on spur twigs along the stems. Provide a moist, well-drained, acid to neutral soil well fortified with compost or peat. Currently available in nurseries are several horticultural variations with only minor differences between them: 'Byer's Golden', 'Fraser's Improved', 'Oklahoma', 'Sundance', and 'Warren's Red'. The variety *longipes* grows between 6 and 12 feet tall (but only from zone 6 southward) with thin leaves 2 to 4½ inches long and with red to purplish fruit suspended on stalks about 1 inch in length. It is often known commonly as Georgia haw or Georgia holly.

Ilex verticillata   (winterberry, common winterberry, black alder, swamp holly)

Zones 4 to 8   8′ to 15′ high x 6′ to 10′ wide   Sun to light shade

This plant has the widest distribution of the North American hollies, with a range from Newfoundland to Minnesota and south to Texas and Georgia. It favors wet to swampy acid locations but adjusts readily to drier conditions, although with some loss in total size and fruit quantity. It was introduced to culture in 1736 and produces either smooth or somewhat hairy spreading branches plus variable foliage from oval to rounded, either dull or semiglossy and from 1½ to 3 inches in length. Its leaves turn black with the first frost. The foliage is double-toothed and often appears with a purplish cast when emerging. Insignificant mid-June flowers produce bright red, globose, often paired, ¼-inch-wide fruit with persistence into midwinter if the birds allow. Use in masses for the finest pollination and berrying. Similar to it is the smooth winterberry, the species *laevigata*, with hardiness just into zone 5; it is native only to the coastal sections from Maine to Georgia. Also comparable is the Japanese species *serrata*, with its smaller-sized leaves and hardiness only from zone 5 southward; here the generous fruiting drops to the ground well before that of *verticillata*. A number of *verticillata* cultivars are known.

Ilex verticillata female fruit

CULTIVAR: 'Christmas Cheer' is upright in form with heavy fruiting.

CULTIVAR: 'Chrysocarpa' produces yellow fruit, but not generously.

CULTIVAR: 'Polycarpa' is vigorous with larger-sized fruit.

CULTIVAR: 'Winter Red' is undoubtedly the best of these with its oversized berries, deep green leaves, and dense, neat habit.

JASMINUM (jasmine, jessamine)   *Oleaceae* (olive) family

An explanation of this genus appears in the "Broadleaf Evergreens" division.

Jasminum nudiflorum   (winter jasmine)

Zones 6 to 9   2′ to 3′ high x 10′ to 15′ wide   Sun to light shade

Here is the hardiest member of this genus, and it behaves as a very adaptable and showy groundcover shrub with a long season of winter bloom. It is one of only two species with opposite foliage (the other is *mesnyi*, or primrose jasmine), and it produces a robust, scrambling, and arching habit suitable for hanging over high walls for a cascading effect or as a tied-in-place espalier. It needs a well-drained, average-fertility soil and much sunlight for continual flowering; however, it can be used successfully on a northern exposure (but out of cold winds) if only foliage is expected. The four-angled, slender, long green stems carry scentless, six-petaled, bright yellow flowering in the leaf axils of the previous year's wood from November into February when grown in the mildest parts of its range; colder sections produce bloom only from middle to late April. The tiny compound foliage is shiny, dark green, and composed of three leaflets in an oval to oblong shape; the entire leaf measures only an inch wide. Native to western China, it came into cultivation during 1844 through the efforts of Robert Fortune. Its variety *aureum* is rare in culture and carries foliage blotched in yellow. There are no particular problems with diseases or insects.

KERRIA (CORCHORUS) (Japanese rose, kerria)   *Rosaceae* (rose) family

Only one species belongs to this genus native to China, although it is identified with Japan and is cultivated extensively there. It was named in 1817 for William Kerr, an eighteenth-century English plant collector who first sent Kew Gardens the double-flowered form in 1805. Grown mainly for its showy yellow blossoming, the plant also derives some appeal from its green stems in winter.

Kerria japonica (Corchorus japonicus) (Japanese rose, kerria)

Zones 5 to 9   5′ to 8′ high x 6′ to 9′ wide   Sun to shade

Remarkably adaptable to great changes in light intensity, this shrub is also very hardy and durable, although it suffers from winter dieback of its thin stem tips in the northern end of its growing range, especially in this single-flowered form. Densely branched and twiggy with slender, shiny, bright green stems showing a graceful and spreading habit, it expands by ready suckering. Provide a well-drained average soil augmented with organic material but avoid an overly rich soil since that tends to promote rank growth at the expense of full flowering. The plant is serviceable in masses, as informal hedges, and as a "facer" for taller and leggier shrubs nearby. Its blossoms tend to bleach in full sun when grown in areas with consistently hot spring weather; provide some afternoon shading in these circumstances. Pests and diseases are rarely a problem. The 1½- to 2-inch flowers bloom in mid-May as clear, golden yellow, single, cup-shaped blossoms with five petals and numerous prominent stamens; they appear on the previous year's growth. Unfortunately, they persist only for a week to 10 days. The fruit is tiny, nutlike, and brown-black. Foliage is alternate, simple, deeply veined, bright green, double-toothed, and lancelike, between 1½ and 4 inches long. The leaves often become oversized on the nonflowering stems. Autumn color is yellow. The following cultivars are usually preferred to the parent.

Kerria japonica cv. 'Picta'

CULTIVAR: 'Aureo-variegata' carries leaves edged nicely in yellow.

CULTIVAR: 'Aureo-vittata' produces twigs striped in green and yellow, producing an outstanding wintertime effect.

CULTIVAR: 'Picta' ('Argenteo-variegata') has foliage attractively edged in white but also develops green-leaved "sport" stems that must be removed quickly or they will dominate the whole plant in a short time. The stems are wiry, and the plant is both lower and wider than the parent.

CULTIVAR: 'Pleniflora' ('Flore Pleno') is the most widely cultivated form and the type originally brought by Mr. Kerr to Kew in 1805; the single-flowered form was not known until 1834. Hardier than the parent, it has double orange-yellow, ball-shaped flowering which creates a somewhat "brassy" accent when in bloom for the usual 3 weeks; it also grows vigorously taller than the parent.

Kerria japonica cv. 'Pleniflora'

KOLKWITZIA (beautybush)   *Caprifoliaceae* (honeysuckle) family

This is another genus with only one representative species. In its showy bloom it has some resemblance to its relation *Weigela*, but it grows more erectly and taller with stem bark which hangs in loose, large shreds. It is named for Richard Kolkwitz, a twentieth-century German botany professor, and it was introduced by Ernest Wilson in 1901 from central China.

Kolkwitzia amabilis (beautybush)

Zones 5 to 8   7' to 15' high x 5' to 10' wide   Sun to light shade

Erect, dense, compact, much branched, and graceful in appearance, this hairy shrub is easy to transplant and also simple to grow in any well-drained, average-fertility soil, either acid or alkaline. It requires no pruning maintenance, has no difficulties with pests or diseases, and serves well as a screen or border specimen. In flower it is attractively showy but afterward tends to be dull in effect. It is florally distinguished from its relation *Weigela* by having only four stamens to *Weigela's* five. These blossoms are profusely set in 3-inch clusters on the previous year's stems; they open by late May as half-inch, bell-shaped, bright pink flowers with yellow throats on very bristly stalks. The egg-shaped, feathery, ¼-inch capsule fruit is also noticeably hairy and is colored brownish to grayish pink when new. Its somewhat fuzzy, dull-looking, dark green foliage has a slight reddish cast and becomes dull red in autumn; it has a length from 1½ to 3 inches and a width of 2 inches. These long-pointed, slightly toothed leaves are carried on hairy stalks. The brown bark peels interestingly in large rolls and flakes on older stems. Its cultivar 'Pink Cloud' displays heavy masses of noticeably deep pink flowering.

Kolkwitzia amabilis

LAGERSTROEMIA (crape myrtle) *Lythraceae* (loosestrife) family

This summer-blooming flamboyant genus contains about fifty species of deciduous and evergreen shrubs or large trees; all are native to the warmer parts of Asia and to the Pacific islands. Only one species is hardy into zone 7, however, and it has long been associated with landscapes in the southern parts of the United States. Full sun and high heat are essential ingredients for good growth with all types. In India the wood of some species is valued for its fine grain and rich brown-red color but especially because it never suffers termite damage, a constant problem there. The exotically showy flowering appears in generous terminal panicles of purple, red, or white with six delicate crinkled petals maturing into nondescript capsules. The leaves are mostly alternate (although occasionally they appear in whorls around the twigs) and simple; they develop on stems with attractively mottled and peeling bark. Of easy culture, they are named for Magnus von Lagerstroem, an eighteenth-century naturalist and friend of the botanist Linnaeus.

Lagerstroemia indica

Lagerstroemia indica (elegans) (crape myrtle)

Zones 7 to 10   12' to 20' high x 8' to 12' wide   Sun

Conspicuous when flowering and noticeable for its flaking bark in other seasons, this species is planted extensively in the southern parts of the United States, especially in the hottest parts of Florida and California, where it thrives. The shrub is valuable as a specimen, for screens and hedges, or as tubbed groupings on large terraces. Long-lived, it is unbothered by city pollution or the reflected heat bounced from pavements and adjacent buildings. These multitrunked, dense shrubs (they occasionally become small trees to 20 feet) are sensitive to any transplanting and cannot be handled when bare-rooted; they move better when balled and burlapped with a generous tight ball of earth dug only in the spring. Provide a moist, organically fortified, well-drained site in full sun for the finest response, although they adapt to drier, poorer soils with some loss of vigor and attractiveness but without extraordinary difficulty. Aphids and powdery mildew are the chief afflictions. This plant came into cultivation in 1747 and is native to China and Korea.

They bloom from July to mid-September with noticeably round buds in loose clusters between 6 and 12 inches long set terminally or axially on the new growth. These buds expand into wrinkled petals about 1 inch long of pink, purple, or white and form ½-inch persistent fruit capsules later. If cut to the ground annually, plants produce increased flowering, but with a great loss of interesting bark and silhouette. The foliage emerges in a bronze tone and matures to medium or dark green with wedge-shaped leaves (sometimes oval) between 1 and 3 inches long showing entire margins and pointed tips. Its autumn color is a vivid mix of orange, red, and yellow, often rivaling that of the tree dogwood, maple, and sumac in some growing areas. The smooth, pinkish brown and gray bark flakes off with age to reveal maroon to pinkish blotches in a compelling fashion. These are exceptionally attractive plants with few problems and with greatly rewarding seasonal effects. The cultivars are even more colorful than the parent.

CULTIVAR: 'Alba' has pure white blossoming.

CULTIVAR: 'Nana Caerulea' has a dwarfed form with blue-toned flowers.

CULTIVAR: 'Purpurea' displays rich purple blooms.

CULTIVAR: 'Prostrata' develops a prostrate habit and pink flowering.

CULTIVAR: 'Rosea' produces blossoms of deep rose.

CULTIVAR: 'Rubra' has reddish purple flowers.

Additional cultivars are usually available from local nurseries in a wider range of colorings and silhouettes since this plant has a popular and commercial appeal.

LIGUSTRUM (privet)   *Oleaceae* (olive) family

An explanation of this genus appears in the "Broadleaf Evergreens" division.

Ligustrum amurense   (Amur privet, Amur river privet)

Zones 4 to 10   8' to 15' high x 6' to 10' wide   Sun to light shade

Durable and hardy are apt descriptions of this dependable plant that is used frequently as an informal or trimmed hedge and screen. Natively found in northern China, it came into cultivation by 1860. It shows a robust, erect, dense, and much branched habit with a pyramidal silhouette. Readily adaptable to any soil, it blooms by mid-June with terminal, hairy clusters up to 2 inches long of white tubular flowers with a heavy perfume (which some find oppressive), followed by oval, ¼-inch, dull-toned black berries that are attractive to birds. The plant somewhat resembles the less hardy *ovalifolium* in general outline and makes a favorable substitute for it in areas where *ovalifolium* is not hardy. The foliage is opposite, clean-looking, deep green, and often semievergreen in mild areas; these flat, 1- to 1½-inch, oblong to oval leaves are dull to semiglossy above with a hairy midrib beneath and show no important color change by autumn.

Ligustrum x ibolium   (Ibolium privet)

Zones 5 to 10   8' to 12' high x 6' to 8' wide   Sun to semishade

More adaptive to shade than many other species, this hybrid of *obtusifolium* and *ovalifolium* came into culture during 1910 as an upright and fast-growing shrub serviceable for hedges and screening. It shows distinctive hairiness on new growth, flowers, and the midribs of the lower leaf surfaces. Its white flowering appears during mid-June in loose, pyramidal, terminal clusterings up to 5 inches in length, and it later produces round, black, ¼-inch fruit in bunches which persist to winter. The plant is also similar in character to *ovalifolium* but is hardier. The cultivar 'Variegated' is not so durable (zone 6) or robust; it has foliage mottled in yellow.

Ligustrum obtusifolium regelianum flowers

Ligustrum obtusifolium regelianum fruit

Ligustrum obtusifolium   (border privet, Ibota privet)

Zones 4 to 10   8′ to 10′ high x 12′ to 15′ wide   Sun to shade

Showing a broad, horizontal, and arching habit that is generally broadest at the top, this very durable privet serves attractively as a barrier hedge or screen in a wide variety of light conditions and soils. The short terminal clusters of white, nodding, showy blossoms appear from mid-June to July, followed by dull black to blue-black berry fruit clusters. Its dark green, wavy-edged, 1- to 1½-inch foliage develops on densely hairy twigs and may turn either russet or purple-brown by autumn; it also may show some winter persistence in mild areas. The popular variety *regelianum* is less hardy (zone 5) but more interesting for its neatly lower silhouette to about 5 feet and "fishbone skeleton" branching that is something like that of *Cotoneaster horizontalis;* the plant is best displayed if kept unsheared. Flower clusters are freely produced terminally at all the short spur growth but are no longer than an inch.

Ligustrum ovalifolium cv. 'Aureo-marginatum'

Ligustrum ovalifolium (californicum)   (California privet, oval-leaf privet)

Zones 6 to 10   10′ to 15′ high x 6′ to 8′ wide   Sun to semishade

Long popular for its especially glossy foliage, narrowly erect but stiff habit, and robust growth even under trying conditions, this shrub has been used (some say overused) for both informal and sheared hedges throughout much of the United States for many generations. It does have an important drawback, however, in that its stems are not reliably hardy, no matter what its age, when temperatures drop below zero for prolonged periods. It will regrow from ground level when winter-killed, but such root vitality offers little consolation to those who use the plant as a screen or boundary hedge. This shrub should not be promoted where this important defect has to be faced on a recurring basis. Tolerant of both shore locations and city pollution along with reduced light, the plant is often mislabeled in catalogs as *ibota*, an inferior-growing species from Japan usually not found cultivated here. Also Japanese in origin, this plant came into culture by 1847. Its profuse mid-June blooms are creamy white in erect 5-inch-high clusters but have a highly disagreeable odor. Generous clusters of black ¼-inch fruit follow soon after, but these are not as prevalent in the northern limits of its range. Its handsome foliage is dark green above and yellowish beneath, broadly oval to 2½ inches long, and point-tipped; it is retained long into the season to become semievergreen in mild locations. The cultivar list is lengthy, but all its members are even less hardy than the parent.

CULTIVAR: 'Albo-marginatum' has leaves pleasantly bordered in white.

CULTIVAR: 'Aureo-marginatum' ('Aureum') is so well liked, it often is found in cut flower arrangements as an attractive foil for other materials; the leaves are broadly and irregularly bordered in yellow.

CULTIVAR: 'Compactum' shows a denser growth habit.

CULTIVAR: 'Globosum' is dwarfed and develops a rounded outline.

CULTIVAR: 'Nanum' is both dwarfed and compact-growing.

CULTIVAR: 'Variegatum' displays foliage marbled with pale yellow.

Ligustrum x vicaryi (Vicary golden privet)

Zones 6 to 10   3′ to 12′ high x 4′ to 15′ wide   Sun to light shade

Ligustrum x vicaryi

Slow-growing, dense, rounded in outline, and capable of a sizable height and spread in the warmest part of its range, here is a bright gold accent plant that is attractive for novelty hedges, tubbed specimens, and border highlights. Blossoming occurs during July as small white panicles without much noticeability, followed by small blue-black fruit clusters. In full sun the leaves are green with an overlayer of bright gold, and they remain unfaded throughout the growing season; if planted in too much shade, they become merely yellow-green. This plant is a hybrid of *ovalifolium cv.* 'Aureo-marginatum' and *vulgare* which originated in England about 1919 and adapts to a variety of soils. The cultivar 'Hillside Strain' is hardier (zone 5) with a brashly yellow coloring that is difficult to assimilate easily among other plants.

Ligustrum vulgare (common privet, European privet, prim, primwort)

Zones 5 to 9   10′ to 15′ high x 10′ to 15′ wide   Sun to light shade

Ligustrum vulgare

Cultivated enthusiastically for centuries, this popular shrub is native to the Mediterranean region and has become naturalized in many parts of the eastern United States since its introduction during colonial times. Greatly appreciated for hedge and specimen use, it is nonetheless of reduced ornamentality compared with some other species; it often behaves as a semievergreen in mild areas. The stout, much branched habit shows an irregularly spreading form with July blossoming of creamy white in dense, pyramidal, terminal panicles between 1½ and 2½ inches tall with an odd scent that some find unacceptable. The foliage is oblong-oval to lancelike, 1 inch to 2½ inches in length, hairless on both surfaces, dark green, and persistent late into the autumn; it shows no important color change in areas where it is deciduous. Its fruit, however, is very conspicuous as long clusters of shiny black with a reliable attraction for birds and other wildlife. This plant adapts well to a wide range of soil conditions, especially alkaline. Powdery mildew and anthracnose disease are serious problems in some growing areas. The cultivar list is extensive.

CULTIVAR: 'Argenteo-variegatum' carries leaves blotched in white.

CULTIVAR: 'Atrovirens' has smaller foliage with deeper coloring.

CULTIVAR: 'Aureum' shows yellow-toned foliage, but it tends to be dull-surfaced and fades appreciably by late July.

CULTIVAR: 'Aureo-variegatum' produces leaves variegated in yellow.

CULTIVAR: 'Buxifolium' behaves as a semievergreen with 1-inch oval leaves and large fruiting.

CULTIVAR: 'Cheyenne' (zone 4) is hardier than the parent, robust, and erect with dark, olive-green leaves.

CULTIVAR: 'Chlorocarpum' develops fruit with a greenish yellow color.

CULTIVAR: 'Foliosum' is more vigorous in all aspects.

CULTIVAR: 'Glaucum' ('Albo-variegatum') produces metallic-toned bluish green leaves edged interestingly in white.

CULTIVAR: 'Italicum' ('Sempervirens') retains its foliage longer.

CULTIVAR: 'Laurifolium' has broadly oval leaves with a laurellike appearance.

CULTIVAR: 'Leucocarpum' produces white fruit.

CULTIVAR: 'Lodense' ('Nanum') is a slow-growing, compact dwarf between 3 and 4 feet tall.

CULTIVAR: 'Pendulum' has noticeably drooping branches.

CULTIVAR: 'Pyramidale' is narrowly pyramidal in habit with strongly erect branching.

CULTIVAR: 'Xanthocarpum' has yellow fruit.

LONICERA (honeysuckle)   *Caprifoliaceae* (honeysuckle) family

Between 150 and 200 species may belong to this large genus of usually deciduous but occasionally semievergreen erect or climbing shrubs. They are cultivated for their showy flowering and often generous fruit crops. Popular, vigorous, and very hardy as a group, these plants grow easily in any average-fertility soil in full sun to light shade, but they react to constant dryness of the air or earth by producing stunted foliage and contorted stems. Native throughout the northern hemisphere, they are fully dependable for annual flowering, although not always for generous fruiting, and some species are especially fragrant. Pests and diseases seem to be more common in the climbing, vine types than in the shrubby forms. The flowers are usually small and tubular, colored pink, white, or red; they appear in pairs at the leaf axils for the most part. Foliage is opposite, simple, and without autumn color. The small berrylike fruit is juicy and attractive to birds; it develops in a palette of red, blue, black, orange, yellow, or white. This genus is named for the sixteenth-century German physician and naturalist Adam Lonicer (sometimes spelled Lonitzer), while the common name comes from the Anglo-Saxon *hunisuce*, an early description for privet, a nonrelation.

Lonicera x amoena   (no common name)

Zones 6 to 9   **7′ to 9′ high x 5′ to 6′ wide**   **Sun to light shade**

Useful in small spaces, this free-flowering and modest-growing shrub is a hybrid of *korolkowii* and *tatarica* that was developed in 1892. It blooms generously during late May with paired, typically pink or white, unscented, ¾-inch flowers that fade to yellow with age; the later fruit is red. Foliage appears on gracefully arching branches and is oval with a length up to 2 inches. The cultivar 'Arnoldiana' has flowering of almost white and is hardy into zone 5, while the cultivar 'Rosea' has deep pink flowering.

Lonicera fragrantissima (fragrant honeysuckle, winter honeysuckle)

Zones 6 to 9   6′ to 8′ high x 8′ to 10′ wide   Sun to semishade

Lonicera fragrantissima

Along with the small-flowered *standishii*, this is the first honeysuckle to bloom, and its cut branches readily force for winter flowering indoors. Especially adaptable to poor soil conditions, this wide-spreading, open shrub is serviceable for informal hedges and masses but has little value for specimen use. Native to eastern China, it was brought into cultivation by Robert Fortune in 1845. The ½-inch, paired, creamy white flowers on the previous year's stems are not particularly showy but are very sweetly scented and open during mid-April (they appear from December to April in mild areas); these are sometimes followed by sparsely set, small red fruit that is hardly ever noticeable. Its leathery, stiff, oval foliage ends in abrupt points and is dark green above but bluish green beneath. These leaves appear on thick stems with exfoliating bark; they produce no autumn color, and in mild sections the plant may retain some into winter.

Lonicera korolkowii (blueleaf honeysuckle)

Zones 5 to 9   8′ to 12′ high x 8′ to 12′ wide   Sun to light shade

Graceful, vigorous, and wide-spreading, this eye-catching shrub makes an attractive specimen or informal hedge. Introduced during 1880 from its native Turkestan, it carries late May, paired, deep rose flowering between ½ and ¾ inch long followed by bright red to orange-red berrylike fruit. Its most noticeable aspect, however, is the oval to oblong bluish green foliage, which is hairy beneath and about an inch long; few shrubs offer such striking color in the leaves. Unfortunately, it is a difficult plant to move at any age and is best handled during spring, and then only when balled and burlapped or containerized while still small. The variety *zabelli* has broadly oval, smooth foliage and darker pink flowering.

Lonicera maackii (Amur honeysuckle)

Zones 3 to 8   10′ to 15′ high x 8′ to 12′ wide   Sun to semishade

Lonicera maackii

This honeysuckle excels in many ways since it is extremely hardy, very tall, easily cultivated, remarkably drought-resistant, and noticeably showy in fruit. Natively found in China and Manchuria, it has been in cultivation since 1880, and it makes a rapid adjustment to transplanting when installed young. Wide and upright (almost treelike when mature), it becomes leggy with age but still serves attractively as a border specimen, mass, or screen. It blooms late (early June) with masses of lightly fragrant, paired, ¾-inch white flowers that fade to yellow with age; these are set regularly spaced in a noticeable fashion all along the stems and are followed by abundant, durable, translucent, dark red fruiting. The fruit points up the neatly formal arrangement of its set in a distinctive way. Both birds and squirrels greatly enjoy these berries as they ripen by midautumn. The foliage is dark green and oval to lancelike with conspicuous tip ends of some length; it grows between 1¾ and 3 inches long and is persistent well into autumn but without any color change of significance. A few variations are known.

CULTIVAR: 'Rem Red' shows a vigorous habit and naturalizes itself easily from self-seeding.

VARIETY: *podocarpa* has slightly less hardiness (zone 4) but may prove semievergreen in the mildest portions of its range. It is tall, graceful, and spreading with a 9-foot width, and it develops heavier flowering and more fruit.

Lonicera morrowii

Lonicera morrowii (Morrow honeysuckle)

Zones 4 to 9   6′ to 8′ high x 10′ to 15′ wide   Sun to light shade

Robust, dense, and moundlike in appearance, the plant shows great hardiness and reasonable drought resistance with more attractive summer foliage than *tatarica*. It is native to Japan and came into cultivation by 1875. It serves well as a screen, informal hedge, barrier, mass, or slope stabilizer since it adjusts satisfactorily and easily to less than ideal growing conditions. The paired, ½-inch, creamy white flowers appear during late May and fade to yellow with maturity. Its fruit is usually dark red and translucent but may vary in intensity even on the same plant. The cultivar 'Xanthocarpa' carries bright yellow fruit, but it is only sparsely set. Both carry oblong, dull green leaves between 1¼ and 2 inches long without autumn color.

Lonicera tatarica fruit

Lonicera tatarica (Tatarian honeysuckle, Tartarian honeysuckle)

Zones 4 to 9   9′ to 12′ high x 9′ to 12′ wide   Sun to semishade

Native to southern Russia across to central Asia, this vigorous shrub has naturalized itself throughout Europe and the United States; it is the common hedgerow honeysuckle. In cultivation since 1752, the plant is upright and strongly multistemmed with arching twigs, but it becomes openly leggy at the base with age. Easily transplanted and grown, it adjusts to all types of growing conditions, especially to reduced light. The late May flowering is paired, bountifully produced, very fragrant, up to an inch long, and colored either pink or white. Bright red berrylike fruit soon develops but is quickly eaten by birds. The leaves are oval to oblong, up to 2½ inches long, and bluish green above (but not as intensely as in *korolkowii*) and paler beneath; they tend to become duller and more greenish by midsummer. Its cultivar list is lengthy.

CULTIVAR: 'Alba' has pure white flowering.

CULTIVAR: 'Angustifolia' produces narrower foliage.

CULTIVAR: 'Arnold Red' displays dark red flowers.

CULTIVAR: 'Grandiflora' has white flowers larger than those of either *cv.* 'Alba' or *cv.* 'Virginalis'.

CULTIVAR: 'Latifolia' ('Pulcherrima') develops leaves up to 4 inches long and 2 inches wide.

CULTIVAR: 'Lutea' bears yellow to orange-yellow fruiting.

CULTIVAR: 'Nana' is low, compact, and slow-growing with heavy flowering.

CULTIVAR: 'Rosea' shows blossoms with rose exteriors and pink interiors.

CULTIVAR: 'Sibirica' ('Rubra') has smaller foliage and deep pink flowering.

CULTIVAR: 'Virginalis' produces white flowers smaller than those of *cv.* 'Grandiflora'.

Lonicera x xylosteoides (no common name)

Zones 5 to 10   6' to 9' high x 4' to 6' wide   Sun to light shade

This is a recent hybrid of *tatarica* and *xylosteum* which has little appeal in itself; it is better known for its more attractive cultivars.

CULTIVAR: 'Clavey's Dwarf' produces a rounded outline and has a slow-growing habit with dense branching to ground level. Its eventual height of 5 feet makes it attractive and popular as a short hedge needing little attention. The foliage is a fresh-looking blue-green, but its late May flowering is not conspicuous since the tiny, paired, obscured blossoms are either creamy or greenish white; little fruit is produced.

CULTIVAR: 'Emerald Mound' is covered with rich-looking emerald-green leaves; it rises only to a 3 foot height with an accompanying spread between 4 and 6 feet. Neither the insignificant flowers nor the scant fruit has any landscape merit. It too can be used attractively as a low-maintenance hedge or as a tubbed accent.

MYRICA (CEROTHAMNUS) (MORELLA) (bayberry, wax myrtle, sweet gale)   *Myrtaceae* (myrtle) family

An explanation of this genus appears in the "Broadleaf Evergreens" division.

Myrica pensylvanica (bayberry, candleberry, swamp candleberry)

Zones 5 to 9   3' to 9' high x 4' to 9' wide   Sun

Myrica pensylvanica fruit

Many authorities believe this to be the species *caroliniensis*, but *Hortus Third* says that that name is not valid here and belongs only with the evergreen species *cerifera*. The shrub is bushy and billowy with a great ability to adapt to shore conditions and is helpful in dune stabilization there since it thrives on dry, poor, sandy soils without loss of its great hardiness. Native from Nova Scotia to Florida and Alabama, it came into cultivation during 1727. The aromatic wax surrounding its clustered, bony, gray-white, ⅛-inch-wide fruit has been used widely to scent candles. These plants are dioecious, however, and only the females bear these long-lasting nutlets. While generally deciduous, some plants often maintain a semievergreen condition through the winter, although the foliage may be heavily scorched at the margins by spring and not appear attractive. These leaves appear on grayish twigs and are broadly wedge-shaped, between 1½ and 4 inches long, dull green above, blunt-tipped, usually untoothed or only slightly indented, and pleasantly fragrant when crushed; they have been used in cooking as a substitute for the more usual bay *(Laurus)* foliage.

PAEONIA (peony)   *Paeoniaceae* (peony) family

Until recently considered a member of the *Ranunculaceae* (buttercup) family, this genus is among the most well known and popular of all plants. Its name honors Paeon, an ancient Greek physician reputed to have first selected these plants for medicinal use. Very hardy and thriving in almost any well-drained soil with adequate light, its thirty-three species vary from stout or coarse perennial herbs to open, spreading shrubs; both are attractive for their conspicuous flowering and are native to western North America and to northern temperate Asia and Europe. The more widely known, herbaceous perennial sorts die to ground level each autumn, but the shrubby forms described here retain their woody stems; both are remarkably long-lived and may continue to give pleasure for a century. Each type normally is planted bare-rooted (unless already containerized) and is best handled in the early autumn as the foliage fades. The roots are thick, tuberous, and easily damaged when handled carelessly; bruised parts should be cut off cleanly before planting or they may develop rot. The plants prefer either full sun (but not in the hot portions of zone 8) or light afternoon shading and enjoy a rich, moist, well-drained, humusy soil with some lime added to acid conditions. They resent exposed, windy sites and do not accept transplanting gracefully when old.

The bowl-shaped flowering occurs during spring and early summer at the ends of new stem growth and appears either solitary or in small clusters as purple, pink, red, yellow, or white blooms. Today the available cultivars offer an expanded color range in an unbelievable assortment of tints, tones, sizes, and shapes. The fruit is a clustering of upright, horizontally spreading, dry, podlike containers botanically called follicles. The foliage is alternate, large, and compound. Insects present far less difficulty than diseases, and generally not even insects are consistently troublesome to these distinguished plants.

Paeonia suffruticosa cultivar

Paeonia suffruticosa cultivar

Paeonia suffruticosa (arborea, moutan) (tree peony, moutan peony)

Zones 5 to 8   4′ to 7′ high x 3′ to 6′ wide   Sun to light shade

Spectacular in flower, very hardy, and long-lived, here is one of the aristocrats of flowering shrubs. The first wild plants were known perhaps 1500 years ago in China, but the cultivated types became fashionable there only at the time of the Tang dynasty in the seventh century A.D. Poets sang its praises, and it was given the emperor's protection. It was painted on walls, silks, and fine papers, and it gradually became an almost-obligatory motif in the decoration of imperial palaces. Peonies were the first plants to be established in the Tang gardens, and when Yung-Lo of the later Ming dynasty moved his court to Peking, he ordered an annual return pilgrimage to observe the flowering of the *Paeonia moutan* (as it was then called), a custom followed faithfully until the nineteenth century. Not many other plants can lay claim to that much devoted attention.

These plants are native to both China and Tibet and came into general knowledge and culture about 1800. Coarsely branched, leggy, and rigid, they dislike nearby root competition from major plants and enjoy a well-drained, organically enriched soil close to neutral conditions (add ground limestone if the pH is very acid) with some light shade in the afternoon when in bloom to prolong the subtle colorings and performance of these overscaled flowers. Choose the permanent location with care since they resent root disturbance as they age. Most are now grafted plants, and it is vital that the swollen junction (or graft union) be set 6 inches below the finished grade of the soil. These plants are heavy feeders and appreciate an annual topdressing of compost around their stems in the autumn; work this carefully into the top layer during early spring along with a light amount of balanced commercial fertilizer. The late May blossoms are normally solitary and appear terminally on new stem growth, which is not very sturdy at this time and may require support staking to prevent the top-heavy flowers from breaking since they range from 6 inches to 1 foot across. Blossoms are crepe-paper-like with thin petals showing raggedly cut edges and appear as rose-pink to white (in the original form) with noticeable maroon blotches at the bases; the center is filled with an abundance of golden stamens. Unfortunately, these blooms are of short duration with a life expectancy of only 10 days; any abnormally hot weather will shorten this span. While they are on display, they cannot be matched readily for their showy nature. The foliage is twice-compound with leaflets deeply cut (and attractive in its own right) in lengths up to 18 inches; it often emerges with reddish overtones and becomes medium to dark green with somewhat hairy undersides but little gloss. Occasionally some autumnal color develops, but it is not intense.

Single and double cultivars by the hundreds are known today, in a listing far too sizable to evaluate here. These range from glistening deep maroon to vibrant yellow in an extraordinary assortment of color mixes and shapes. The newest cultivars can be highly expensive when first introduced, but older types are only modest in cost. Regardless of the price, tree peonies are an investment of permanent and expanding attractiveness, worth including in any landscape design.

PHILADELPHUS (mock orange)   *Saxifragaceae* (saxifrage) family

Between sixty-five and seventy-five species (depending on the authority) of mainly deciduous shrubs with erect habits and arching branches exist in this genus that is distributed generally in eastern North America, southern Asia, and southeastern Europe (a few evergreen sorts are found in Central America). Most are hardy and vigorous but tend to become leggy with age; they bloom, however, at an early stage and often display attractively fragrant and showy flowering (the perfume industry cultivates this genus on an industrial scale). Most tend to cross-fertilize with each other readily, creating some botanic confusion about the actual size and coloring of some species. Easy to grow in almost any climate, this group enjoys an average-fertility, moist, well-drained soil fortified with organic matter in sun or light shade; most accept dryness well, but none likes soggy soil. Flowering appears during early summer in white, usually with four petals and, on the single-bloom types, masses of golden yellow stamens; these are either solitary or in small clusters on the wood of the previous year. Double-flowered sorts remain in bloom longer. Most of the recent cultivars are the work of the Lemoine nursery in France, which also hybridized many *Deutzia*, a close relation. Fruit is a dry capsule without landscape merit. The leaves are opposite, simple, and dull green; they lack autumnal color. They develop either entire or toothed, and some species disperse the odor of ripe cucumber when the leaves are crushed. Pests and diseases are not a major problem. The genus name may commemorate Ptolemy Philadelphus, a king of the third century B.C. with a fondness for gardening, or it may come from the Greek word for "brotherly love," an obscure allusion. These plants are often commonly called "syringa," which is confusing since that name is currently restricted to the genus of the unrelated lilac.

Philadelphus coronarius   (sweet mock orange, false syringa)

Zones 5 to 8   **7′ to 10′ high × 7′ to 10′ wide**   **Sun to light shade**

Widely cultivated and a parent of most *Philadelphus* hybrids we know today, this shrub has maintained popular appeal since the sixteenth century, when it first was cultivated. Its species name means "used for crowning or garlanding." Natively found in southwestern Asia and southeastern Europe (where it is the only native species known), the plant grows vigorously erect and dense but becomes rigid, coarse-looking, and leggy when mature. It has wide-ranging, competitive roots and easily accepts very dry locations (but only when watered regularly after transplanting to establish it). The bloom appears by early June as creamy white, very sweet-scented, 1 to 1½-inch-wide flowers held in terminal clusters of five to seven all along the outer stems. Its foliage is dull green, oval to oblong, 1½ to 3 inches in length, slightly toothed

Philadelphus coronarius

but with prominent veining, and supported by hairy leaf stalks. The cultivar list is extensive.

CULTIVAR: 'Aureus' ('Foliis Aureis') has a dense, compact, and rounded habit with insignificant flower displays and leaves that are bright yellow when emerging; these often fade by midsummer to yellow-green with little appeal. It appears that this plant requires some afternoon shade to keep its yellow coloring prominent.

CULTIVAR: 'Deutziiflorus' ('Multiflorus plenus') is dwarfed and has double flowers which carry narrow, pointed petals.

CULTIVAR: 'Dianthiflorus' is another dwarf with double blooms, but here the petals are rounded (see *cv.* 'Deutziiflorus').

CULTIVAR: 'Duplex' ('Flore-pleno', 'Nanus', 'Pumilus') grows only to 3 feet tall with double or semidouble blooms on hairy flower stalks; it does not begin to flower until it is several years old.

CULTIVAR: 'Primuliflorus' ('Rosiflorus Plenus') grows taller than *cv.* 'Dianthiflorus'; it is otherwise similar in habit but with slightly wider flower petals.

CULTIVAR: 'Salicifolius' behaves in a distinct manner with its narrow lancelike (or willowlike) foliage 4 inches long and ½ inch wide.

CULTIVAR: 'Speciosissimus' *(var. speciosissimus)* is low-growing with smaller leaves than the parent.

CULTIVAR: 'Variegatus' has been cultivated since 1770 as an upright, slow-growing, double-flowered form with leaves irregularly but attractively bordered in white.

CULTIVAR: 'Zeyheri' displays an erect silhouette to 6 feet with single flowers 1 inch wide.

Philadelphus x lemoinei   (Lemoine mock orange)

Zones 5 to 8   **3′ to 4′ high x 4′ to 5′ wide**   **Sun to light shade**

Dense, mounded, and highly fragrant, this shrub is the original hybrid from which many popular cultivars have been selected. It is a cross between *coronarius* and *microphyllus* made by the Lemoine nursery of France; it was introduced in 1884. The mid-June flowering is white, up to 1½ inches wide, and clustered in groups of three to seven blossoms; it seems to flower almost as well in modest shade. The oval to oblong leaves are dull green and about 2 inches long with slightly hairy undersides. Several attractive and popular cultivars are available.

CULTIVAR: 'Avalanche' (1896) behaves in a semierect fashion to a 4-foot height with arching branches and smaller leaves than those of the parent. It is prolific and very fragrant in flower; the blooms are single and an inch across.

CULTIVAR: 'Belle Etoile' (1925) grows compactly to 6 feet with attractively fragrant, single, fringed flowers opening to a sizable 2¼ inches wide and showing a maroon flush at the centers.

CULTIVAR: 'Boule d'Argent' (1894) is the hardiest member of this group. It expands only to a 5-foot height with double or semidouble, pure white, slightly scented blossoms that are 2 inches across. The flowering is both prolific and heavily produced; this is a very showy plant.

CULTIVAR: 'Erectus' (1894) has a compact and noticeably upright habit to 4 feet with much smaller dark green leaves than the parent. The profuse blooms are single, fragrant, and an inch wide; it closely resembles *cv.* 'Avalanche' except for its habit.

CULTIVAR: 'Innocence' (1927) grows 8 feet tall with leaves often variegated in creamy white and displaying single, highly scented 1¾-inch blossoms that are very freely produced.

CULTIVAR: 'Manteau d'Hermine' remains compactly low to 3 feet with double to semidouble, creamy white, scented flowers that often are hidden by the heavy foliage.

CULTIVAR: 'Mont Blanc' (1896) is moundlike to 4 feet and exceptionally hardy. It carries single, 1¼-inch-wide, fragrant blooms with widely spaced drooping petals.

Philadelphus x virginalis (virginalis mock orange)

Zones 5 to 8   5′ to 9′ high x 4′ to 7′ wide   Sun to light shade

Robust and erect, this hybrid of *x lemoinei* and perhaps *nivalis plenus* originated before 1910 at the Lemoine nursery in France. It blooms during mid-June with double or semidouble flowers 1 to 2 inches wide in clusters of three to seven. The leaves are oval and about 3 inches wide with hairy undersides. Less fragrant than either *coronarius* or *x lemoinei* but hardier than both, this plant is the parent of a host of attractive cultivars.

CULTIVAR: 'Argentine' (1914) shows double blossoms 2 inches wide in small clusters of three on a 4-foot plant.

CULTIVAR: 'Bouquet Blanc' (1894) is moundlike with a 6-foot height; it carries 1-inch, single, fragrant blooms.

CULTIVAR: 'Burfordiensis' ('Burford') (1921) grows erect to 6 feet with single, cup-shaped, 1¾-inch-wide flowers showing conspicuous masses of stamens. It was developed in England by Sir William Lawrence.

CULTIVAR: 'Enchantment' shows a graceful, 5-foot-high silhouette and sweetly scented double flowering with fringed petals held in loose clusters.

CULTIVAR: 'Frosty Morn' (1953) is very hardy (zone 4) and heavily scented. It grows to 4 feet with double blossoms. It was originated by Guy Bush of Minnesota.

CULTIVAR: 'Girandole' (1916) carries very double, fragrant, 1¾-inch-wide flowers on a 4-foot plant.

CULTIVAR: 'Glacier' (1914) blooms later than most with fragrant, very double, 1¼-inch-wide blossoms; it develops smaller leaves.

CULTIVAR: 'Minnesota Snowflake' (1935) is another of the very hardy (zone 4) introductions from Guy Bush of Minnesota (see *cv.* 'Frosty Morn'). This one grows as tall as 8 feet with arching branches clothed right to the ground and double, 2-inch-wide, fragrant blooms.

CULTIVAR: 'Virginal' (1907) is undoubtedly the best double-flowered cultivar known; it certainly is the most widely grown and admired. Robust, erect to 9 feet, but leggy at maturity, it produces intensely scented double to semidouble flowers 2 inches wide that are set attractively on the many branches.

Philadelphus x virginalis cv. 'Minnesota Snowflake'

POTENTILLA (DRYMOCALLIS) (cinquefoil, five fingers)   *Rosaceae* (rose) family

Some 500 species of annual and perennial herbs plus a few shrubs belong to this genus that is native mostly to both the north temperate and the arctic regions. They enjoy full sun when raised in the north but prefer light shading in the south. Easy to grow well and adaptable to some dryness, these plants like cool, deep, moderately moist, acid or alkaline soils. The familiar shrub forms carry blossoms resembling single roses (they are related, but distantly), show a lengthy blooming period, and are very drought-resistant. These also have dark brown stems with somewhat less appeal than many other plants during winter. The flowers are yellow, white, or red with five broad petals; these develop thin-walled, dry fruit botanically called achenes; they are generally without landscape appeal. The leaves are compound—either pinnate or palmate—and usually toothed. Diseases and insect pests are rarely bothersome. The name comes from the Latin *potens* ("powerful") and probably refers to ancient medicinal qualities of some sort. The common name "cinquefoil" is French for "five leaves," which is the common palmate form seen on these plants.

Potentilla fruticosa (shrubby cinquefoil, golden hardhack, widdy)

Zones 2 to 8   2' to 4' high x 2' to 4' wide   Sun to light shade

Cultivated since 1700 and native to the north temperate regions as well as the polar ones, these shrubs are carefree, very hardy, and drought-tolerant with a basically generous bloom in late May that is followed by intermittent flowering for the rest of the summer. They accept any soil from wet to dry and from heavy to sandy, yet they do not seem to prosper along the Gulf coast or in Florida. Much branched and densely leafy, this shrub develops a rounded form and a fine-textured appearance; the flaky or peeling bark is deep brown. Pinnately compound leaves are bright green and long-stalked with five oval to wedge-shaped, toothless leaflets between ½ and ¾ inch long showing inturned margins. Some cultivars once listed here now are divided between *davurica* and *parvifolia*.

Potentilla parvifolia (small leaf cinquefoil)

Zones 4 to 8   2' to 3' high x 2' to 3' wide   Sun to light shade

The plant differs from *fruticosa* in its more uniformly fine foliage with seven somewhat hairy, narrow, medium green, ¼-inch leaflets; *fruticosa* has only five leaflets. These leaves are densely set along the stems, which are semierect. The mid-June flowering is golden yellow or deep orange, up to an inch wide, and produced abundantly. Adaptable to almost any soil, they accept drought well and even flower satisfactorily with some modest shading. A few cultivars are available.

CULTIVAR: 'Gold Drop' ('Farreri') is compact, dwarfed, and hardy into zone 3. It carries leaflets between ¼ and ¾ inch long plus small flowers of deep yellow.

CULTIVAR: 'Pumila' is very low and dwarfed with noticeably silky-haired foliage between ⅛ and ¼ inch in length.

CULTIVAR: 'Tenuiloba' has almost linear leaflets and is more hairy than the parent.

Potentilla cv. 'Primrose Beauty'

Potentilla selections

Zones 3 to 8 (variable)   Variable sizes   Sun to light shade

These are either garden discoveries or created hybrids that come from *davurica, fruticosa, parvifolia* (and other species) without clear parental histories at this time. They differ somewhat from each other in their hardiness and require some trial-and-error planting (much like the *Chaenomeles x superba* types) to determine their adaptability to local growing areas. Widely available in nurseries, they offer attractive forms and flowering in a wide selection of color values.

CULTIVAR: 'Beanii' displays a dwarfed form with very green leaves and white flowers.

CULTIVAR: 'Farrar's White' has a compact and dense habit with generous white blossoming all summer.

CULTIVAR: 'Friedrichsenii' ('Berlin Beauty') shows a robust and erect habit to 6 feet with somewhat gray-green leaves and an irregular outline that may be suitable as an informal hedge. It flowers throughout the summer with pale yellow blooms.

CULTIVAR: 'Grandiflora' is erect and strong-growing to 5 feet with large sage-green leaves and dense clusters of 1¼-inch canary-yellow flowers.

CULTIVAR: 'Katherine Dykes' ('Kathryn Dykes') produces silvery foliage and an abundance of primrose-yellow blossoms all summer on a plant 6 feet high.

CULTIVAR: 'Klondike' ('Klondyke') has a dwarfed habit. It is very similar to *parvifolia cv.* 'Gold Drop' but produces larger, deep yellow blossoming.

CULTIVAR: 'Longacre' maintains a matlike, dwarfed appearance and carries large, bright, sulfur-yellow flowers.

CULTIVAR: 'Maanelys' ('Moonlight') is erect to 3 feet with dark blue-green leaves and pale yellow blossoms intermittently carried throughout the summer.

CULTIVAR: 'Mount Everest' has a densely compact habit with some vigor to become 5 feet high. The dark green foliage sets off the 1¼-inch-wide blossoms attractively, but they are produced only intermittently during the summer months.

CULTIVAR: 'Ochroleuca' has cream-colored blooms and a general resemblance to *cv.* 'Friedrichsenii' in habit; it also may prove useful as an informal hedge.

CULTIVAR: 'Primrose Beauty' is a superior cultivar with a free-flowering habit and yellow blossoms with deeper yellow centers. The foliage is gray-green and small-sized, appearing on arching branches.

CULTIVAR: 'Rehderana' grows to 4 feet with very tiny leaves and light yellow flowers.

CULTIVAR: 'Red Ace' is a recently introduced form with tomato-red flowering; it may require some shading to keep that intensity from fading.

CULTIVAR: 'Tangerine' shows a dwarfed, wide-spreading, mounded habit and pale copper-yellow blossoms when given partial shade; in full sun the flowers fade to just yellow.

PRUNUS (LAUROCERASUS) (no one common name)   *Rosaceae* (rose) family

An explanation of this genus appears in the "Broadleaf Evergreens" division.

Prunus x cistena (purpleleaf sand cherry)

Zones 3 to 7   5' to 8' high x 4' to 6' wide   Sun

Perhaps even hardier than described here, the plant is particularly suited to the cold winters and hot summers of the central and northern plains of the United States and lower Canada. Upright and robust with an irregular outline, it is a hybrid cross of *cerasifera* and *atropurpurea*, which came from South Dakota about 1910. It behaves exceptionally well as a hedge or border accent since it adapts to any well-drained soil. The mid-May flowering is white to pink-toned, fragrant, single, and ½ inch wide; it appears on the previous year's wood. Foliage is 1 to 2 inches long, toothed, and rich red all summer; there is no autumnal change. Its edible fruit is typically cherrylike as a drupe; it is ½ inch long and blackish purple.

Prunus x cistena

Prunus glandulosa (flowering almond, dwarf flowering almond, Chinese bush cherry)

Zones 4 to 8   3' to 5' high x 3' to 5' wide   Sun

Native to central and northern China as well as to Japan, this handsome shrub has been cultivated since 1835 for its attractive spring flowering, but only as the double-flowered cultivar. Today the typical single-flowered form is very rare in nurseries. Upright and open with slender stems coming directly from the ground with little branching, the plant has a somewhat rounded outline

Prunus glandulosa (Cont.)

Prunus glandulosa cv. 'Sinensis'

and only one season of interest: the blooming time, which is usually early May. These flowers are pink or white, single, nearly an inch wide, and set closely all along the stems of the previous season. Its dark red, ½-inch, round fruit is rarely seen (the double forms do not produce fruit). The foliage is thin, light green, almost oblong, 1½ to 4 inches long, point-tipped, and round-toothed; it provides no autumn color. Fire blight disease is prevalent with this shrub and spreads rapidly once infection occurs. Pruning immediately and drastically after flowering may arrest the disease before it becomes rampant; this technique is also worthwhile to increase new stem development, and it induces subsequently greater flowering as well. Adaptable to many soil types, it favors a consistently moist, humusy, well-drained site. Several important cultivars are available.

CULTIVAR: 'Alboplena' originated in 1852; it produces heavy flowering of double, white, pomponlike blooms.

CULTIVAR: 'Rosea' has single pink flowers.

CULTIVAR: 'Sinensis' *(P. sinensis)* is by far the most popular sort with its deep green foliage and generous, bright pink, double blossoms; it was a garden staple of most Victorian and Edwardian landscapes in England.

Prunus maritima fruit

Prunus maritima (acuminata) (beach plum, shore plum, black plum)

Zones 4 to 7   3' to 7' high x 5' to 10' wide   Sun

Attractive as a shoreline plant that is readily adaptable to both salt spray and sandy soil, this rounded, dense shrub is native to the sandy coastal areas from Maine to Delaware. In culture since 1818, it is simple to grow well, and it produces a marketable fruit suitable for jellies and jams. The early May flowers appear before leaf development as white, single (sometimes semidouble), ¾-inch-wide blossoms in clusters of two or three in the leaf axils of the previous year's stems. Foliage is oval to wedge-shaped, sharply toothed with hairy undersides, dull green, and 1 inch to 2½ inches long; it has no autumnal color value. The edible, dull purple to red, ½- to 1-inch-wide fruit is a spherical drupe (a typical plum). The cultivars 'Eastham', 'Hancock', and 'Premier' are superior types selected for the quality and larger size of the fruit; they show only minor differences from a landscape standpoint.

PUNICA (pomegranate)   *Punicaceae* (pomegranate) family

Only two species of deciduous shrubs (or small trees) are included in this genus native to southeastern Europe and southern Asia, and the family has only this genus. Grown since antiquity for the large, edible fruit, the plant is mentioned approvingly many times in the Old Testament, especially for its prolific seeds, which are cited often in the "one-from-many" parables that early cultures found endearing. The flared design of the dried sepal parts of the end of the fruit is said to have influenced King Solomon in the construction of his own crown (which other, later rulers seem to have adopted as well). In the Middle East today it is believed that Eve offered Adam one of these fruits, not an apple. Many cultures value this plant as a promoter of good luck, while others (especially in the Mediterranean area) see the juicy, edible pulp surrounding the myriad red seeds of the fruit as a symbol of fertility. The fruit silhouette is boldly incorporated into the official emblem of Granada, Spain, where these plants were installed profusely by the Moors during the centuries they held the land. There can be no question that this plant has made a lasting impression. The common name derives from the Latin *pomum* ("apple") and *granatum* ("with many seeds"), an appropriate description of its nature. The genus name, *Punica*, comes from the Latin term *malum punicum*, or "apple of Carthage"; Carthage was known to the Romans as Punicus, and this plant obviously grew and thrived there.

The solitary or clustered flowering grows at the tips of stems and persists noticeably in the five sepal parts (Solomon's crown design) of the later fruit, which is a leathery-skinned, edible berry with many seeds in conspicuous compartments surrounded by juicy red flesh. The foliage is mostly opposite, simple, and entire and is often clustered on the twigs; when emerging, it is generally copper-toned. These shrubs grow best in a deep, heavy loam and rarely need pruning. Few insects or diseases are bothersome.

Punica granatum (pomegranate)

Zones 9 and 10   15′ to 25′ high x 10′ to 15′ wide   Sun

Developing either as a dense, twiggy, large-scaled shrub (the norm) or as a small, bushy tree, this anciently cultivated plant has fountainlike arching branches and is naturalized now in much of southeastern Europe and across Asia to the Himalayas. Highly popular today as an ornamental in the southern and southwestern parts of the United States for use as hedges or specimens, it is especially tolerant of heat, drought, and alkaline conditions, yet for high-quality fruit development it requires regular and deep watering plus a well-drained soil. The funnel-shaped, 1¼- to 4-inch-wide flowers open during late summer or early autumn and are a bright, waxy orange-red with thick, crumpled petals and purplish sepals, producing a somewhat gaudy show on its new wood; occasionally these blossoms are yellow or cream, and any plant may develop spiny tips at the twig ends. The almost-round, 2½- to 5-inch-wide, thick-skinned fruit varies in color from purplish red to brownish yellow with pronounced, flared sepal remains at the terminal ends; these insist on a long hot summer season to mature properly and be edible. The oblong to lancelike foliage is 1 to 3 inches in length, entire, glossy, deep green, and blunt-tipped; it turns a bright golden yellow in the autumn. The following popular cultivars are not always as hardy as the parent.

CULTIVAR: 'Alba Plena' ('Albo Plena', 'Multiplex') carries double blossoms in white and remains low-growing between 6 and 8 feet tall.

CULTIVAR: 'Chico' matures at a height between 4 and 8 feet with 1- to 2-inch-wide double flowers of orange-red which bloom through the summer but develop no fruiting; the leaves grow only up to 1½ inches long.

CULTIVAR: 'Flore Pleno' ('Pleniflora', 'Rubra Plena') has showy double flowering of rich red.

CULTIVAR: 'Legrellei' ('Mme. Legrelle') produces double orange-red blossoms streaked and margined in yellowish white; it also sets occasional flowers of scarlet with irregular variegations.

CULTIVAR: 'Nana' (*var. nana*) is dwarfed, twiggy, and compact to a height between 3 and 6 feet; it is slightly hardier than the parent and is often used for hedges and pot plants. It blooms when very young and sets single, 1-inch-wide, red-orange flowers during September and October; the leaves vary from ¾ inch to 1½ inches long. The fruit is only 2 inches wide.

CULTIVAR: 'Wonderful' has become a very popular type for its 5-inch-wide fruit with commercial uses. The orange-red double flowers appear on a plant that matures to about 10 feet.

RHAMNUS (buckthorn)   *Rhamnaceae* (buckthorn) family

About 150 species of mostly deciduous shrubs and small trees are contained in this adaptable genus native generally to the temperate regions of the northern hemisphere; a few are found in Brazil or South Africa. The twig tips often end in a sharp point, which accounts for the "thorn" part of the name, and the majority are grown for their foliage effects as screens or barriers; a few are cultivated for medicinal properties. All species are banned from growing in Canada since they are alternate hosts for the devastating crown rust of wheat, an important crop there. These plants adjust to any soil, even wet, and accept either full sun or semishade. The flowers are insignificantly small and green-toned, appearing in the leaf axils. Its fruiting develops either as a small capsule or as a fleshy drupe and is enjoyed by wildlife; these plants often overseed generously to form thickets or large masses. The simple foliage is either opposite or alternate with conspicuous parallel veining. Pests and diseases are not uncommon with some species, but none is especially disfiguring on a regular basis.

Rhamnus frangula (alder buckthorn, glossy buckthorn)

Zones 3 to 8   10′ to 18′ high x 10′ to 18′ wide   Sun to light shade

This widely distributed and readily grown shrub may be hardy even into parts of zone 2 since it also is found natively in bleak locations of the British Isles, Europe, northern Africa, and Asia and has been naturalized in the eastern part of North America, particularly in wet places. Dense, robust, and self-seeding, it has been known here since the colonial era. Its fruit is welcomed by birds, which distribute the seeds far and wide, making the plant a dominating pest in some areas. The twig ends here do not have sharpened tips. Its dried bark is commercially used as a laxative (as is that from the sharp-tipped, less attractive common buckthorn, *cathartica*). The diminutive flowering begins during June and continues through much of the summer; these are pale green and come in clusters of eight to ten blossoms at the leaf axils on new growth. Fruit formation quickly follows and continues for many weeks, maturing at different times and presenting a varied color range from the initial green to cream to red to a final black-purple. Any average-fertility soil is acceptable. Japanese beetles have a decided liking for the broadly oval, lustrous, dark green, toothless leaves, which range between 1½ and 2½ inches long and have conspicuous parallel veining with eight to nine pairs of lines; its autumn coloring is yellow. The parent is rarely cultivated, but the following cultivars are.

CULTIVAR: 'Asplenifolia' develops a rounded habit and carries ¼-inch-wide threadlike foliage with wavy edges.

CULTIVAR: 'Tallhedge' ('Columnaris') is a patented plant (1955) and the most popular form because of its distinctly erect, dense, narrow habit with a width of only 4 feet. It is extensively used now for hedges or screens and requires little pruning to hold its form, although it can be sheared tightly without harm.

RHODODENDRON (rhododendron, azalea)   *Ericaceae* (heath) family

An explanation of this genus appears in the "Broadleaf Evergreens" division.

Rhododendron arborescens (Azalea arborescens)
(smooth azalea, sweet azalea, tree azalea)

Zones 5 to 8   **8′ to 20′ high x 10′ to 25′ wide**   **Sun to light shade**

Native to mountain stream areas from Pennsylvania to Georgia and Alabama, this desirable large shrub has been in culture since 1818. It offers attractively fragrant, conspicuous flowering during mid-June and deep red, glossy autumn color. Generally much smaller when cultivated, the plant enjoys a humusy, consistently moist soil and room to expand properly. The twigs are hairless and produce heliotrope-scented, 1-inch-long, white or pink-toned funnel-shaped flowers with very long red stamens; these blooms are very sticky on the exteriors, are up to 2 inches wide at the mouth, and come in terminal clusterings of three to six, producing a showy and colorful effect. Fruit is a narrowly egg-shaped, densely hairy capsule between ½ and ¾ inch long. The smooth, thick, wedge-shaped to lancelike foliage varies from 1½ to 3 inches in length and is a shiny, bright green. This plant differs from its near-relation *viscosum* in its earlier bloom plus its smooth stems and leaves.

Rhododendron calendulaceum (Azalea calendulaceum)
(flame azalea, yellow azalea)

Zones 5 to 8   **5′ to 10′ high x 5′ to 10′ wide**   **Sun to light shade**

Considered one of the most vividly colorful of all wild azaleas, especially for its late displays, this horizontally branched shrub is one of the many parents used in the creation of the showy Ghent and recent Exbury hybrids. The species name translates to "like a calendula," reflecting its color range mostly in yellows and oranges (occasionally red); when in bloom during early June the flowers can submerge the developing leaves completely. Natively found from southwestern Pennsylvania and Ohio to Georgia, the plant has been cultivated since 1806 because the blooms hold their brilliance even in full sun and the colorings persist up to 2 weeks. New twigs are downy and produce oval to oblong bright green foliage which is hairy beneath, 1½ to 3 inches long, and colored dull yellow or bronze in the autumn. The funnelform, usually unscented blossoms are 2 inches wide at the mouth and have hairy exteriors plus conspicuously long, projecting stamens. Blooms develop as clusters of five to seven in orange, yellow, and sometimes scarlet colorings. The fruit is narrowly egg-shaped, downy, and about ¾ inch long. Several variations are known.

CULTIVAR: 'Auranticum' produces a color range from orange to scarlet.

CULTIVAR: 'Croceum' has blossoms varying from yellow to orange-buff.

VARIETY: *bakeri (cumberlandense)* is very similar in form to the parent but blooms about 3 weeks later in deep orange to red-orange.

Rhododendron calendulaceum

Rhododendron calendulaceum

Rhododendron x gandavensis

Rhododendron x gandavensis cv. 'Narcissiflora'

Rhododendron x gandavensis (Azalea x gandavensis)
(Ghent azalea, Ghent hybrid azalea)

Zones 5 to 7   6' to 10' high x 6' to 10' wide   Light shade

This importantly showy group is the result of a series of crossings between *luteum* and *calendulaceum, molle, periclymenoides,* plus *viscosum* made mostly between 1830 and 1850 in Belgium and England. These shrubs are tall, erect, and very hardy (some will do well even in zone 4) with a preference for less than full sun. The late May, fragrant flowers are honeysucklelike and funnelform with mouths 1½ to 2½ inches wide on both the single and the double forms in main colorings of white, pale yellow, orange, red, or red-violet with additional shadings or blotches of at least one of these colors as an accent. The foliage is variable in both size and color value between cultivars during summer as well as at the autumn changeover. The following selection places the single-flowered types first.

CULTIVAR: 'Altaclarensis' shows basic orange-yellow color with a darker throat blotch.

CULTIVAR: 'Bouquet de Flore' is bright pink with a yellow center.

CULTIVAR: 'Coccinea Speciosa' flowers glowingly in orange-red.

CULTIVAR: 'Daviesi' has white blossoms blotched in yellow.

CULTIVAR: 'Gloria Mundi' is bright orange with the upper petal yellow and frilled.

CULTIVAR: 'Nancy Waterer' displays large golden yellow blooms.

CULTIVAR: 'Pallas' carries orange-red flowering with an orange-yellow upper petal.

These are the double-flowered types:

CULTIVAR: 'Narcissiflora' develops a robust but compact habit and displays sweetly-scented, sulfur-yellow double blossoms.

CULTIVAR: 'Raphael de Smet' has white flowers flushed with rose and offers superior autumn color.

Rhododendron 'Knap Hill–Exbury Hybrid' cultivar

Rhododendron 'Knap Hill–Exbury Hybrids' (*Azalea* 'Knap Hill–Exbury Hybrids')

Zones 6 to 8   4' to 8' high x 4' to 8' wide   Sun to light shade

These plants were originally developed at the English Knap Hill nursery as far back as 1870 and more recently at the Exbury estate (near Southampton, England) of Lionel de Rothschild; some of the newest forms have even been hybridized in New Zealand. Most are crosses between *x kosteranum* and *x gandavensis* cultivars and display enormous but generally scentless blossoms in large clusters showing uniquely attractive color combinations. They present vividly showy displays during late May and early June, but none thrives beyond zone 8 of their range, although a few accept colder conditions. An important drawback is the tendency of some cultivars to contract powdery mildew on the sizable leaves, especially in areas where summers are hot and humid for prolonged periods. While most are erect and some are low but spreading in habit, all are characterized by trumpet-shaped blossoms with mouths between 2 and 3 inches wide; they are clustered terminally in generous heads containing anywhere from eighteen to thirty individual blossoms. These range in color between white, cream, yellow, orange, pink, rose-red, and vivid red, but nearly all are a blended mix of several colorations. Depending on the cultivar, the medium green foliage changes to bright yellow, orange, or red in the autumn. Without a doubt these are desirable additions to any location where they grow suitably. The cultivar list is huge and continually expanding, but the following ones are currently popular.

CULTIVAR: 'Balzac' is fragrant and has orange-red flowers with an orange flare.

CULTIVAR: 'Berryrose' develops copper-toned new leaves and rose-pink blossoms with yellow flashes.

CULTIVAR: 'Brazil' displays frilled petals and a bright tangerine-red coloring.

CULTIVAR: 'Buzzard' is both vigorous and fragrant with pale yellow blooms edged and tinted pink with deep yellow flares.

CULTIVAR: 'Debutante' flowers in rose-pink.

CULTIVAR: 'Eisenhower' is fiery red with an orange blotch.

CULTIVAR: 'Fireball' has copper-toned new foliage and deep orange-red blossoms with reflexed petals.

CULTIVAR: 'Fireglow' is colored orange-vermilion.

CULTIVAR: 'Gibraltar' has become a very popular type with its vigorous, upright, and wide-spreading habit plus brilliantly orange flowers showing crinkly petals.

CULTIVAR: 'Gold Dust' blooms earlier than most with pale yellow blossoms having gold flares.

CULTIVAR: 'Golden Oriole' produces bronze new leaves and deeply golden flowering with orange flares.

CULTIVAR: 'Klondyke' is striking with its emerging copper-red foliage and large blossoms of glowing orange-gold.

CULTIVAR: 'Royal Lodge' blooms later than most others in deep, vermilion-red with noticeably long, projecting stamens.

CULTIVAR: 'Satan' becomes strongly upright and has scarlet flowers.

CULTIVAR: 'Strawberry Ice' carries blossoms of flesh pink with gold flares.

CULTIVAR: 'Toucan' is robust and fragrant with pale yellow or cream flowers edged in pink with dark yellow flares.

CULTIVAR: 'Tunis' is wide-spreading, upright, and vigorous with deep crimson flowering carrying orange flares.

CULTIVAR: 'White Swan' displays white blooms with yellow flares.

CULTIVAR: 'Whitethroat' blooms late; its double, pure white flowers have frilled petals; it has a compact habit and attractive red autumn coloring.

Rhododendron x kosteranum (Azalea x kosteranum)
(Molle hybrid azalea, Mollis hybrid azalea)

Zones 6 and 7   3′ to 8′ high x 3′ to 8′ wide   Sun to light shade

Rhododendron x kosteranum cultivar

This plant and its cultivars are similar to the Ghents but lack their hardiness and long life. A cross between *japonica* and *molle* developed in Belgium about 1873, the shrub is stiffly erect, modest in growth, and rounded in outline; it blooms by late May before the leaves emerge fully. Its coarse foliage is variable in size and is usually found clustered near the twig ends; these leaves show prominent veining and curled edges with yellow and occasionally orange autumn color. The flowers are always single and about 2½ inches wide at the mouth in white, yellow, pink, or red; they come in clusters of seven to thirteen and emit a conspicuous musky odor with little appeal. The following cultivars are known.

CULTIVAR: 'Comte de Gomer' blooms rose-pink with orange flares.

CULTIVAR: 'Comte de Papadopoli' flowers bright pink shaded orange.

CULTIVAR: 'Hugo Koster' carries 3-inch-wide blossoms of salmon-orange flushed red.

CULTIVAR: 'Miss Louisa Hunnewell' is colored orange-yellow and has flowering 3 inches across.

CULTIVAR: 'Snowdrift' develops slender-tubed white blossoms with deep yellow flashes.

Rhododendron mucronulatum (dauricum mucronulatum) (Azalea mucronulata)
(Korean rhododendron, Mongolian azalea)

Zones 5 to 8   4' to 8' high x 4' to 8' wide   Light to semishade

This is the first hardy rhododendron (azalea) to bloom; its bright rosy-purple flowering appears by late March or early April (earlier in southern locations), often as a companion to some species of *Forsythia*. Cut branches taken in late winter force easily for indoor use. Because it blooms so early, however, the exposed buds may be lost to a sudden spring freeze. Avoid placing this shrub where the heat from late winter sun may encourage earlier flowering than normal (a northeast corner may prove workable) and make sure to provide shelter from constantly cold winds. Natively distributed in Japan, Korea, and China, it has been in cultivation since 1882 and possesses a slenderly upright form in most areas. The flowers are broadly funnelform, scentless, and 1¾ inches wide in clusterings of six or less. The thin wedge-shaped to lancelike foliage is soft green, scaly on both surfaces, and between 1¼ and 3 inches long; it attractively colors yellow to bronze-red in the autumn. The popular cultivar 'Cornell Pink' carries clear pink flowering.

Rhododendron periclymenoides

Rhododendron periclymenoides (nudiflorum) (Azalea nudiflora)
(pinxterbloom, pinxter flower, wild honeysuckle, purple honeysuckle, election pink)

Zones 4 to 8   4' to 6' high x 4' to 6' wide   Sun to light shade

Unique for its genus, this plant readily accepts dry, sandy locations. Native from Maine to South Carolina and Tennessee, it has been known to cultivation since 1734 and is the parent of many of the Ghent hybrids. These shrubs are usually low and much branched with a neat appearance; the smooth stems carry oval to oblong, 1¼- to 3-inch, hairless leaves of bright green which turn only dull, yellow-brown in the autumn. Its early to mid-May flowering develops before the foliage appears and carries a faint to delicate scent (depending on its growing area) from funnelform, 1½-inch-wide, pink or purplish (and perhaps nearly white) blossoms with elongated projecting stamens; these blooms appear in clusters of six to twelve. The early Dutch settlers of Pennsylvania provided the common name "pinxter" since the plant blooms there at Pentecost or Whitsuntide, which the Dutch call Pingster; thus, to them the plant was known as *pingsterbloem*. It has suffered only slightly in translation.

Rhododendron prinophyllum (roseum, nudiflorum rosea) (Azalea roseum) (roseshell azalea, downy pinxterbloom, early azalea, Piedmont azalea, Mayflower azalea)

Zones 4 to 8   5′ to 9′ high x 5′ to 9′ wide   Sun to light shade

Closely resembling *periclymenoides* in form, this shrub differs in the prominent clove scent of its flowers and the hairy undersides of the leaves. Native from southern Quebec and Maine to southwest Virginia and west to Ohio and Oklahoma, it has been cultivated at least since 1812 for its highly attractive blossoms and noticeable red autumn color. Both the buds and twigs are gray-hairy, and the oval to oblong 2- to 3-inch-long leaves are a dull bluish green with dense gray hairs beneath. Its late May flowers appear with the foliage and have funnel shapes, widths about 1½ inches across, and clusterings of five to nine blossoms; these are bright pink (occasionally pale pink to almost white) and carry the spicy smell of cloves.

Rhododendron schlippenbachi (Azalea schlippenbachi) (royal azalea)

Zones 5 to 8   9′ to 15′ high x 6′ to 8′ wide   Sun to light shade

Native to Manchuria, Korea, and Japan, this large-flowered regal shrub was discovered by Baron Schlippenbach in 1854, but it was not cultivated until 1893. Upright but rounded in form, it has wedge-shaped large foliage and oversized blossoms during mid-May as the leaves emerge. Slightly fragrant, these 2- to 3½-inch-wide flowers vary in color from pale pink to rosy pink and are freckled with light red-brown spotting; the clusters hold three to six blooms. The foliage develops in tight whorls of five atop the smooth stems. These thin leaves are deep, dull green and can become up to 5 inches long; they turn rich yellow or orange by autumn, provided the summer weather has not been overly dry. If it has been, they usually become muddy-toned.

Rhododendron vaseyi (Azalea vaseyi) (pinkshell azalea)

Zones 5 to 8   5′ to 15′ high x 4′ to 6′ wide   Sun to semishade

Surprisingly adaptive to either moist or somewhat dry soils as well as to reduced light, this delicate-flowered shrub is native to wet places in North Carolina and has been cultivated since 1880. Upright, bushy, and slender-stemmed, it blooms by mid-May before the foliage develops. The flowers are unscented, pale pink to rose with brown spotting, about 1½ inches wide, and broadly funnel-shaped in clusterings of five to eight. The winter buds are terminal and ⅜ inch long; they are egg-shaped, as are those of so many other azaleas, but here they perch atop the very thin twigs in such a seemingly precarious position that they become noticeable. Narrowly oval to oblong, dark green, thin leaves expand to about 5 inches in length and color rich red in the autumn, provided that (as with *schlippenbachi*) the summer was not extremely dry. In that case, these leaves will be only brownish red and without merit. The variety *album* carries pure white flowering but has been difficult to locate in nurseries.

Rhododendron vaseyi

Rhododendron viscosum

Rhododendron viscosum (Azalea viscosa)
(swamp azalea, white swamp azalea, swamp
honeysuckle, clammy azalea)

Zones 4 to 8   3′ to 8′ high x 3′ to 8′ wide   Sun to semishade

This is the last azalea to bloom, and it carries early July flowering that is
heavily scented with the spicy odor of cloves. The white to pale pink blossoms
are narrowly funnelform to an inch long in clusters of four to nine; these are
not annually distributed in any regular fashion throughout the plant. Native
to swampy areas from Maine to South Carolina, this hardy shrub enjoys
wetness, yet it also accepts somewhat drier conditions well. Bushy but loose
and open, it has narrowly oval to lancelike dark green leaves with gray-green
undersides in lengths up to 2½ inches; the autumn color varies from orange to
bronze-red. Its variety *aemulans* blooms earlier with larger clusters of flowers,
while *montanum* has a low, densely branched, suckering habit. All will grow
attractively in reduced light conditions.

Rhododendron yedoense (yodogava) (Azalea
yodogava)   (Yodogawa azalea)

Zones 6 to 8   2′ to 3′ high x 5′ to 6′ wide   Sun to light shade

Here is another naming situation in which the double-flowered form was
discovered well (almost 20 years) before the single type was known to exist.
Now we have a somewhat backward label arrangement since the double-
flowered plant has the *single* or species name, while the single-blooming plant
has the *double* or varietal name. Natively found in Korea and Japan, the
species has been known since 1884. It presents a low, dense, twiggy, wide-
spreading appearance. Blossoms appear by mid-May (but are not always
profuse each year) as funnel-shaped, 2-inch-wide double flowers of rosy-
purple spotted in dark purple. The dark green, narrowly oval to lancelike
leaves grow up to 3 inches long with pale and hairy undersides. Often this
plant behaves as a semievergreen in milder growing locations, but where it is
fully deciduous, the autumn color is purple-toned.

Its variety *poukhanense (Azalea poukhanensis)* is also a spreading plant but
is not always as low-growing as the parent since it can reach a 6-foot height
when grown in shade. It has single, fragrant blossoms which develop annually
and fully even on small plants; these flowers are up to 2 inches across in pale
lilac-purple with brown freckles and appear in clusters of two or more just as
the leaves emerge. The foliage is dark green and up to 3½ inches in length; it
turns purple-crimson in the autumn. This shrub is rarely semievergreen, but it
is hardier than the species and easily accepts semishaded conditions. It did not
become known until 1905, well after it was found in Korea.

ROSA (rose)   Rosaceae (rose) family

Roses have maintained consistent worldwide appeal since antiquity and
often are called "queen of the flowers" for their encouraging durability,
enticing fragrance, generally repetitive blooming, and attractive forms.
Possibly 200 distinct species exist today, although no one is certain, and at
least 20,000 cultivars of them are currently known and cataloged officially.
So many millions of words have been published about their selection and
culture that they cannot be intelligently condensed here; libraries of even
the smallest size carry many volumes which offer a better guide than can
be provided in this book.

Briefly, these plants want the fullest amount of sun (yet are tolerant of
some light shade) and a fertile, well-drained, moist soil neither strongly

acid nor overly alkaline. If bare-rooted, they are best installed when fully dormant, which can be late autumn or early spring; however, containerized plants can be installed at any convenient time when the ground is workable. These plants suffer numerous and continual pests and diseases, but few are unmanageable with reasonable and prompt attention. Roses are generally considered worth the effort of raising them.

The first historical record of roses dates back 5000 years to King Sargon I of Mesopotamia, who brought home from an expedition beyond the Tigris River "vines, figs, and rose trees." The name is from the ancient Celtic word *rhodd* or *rhudd* ("red"), and the Greek word *rhodon* ("rose") may be derived from it. Today roses can be divided into three main groups: (1) the cut-flower or display sorts that are hybridized and marketed by the hundreds annually (these are called the "contemporary" roses), (2) those with a reduced interest among growers and the public which no longer are being hybridized extensively (in general, the "old garden" types popular before 1900), and (3) the species and their variations. The selections here will be restricted to the species or to shrub roses which serve well as specimens, screens, masses, groundcovers, or hedges even if their flowering period is briefly set for one main show. These shrubs offer less demanding requirements for winter protection, insect and disease controls, and pruning. Many also develop attractively showy and persistent fruit plus autumn foliage color and winter stem interest. Any of these will thrive under reduced general maintenance requirements if correctly chosen for its attributes. The majority maintain vigorous natures, and quite a few have single flowers in the basic pattern of five sepals, five petals, and a central mass of different colored stamens. Where flowers are double, little or no fruit develops.

Rose fruit is round to oval, usually red or some mix of red, generally rich in vitamin C, and often long-lasting and decorative. They are given the special name of "hip" ("hep" in Europe and the British Isles) and are normally found clustered. The foliage is pinnately compound and toothed, mainly green and somewhat glossy (although some types have gray-toned or red-flushed leaves). The stems are generally equipped with sharp prickles or thorns, adding to the barrier quality of these multistemmed plants. Shrub roses are considered very hardy and adaptable plants.

Rosa blanda   (meadow rose, smooth wild rose)

Zones 2 to 7   6' to 8' high x 4' to 6' wide   Sun

Native to moist and rocky places in the northeastern portion of North America, this plant came into culture during 1773 and is one of the largest-flowered of all the species. It serves admirably as a groundcover, barrier, or mass and has a suckering nature. The slender brown stems are erect and twiggy with only a few prickles. Its early June flowering presents single rose-pink blossoms up to 2½ inches across, usually in clusters of about eight and heavily produced. The fruit is smooth, round or oval, scarlet, and ½ inch wide. Foliage varies from five to seven oval, sharply toothed leaflets between ½ inch and 1¼ inches long in dull green with somewhat hairy undersides. There is no autumn leaf color.

Rosa californica (California rose)

Zones 5 to 8   6′ to 8′ high x 4′ to 6′ wide   Sun

Vigorous with stout, flattened, recurved, ¼-inch prickles (thorns) on its many stems, this native from Oregon to lower California enjoys moist locations and flowers attractively in June with deep, carmine-pink, 1½-inch-wide blossoms in large clusters of ten to fifteen. The red, globose fruit has a distinct neck. Foliage leaflets are broadly oval, ½ to 1 inch long, and dull green above but hairy beneath. The cultivar 'Plena' is the preferred type with its semidouble, freely produced, well-scented, showy, dark pink flowers which fade to rose and purple.

Rosa carolina (Carolina rose, low rose)

Zones 4 to 8   1½′ to 2½′ high x 4′ to 6′ wide   Sun

Dense, compact, and low-spreading, the shrub is native to dry, open woods from Nova Scotia to Minnesota and Nebraska and south to Texas and Florida. Tolerant of much aridity, it serves attractively as a groundcover or steep embankment stabilizer. The late June blooms are solitary, fragrant, 2 inches wide, and rose-pink in color. The fruit is red, roundish, and ½ inch wide. Its five egg-shaped, sharply toothed leaflets are dull green and between ¾ inch and 1¼ inches long. Stems are armed with needlelike prickles and are very bristly when new.

Rosa foetida (Austrian brier)

Zones 4 to 9   6′ to 10′ high x 8′ to 12′ wide   Sun

Popular since the sixteenth century and used in hybridization for many of today's cultivars, this native of western Asia has been naturalized in central and southern Europe. It has slender, erect brown stems with straight prickles and a dense, twiggy, suckering habit. The solitary (occasionally several) flowers that appear by early June are deep yellow, single, and 2 to 3 inches wide; they possess an oddly pungent smell which some find disagreeable. Its fruit is round and dull red but of little interest. The leaves are bright green and carry five to nine broadly oval leaflets that are doubly toothed; these are ½ inch to 1½ inches in length with deep green tops and gray-hairy undersides. Aside from the fetid odor of the blooms, the greatest difficulty with this rose and its cultivars is its assured propensity for contracting black spot disease on the foliage: it will in turn infect any other rose nearby. The cultivars are preferred to the parent.

CULTIVAR: 'Bicolor' grows tall and erect. It has had popular appeal since its introduction in 1590 for the brilliantly copper-red single flowers showing deep gold exteriors. It also develops showy red hips.

CULTIVAR: 'Persiana' is also upright and tall but has double, golden yellow, smaller flowering than the parent. Known since 1838, it never has been seen growing in the wild. Similar to it is a shorter type, x *harisonii*, which is a cross between *foetida* and *spinosissima* with paler yellow and less-double blooms; its fruit is black.

Rosa hugonis (Father Hugo rose)

Zones 5 to 10   6′ to 8′ high x 6′ to 8′ wide   Sun

Beautiful in both leaf and flower, here is the most popular and best-performing single yellow species rose known. Iron-hardy, it serves attractively as a screen, accent, or informal hedge. Native to central China, it was discovered there in 1899 by Father Hugo Scanlon, a missionary with botanic interests. The solitary, fragrant, 2-inch-wide, soft yellow blossoms appear in late May all along the gracefully arching stems of this rapidly growing, free-flowering, rounded shrub. Its dark reddish stems carry straight prickles mixed with softer bristles. The rounded ½-inch-wide hips vary from deep scarlet to blackish red and are generally not numerous. Foliage is decidedly fernlike and vivid green (reddish orange in autumn) with five to thirteen oval, finely toothed leaflets only between ⅓ and ¾ inch long.

Rosa hugonis

Rosa rubrifolia (glauca, ferruginea) (redleaf rose)

Zones 2 to 8   5′ to 6′ high x 5′ to 6′ wide   Sun

Trouble-free, very hardy, and valuable for its distinctive foliage, the plant is native to the mountains of central and southern Europe; it came into cultivation about 1814. It is remarkably adaptable to the windswept prairie regions in the United States and lower Canada. This shrub should not be confused, however, with the totally different *rubifolia*, one of the earlier species names for the present-day *setigera*. *Rubrifolia* displays slender, purple-toned, almost thornless stems and carries early June, inconspicuous, small (1 inch to 1½ inches wide) flowers of clear, deep pink in clusters of only two or three blossoms; it sporadically reblooms through the summer. The ovoid, bright red, ⅜-inch-wide fruit fades to deep, dull red by autumn. Its showiest characteristic is the bluish green foliage tinged in purplish red, a color value not often seen in roses. These leaves are composed of seven to nine oval, toothed leaflets between 1 inch and 1½ inches in length. There is no appreciable change in autumn.

Rosa rubrifolia flowers

Rosa rubrifolia fruit

Rosa rugosa flowers

Rosa rugosa fruit

Rosa rugosa cv. 'Blanc Double de Coubert'

Rosa rugosa (rugosa rose, sea tomato, beach rose)

Zones 2 to 10   **6′ to 8′ high x 8′ to 10′ wide**   **Sun**

Natively found in Japan, Korea, and China (where it has been in cultivation for 800 years), this ruggedly hardy and popular rose was introduced by Dr. Siebold in 1845. The parent of a vast progeny of hybrids, it probably is the easiest rose to grow well, and it is now distributed over a wide area of the world. Adaptable to difficult, rocky, or sandy soil, it thrives at shore locations and can grow in pure sand at just about dune level. Its erect, dense form is vigorous and suckering with stout stems heavily covered by stiff prickles (thorns), making this shrub well suited for use as a barrier, a trimmed or informal hedge, and a groundcover mass. The early June blossoms are fuchsia-pink to white, single, attractively scented, 2 to 3½ inches wide, and either solitary or clustered in small groups. They continue flowering intermittently and noticeably all summer, but Japanese beetles have a decided liking for the blooms. Its brick-red, edible, up to 1-inch-wide, tomato-shaped fruit was once used as a source of vitamin C during the long journeys of nineteenth-century clipper ships; the fruit was packed in moist sand and then barreled for later consumption. Because the plant is a repeat bloomer, ripening fruit and some flowers are evident by late summer. Many cultivars of interest are now available.

CULTIVAR: 'Alba' has a more upright and very vigorous habit with pure white blossoms.

CULTIVAR: 'Blanc Double de Coubert' carries semidouble, scented, white blossoms; it has been known since 1892.

CULTIVAR: 'Frau Dagmar Hastrop' came into culture during 1914 and is compact to a 5-foot height with a slow-growing manner and noticeably lush foliage. The flowers are pleasantly scented, repeat-blooming, and pale rose-pink.

CULTIVAR: 'Plena' ('Roseraie de l'Hay') grows robustly to 5 feet in width and displays double crimson-purple blossoms.

CULTIVAR: 'Rubra' produces large, single, wine-pink flowers and conspicuous fruiting.

CULTIVAR: 'Sir Thomas Lipton' is double, white, very fragrant, and a repeat bloomer.

A popular cultivar of *rugosa* and *wichuriana* is 'Max Graf', which has growth characteristics wholly unlike any of the above cultivars since it is a sprawling groundcover form used for covering large embankments quickly. This prostrate shrub can expand 8 feet in a single season and needs very careful placement when not located in a large space. The small rose-pink flowers bloom over a long period and are considered sterile; thus there is no fruiting. The foliage is attractively glossy.

Rosa spinosissima altaica

Rosa spinosissima (pimpinellifolia) (Scotch rose, Scots rose, burnet)

Zones 4 to 10   **2′ to 3′ high x 3′ to 4′ wide**   **Sun**

The parent of many hybrids, this durable and hardy plant is the only rose native to Ireland. Found wild in many parts of the British Isles, Europe, and northern Asia, it has been cultivated since 1600 and is often employed as a sturdy groundcover since it easily endures strong wind, poor or very sandy soil, and salt spray without a qualm. Dense, mounded, vigorous, and suckering, the shrub has slender, somewhat arching stems. It shows a heavy production of downturned prickles. (Compare it with the taller but similarly foliaged *hugonis*, which has straight thorns.) Its early June flowering becomes white or pale pink, 1½ to 2 inches wide, single, and fragrant but not long enduring; these blooms appear all along the stems. The fruit is round, ⅜ inch across, black to deep brown, and not very ornamental. Its fernlike smooth foliage is composed of five to eleven (but normally seven to nine) finely toothed, oval, deep green leaflets between ⅛ and ¼ inch long; they offer little autumnal coloring. A number of interesting variations are known.

CULTIVAR: 'Lutea' grows 3 feet high with bright foliage and develops single buttercup yellow flowers 2 inches wide.

CULTIVAR: 'Lutea Plena' carries double flowers of mimosa yellow.

VARIETY: *altaica* was discovered in Siberia during 1820 and shows a more robust and suckering habit than the parent with gracefully arching stems to a height of 8 feet in mild areas. Less thorny on the average, it has greater hardiness as well. The 2- to 2½-inch flowers are creamy white and attractively scented, appearing all along the stems.

VARIETY: *hispida* came from Russia and is upright to 6 feet with many soft-to-touch bristles (plus some prickles) and pale yellow blossoms about 2 inches wide.

Rosa virginiana (Virginia rose)

Zones 4 to 10   4′ to 6′ high x 6′ to 8′ wide   Sun

Rewardingly attractive year-round, this rose is considered by many to be the best native on this continent. It is reputed to be the first species brought back to England for cultivation in 1800. Natively found from Newfoundland to Virginia, it is also wild down to Alabama and west to Missouri. Easy to grow well in any porous soil, this shrub is remarkably free of problems from either insects or diseases. Sturdily adaptable to shore conditions, it also can be formed into a low hedge with pruning or installed as a suckering, reliable groundcover. It accepts ground-level pruning every few years for quick and vigorous regrowth. Dense, erect, graceful, and rounded in outline, the shrub has slender reddish stems with a minimum number of prickles. Its main bloom occurs by mid-June, but it also blooms sporadically throughout the summer with single, 2-inch-wide, lively magenta to pink flowers either in clusters of three or solitary. The hips are generously set and are globose, shiny red, ½ inch wide, and usually long-lasting into winter. Foliage is dark green and glossy with oval and toothed leaflets numbering seven to nine between ¾ inch and 2¼ inches in length. The autumn coloring is purple or scarlet or even orange—perhaps all mixed at once—providing a showy finale to the season.

Rosa wichuriana (luciae wichuriana) (memorial rose)

Zones 6 to 10   1′ to 1½′ high x 12′ to 15′ wide   Sun

Here is the only *Rosa* species that is truly recumbent and sprawling (although the *rugosa* hybrid 'Max Graf' also can be called rampantly spreading), and it is one of the parents of many recent rambler cultivars. Although now separated by botanists, it is related closely to *luciae*, which is an upright species that blooms at the same time and produces similar flowering. Dense, robust, and ever expanding by its elongated stems with stiff, curved thorns (which trap debris easily and release it slowly), the shrub trails over the ground and roots wherever the stems touch open earth. It has an obvious use as a rapid, all-encompassing groundcover for embankments and rocky slopes in full sun. Native to Japan, Korea, and Taiwan plus eastern China, it has been in cultivation since 1891 and adapts to a wide range of soil types. The pure white, single, noticeably scented, up to 2-inch-wide flowers appear by early July in erect, conical clusters of six to ten blossoms. The dark red, globose, ⅛-inch-wide fruiting is not conspicuous. Foliage is glossy, deep green, broadly oval, and coarsely toothed; it is formulated with seven to nine leaflets about an inch long. It develops no autumn color change. In some mild-climate areas this plant may remain semievergreen.

SALIX (willow, osier)   *Salicaceae* (willow) family

Between 300 and 500 species may belong here (authorities cite widely discrepant numbers), and the only definite fact seems to be that they all are soft-wooded and adaptable to very moist or wet soils and grow vigorously. The genus name is an ancient one for these plants. They appear on all continents except Australia and are native to both temperate and colder areas, although none favors thin, sandy soil. The flowers appear by late winter to early spring with the sexes on different plants. Males are usually showier (and are therefore more widely cultivated), while the females are nondescript in bloom; both are wind-pollinated. The female fruiting is a small capsule with hairy seeds. Male blossoms are borne in dense, silky-hairy, egg-shaped to cylindrical catkins and develop either before or just after the leaves emerge in a show of flowering interest. The foliage is entire, mainly lancelike, and alternately placed. These deciduous shrubs (only a few are evergreen) adjust to a wide variety of soils easily. While they endure a number of insect problems on the foliage, they are more plagued by stem borers.

   Salix is the source of a well-known and remarkable remedy for the common headache. Early in the nineteenth century a French chemist sought to isolate the pain-relieving agent thought to be in willows and other plants. He succeeded with a product he called "salacin," which is derived from the genus name, *Salix*. In 1899 a German chemist isolated from the bark of willows the related acid called "acetylsalicylic," and because this was an unwieldy term, he abbreviated it to "aspirin."

Salix caprea   (goat willow, French pussy willow, florist's willow, sallow)

Zones 5 to 9   15′ to 25′ high x 10′ to 20′ wide   Sun

Here is a difficult shrub to endorse since it is unkempt, short-lived, prone to defoliation where Japanese beetles abound, and dull-looking after flowering. It has popular appeal, though, as a result of its spring catkins and is extremely simple to cultivate, although it appears to be laggard in adjusting to the Gulf coast and most of Florida. The cut branches are highly desirable in late winter either as a florist's item or as pruned elements from the garden. If given sufficient room, this robust and sizable shrub can become useful as a screen or hedge, but it does not deserve space in a border except for the diehard enthusiast. Native to Europe and northern Asia, it has been in cultivation for centuries. While adapting easily to many soil conditions, it prefers a constantly moist location with an abundance of organic matter and full sun. Its typical spring bloom comes early in March (sooner in milder locales) as male catkins maturing from red-capped buds on the previous year's stems; they expand to 1½ inches in length, which is large for this genus, in a silvery-pink color studded with golden stamen tips. The female fruit on separated plants is an undistinguished tiny capsule. Foliage is dark green, broadly oval to oblong, 2½ to 4 inches long, slightly toothed, and gray-hairy beneath; it provides no autumn coloring. To keep plants healthy and productive, cut them to ground level every few years; they regrow eagerly. Several cultivars are known.

CULTIVAR: 'Pendula' *(var. pendula)* carries stiff, crooked, drooping branches in a low silhouette; it is useful as a very unusual groundcover. Often it is grafted by nurseries to a taller sort to produce a weeping tree form. Neither flowers in an interesting fashion.

CULTIVAR: 'Variegata' *(var. variegata)* develops leaves mottled in white, but it is not as hardy as the parent.

Salix purpurea   (purple osier, basket willow)

Zones 5 to 9   7' to 9' high x 7' to 9' wide   Sun

Serviceable as a modest-sized hedge, the shrub adjusts to frequent shearing without difficulty, but it also can be used in masses or as an informal screen. Slender, flexible, glossy, and graceful stems are purple when new and later become olive-gray; they often are cut for use in basketry. Its silhouette is dense, twiggy, and irregularly rounded to the extent that the uneven appearance becomes distracting after a few years; prune to ground level then for quick rejuvenation as a regular outline. Its small, narrow, curved, male catkins open in March (often sooner in mild climates) and show red stamens. Leaves are slenderly oblong, from 1 to 4 inches long, dull blue-green, and set oppositely, an unusual deviation from other species. A few variations are known.

CULTIVAR: 'Gracilis' ('Nana') is dwarfed and compact to 3 feet with slender stems and narrower foliage but has significant flowering. It can be useful as a low hedge in constantly damp locations.

CULTIVAR: 'Pendula' *(var. pendula)* carries long, thin, drooping branches.

VARIETY: *lambertiana* produces oblong foliage with teeth all along the margins.

SPIRAEA (spirea, bridalwreath)   *Rosaceae* (rose) family

One hundred species of vigorous deciduous shrubs with slim stems belong here, and many are highly ornamental in flower. They are native to the northern hemisphere and are very much at home in cool mountainous regions with open air circulation and full sun; when placed in hot, dry locations, they prefer some shading. All are simple to transplant as a result of their generous fibrous rooting, and they grow easily in any fertile soil, even in urban pollution. Few insects or diseases are bothersome. Suitable for either clipped or informal hedges, they are less satisfactory as specimens because only the short blooming season produces any showy effect; however, since both spring- and summer-flowering types are commonly available, the flowering displays can be extended over several weeks. Blossoms are individually tiny in white, pink, or red and are noticeably grouped either all along the graceful stems of the previous year (in the spring-flowered sorts) or terminally on new growth (in the summer-blooming types). None offers decorative fruiting—only minute, dry capsules. The majority of these shrubs are dioecious, but this has no important effect on the showiness of the blossoming, and growers make no distinction between male and female plants for propagation. The foliage is simple, alternate, and only occasionally of autumnal interest. Its name comes from the Greek *speira* ("coil" or "wreath") and indicates a long-established association with wreath making. Note that the correct common name spelling omits one of the letters "a" found in the genus name.

Spiraea albiflora (japonica alba) (Japanese white spirea)

Zones 5 to 10   1½' to 2' high x 2' to 2½' wide   Sun

Although native to Japan, this low shrub has never been found in a wild state; yet it has been cultivated for its early summer bloom since about 1868. The plant combines well with both *x bumalda* and *japonica* forms because of its profusely set, white, small flowering in heavy, flat clusterings to 2 inches wide on current growth during late June. It has a dense, compact, and neat-looking habit with a rounded outline and somewhat angled stems. The foliage becomes lancelike, smooth, double-toothed, and about 2 inches long in rich green with gray-toned undersides, but it develops no autumn coloring. Adaptable to many soils, it does not perform well on highly alkaline sites.

Spiraea x arguta (garland spirea, foam of May, bridalwreath)

Zones 5 to 10   3' to 6' high x 3' to 6' wide   Sun

Noteworthy for its free-flowering nature during early May, this plant blooms later than the also popular *thunbergii* and thus avoids damage from sudden spring frost. A cross between *x multiflora* and *thunbergii*, it is a robust, dense, erect, and rounded shrub introduced in 1884; it grows suitably in all types of soils except alkaline ones. The blossoming is notably generous from tiny, pure white flowers appearing in flat 2-inch clusters all along the arching stems of the previous season as the leaves emerge. This foliage is mid-green, narrowly oval but acutely pointed, often double-toothed, about 1½ inches long, and both showy and enduring in the autumn. It is an appealing border plant.

Spiraea x billiardii (Billiard spirea)

Zones 5 to 10   4' to 6' high x 4' to 6' wide   Sun

A cross between *douglasii* and *salicifolia* made before 1854, here is an easy-to-grow hybrid with erect stems which suckers widely to use as a groundcover, especially for embankment stabilization. Accepting any but highly alkaline conditions, it produces late June blossoming in narrow, fluffy spikes between 4 and 8 inches high of deep, purplish pink. The pointed oval foliage has sharp teeth, ranges between 2 and 3 inches in length, and is gray-haired beneath; it appears on hairy stems. A few cultivars are available.

CULTIVAR: 'Alba' has white flowers.

CULTIVAR: 'Triumphans' *(manziesii cv.* 'Triumphans') forms densely pyramidal 8-inch-tall spikes about 4 inches wide of rose-colored blossoms with prolonged reblooming throughout the summer. Its foliage varies from pale to mid-green.

Spiraea x bumalda (Bumalda spirea)

Zones 5 to 10   1½' to 2' high x 1½' to 2' wide   Sun

Popular for its many attractive cultivars, this is an erect, low shrub with maroon, noticeably striped stems; it adapts easily to grow in a variety of soils. A cross between *albiflora* and *japonica* made before 1900, the plant (including its cultivars) occasionally self-seeds into other areas. White to deep pink flowers appear in late June or early July as flat terminal clusters between 2 and 3 inches across on current growth. The oval and lancelike, double-toothed, hairless leaves vary from 2 to 3 inches in length and are gray-green. Many cultivars extend its appeal.

CULTIVAR: 'Anthony Waterer' is the best known and currently the most widely grown type with its mounded form to 2 feet high with a 4-foot width. It carries bright crimson blossoming in large clusters about 6 inches wide and continues flowering intermittently all summer. The leaves are pink-toned when new and often develop cream-and-pink variegations later.

CULTIVAR: 'Atrorosea' shows a rounded form with 3-inch leaves and dark pink flowering.

CULTIVAR: 'Crispa' produces deeply cut foliage which emerges red, but the plant is less vigorous than many other cultivars and reaches only a 2-foot height.

CULTIVAR: 'Froebelii' (var. froebelii) has a vigorous habit to a 3- or 4-foot height with showy crimson flower clusters which appear later than those of cv. 'Anthony Waterer'. It reblooms generously all summer and masks its spent flowering attractively with the new blossoms in a neat fashion. This cultivar is likely to surpass cv. 'Anthony Waterer' in popular appeal soon.

CULTIVAR: 'Gold Flame' offers foliage novelty in spring since the new leaves are conspicuously mottled in red, copper, yellow, and orange on a rounded, neat plant about 3 feet tall. By midsummer these fade to mid-green, but some plants recolor during early autumn. The flowers are deep pink. It occasionally self-seeds true to type.

CULTIVAR: 'Nyeswood' forms a dense, compact, mounded outline to an 18-inch height with blue-green foliage and attractively pink flowering.

CULTIVAR: 'Wallufii' has a compact form with red new foliage and pale pink blossoms.

Spiraea x bumalda cv. 'Anthony Waterer'

Spiraea x bumalda cv. 'Gold Flame'

Spiraea cantoniensis (reevesiana) (Reeves spirea)

Zones 7 to 10   4' to 5' high x 5' to 6' wide   Sun

Perhaps the most elegant-looking species, this shrub has become the best spirea for growing in the southern United States. Native to China but long cultivated in Japan, it came into cultivation during 1824. It presents a uniformly graceful and spreading outline with slender, arching branches similar to x vanhouttei (the most popular form in the north). Domed 2-inch-wide clusters of white flowers appear in late May all along the dark brown stems of the previous year together with lancelike, somewhat oval, deeply toothed leaves 1 to 2 inches long, colored deep green above and blue-green beneath. In the mildest areas the plant tends to be semievergreen, but elsewhere the foliage turns reddish in the autumn. Its cultivar 'Lanceata' ('Flore Pleno') carries double flowers and noticeably lancelike leaves.

Spiraea japonica (callosa) (Japanese spirea)

Zones 6 to 10   3' to 6' high x 3' to 6' wide   Sun to semishade

Very similar in all respects to x bumalda except for height and much greater tolerance of shade, this shrub develops stiffly erect, shiny stems with little branching and a mounded habit. Native to temperate eastern Asia, it has been in culture since 1870 and adapts to any soil condition with consistent soil

Spiraea japonica (Cont.)

Spiraea japonica cv. 'Alpina'

moisture. The mid-June pink blossoming becomes 4 to 5 inches wide as flat terminal clusters with leafy bases on the new growth. The narrowly oval to lancelike, sharply double-toothed leaves vary from 1 to 4 inches long and are colored rich green above and grayish beneath. It provides a wide selection of options.

CULTIVAR: 'Alpina' is a dwarfed, densely mounded, very twiggy form with a height of about a foot showing sluggish growth and rebloom of light pink flowers throughout the summer. It has some merit as a slowly expanding groundcover.

CULTIVAR: 'Atrosanguinea' offers an upright form to 4 feet with a more open silhouette than that of *x bumalda cv.* 'Anthony Waterer'. The new leaves are red, and its densely hairy flower clusters open as a very dark purplish red in a width up to 5 inches.

CULTIVAR: 'Macrophylla' carries oval leaves up to 6 inches long and 3 inches wide on upright branching with pink flowering; it has showy autumn foliage coloring.

CULTIVAR: 'Ruberrima' grows to a 3-foot height with a dense, rounded silhouette; it produces dark pink flowers.

VARIETY: *fortunei* is taller than the parent with foliage that is up to 4 inches long and smooth beneath.

VARIETY: *ovalifolium* has oval, hairless leaves that are blue-toned on the undersides and white flowering.

Spiraea nipponica cv. 'Snowmound'

Spiraea nipponica   (Tosa spirea, Nippon spirea)

Zones 5 to 10   5′ to 8′ high x 6′ to 10′ wide   Sun

Some consider this vigorous species more attractive in flower than the popular *x vanhouttei*, but *nipponica* is not as graceful. Since it blooms later than *x vanhouttei*, it offers an expanded flowering period of similar form when both are used in the same landscape layout. The branches are arching but stiffly held, and its dense, twiggy outline is useful for screens or hedges, especially since the plant adapts readily to many soil conditions. Where it thrives, it tends to self-seed occasionally. The early June blossoming is white in 1½-inch domed clusters with tiny leaf bracts beneath each ⅓-inch flower; they appear all along the stems of the previous season. Native to the mountains of Japan, it came into cultivation about 1882 and has wedgelike to oval, few-toothed, ½-inch to 1½-inch leaves that are dark green above and blue-green beneath; these remain long into the autumn but do not color appreciably. A few variations are known.

CULTIVAR: 'Snowmound' *(var. tosaensis)* is popularly called the "boxleaf spirea" for its smaller, more lancelike, blue-green foliage and uniformly neat outline. Growing 5 feet high and about 7 feet wide at maturity, it has a dense and multistemmed habit with smaller flower clusters crowded profusely along the cinnamon-brown stems; it also tends to self-seed under some circumstances.

VARIETY: *rotundifolia* behaves robustly with larger, broader leaves.

Spiraea prunifolia (prunifolia cv. 'Plena')   (bridalwreath)

Zones 5 to 10   6′ to 8′ high x 6′ to 8′ wide   Sun

Very ornamental and popular, this species blooms with many of the early azaleas and contributes a wandlike, open form to the shrub border. It shows yet another example of botanic naming difficulties (see *Rhododendron yedoense*) since this double form was discovered growing in a Chinese garden during 1843, but its single-flowered type, native to Korea, China, and Taiwan, was not learned about until 1864. The very double, pure white, ½-inch-wide, buttonlike flowers are produced heavily in mid-May on the previous year's stems before foliage emerges fully. Slow-growing, it is erect with slender, arching, dark brown, finely hairy (when new) stems and develops a somewhat unkempt and loose form which becomes leggy at the base with age. The lustrous, finely toothed oval foliage carries soft hairs beneath and expands to about 1½ inches; it is unusual for becoming richly vivid in red, orange, and bronze by autumn. The variety (or forma) *simpliciflora* is the wild single-flowered form, but it is horticulturally inferior and rarely is cultivated today.

Spiraea thunbergii (Thunberg spirea, baby's breath spirea)

Zones 5 to 10   4′ to 5′ high x 6′ to 7′ wide   Sun

Here is the earliest flowering spirea, but since it blooms by mid-April (earlier farther south in its range), it can be damaged by spring frost. Although popular for its bloom, the plant is short-lived and tends to have much twig die-back each season. Fine-textured, very bushy, and broadly rounded but open in form, this slow-growing shrub carries wiry, arching, downy stems and delicate, pure white, starlike single flowers in small clusters of two to five on the previous season's growth; it presents a feathery appearance when in bloom. The foliage is narrowly lancelike in light, yellow-green or pale green, ½ inch to 1¼ inches long, and double-toothed; occasionally these leaves convert to orange or yellow tones by autumn. It has appeal for borders and hedges.

Spirea x vanhouttei (bridalwreath, Vanhoutte spirea)

Zones 5 to 10   6′ to 8′ high x 8′ to 10′ wide   Sun

Highly regarded as a specimen, hedge, or screen, this showy-flowered and very hardy species has been well liked since its development in France during 1862 as a cross between *cantoniensis* and *trilobata*. Of easy culture, it flowers profusely in late May and usually offers some reddish or orange-toned autumnal color. Fast-growing and durable, the shrub develops a fountainlike outline from long, deep brown, gracefully arching stems which often reach to the ground as the plant matures. Its pure white ¼-inch flowers appear in flat clusters between 1 and 2 inches wide along the stems of the previous year. The lozenge-shaped to oval, coarsely toothed foliage has three to five shallow lobes and expands to about 1½ inches long with deep green tops and gray-toned undersides. This graceful shrub looks best when it is not sheared.

Spiraea x vanhouttei

STEWARTIA (MALACHODENDRON) (Stewartia)
Theaceae (tea) family

Six to seven species of deciduous shrubs or small trees make up this genus native to temperate eastern Asia as well as eastern North America. It is named (but not precisely) for John Stuart, earl of Bute, an eighteenth-century English patron of botany. A relative of *Camellia*, this genus contains plants useful as showy-flowered summertime additions to the landscape for border specimens or naturalized at the edges of deciduous woodlots in sun to semishade. If placed in full sun, however, each requires some additional shading over the roots, perhaps supplied by a low groundcover or a cooperative shrub. Provide a lime-free soil with consistent moisture and a high humus content out of strong winds. Resentful of transplanting, they move best when small and in the spring; keep them regularly watered until established. The plant remains long in bloom from July to late August, but

Spiraea x vanhouttei

the individual blossoms are short-lived. These flowers are white, solitary at the leaf axils, and cup-shaped or flattened with generally five equally large petals; they are conspicuous from masses of colorful stamens. Plants are of separated sexes, and females later produce fair-sized woody, persistent capsules of some ornamental value. The alternate, simple, toothed, deep green, attractive leaves often color richly by autumn. Pests and diseases are not a frequent problem. The stems are smooth and flaky, often displaying colorfully mottled bark. Where they grow successfully, these plants are choice additions to the landscape scene.

Stewartia ovata (pentagyna) (Mountain camellia, mountain stewartia)

Zones 6 to 9   10′ to 15′ high x 8′ to 12′ wide   Sun to light

Native to the streamside, richly wooded mountain areas of Kentucky and Virginia and south to Georgia, this popular shrub is often hardy into some of the milder parts of New England. It has been cultivated since 1800 for its early July to late August flowering and handsome flaking bark. The solitary 3-inch-wide blossoms appear in the leaf axils of the hairless stems with five or six white, cupped petals and white, orange-toned masses of stamens. Females produce egg-shaped (hence the species name), pointed, flared, and enduring capsule fruit. The oval foliage is between 2 and 5 inches long with sharply pointed tips in dark green with gray-toned undersides; these color orange to scarlet by autumn. Its variety *grandiflora* carries flowers 4 inches wide with purple-orange stamens. Both enjoy moist, acid, humusy sites.

Stewartia pseudocamellia bark

Stewartia pseudocamellia fruit

Stewartia pseudocamellia (Japanese stewartia)

Zones 6 to 9   20′ to 30′ high x 10′ to 15′ wide   Sun

Potentially able to reach a tree size of 50 feet where it grows ideally, the plant is usually much lower-growing and more openly bushy in habit. The twigs are smooth, while the bark is attractively red-toned, flaking, and ornamental of itself, making this species superior as a border accent or specimen. Native to Japan and cultivated since 1878, it accepts sun if provided with some shading during the hot afternoons of summer. The somewhat cup-shaped solitary flowers are 2 to 2 ½ inches across and show furry exteriors to the white petals; these carry small, bright yellow stamens and appear during July and August. The foliage is deep green, tip-pointed, oval, smooth beneath, and up to 3 inches long; it usually colors deep purple (occasionally yellowish) by autumn. As with the others, it prefers a moist, acid, humus-laden soil.

SYMPHORICARPOS (SYMPHORIA) (snowberry, waxberry)   *Caprifoliaceae* (honeysuckle) family

Either sixteen or eighteen species of deciduous shrubs make up this genus of ornamentally fruited or attractively foliaged plants much enjoyed as hedges, masses, and embankment stabilizers. None is particular about soil type, while all transplant and grow easily, have pleasant habits, accept placement near the competitive roots of other plant materials, and thrive in either sun or semishade. Few insects or diseases ever become a serious problem. The majority are native to North America; one is from China. Its name is from the Greek *symphorein* ("to cluster together") and *karpos* ("fruit"), referring to the closely grouped fruit crops. The flowers are small, white or pink, clustered or in spikes, and rarely significant for notice. Any fruit is a white or colored berry produced heavily in terminal locations; it is often both showy and persistent but has no attraction for birds. The foliage is opposite, simple, and entire.

Symphoricarpos albus (racemosus)
(snowberry, waxberry)

Zones 3 to 9   **2′ to 3′ high x 3′ to 6′ wide**   **Sun to light shade**

Symphoricarpos albus fruit

Natively found on dry, rocky soil from Quebec to Minnesota and south to Pennsylvania and Virginia, this bushy shrub has been cultivated since about 1879. It develops upright stems without a suckering habit. The nondescript flowering occurs in mid-June as paired, pinkish, bell-shaped, ¼-inch-long blossoms on short terminal spikes. Its round, snow-white to creamy-white fruit is ¼ to ½ inch wide in large clusterings persisting into winter; unfortunately, anthracnose disease in early autumn usually turns them brown. The foliage is deep green, hairy beneath, occasionally lobed on the vigorous shoots, between 1 and 2 inches long, oval, and blunt-tipped; it has no autumn coloring. The plant is suited for all soils, including dry ones, and often is planted as a hedge, mass, or border specimen. Some nurseries confuse it with the species *rivularis*, which is similarly fruited but taller-growing.

Symphoricarpos x chenaultii   (Chenault coralberry)

Zones 5 to 9   **2′ to 3′ high x 8′ to 10′ wide**   **Sun to light shade**

A cross between the Mexican species *microphyllus* and *orbiculatus* developed about 1910, this plant becomes erect and dense with a wide-spreading and suckering habit. It adapts admirably to difficult sites but prefers a fertile well-drained soil for the finest performance. Its minute flowering emerges in mid-July as small pink spikes, followed by terminal clusters of attractive, purplish red, ¼-inch, round fruit whitened on the sides away from the sun. Foliage has a bluish green cast; it is hairy beneath, oval, up to ¾ inch long, and without autumn coloring. The cultivar 'Hancock' is robust and hardier than the parent and has long, prostrate, rooting stems in a low, spreading form only 2 feet high. It performs admirably as a mass on embankments, as a groundcover beneath many deciduous trees, and as a feature set to drape gracefully over high walls. The foliage is bright green, while its fruit is pink-white.

Symphoricarpos x doorenbosii   cultivars

Zones 5 to 9   **3′ to 5′ high x 4′ to 5′ wide**   **Sun to light shade**

Introduced during the 1960s by Dr. Doorenbos of Holland, the parent is a cross between *x chenaultii* and *rivularis* with strongly upright characteristics and a blooming time of mid-July. Of itself the parent is not cultivated, and the selections made by Dr. Doorenbos are the ones which are available.

CULTIVAR: 'Magic Berry' is compact with a spreading habit and a height of only 3 feet; it produces large quantities of rose-pink berries for a conspicuous autumnal display.

CULTIVAR: 'Mother of Pearl' develops either pale pink or white tinged-rose fruiting in generous clusters.

CULTIVAR: 'White Hedge' has a decidedly erect and compact growth habit unexcelled for creating a sturdy hedge; it produces upright clusterings of small white fruit.

Symphoricarpos orbiculatus fruit

Symphoricarpos orbiculatus (vulgaris) (Indian currant, coralberry, snapberry)

Zones 3 to 9   3' to 6' high x 4' to 8' wide   Sun to shade

Remarkably tolerant of shade and able to grow in any soil condition, this shrub is a rampant, dense, irregularly bushy, fine-twigged plant serviceable for naturalizing and for erosion control on slopes. It spreads freely by suckering and has slender, downy, arching stems plus heavy masses of leaves. Cultivated since 1730, it is native from New York to Colorado and south to New Mexico, Texas, and Florida. During the eighteenth century its dried and powdered roots were believed to hold a guaranteed cure for malaria; today it is regarded simply as an interesting ornamental. The mid-July, ⅛-inch, bell-shaped flowers are an insignificant yellowish white in dense and pendant clusters, followed by rounded to oval, ¼-inch-long, coral-red to purplish red fruit created as generous, angular clusters all along the stem tips; they persist through the winter. Its blunt-tipped, egg-shaped, dull green foliage varies from ½ inch to 2 inches in length and is often hairy beneath; there is no autumn color. The cultivar 'Leucocarpus' has white fruit, while *cv.* 'Variegatus' carries smaller leaves that are pleasantly variegated in yellow when grown in full sun. These may revert to all green if given too much shade.

Symphoricarpos rivularis (albus laevigatus, ovatus) (snowberry)

Zones 2 to 9   3' to 10' high x 3' to 10' wide   Sun to semishade

This plant has larger-sized leaves and fruit than its look-alike *albus*, and the two plants often are confused in nurseries. Native from southeastern Alaska to Montana and California, this shrub has been cultivated since 1817. It makes dense thickets of erect, smooth stems showing strong development. Generous flowering appears by mid-June in short terminal spikes of rose-pink to white blossoms that are ¼ inch long. These soon are followed by great masses of white, rounded, ½- to ¾-inch-wide glistening fruit much resembling large marbles. Adaptable for poor soils and much shade, the plant carries oval dark green leaves showing hairy undersides with lengths between ¾ inch and 2½ inches; no color is produced in autumn. Its cultivar 'Nana' is dwarfed in form.

SYRINGA (lilac)   *Oleaceae* (olive) family

Thirty species of deciduous shrubs or small trees native to eastern Asia, the Himalayas, and southeastern Europe belong here. All prefer full sun with an open, airy location. Grown since time immemorial for their attractively and heavily fragrant flowers, they are very hardy in the north and usually behave with great vigor. Their preference is for a fertile, consistently moist, well-drained soil between neutral and alkaline; however, they adapt well to less amenable conditions and benefit from an annual top-dressing of compost or rotted manure in autumn or late winter. Easily grown and transplanted, most are not successful where there is little or no frost in the dormant period. All recover well from drastic pruning when overgrown or when damaged by storms. Where possible, remedial pruning should take place right after flowering has occurred; otherwise, flower buds will be lost. The greatest difficulties are with powdery mildew on the foliage and borers and scale insects throughout the stems. If just the species adaptable to a region are used, colorful blooms can be maintained for about 6 weeks in many growing areas.

Its name comes from the Greek *syrinx* ("pipe"), which is possibly a reference to the hollow new shoots. However, this genus name is often misapplied as the *common* name for the mock orange *(Philadelphus)*, perhaps in the beginning because of the similarity of their sweet scents. Now, however, we know better about this detail. The first lilac introduced to Europe was the very fragrant *vulgaris* species, which arrived from Turkey (not its true homeland) in the sixteenth century. *Syringa* first appeared in print during 1565 as an entry in Matthiolus's *Commentarii*, but it took until 1828 to learn that the native habitat of the plant was actually the Balkan peninsula, particularly Yugoslavia and Bulgaria. No member of this genus is indigenous to North America, and the plant probably arrived with some of the first European settlers since it transports well even bare-rooted. Their appeal and ability to thrive here rapidly brought them to the interest of other immigrants, and as early as the beginning of the nineteenth century lilacs were present in almost every Canadian garden. Without doubt, they are still cherished as a garden ornament wherever they can grow contentedly.

The small tubular flowers have four petals and appear in showy terminal or axillary panicles of white, lilac, pink, red, or purple, often with darker-toned budding. All species produce a scent, but not all have an enticing fragrance. The fruit is a leathery capsule of no decorative importance and constitutes a distinguishing mark of difference between lilac and its important near relation privet *(Ligustrum)*, with its fleshy, rounded fruiting.

Many lilac cultivars today are grafted to the roots of privet species for speed and convenience in marketing the plants; this below-ground association should clarify the unexpected production of privet stems and foliage interwoven with the lilac growth of plants damaged at this graft union by disease, insects, or mechanical injury. Promptly remove such extraneous growth by pruning below ground level. Lilac foliage is opposite, mainly simple in outline, entire or cut, and without any autumnal coloring.

Syringa x chinensis (rothomagensis) (Chinese lilac, Rouen lilac)

Zones 3 to 7   8′ to 15′ high x 5′ to 7′ wide   Sun

Useful as a screen or border specimen, this cross between *laciniata* and *vulgaris* is acknowledged as having occurred in the botanic garden at Rouen, France, in 1777. Upright, dense, and bushy, the shrub has a graceful outline with slender, arching stems and blooms in late May with profuse, very fragrant flowers of rich lilac or purple. The ½-inch florets are set on broad, terminal, pyramidal, drooping panicles about 6 inches long and 4 inches wide. Its leaves are oval to lancelike with a tapering point, smooth on both sides, and up to 3 inches long. Several interesting cultivars are known.

CULTIVAR: 'Alba' has flowers that are almost white.

CULTIVAR: 'Duplex' carries double flowering of purplish lilac.

CULTIVAR: 'Metensis' displays pale rose-lilac blossoms.

CULTIVAR: 'Nana' is a dwarfed plant.

CULTIVAR: 'Saugeana' ('Rubra') develops lilac-red flowering but often is mislabeled in catalogs as *cv.* 'Sanguinea'.

Syringa x hyacinthiflora (no common name)

Zones 4 to 7   10′ to 15′ high x 7′ to 10′ wide   Sun

Resembling *vulgaris* in leaf appearance and habit, here is a very attractive cross between *oblata* and *vulgaris* made at the Lemoine nursery of France about 1876. More recent hybrids have been created in California by W. B. Clarke using *oblata giraldii*. Blooming occurs by early May, a week or so before *vulgaris* flowers. The plant is not cultivated for itself today, and the following cultivars are the preferred choices.

CULTIVAR: 'Alice Eastwood' is double with reddish purple flowering.

CULTIVAR: 'Blue Hyacinth' carries single mauve to pale blue flowers.

CULTIVAR: 'Buffon' develops light pink, slightly fragrant single blossoms.

CULTIVAR: 'Clarke's Giant' shows single lilac-blue flowering of large florets in panicles up to a foot in length.

CULTIVAR: 'Esther Staley' produces abundant, single, attractively pink blossoming.

CULTIVAR: 'Lamartine' has bronzed new growth and sizable clusters of lilac-blue single flowers.

CULTIVAR: 'Plena' is the original Lemoine hybrid creation; it shows a double, delicate, violet bloom with bright purple budding.

CULTIVAR: 'Purple Heart' carries large panicles of single deep purple blooms.

Syringa laciniata (persica laciniata) (cutleaf lilac)

Zones 5 to 7   5′ to 6′ high x 4′ to 6′ wide   Sun

Cultivated since 1614 and misnamed originally, this species recently was proved to reproduce easily from seed, while its former parent *x persica* is known to be sterile. Such information forced a botanic renaming that now makes *x persica* only a hybrid of *laciniata*. The shrub is upright and graceful with late May flowering of pale lilac in fragrant loose clusters only 3 inches long, set generously all along the lengthy, arching stems. The 2½-inch-long cut foliage is pinnately and finely dissected to the midrib with three to nine lobes; however, entire leaves on some shoots are not rare. This species is native to northwestern China.

Syringa meyeri (velutina, palibiniana, patula) (Meyer's lilac, Korean lilac)

Zones 6 and 7   4′ to 5′ high x 5′ to 6′ wide   Sun

Syringa meyeri cv. 'Palabin'

There has been some recent confusion about where this unusual species belongs botanically. The situation may not yet be fully resolved, since it is similar in both size and habit to *microphylla* when small (but lacks its pleasing fragrance), so that nurseries often confuse the two. The shrub probably came, as a mildew-free distinct form, from a Chinese garden between 1908 and 1910 through the efforts of F. N. Meyer, yet it never has been seen growing wild. It now is considered a native of Korea, and it serves as an admirable border specimen, mass planting, or informal hedge. The shrub is dense, compact, and slow-growing with upright branching of gray-brown twigs of a slim nature. The flowering appears by late May in pale lilac or lilac-pink, heavily produced laterally—rarely in terminal locations—as short, 3- to 4-inch, upright clusters even on very young plants. They often rebloom by early September, which accounts for the lack of terminal flowering in the spring. Its fragrance is not sweet but more like that of the pungent privet *(Ligustrum)* species. Foliage varies from oval to rounded to rhomboidal with wavy margins in deep green with unusual parallel veining different from that of other species. Often these leaves turn bronze-toned in the autumn (another novelty), and they generally persist long into the season. The most popular form is the cultivar 'Palibin' (named for the Russian botanist) with its low, spreading silhouette to 5 feet and sluggish growth. It also adapts easily to light shade without any special loss of flowering appeal.

Recently increased planting of this cultivar has brought scattered reports of even greater size limits and expanded growing areas beyond those listed here. More popular investigation of this lilac is deserved.

Syringa meyeri cv. 'Palabin'

Syringa microphylla (littleleaf lilac)

Zones 4 to 7   5′ to 6′ high x 9′ to 12′ wide   Sun

No other lilac grows as broad as this species, which produces a dense pyramidal habit with upright stems and slim, arching branches down to ground level. Native to northern and western China, it came into cultivation during 1910. It flowers by late May and often repeats, but sparsely, in mid-September. The blossoms are pale rosy-lilac with a desirable scent in small clusters up to 3 inches tall. The medium-green foliage is somewhat hairy beneath, oval, between ½ and 1½ inches long, tapered at the tips, and closely set along the stems. Its cultivar 'Superba' has deep pink flowering and also repeat-blooms in early autumn.

Syringa x persica (Persian lilac)

Zones 5 to 7   6′ to 7′ high x 6′ to 7′ wide   Sun

Established now as a cross between *afghanica* and *laciniata* (see the data under *laciniata*), here is a lilac with a dense, rounded, bushy habit carrying lilac-colored fragrant blossoms by late May in 2- to 3-inch panicles set generously on the slim branching. Because these are sterile flowers, no fruit develops. The leaves are narrowly lanceolate, dark green, smooth, and up to 2½ inches long. Its cultivar 'Alba' has white flowering in 8-inch clusters on even slenderer stems.

Syringa x persica

Syringa x persica

Syringa potaninii

Syringa potaninii (daphne lilac, Potanin lilac)

Zones 6 and 7   6′ to 12′ high x 4 to 6′ wide   Sun

Erectly graceful and attractively slim, this native of western China came into cultivation during 1905. The new growth is hairy and develops flowering in mid-May with white to rose-purple, fragrant, loosely held blossoms in erect, stubby panicles that grow up to 4 inches long. The leaves are oval, gray-toned on both surfaces, slender-pointed, and between 1½ and 3 inches long.

Syringa x prestoniae cultivar

Syringa x prestoniae (Preston lilac)

Zones 2 to 7   6′ to 9′ high x 8′ to 10′ wide   Sun

Vigorous, dense, upright with stout branching, and large-foliaged, this very hardy shrub produces heavy flowering by early to mid-June and is very showy in bloom. It acts dependably as a windbreak or hedge, but only occasionally is it serviceable as a specimen as a result of its coarse appearance. The plant was developed by Dr. Isabella Preston about 1925 in Ottawa, Canada, as a cross between *reflexa* and *villosa;* the initial group carries a predominantly red-purple coloring. Since then, her own and other breeders' hybrids have expanded the color range. The fragrance of any type, however, is not sweet and may be nondescript at times. The bloom is terminal on new growth (fairly often developed as threes from the shoot ends), 6 to 8 inches tall, and erect or drooping in pyramidal clusterings with slender, tubular florets of pale pink to pink-lilac. The leaves are oval to oblong, pointed, up to a full 7 inches long at times, and colored dull mid-green to deep green; they offer no autumn color of notice. The cultivars are much preferred to the parent.

CULTIVAR: 'Audrey' carries deep pink flowering in dense, wide clusters.

CULTIVAR: 'Coral' has coral-pink budding and pink clusters up to 7 inches long.

CULTIVAR: 'Isabella' develops oversized erect panicles of warmly pink flowers up to a foot square with bright green foliage.

CULTIVAR: 'James MacFarlane' is slender-growing and forms bright pink blossoming.

CULTIVAR: 'Royalty' has violet-purple conspicuous blooms.

Syringa vulgaris

Syringa vulgaris (common lilac)

Zones 4 to 7   15′ to 20′ high x 8′ to 10′ wide   Sun

Cultivated since 1563 and one of the earliest plants of Europe to reach the North American continent, this strongly erect species from the Balkan peninsula has popular appeal for its consistently gratifying flower scent. As with all the others, it is simple to cultivate in areas where seasonal changes are distinct and some frost can be expected. However, a few new cultivars have proved themselves able to cope with the warmer areas in some parts of zone 8 and should be tried more frequently there: 'Blue Boy', 'Chiffon', 'Lavender Lady', and 'Sylvan Beauty'. As a group these shrubs often are called "French" lilacs because so many of the choice cultivars appeared during the nineteenth or early twentieth century from the Lemoine nursery of France, that exceptional purveyor of so many shrub improvements. Today large collections of lilacs are available for review by mid-May at both the Arnold Arboretum of Boston and Highland Park in Rochester, New York.

While compelling in bloom, these plants offer little else for the balance of the year (except screening possibilities) because they develop no fruit of any distinction, have no autumn color, and are continually prone to severe attacks of powdery mildew in late summer. Perhaps they are best placed at some distance from the main living areas for those reasons, especially since the desirable fragrance is known to travel across great distances.

Responsive to drastic pruning when overgrown or damaged, this species often requires revitalization on a regular basis since it expands rapidly by suckering. Diseased, weakened, and nonflowering stems should be cut to 4 inches above ground level or to an important stem junction immediately after the bloom is completed. This program also provides additional and useful air circulation through the plant and may help reduce mildew problems; however, chemical spraying and collecting and destroying fallen leaves in autumn are more valid controls for disrupting the cycle of the mildew infection. All lilacs do well if provided with a neutral soil (add limestone if very acid conditions prevail) that is rich, moist, humusy, and in full sun; increased shading by trees or buildings that are close at hand is the chief reason so many older plants do not bloom as well as they once did.

The flowering appears from mid-May to early June in dense, erect, terminal, and conical panicles of single florets shaded in lavender with a heady and pleasant fragrance superior to that of all other species. Its gray-green to deep green leaves (perhaps bluish on some plants) are semiglossy and somewhat heart-shaped with pointed tips; they range from 2 to 5 inches in length. The variety *alba* is more upright and slender in its outline with a somewhat greater height potential; it carries pure white blossoms and is the oldest white-flowering lilac known. More stimulating are the many cultivars available today; these are often grafted plants (a few nurseries offer "own root" plants) on the roots of the related privet *(Ligustrum)* since these two genera are compatible with this mechanical system. Any damage to the graft junction, however, probably will result in stimulation of dormant budding on the privet with the resultant dominance of privet stems throughout the lilac in a short time. Such mixed-up plants can be pruned of the extraneous privet below ground level, but if this fails to stop the growth, the plants should perhaps be discarded entirely.

Named cultivars are very numerous today, but many are only subtly different from each other, requiring expert knowledge to separate satisfactorily. The listings provided here are for those most recommended for planting by the experts, and all are attractively fragrant.

Syringa vulgaris with powdery mildew

Syringa vulgaris cultivar

Syringa vulgaris cv. 'Madame Lemoine'

WHITE, SINGLE: 'Jan Van Tol', 'Maud Notcutt', 'Mont Blanc', and 'Vestale'

WHITE, DOUBLE: 'Edith Cavell', 'Ellen Willmott', 'Madame Lemoine', 'Monique Lemoine', and 'Saint Joan'

VIOLET, SINGLE: 'Cavour' and 'De Miribel'

VIOLET, DOUBLE: 'Marechal Lannes' and 'Violetta'

BLUE, SINGLE: 'Descaisne', 'Firmament', and 'President Lincoln'

BLUE, DOUBLE: 'Ami Schott', 'Olivier de Serres', and 'President Grevy'

LILAC, SINGLE: 'Cristophe Colomb' and 'Jacques Callot'

LILAC, DOUBLE: 'Alphonse Lavalee', 'Henri Martin', 'Leon Gambetta', and 'Victor Lemoine'

PINK, SINGLE: 'Charm', 'Lucie Baltet', 'Macrostachya', and 'Mrs. Harry Bickle'

PINK, DOUBLE: 'Belle de Nancy', 'Katherine Havemeyer', 'Madame Antoine Buchner', and 'Montaigne'

MAGENTA, SINGLE: 'Captain Baltet', 'Congo', and 'Madame F. Morel'

MAGENTA, DOUBLE: 'Charles Joly', 'My Favorite', 'Paul Thiron', and 'President Poincare'

PURPLE, SINGLE: 'Ludwig Spaeth', 'Monge', 'Mrs. W. E. Marshall', 'Night', and 'Sensation'

PURPLE, DOUBLE: 'Adelaide Dunbar', 'Anne Tighe', and 'Paul Hariot'

VIBURNUM (viburnum)   *Caprifoliaceae* (honeysuckle) family

An explanation of this genus appears in the "Broadleaf Evergreens" division.

Viburnum acerifolium (maple-leaved viburnum, dockmackie, arrowwood, possum haw)

Zones 4 to 8   4' to 6' high x 3' to 4' wide   Sun to shade

Somewhat limited in ornamental appeal, this hardy shrub offers wide adaptability to both reduced light and varying soil conditions as a naturalizing plant well suited to moist and shady places. Readily suckering into broad colonies, it is native from New Brunswick to North Carolina and west to Minnesota. Cultivated since 1736, the plant is upright, neat-looking, and sparsely branched with an attractive autumn coloring of pink-toned to magenta variations. The mid-June flowering is not especially striking with its small, yellowish to white, long-stalked, flat, terminal blossom clusters up to 3 inches wide; the later fruit is meagerly set, oval, about ⅓ inch across, and red turning to purple-black at maturity. The foliage is bright to deep green (depending on the amount of light provided) and egg-shaped in outline with three noticeable lobes —very similar in appearance to the leaves of red maple *(Acer rubrum)*—between 3 and 5 inches long, coarsely toothed, and densely covered with hairs on the undersides and the leaf stalks.

Viburnum x carlecephalum

Viburnum x carlecephalum (fragrant snowball)

Zones 5 to 9   6' to 8' high x 6' to 8' wide   Sun

Resembling the popular *carlesii* (one of its parents) in both habit and foliage, this scented viburnum is desirable as a border accent but is difficult to transplant and establish easily; for best results, install only small containerized or balled-and-burlapped plants. A cross between *carlesii* and *macrocephalum* made in England during the 1930s, it forms a fast-growing, loose, open silhouette and needs ample room for proper expansion. The late May blossoms come from winter-exposed budding at the ends of the twigs and develop into huge, densely packed, globular heads (similar to popcorn balls) of tubular white florets tinged red on the outsides of the petals. These become up to 5 inches across and are nicely fragrant with the scent of cloves, although these flowers are not as intensely memorable as those of *carlesii*. The fruit is usually sparse in clusters of red berries which later become black. The somewhat glossy foliage is toothed, oval, hairy beneath, and between 3 and 4 inches long; it often changes to bright red in the autumn.

Viburnum carlesii (Koreanspice viburnum, Mayflower viburnum)

Zones 5 to 8   5′ to 8′ x 5′ to 8′ wide   Sun to light shade

This is one of the most popular of all shrubs for its special fragrance in mid-May on a slow-growing, neat, upright plant with a rounded silhouette. Simple to grow and relatively easy to establish, it is native to Korea and has been cultivated since 1902 (although it was known by 1885 as a discovery in a Japanese garden). Winter-exposed terminal flower buds develop into dense, rounded heads up to 3 inches wide of spicy but sweet-smelling blush-toned florets which fade to white at maturity; individual flowers resemble those of Mayflower *(Arbutus)* in both shape and scent. The fruiting is often sparse as blue-black drupes with little ornamental value. Its dull, deep green, oval, and toothed leaves are between 2 and 4 inches long with hairiness on both surfaces; their autumn color is reddish or purple-red and muted. The cultivar 'Compactum' is a Rhode Island nursery find discovered in 1956 with deeper green foliage, heavier flowering as the plant matures, a compact habit, and a height of only 3½ feet. This and the parent now often are grafted to the rootstock of the species *lantana* since cuttings have a high mortality rate; however, the system has serious drawbacks because an incurable graft blight causing death of the entire plant is common even in nurseries.

Viburnum carlesii

Viburnum dentatum (pubescens) (arrowwood, southern arrowwood)

Zones 3 to 9   5′ to 10′ high x 8′ to 15′ wide   Sun to semishade

The strong, very straight, basal stems of this shrub are said to have been used in making arrow shafts by American Indians; this has provided the common name. Today the plant is used as a dependably durable hedge, screen, or naturalized mass. It grows readily in any soil but thrives where consistent moisture is available. Rapid and vigorous, the shrub develops rounded thickets easily in a variety of light exposures. Native from New Brunswick to Florida and Texas, it has been cultivated since 1736. It produces edible fruit by midsummer. The early June flowering is creamy white in flat clusters about 3 inches wide with florets carrying noticeably long and projecting stamens. Its abundant fruiting is egg-shaped, blue to blue-black, and much favored by birds. In some parts of western Europe this plant is cultivated for the fruit, which is used in baking in much the same way Americans use blueberries. The foliage is glossy, dark green, generally oval in outline with noticeably coarse teeth and deep-set veining, about 3 inches in length, and colored anywhere from rust-red to dull yellow by autumn.

Viburnum dentatum

Viburnum dentatum flowers

Viburnum dentatum fruit

Viburnum dilatatum

Viburnum dilatatum (linden viburnum)

Zones 5 to 8   6′ to 10′ high x 5′ to 8′ wide   Sun to light shade

Generous and conspicuous fruiting is the attraction of this shrub, but for assured crops annually, install several plants close at hand for greater pollination. Native to Japan, this dense, rounded, and compact shrub has been in culture since at least 1845. It prefers a moist, average-fertility soil and is appealing as a border specimen, informal hedge, or naturalized screen. The upright, sturdy stems are deep red-brown and carry creamy white early June flowering in hairy, flat clusters up to 5 inches across; their odor tends to be strong but not unpleasant. Large fruit clusters develop by midsummer as oval, scarlet, ⅓-inch drupes with persistence in reasonably attractive condition through the winter months. Birds appear to prefer the fruit well aged since they consume it mainly in February and March; however, they may have to pay a penalty for this preference since it is not unusual to find intoxicated robins near the plants at such feeding times. The foliage is mostly oval, variable to 5 inches long, coarsely toothed, and hairy on both sides, with a reasonable resemblance to linden leaves; its autumn coloring is russet-red to purple. The cultivar 'Xanthocarpum' develops pallid yellow fruiting, but only sparsely.

Viburnum dilatatum flowers

Viburnum dilatatum fruit

Viburnum x juddii (Judd viburnum)

Zones 5 to 10   6′ to 10′ high x 8′ to 12′ wide   Sun to light shade

This is a cross between *bitchiuense* and *carlesii* developed in 1920 at the Arnold Arboretum of Boston and named to commemorate William Judd, a propagator there. Dense, bushy, and broadly spreading, the plant has freely produced mid-May flowering in loose clusters about 3½ inches wide of pink fading to white with a pleasant fragrance. This hybrid blooms with *carlesii* and is hardier than it, but the scent is not as strongly perfumed. It does, however, appear to fruit more heavily then *carlesii* with reddish black ornamental clusters that are enjoyed by birds. The dark green foliage is oval, up to 3½ inches long, shallowly toothed, hairy beneath, and more lustrous than that of the parents.

Viburnum lentago (sheepberry, nannyberry, black haw, cowberry, nanny plum, sweetberry, wild raisin, sweet viburnum)

Zones 3 to 9   15' to 30' high x 15' to 30' wide   Sun to light shade

Natively found along moist stream banks from the Hudson Bay to Georgia and Mississippi, this plant has been cultivated since 1761. It develops a vigorous, suckering, and wide-spreading habit with a tendency to become more open at maturity. This is a sizable, dense shrub with slender, erect stems that eventually arch to the ground and often root. The late May flowers are showy on flat clusters of creamy white that are between 3 and 4½ inches wide and have an agreeable scent. The noticeable and edible fruit is shiny, blue-black, ½ inch long, and oval; it is produced in generous 3-inch clusterings eagerly sought by birds. The foliage is a soft yellow-green when emerging but later becomes glossy, deep green, slenderly oval with lengths between 1 inch and 4 inches, toothed, and long-pointed at the tips. Each leaf stalk produces a distinctively conspicuous set of small wings along its length. The autumn color varies from purplish red to dull orange. This plant serves pleasantly as a tall background screen or as a naturalized mass in deciduous woodlots. Mildew on the leaves is the chief problem in some growing areas.

Viburnum macrocephalum (Chinese snowball)

Zones 7 to 10   6' to 12' high x 6' to 12' wide   Sun to light shade

Here is the viburnum with the largest flowering of all; its showy, globose heads grow between 4 and 8 inches wide during late May. These are composed entirely of large, sterile florets with no possibility of fruiting; the blossoms closely resemble those of *Hydrangea macrophylla*. Well adapted for the mild areas of the southern United States, the plant is often semievergreen there and shows an upright and spreading nature with a dense and rounded silhouette requiring adequate space for enlargement. Native to China and introduced by Robert Fortune in 1844, this shrub is one of the parents of the hybrid species *x carlecephalum*. It demands a rich, well-drained soil and must be sheltered from winter wind at the northern end of its growing range. The leaves are dull, oval, 2½ to 4 inches long, finely toothed, and hairy on both sides; they offer no autumn coloring. The variety *keteleeri* is a wild form hardy into zone 6 with only a few sterile florets as a halo around the mass of fertile flowering; it rarely is cultivated.

Viburnum macrocephalum

Viburnum opulus (cranberry bush, European cranberry bush, Guelder rose, whitten tree)

Zones 3 to 10   8' to 12' high x 8' to 12' wide   Sun to semishade

Perhaps the best known of all the viburnums, the shrub has been in cultivation many hundreds of years for its decorative values and edible fruit. This very hardy species differs from its close relation *trilobum* in its shallowly grooved petioles with large nectar glands near the stem junctions. (Some authorities believe that the species *trilobum* is only a form of *opulus* which developed here some time after *opulus* was introduced by early settlers.) Very easily grown in almost any soil and with any light intensity, this shrub is also resistent to city pollution and is readily tolerant of summer heat and dry earth. Aphids are its only serious affliction, and their inroads can distort new soft growth appreciably unless controlled by spraying. Erect, dense, robust, suckering, and rounded in outline, the plant has gray to tan stems and blooms late in May with creamy white, flat, 4-inch-wide clusters of heavily scented flowers showing occasional marginal, sterile florets almost an inch across at the outer edges. It is native to the British Isles, Europe (even into the Arctic Circle), northern Africa, and northern Asia; it is generally rampant where the ground is wet and boggy. The fruit is prolific, pendant, very decorative, and persistent through the winter since birds find its bitter taste unpalatable. While edible by humans, it is considered much less desirable for flavor than the fruit of *trilobum*. These cranberry like drupes are translucent, shiny, oval, scarlet, and ⅓ inch long in clusters from 2 to 3 inches wide. The glossy, dark green leaves are maplelike in appearance with three to five lobes, coarse teeth, and dimensions between 3 and 4 inches for width and length. They are hairy beneath and change to yellow-red or purple-red during autumn. Many cultivars are currently available.

CULTIVAR: 'Aureum' is a rugged, compact plant with new leaves that are bronze, becoming deep yellow, then bright yellow, and finally green for the summer.

CULTIVAR: 'Compactum' is less hardy (zone 5) with a densely compact habit to 5 feet but with a free-flowering and heavy-fruiting nature even when young.

CULTIVAR: 'Nanum' serves attractively as a low hedge with its mounded, dwarfed habit to 2 feet tall with small leaves; it rarely blooms or fruits, however, and offers no autumn color.

CULTIVAR: 'Notcutt' possesses a robust nature and produces more flowers and fruiting.

CULTIVAR: 'Roseum' ('Sterile') carries only sterile flowering in globose heads and remains the favorite cultivar; nevertheless, it can be disfigured by aphid infestations on all new stems and leaves, and it has no autumn coloring. These blossoms are first lime-green and then turn pure white as an unusual accent of flowering. This plant usually is known as the "Guelder rose," a name derived from Guelderland, Holland, where it may have originated several centuries ago.

CULTIVAR: 'Xanthocarpum' develops clear, golden yellow, ¼-inch fruiting.

Viburnum plicatum

Viburnum plicatum (tomentosum plicatum, tomentosum sterile)   (Japanese snowball)

Zones 5 to 9   8′ to 10′ high x 8′ to 10′ wide   Sun to light shade

This showy plant is in the front rank for popularity, durable hardiness, and ornamental assets; few other shrubs have so many attractive qualities throughout the year. Unexcelled as a specimen or a wide screen or for massing, it is easy to grow in any fertile, moist, well-drained location, but it does not accept wet, heavy soil. Less troubled by aphids than *opulus* and its cultivars, this modest-growing shrub forms a dense, broadly spreading and arching outline with horizontal main branching somewhat like that of the tree dogwood, *Cornus florida*. Its profuse late May flowering appears in opposite double rows all along the stems of the previous season at the leaf axils. These long-lasting blooms are creamy white and totally sterile in the typical form and appear as conspicuous globose clusters between 2 and 3 inches across; they cannot produce fruit. The pleated foliage is dull to bright green, oval, 3 to 4 inches long, toothed, somewhat hairy beneath, and rust-red to purple-red in the autumn.

Native to both China and Japan, the plant was introduced by Robert Fortune in 1844 from a Japanese garden several decades before the wild form, *tomentosum*, was known to exist. Again, a problem existed for botanists in terms of how to catalog this plant correctly since it was assumed that a completely sterile form must have a fertile counterpart somewhere; while they waited for news of its discovery, they named this shrub *tomentosum plicatum* (as well as *tomentosum sterile*). It took until 1865 for the fertile type to be located, but by then the botanic laws of precedence awarded the *plicatum* label to this totally sterile plant so that the fertile form is now only a variety of it, instead of the other way around as is usually the case. Many attractive options are now available from the *variety*—not the species.

VARIETY: *tomentosum* (*V. tomentosum*) is commonly known as the "doublefile viburnum." It is the wild, fertile form with the same attractive form and blooming habit as the species; here, however, the mass of fertile flowering is surrounded only by an outer ring of sterile florets. Bright red oval fruit develops later and is positioned strongly upright from the leaf axils to become very conspicuous in late summer with its double-file placement along the stems. These change to black at maturity and are favored by birds.

CULTIVAR: 'Lanarth' is vigorous, taller, and graceful with more upright but still mainly horizontal branching and larger, sterile florets around the outer margins.

CULTIVAR: 'Mariesii' carries longer, drooping, horizontal branches and showier flower clusters with up to 2-inch-wide sterile florets circling the fertile inner ones. It also develops larger fruit than *tomentosum*, but the fruit is not always prolific.

CULTIVAR: 'Pink Beauty' ('Roseum') displays smaller leaves and flowers which become deep pink as they age; this color change is not reliable, however, in all soils.

Viburnum plicatum tomentosum flowers

Viburnum plicatum tomentosum fruit

Viburnum prunifolium (black haw, sweet haw, sheepberry, nannyberry, stagbush)

Zones 3 to 9   10′ to 15′ high x 10′ to 15′ wide   Sun to semishade

Generally used as a shrubby specimen, screen, or mass, this plant can be pruned successfully into a tree form in certain situations. Natively found from Connecticut to Michigan and south to Texas and Florida, it has been cultivated since 1731 for its desirable fruiting. Adapting well to dry locations, it produces a rounded, multistemmed outline with slim, stiff branching. The mid-May flowers are creamy white in flat clusters up to 4 inches wide and are followed by profuse bunches of oval fruit set on red supports; fruit is first green, then yellow, and finally blue-black. They are the largest fruit produced by any viburnum with lengths about ½ inch and widths to ¼ inch. After a frost they become sweetly edible and have been used since the eighteenth century for making jams and jellies. The blunt-tipped, oval to egg-shaped, glossy leaves are deep green, 2 to 3 inches long, and finely toothed; they turn purple or rich red in the autumn. The roots of this shrub have been used medicinally.

Viburnum setigerum fruit

Viburnum setigerum (theiferum) (tea viburnum)

Zones 6 to 9   8′ to 12′ high x 6′ to 8′ wide   Sun to light shade

A distinctive and attractive shrub with its colorful summertime fruiting and drooping leaves, this plant is native to central and western China; it was introduced by Ernest Wilson in 1901. Narrowly upright with an open habit and arching branches, it may become leggy with age; young plants tend to grow vigorously. The early June flowers are fragrant and creamy white in flat clusters only 2 inches wide; these are followed by generous orange or reddish orange oval fruit about ⅜ inch long which becomes translucent with frost and then turns brown. Birds appear to like them before they age. The foliage has a metallic sheen in blue-green to deep green, and the slightly toothed, narrowly oval leaves vary from 3 to 5 inches in length and hang pendantly. Its autumn coloring may fluctuate from yellow-orange to red. Tea is made from the dried leaves by Chinese monks in some parts of that country. The cultivar 'Aurantiacum' was discovered in 1907 and develops orange-yellow fruiting.

Viburnum sieboldii

Viburnum sieboldii flowers

Viburnum sieboldii fruit

Viburnum sieboldii (Siebold viburnum)

Zones 5 to 9   15′ to 25′ high x 10′ to 15′ wide   Sun to light shade

Robust and wide-spreading by nature, here is another shrub which can be trained satisfactorily as a small tree by regular pruning. Upright and open with stout, stiff branching and conspicuous, half-inch, tan or grayish winter buds, this native from Japan came into culture during 1880 and performs admirably as a large specimen, tall screen, or mass planting. Its fruiting displays are noticeable for a long period with or without the actual fruit. The plant blooms in late May with creamy to yellowish green flat clusters between 3 and 4 inches wide which carry a strong, almost offensive odor. The ensuing oval fruit is green, then pink, then red, and finally black on showy red supports which remain in place for several weeks after the fruit is gone (mainly to birds). Its crinkled, thick, pleated leaves are yellow-toned to deep green; they are lustrous above and yellow-hairy beneath in an oval to wedge shape. They can extend to 6 inches long with coarse teeth and have a disagreeable smell when crushed; they turn bronze in the autumn.

Viburnum trilobum (americanum, opulus americanum)

(cranberry bush, American cranberry bush, highbush cranberry, crampbark, grouseberry, squawbush)

Zones 2 to 9   8′ to 12′ high x 8′ to 12′ wide   Sun to semishade

Viburnum trilobum flowers

In form, flowering, and fruiting, this species is very similar to *opulus*, differing from it by greater hardiness, petiole design, and hairless, three-pointed leaves. Several authorities contend that it is just a naturalized form of *opulus* developed from the fruit of early settlers' plants, but the only point which is certain is that nurseries today grow less *trilobum* than *opulus*. This vigorous shrub is upright with open, spreading branches and is native to the cool woods and streamsides of southern Canada and the northeastern United States. The flowers appear in late May as white, flat, fertile clusters 2 to 4 inches wide surrounded by outer rings of sterile florets. The fruit is oval, scarlet, and cranberrylike in 2- to 3-inch bunches which persist since birds find them too tart to eat. They are edible for humans, however, and make very acceptable jellies and preserves (this is not so with *opulus*). The smooth, hairless, up to 5-inch-long leaves are broadly oval with three lobes in a maplelike appearance with coarsely toothed margins; they offer little autumn color. Leaf petioles are broadly grooved and have small nectar glands (smaller than those of *opulus*). Useful for hedges, screens, or naturalized masses on a variety of soils and with varying light conditions, the shrub is remarkably hardy over a wide area and has few problems with pests or diseases. The cultivar 'Compactum' is slow-growing to 5 feet and has a denser, oval outline.

Viburnum trilobum fruit

Viburnum wrightii   (Wright viburnum, leatherleaf)

Zones 5 to 9   6′ to 10′ high x 5′ to 8′ wide   Sun to light shade

Very similar in general appearance to *dilatatum*, this shrub differs in its nearly hairless leaves and briefly enduring fruit crops. Native to Japan, Korea, and China, it came into cultivation during 1892 and blooms in late May with creamy white flat clusters between 2 and 4 inches across. The bright red, glossy fruit forms early in August but persists only into November; it is both larger and more profuse than that of *dilatatum*. The metallic-green foliage is only barely hairy on the undersides (at the midveins) and is oval to rounded, 3 to 6 inches long, coarsely toothed, abruptly tip-pointed, and bronze-toned in autumn. The cultivar 'Hessei' *(var. hessei)* has a dwarfed compact habit to 3 feet with smaller but annually dependable flowering and fruiting; its leaves have few teeth.

Viburnum wrightii fruit

VITEX (Chaste tree, tree of chastity, hemptree)
Verbenaceae (vervain or verbena) family

About 270 species of deciduous and evergreen trees and shrubs that are native mostly to tropical and subtropical regions exist in this genus. Many have been cultivated since ancient times and tend to be long-lived. These plants grow in any fertile soil that is well drained, and they thrive in hot weather. The name is an old Latin one for these plants. Flowers are white, yellow, red, blue, or purple and develop either in panicles or in small spikes of bell-shaped florets. The fruit is a small drupe (like a plum). Leaves are often aromatic, oppositely placed, palmately compound with three to seven leaflets, and generally darker above than below; they form on four-angled, hairy stems. These plants usually perform best (at least in this country) when in full sun. Few pests or diseases are a problem.

Vitex agnus-castus

Vitex agnus-castus   (chaste tree, lilac chaste tree, hemptree, monk's pepper tree, sage tree, wild pepper)

Zones 7 to 10   10′ to 20′ high x 10′ to 20′ wide   Sun

These are certainly long-lived plants. A vigorous specimen that still exists today in the botanic garden of Padua, Italy, was installed in 1560. While native to the Mediterranean region, they are adaptable to less desirable growing conditions even though a side effect in very cold areas can be dieback to ground level. The plant likes a fertile, moderately dry, well-drained location and enjoys placement near shorelines. Its late blooming makes it popular at beach sites. In the northern end of the range, they may require winter mulching and wind protection, but since their horticultural care often involves reducing the stems to ground level to induce better flowering, it seems wiser to treat these shrubs as herbaceous perennials no matter where they are raised. This culture is similar to that for *Buddleia davidii,* and both will leave gaps in northern borders where they are so used.

Robust, spreading, and loose in outline, this shrub was introduced to culture in 1570 in the British Isles. It has a curious history since everything written about it in the past seems to relate to chastity and lust. The species name comes from the Greek *agnos* ("without descent") and the Latin *castus* ("chaste"), which probably means that the presence of the plant suppressed carnal desire. The ancient Greeks are said to have scattered dried leaves of it on the beds of virgins to curb the heat of lust (exactly *whose* lust is not clear), and the seed is also held to possess antiaphrodisiac properties. Fashion and preferences about such matters do appear to change with the times.

Flowers occur on new growth during August and continue until October (later in mild climates) as fragrant, long-lasting, ⅛-inch, lilac to lavender blossoms on slender spikes between 5 and 12 inches long, crowded terminally as well as in the forward leaf axils. The fruit is a very small drupe resembling a peppercorn. Its twigs and leaves are strongly but pleasantly aromatic when bruised, and the lancelike leaflets are generally arranged in fives (occasionally seven) of a very deep green coloring above and gray-hairy beneath with notably extended leaf stalks. These grow between 3 and 4 inches long and are nearly entire with but a few teeth at the tips; they produce no autumn coloring. A few cultivars are known.

CULTIVAR: 'Alba' *(var. alba)* carries white flowers.

CULTIVAR: 'Latifolia' *(var. latifolia, macrophylla)* is hardier and more robust than the parent with shorter and broader leaflets; it may grow satisfactorily into zone 6.

CULTIVAR: 'Rosea' produces pink-toned flowering.

CULTIVAR: 'Variegata' has variegated leaves of cream and green.

Vitex negundo (cutleaf chaste tree)

Zones 6 to 9   10′ to 15′ high x 8′ to 10′ wide   Sun

Vitex negundo heterophylla

Similar to *agnus-castus* except for lighter green foliage and a less rigid outline, this openly graceful, aromatic shrub is a fast-growing native from southeastern Africa, Madagascar, eastern Asia, the Philippines, and Guam that was introduced in 1697. Its flowers appear from August to October as loose scented spikes to a height of 8 inches with ¼-inch florets in lilac to lavender appearing on new growth. The stems are pungently fragrant when bruised and produce long-stalked leaves that are similarly aromatic with three to five lancelike to oval leaflets between 1½ and 4 inches long. They develop with entire margins or show some lobes, and they are deep green above with gray-hairy undersides, there is no color change in autumn. The variety *heterophylla (incisa, laciniata)* is hardier than the parent; it carries smaller, deeply cut leaves but has less showy flowering.

WEIGELA (weigela)   *Caprifoliaceae* (honeysuckle) family

Between ten and twelve species of sun-loving deciduous shrubs native to Asia belong to this genus, but they formerly were assigned to *Diervilla*, which is a group that expands by suckering, whereas these do not. Easily transplanted and grown in any moist and fertile soil, they all accept city pollution well and serve usefully as vigorous, showy-flowered border specimens or masses. They have no bothersome diseases or insect pests, but while generally hardy, they can be injured by cold in the northern end of their growing range. Unfortunately, all species crossbreed easily, creating some confusion about the true dimensions and flower color of any one type. The plant is named for an eighteenth-century German professor of botany, Christian von Weigel, who published *Flora Pomerana Rugica* in 1769; the genus often is misspelled in catalogs as "Weigelia." The Chinese called them "flowers of the embroidered girdle" or "flowers of the silken ribbons," no doubt because they were thought attractive when depicted as woven embellishments on clothing.

Bloom occurs in May and June (along with mock orange, early deutzia, and late lilac) as tubular, foxglovelike, 1½-inch, conspicuous flowers of red, pink, or white, mostly clustered on short, leafy spurs of the previous year's growth. The fruit is an oblong woody capsule with no landscape value. Its opposite foliage is simple and toothed but has no autumn coloring. These popular plants are valued chiefly for their profuse, showy, spring blossoming.

Weigela florida (amabilis, rosea)   (oldfashioned weigela)

Zones 5 to 8   6′ to 8′ high x 6′ to 8′ wide   Sun to light shade

Weigela florida

The parent of many hybrids, here is the most common of all in old garden developments, but it is very variable in color and performance. The shrub enjoys a moist, average-fertility, well-drained site and produces a coarse, rangy, wide-spreading, and rounded outline requiring much annual pruning attention for presentability. The late May and early June unscented blossoms are very showy and profusely set with broadly funnelform, 1¼-inch-long, reddish to rose-pink flowers crowded in groups of three or four on short, gray-tan twigs. The light green, oval to wedge-shaped leaves are 2 to 4 inches long, tip-pointed, toothed, and prominently veined; they offer little autumn color.

Weigela florida   (Cont.)

Weigela florida

Weigela florida cv. 'Alba'

Weigela florida cv. 'Foliis-purpureis'

Weigela florida cv. 'Variegata'

This plant is native to Japan, Manchuria, northern China, and Korea; it was brought into culture by Robert Fortune during 1845. Several variations are available.

CULTIVAR: 'Alba' has white flowering fading to light pink with age.

CULTIVAR: 'Foliis-purpureis' grows compactly and slowly to 4 feet with dark purplish leaves and pink blossoms.

CULTIVAR: 'Variegata' offers compact growth to a height of 4 or 5 feet and foliage edged broadly in yellow to creamy white; its flowers are pink. While highly noticeable, this is a difficult plant to assimilate satisfactorily into a design.

VARIETY: *venusta* is very hardy (zone 4) and was discovered in Korea during 1905. It grows to 6 feet with graceful stems and presents earlier flowering of larger size and deeper pink color than the parent.

Weigela hybrids and cultivars

Zones 5 to 8   Variable from 5′ to 10′ high and wide   Sun to light shade

Weigela cv. 'Bristol Ruby'

The plants listed here are attractive and popular sorts difficult to separate botanically as either hybrids or cultivars. They have mixed parentage involving *florida, coraeensis,* or *floribunda.* Many came from the Lemoine nursery in France.

'Abel Carriere' blooms early with large, bright, rose-carmine flowers flecked with yellow at the throats.

'Bristol Ruby' is vigorous and erect to 10 feet with sparkling ruby-red blossoming.

'Bristol Snowflake' is the white counterpart to *cv.* 'Bristol Ruby' with some pink tones to the flowers as they fade.

'Candida' produces a compact form with light green leaves and pure white flowering.

'Conquete' ('Conquerant') has 2-inch blossoms of deep rose-pink.

'Dame Blanche' carries large white flowers blushed with pink on the exteriors.

'Eva Rathke' grows slowly and compactly to a 5-foot height with bright crimson-red flowers opening over a long period.

'Eva Supreme' is compactly neat to 5 feet with profuse deep red blossoms.

'Floreal' blossoms early and carries large carmine-pink flowering with crimson-red throats.

'Gracieux' is erect to 8 feet with large blossoms of salmon-rose showing sulfur-yellow throats.

'Madame Tellier' has large white flowers suffused in pink.

'Mont Blanc' grows vigorously to 10 feet with large, white, scented flowers fading to pale pink.

'Perle' is robust and carries sizable pale cream flowering with rose edges and clear yellow mouths.

'Seduction' flowers early and shows magenta-rose blossoms.

'Styriaca' has arching vigorous growth and showy carmine-red flowers.

'Vanicek' ('Newport Red', 'Rhode Island Red') is hardier than *cv.* 'Bristol Ruby' and more upright than *cv.* 'Eva Rathke'; it has large violet-red blossoming and green winter stems.

SHRUBS WITH POTENTIAL HEIGHTS UP TO 3 FEET

Needle Evergreens

Abies balsamea cv. 'Hudsonia'
Abies balsamea cv. 'Nana'
Cephalotaxus fortunei cv. 'Prostrate Spreader'
Chamaecyparis obtusa cv. 'Kosteri'
Chamaecyparis obtusa cv. 'Nana'
Chamaecyparis obtusa cv. 'Nana Aurea'
Chamaecyparis obtusa cv. 'Nana Pyramidalis'
Chamaecyparis pisifera cv. 'Filifera Aurea'
Chamaecyparis pisifera cv. 'Filifera Nana'
Chamaecyparis pisifera cv. 'Squarrosa Minima'
Juniperus chinensis cv. 'Mint Julep'
Juniperus chinensis cv. 'San Jose'
Juniperus chinensis procumbens and cultivars
Juniperus chinensis sargentii and cultivars
Juniperus communis cultivars
Juniperus conferta and cultivars
Juniperus horizontalis and cultivars
Juniperus sabina and cultivars
Juniperus squamata cv. 'Blue Star'
Juniperus virginiana cv. 'Silver Spreader'

Picea abies cv. 'Gregoryana'
Picea abies cv. 'Maxwellii'
Picea abies cv. 'Procumbens'
Pinus mugo pumilo
Pinus sylvestris cv. 'Repens'
Platycladus orientalis cv. 'Decussatus'
Platycladus orientalis cv. 'Rosedalis'
Taxus baccata cv. 'Cavendishii'
Taxus cuspidata cv. 'Aurescens'
Taxus x media cv. 'Tauntonii'
Thuja occidentalis cv. 'Caespitosa'
Thuja occidentalis cv. 'Little Gem'
Thuja occidentalis cv. 'Rheingold'
Tsuga canadensis cv. 'Cole'

Broadleaf Evergreens

Abelia x grandiflora cv. 'Prostrata'
Abelia x grandiflora cv. 'Sherwoodii'
Berberis candidula
Berberis darwinii cv. 'Depressa'
Berberis darwinii cv. 'Nana'
Berberis x stenophylla cv. 'Coccinea'
Berberis x stenophylla cv. 'Gracilis Nana'
Buxus microphylla and cultivars
Calluna vulgaris and cultivars
Cotoneaster dammeri

Cotoneaster microphyllus
Cotoneaster salicifolius repens
Daphne cneorum and cultivars
Erica carnea and cultivars
Erica cinerea
Erica vagrans and cultivars
Euonymus fortunei cultivars
Gardenia jasminoides cv. 'Prostrata'
Hypericum calycinum
Hypericum cv. 'Hidcote'
Hypericum moseranum
Ilex crenata cv. 'Helleri'
Ilex crenata cv. 'Mariesii'
Leucothoe fontanesiana cv. 'Nana'
Mahonia repens
Nandina domestica cv. 'Nana Purpurea'
Pieris japonica cultivars
Pyracantha koidzumii cv. 'Santa Cruz'
Rhododendron obtusum and 'Kurume Hybrids'
Skimmia reevesiana
Vaccinium delavayi
Vaccinium vitis-idaea and varieties
Viburnum davidii

Deciduous Shrubs

Aronia melanocarpa
Berberis thunbergii cultivars

Caragana arborescens nana
Caryopteris x clandoniensis and cultivars
Chaenomeles japonica and cultivars
Chaenomeles speciosa cultivars
Chaenomeles x superba cultivars
Cotoneaster apiculatus
Cotoneaster horizontalis
Cytisus x kewensis
Cytisus purpureus
Jasminum nudiflorum
Philadelphus coronarius cv. 'Duplex'
Philadelphus x lemoinei cv. 'Manteau d'Hermine'
Potentilla fruticosa
Potentilla parvifolia and cultivars
Potentilla selections
Rhododendron yedoense
Rosa carolina
Rosa rugosa cv. 'Max Graf'
Rosa spinosissima and cultivars
Rosa wichuriana
Salix purpurea cv. 'Gracilis'
Spiraea albiflora
Spiraea x bumalda and cultivars
Spiraea japonica cv. 'Alpina'
Symphoricarpos albus
Symphoricarpos x chenaultii

SHRUBS WITH POTENTIAL HEIGHTS FROM 3 TO 6 FEET

Needle Evergreens

Abies concolor cv. 'Compacta'
Abies koreana cv. 'Compact Dwarf'
Abies koreana cv. 'Prostrate Beauty'
Cephalotaxus fortunei drupacea
Chamaecyparis obtusa cultivars

Juniperus chinensis cultivars
Picea abies cv. 'Nidiformis'
Picea pungens cultivars
Pinus mugo cv. 'Compacta'
Pinus mugo mugo
Pinus sylvestris cv. 'Beauvronensis'
Platycladus orientalis cultivars
Pseudotsuga menziesii cv. 'Nana'

Taxus baccata cultivars
Taxus cuspidata cv. 'Densa'
Thuja occidentalis cultivars
Tsuga canadensis cultivars

Broadleaf Evergreens

Abelia x grandiflora and cultivars
Berberis x chenaultii

Berberis x mentorensis
Berberis x stenophylla cultivars
Berberis verruculosa
Buxus microphylla varieties
Buxus sempervirens cv. 'Suffruticosa'
Buxus sempervirens cv. 'Vardar Valley'

Calliandra tweedii
Codiaeum variegatum pictum and
cultivars
Daphne x hybrida
Daphne odora and cultivars
Erica canaliculata and cultivars
Euonymus fortunei cultivars
Euonymus fortunei vegeta
Gardenia jasminoides and
cultivars
Ilex cornuta cultivars
Ilex glabra cv. 'Compacta'
Ixora coccinea
Leucothoe axillaris
Leucothoe fontanesiana
Ligustrum japonicum cv.
'Suwanne River'
Mahonia aquifolium and cultivars
Nandina domestica
Pieris floribunda
Rhododendron carolinianum and
cultivars
Rhododendron indicum and
cultivars
Rhododendron laetivirens
Rhododendron micranthum
Rhododendron minus cv.
'Compacta'

Rhododendron mucronatum and
cultivars
Sarcococca ruscifolia
Skimmia japonica
Vaccinium ovatum
Viburnum x burkwoodii
Viburnum suspensum

Deciduous Shrubs

Abeliophyllum distichum
Berberis koreana
Berberis thunbergii and cultivars
Chaenomeles x superba and
cultivars
Cornus sericea cv. 'Kelseyi'
Cotoneaster dielsiana and varieties
Cotoneaster divaricatus
Cotoneaster racemiflorus
royaleanus
Cytisus nigricans
Daphne x burkwoodi
Daphne mezereum and cultivars
Deutzia gracilis
Enkianthus perulatus
Euonymus europaea cv.
'Pumilus'
Fothergilla monticola

Hydrangea arborescens and
cultivars
Hydrangea quercifolia
Hypericum frondosum
Hypericum prolificum
Ligustrum obtusifolium
regelianum
Ligustrum ovalifolium cv.
'Globosum'
Ligustrum ovalifolium cv.
'Nanum'
Ligustrum vulgare cv. 'Lodense'
Lonicera tatarica cv. 'Nana'
Lonicera x xylosteoides cv.
'Clavey's Dwarf'
Lonicera x xylosteoides cv.
'Emerald Mound'
Paeonia suffruticosa and cultivars
Philadelphus coronarius cultivars
Philadelphus x lemoinei and
cultivars
Philadelphus x virginalis and
cultivars
Potentilla selections
Prunus glandulosa and cultivars
Prunus maritima
Punica granatum cultivars
Rhododendron periclymenoides

Rhododendron viscosum
Rhododendron yedoense
poukhanense
Rosa rubrifolia
Rosa rugosa cv. 'Frau Dagmar
Hastrop'
Rosa virginiana
Spiraea x arguta
Spiraea x billiardii
Spiraea cantoniensis
Spiraea japonica and cultivars
Spiraea nipponica cv.
'Snowmound'
Spiraea thunbergii
Symphoricarpos x doorenbosii
cultivars
Symphoricarpos orbiculatus
Symphoricarpos rivularis
Syringa x chinensis cv. 'Nana'
Syringa laciniata
Syringa microphylla
Syringa meyeri
Viburnum acerifolium
Viburnum opulus cultivars
Weigela florida cultivars
Weigela hybrids and cultivars

SHRUBS WITH POTENTIAL HEIGHTS FROM 6 TO 10 FEET

Needle Evergreens

Juniperus chinensis cv. 'Hetzii'
Juniperus chinensis cv. 'Pfitzeriana
Glauca'
Juniperus squamata cv. 'Meyeri'
Picea abies cultivars
Picea pungens cv. 'Compacta'
Pinus mugo
Platycladus orientalis cv. 'Semper-
aurescens'
Taxus baccata cv. 'Fowle'
Taxus cuspidata cv. 'Nana'
Taxus x media cultivars
Thuja occidentalis cv.
'Ellwangerana Aurea'
Thuja occidentalis cv. 'Hoveyii'

Broadleaf Evergreens

Berberis darwinii and cultivars
Berberis gagnepainii and varieties
Berberis julianae
Berberis x stenophylla and
cultivars
Codiaeum variegatum pictum and
cultivars
Cotoneaster franchettii and
varieties
Cotoneaster glaucophyllus
Euonymus fortunei
x Fatshedera lizei
Ilex cornuta and cultivars

Ilex crenata
Ilex glabra
Ilex x meserveae cultivars
Kalmia latifolia and cultivars
Ligustrum japonicum
Mahonia bealii
Myrtus communis and cultivars
Nerium oleander and cultivars
Pieris taiwanensis
Pittosporum tobira
Prunus laurocerasus and
cultivars
Pyracantha coccinea
Pyracantha fortuneana
Pyracantha koidzumii
Rhododendron macrophyllum
Rhododendron minus
Rhododendron smirnowii
Viburnum japonicum
Viburnum tinus and cultivars

Deciduous Shrubs

Acanthopanax sieboldianus
Aronia arbutifolia
Aronia melanocarpa grandifolia
Buddleia davidii and cultivars
Calycanthus floridus
Chaenomeles speciosa and
cultivars
Clethra alnifolia
Cornus alba and cultivars

Cornus mas cv. 'Nana'
Cornus sericea and cultivars
Cotoneaster lucidus
Cotoneaster racemiflorus and
varieties
Cytisus x praecox
Cytisus scoparius and cultivars
Deutzia scabra and cultivars
Elaeagnus multiflorus
Euonymus alata and cultivars
Euonymus sachalinensis
Forsythia x intermedia and
cultivars
Forsythia suspensa and cultivars
Fothergilla major
Hamamelis vernalis
Hydrangea macrophylla
Kerria japonica and cultivars
Ligustrum obtusifolium
Lonicera x amoena
Lonicera fragrantissima
Lonicera korolkowii
Lonicera morrowii
Myrica pensylvanica
Philadelphus coronarius and
cultivars
Philadelphus x virginalis and
cultivars
Prunus x cistena
Rhododendron calendulaceum and
cultivars
Rhododendron gandavensis and
cultivars

Rhododendron 'Knap Hill–Exbury
Hybrids'
Rhododendron x kosteranum and
cultivars
Rhododendron mucronulatum
Rhododendron prinophyllum
Rhododendron vaseyi
Rosa blanda
Rosa californica
Rosa foetida and cultivars
Rosa hugonis
Rosa rugosa and cultivars
Rosa spinosissima altaica
Rosa spinosissima hispida
Salix purpurea
Spiraea nipponica
Spiraea prunifolia
Spiraea x vanhouttei
Syringa x persica
Syringa potaninii
Syringa x prestoniae and cultivars
Viburnum x carlecephalum
Viburnum carlesii
Viburnum dentatum
Viburnum dilatatum
Viburnum x juddii
Viburnum macrocephalum
Viburnum plicatum and cultivars
Viburnum wrightii
Weigela florida and cultivars
Weigela hybrids and cultivars

SHRUBS WITH POTENTIAL HEIGHTS FROM 10 to 15 FEET

Needle Evergreens

Cephalotaxus fortunei cv. 'Fastigiata'
Chamaecyparis obtusa cv. 'Tetragona Aurea'
Taxus baccata cv. 'Aurea'
Taxus baccata cv. 'Elegantissima'
Taxus baccata cv. 'Overeynderi'
Taxus cuspidata cv. 'Nana Pyramidalis'
Taxus x media cv. 'Hatfieldii'

Broadleaf Evergreens

Aucuba japonica and cultivars
Buxus sempervirens and cultivars
Calliandra haematocephela
Camellia sasanqua and cultivars
Carissa grandiflora and cultivars
Cotoneaster lacteus
Cotoneaster salicifolius
Elaeagnus pungens and cultivars
Euonymus japonica and cultivars
Euonymus kiautschovica
Fatsia japonica and cultivars
Pieris japonica
Pittosporum crasifolium
Prunus ilicifolia
Pyracantha atalantiodes
Rhododendron catawbiense and cultivars
Rhododendron griffithianum
Rhododendron maximum
Viburnum rhytidophyllum

Deciduous Shrubs

Aesculus parviflora
Buddleia alternifolia
Caragana arborescens
Chionanthus retusus
Cotinus coggria and cultivars
Elaeagnus umbellata
Euonymus europaea and cultivars
Hamamelis mollis and cultivars
Hibiscus syriacus and cultivars
Ilex decidua
Ilex verticillata and cultivars
Kolkwitzia amabilis
Ligustrum amurense
Ligustrum x ibolium
Ligustrum ovalifolium and cultivars
Ligustrum vulgare and cultivars
Lonicera maackii
Lonicera tatarica and cultivars
Rhamnus frangula and cultivars
Rhododendron arborescens
Rhododendron schlippenbachi
Stewartia ovata
Syringa x chinensis and cultivars
Syringa x hyacinthiflora and cultivars
Viburnum lantana and cultivars
Viburnum opulus and cultivars
Viburnum prunifolium
Viburnum setigerum
Viburnum trilobum
Vitex agnus-castus and cultivars
Vitex negundo

SHRUBS WITH POTENTIAL HEIGHTS BEYOND 15 FEET

Needle Evergreens

Cephalotaxus fortunei
Cephalotaxus harringtonia
Platycladus orientalis cv. 'Elegantissima'
Taxus baccata and cultivars
Taxus cuspidata and cultivars
Taxus x media and cultivars

Broadleaf Evergreens

Callistemon citrinus and cultivars
Camellia japonica and cultivars
Ilex pernyi and cultivars
Ligustrum lucidum and cultivars
Myrica cerifera
Osmanthus x fortunei
Osmanthus fragrans
Osmanthus heterophyllus and cultivars
Photinia x fraseri and cultivars
Photinia serrulata
Viburnum odoratissimum

Deciduous Shrubs

Aralia elata and cultivars
Aralia spinosa
Chionanthus virginicus
Cornus mas and cultivars
Elaeagnus angustifolia
Enkianthus campanulatus
Hamamelis x intermedia and cultivars
Hamamelis virginiana
Hippophae rhamnoides
Hydrangea paniculata and cultivars
Lagerstroemia indica and cultivars
Punica granatum and cultivars
Salix caprea
Stewartia pseudocamellia
Syringa vulgaris and cultivars
Viburnum lentago
Viburnum sieboldii

SHRUBS WITH SHOWY FLOWERING

Needle Evergreens

(None included in this book)

Broadleaf Evergreens

Abelia x grandiflora and cultivars
Berberis darwinii and cultivars
Calliandra species
Callistemon citrinus and cultivars
Calluna vulgaris and cultivars
Camellia species and cultivars
Daphne species
Erica species and cultivars
Gardenia jasminoides and cultivars
Hypericum species
Ixora coccinea and cultivars
Jasminum species
Kalmia latifolia and cultivars
Mahonia species
Myrtus communis and cultivars
Nandina domestica
Nerium oleander and cultivars
Pieris species
Prunus laurocerasus and cultivars
Rhododendron species and cultivars
Viburnum species and cultivars

Deciduous Shrubs

Abeliophyllum distichum
Aesculus parviflora
Aralia species and cultivars
Buddleia species and cultivars
Caragana arborescens
Chaenomeles species and cultivars
Chionanthus species
Clethra alnifolia and cultivars
Cotoneaster multiflorus
Cytisus species and cultivars
Daphne species and cultivars
Deutzia species and cultivars
Enkianthus species
Forsythia species and cultivars
Fothergilla species
Hamamelis species and cultivars
Hibiscus syriacus cultivars
Hydrangea species and cultivars
Hypericum species
Jasminum nudiflorum
Kerria japonica and cultivars
Kolkwitzia amabilis and cultivars
Lagerstroemia indica and cultivars
Lonicera species and cultivars
Paeonia suffruticosa cultivars
Philadelphus species and cultivars
Potentilla species and cultivars
Prunus glandulosa cultivars
Rhododendron species and cultivars
Rosa species and cultivars
Spiraea species and cultivars
Stewartia species
Syringa species and cultivars
Viburnum species and cultivars
Vitex species and cultivars
Weigela species and cultivars

SHRUBS WITH FRAGRANT FLOWERING

Needle Evergreens

(None included in this book)

Broadleaf Evergreens

Berberis x stenophylla
Berberis verruculosa
Buxus species
Camellia japonica cv. 'Kramer's Supreme'
Carissa grandiflora
Daphne species
Elaeagnus pungens
Gardenia jasminoides
Mahonia bealii
Myrtus communis
Osmanthus species
Pieris japonica
Pittosporum tobira
Prunus laurocerasus
Sarcococca ruscifolia
Skimmia species
Viburnum x burkwoodii
Viburnum odoratissimum
Viburnum suspensum

Deciduous Shrubs

Buddleia species
Calycanthus floridus

Chionanthus species
Clethra alnifolia
Daphne species
Elaeagnus species
Fothergilla species
Hamamelis species
Lonicera fragrantissima

Philadelphus species
Prunus x cistena
Rhododendron arborescens
Rhododendron x gandavensis
Rhododendron 'Knap Hill–Exbury Hybrids'
Rhododendron prinophyllum

Rhododendron viscosum
Rhododendron yedoense poukhanense
Rosa species
Syringa species
Viburnum x carlecephalum
Viburnum carlesii

Viburnum x juddii
Viburnum opulus

SHRUBS WITH ORNAMENTAL FRUITING

Needle Evergreens

Juniperus chinensis cv. 'Pfitzeriana'
Juniperus chinensis cv. 'Pfitzeriana Glauca'
Taxus species and cultivars (female plants only)

Broadleaf Evergreens

Berberis species and cultivars
Carissa grandiflora

Cotoneaster species and cultivars
Euonymus fortunei vegeta
Fatsia japonica and cultivars
Hypericum calycinum
Ilex species and cultivars (female plants only)
Ligustrum species and cultivars
Mahonia species and cultivars
Myrica species
Nandina domestica
Pyracantha species and cultivars
Skimmia species
Vaccinium vitis-idaea and varieties

Viburnum davidii
Viburnum rhytidophyllum

Deciduous Shrubs

Aralia species and cultivars
Aronia species
Berberis species and cultivars
Cornus mas and cultivars
Cotinus coggyria and cultivars (actually expanded flower parts)
Cotoneaster species and cultivars

Euonymus europaea and cultivars
Euonymus sachalinensis
Hippophae rhamnoides
Ilex species and cultivars (female plants only)
Ligustrum species and cultivars
Lonicera species and cultivars
Myrica pensylvanica
Punica granatum and cultivars
Rosa species and cultivars
Stewartia species
Symphoricarpos species and cultivars
Viburnum species and cultivars

SHRUBS WITH VARICOLORED FOLIAGE

Needle Evergreens

Abies concolor cultivars
Chamaecyparis pisifera cultivars
Juniperus chinensis cultivars
Juniperus communis cultivars
Juniperus conferta cultivars
Juniperus horizontalis cultivars
Juniperus sabina cultivars
Juniperus scopulorum cultivars
Juniperus squamata cultivars
Juniperus virginiana cultivars
Picea pungens cultivars
Pinus sylvestris cultivars
Platycladus orientalis cultivars
Taxus baccata cultivars
Thuja occidentalis cultivars
Tsuga canadensis cultivars

Broadleaf Evergreens

Aucuba japonica cultivars
Buddleia alternifolia cv. 'Argentea'
Buxus sempervirens cultivars
Calluna vulgaris cultivars
Codiaeum variegatum pictum cultivars
Daphne cneorum cultivars
Daphne odora cultivars
Elaeagnus pungens cultivars
Euonymus fortunei cultivars
Euonymus japonica cultivars
x Fatshedera lizei cv. 'Variegata'
Fatsia japonica cv. 'Variegata'
Leucothoe fontanesiana cultivars
Ligustrum japonicum cv. 'Variegatum'
Ligustrum lucidum cultivars

Mahonia aquifolium cultivars
Mahonia bealii
Mahonia lomariifolia
Mahonia repens
Myrtus communis cv. 'Variegata'
Osmanthus x fortunei cv. 'Aurea'
Osmanthus heterophyllus cultivars
Photinia species
Pieris japonica cultivars
Pittosporum crasifolium cv. 'Variegatum'
Pittosporum tobira cv. 'Variegata'
Viburnum tinus cv. 'Variegatum'

Deciduous Shrubs

Aralia elata cultivars
Berberis thunbergii cultivars
Calycanthus floridus cv. 'Purpureus'

Cornus alba cultivars
Cornus mas cultivars
Cotinus coggyria cultivars
Hippophae rhamnoides
Jasminum nudiflorum aureum
Kerria japonica cultivars
Ligustrum x ibolium cv. 'Variegated'
Ligustrum ovalifolium cultivars
Ligustrum x vicaryi
Ligustrum vulgare cultivars
Philadelphus coronarius cultivars
Potentilla selections
Prunus x cistena
Rosa rubrifolia
Spiraea x bumalda cultivars
Spiraea japonica cv. 'Atrosanguinea'
Vitex agnus-castus cv. 'Variegata'
Weigela florida cultivars

DECIDUOUS SHRUBS WITH AUTUMN FOLIAGE COLOR

Aesculus parviflora (yellow)
Aralia elata (red-orange)
Aralia spinosa (purple-red)
Aronia arbutifolia (red)
Aronia melanocarpa (purple-red)
Berberis koreana (orange-red)
Berberis thunbergii (scarlet)
Chionanthus species (yellow)
Clethra species (yellow)
Cornus alba (purple-red)
Cornus mas (reddish purple to bronze)
Cornus sericea (purplish red)
Cotinus species (yellow to orange-yellow)
Cotoneaster apiculatus (scarlet)
Cotoneaster dielsiana (orange-red)

Cotoneaster divaricatus (orange-red)
Cotoneaster horizontalis (crimson)
Cotoneaster lucidus (yellow and red)
Enkianthus species (red to yellow-red)
Euonymus alata (crimson)
Euonymus sachalinensis (yellow)
Forsythia species (bronze to purple)
Fothergilla species (yellow, orange, and red)
Hamamelis species (yellow and orange)
Hydrangea quercifolia (orange, purple, and bronze)

Kerria species (yellow)
Lagerstroemia species (yellow, orange, and red)
Ligustrum obtusifolium (russet)
Punica granatum (gold)
Rhamnus frangula (yellow)
Rhododendron arborescens (red)
Rhododendron calendulaceum (bronze)
Rhododendron x kosteranum (yellow)
Rhododendron mucronulatum (yellow to bronze-red)
Rhododendron prinophyllum (red)
Rhododendron schlippenbachi (yellow to orange)
Rhododendron vaseyi (red)

Rhododendron viscosum (orange to bronze-red)
Rhododendron yedoense (purple)
Rhododendron yedoense poukhanense (purple-crimson)
Rosa hugonis (red-orange)
Rosa nitida (crimson)
Rosa virginiana (purple, scarlet, and orange)
Spiraea x arguta (yellow and orange)
Spiraea cantoniensis (red-bronze)
Spiraea prunifolia (red, orange, and bronze)
Spiraea thunbergii (orange to yellow)
Stewartia ovata (orange to scarlet)

Stewartia pseudocamellia (purple)
Syringa meyeri (bronze)
Viburnum acerifolium (pink to magenta)
Viburnum x carlecephalum (red)

Viburnum carlesii (purple-red)
Viburnum dentatum (rust-red to yellow)
Viburnum dilatatum (russet)
Viburnum lentago (purple-red to orange)

Viburnum opulus (yellow-red to purple-red)
Viburnum plicatum (rust-red to purple-red)
Viburnum prunifolium (purple to red)

Viburnum setigerum (yellow-orange to red)
Viburnum sieboldii (bronze)
Viburnum wrightii (bronze)

SHRUBS WITH COLORFUL STEMS OR EXFOLIATING BARK

Needle Evergreens

(None included in this book)

Broadleaf Evergreens (effect obscured by the persistent leaves)

Cotoneaster lacteus
Elaeagnus pungens and cultivars

Photinia species and cultivars
Pyracantha koidzumii
Rhododendron griffithianum

Deciduous Shrubs

Cornus alba and cultivars
Cornus sericea and cultivars
Cytisus species and cultivars

Jasminum nudiflorum
Kerria japonica cv. 'Aureo-vittata'
Kolkwitzia amabilis and cultivars
Lagerstroemia indica and cultivars
Rosa virginiana
Stewartia species

SHRUBS TOLERANT TO OR PREFERRING SOME SHADE

Needle Evergreens

Abies concolor cultivars (semishade)
Abies koreana cultivars (semishade)
Cephalotaxus fortunei cultivars (semishade)
Cephalotaxus harringtonia cultivars (full)
Chamaecyparis obtusa cultivars (light)
Chamaecyparis pisifera cultivars (light)
Juniperus chinensis cultivars (light to semishade)
Juniperus horizontalis cultivars (light)
Juniperus squamata cultivars (light)
Juniperus virginiana cultivars (light)
Picea abies cultivars (light)
Pinus mugo cultivars (light)
Platycladus orientalis cultivars (light)
Taxus species and cultivars (light to semishade)
Thuja occidentalis cultivars (light)
Thuja plicata cultivars (semishade)
Tsuga canadensis cultivars (semishade)

Broadleaf Evergreens

Abelia x grandiflora and cultivars (light)
Aucuba japonica and cultivars (full)
Berberis candidula (light)
Berberis x chenaultii (light)
Berberis darwinii (semishade)
Berberis gagnepainii (light)
Berberis julianae (light)
Berberis verruculosa (light)
Buxus microphylla and cultivars (semishade)
Buxus sempervirens and cultivars (light)

Calliandra haematocephela (light)
Calliandra tweedii (light)
Camellia japonica cultivars (semishade)
Camellia reticulata cultivars (semishade)
Camellia sasanqua cultivars (light)
Carissa grandiflora cultivars (semishade)
Codiaeum variegatum pictum cultivars (semishade)
Daphne x hybrida (light)
Daphne odora cultivars (light)
Elaeagnus pungens cultivars (light)
Euonymus fortunei cultivars (semishade)
Euonymus japonica cultivars (full)
x Fatshedera lizei (semishade)
Fatsia japonica and cultivars (semishade)
Gardenia jasminoides and cultivars (light)
Hypericum calycinum (semishade)
Hypericum cv. 'Hidcote' (light)
Hypericum moseranum (light)
Ilex species and cultivars (light)
Kalmia latifolia and cultivars (light to semishade)
Leucothoe species and cultivars (light)
Ligustrum species and cultivars (light)
Mahonia species and cultivars (light to semishade)
Nandina domestica and cultivars (semishade)
Osmanthus species and cultivars (light)
Pieris species and cultivars (semishade)
Pittosporum species and cultivars (light to semishade)
Prunus laurocerasus and cultivars (semishade)
Rhododendron species and cultivars (light to semishade)

Sarcococca ruscifolia (semishade)
Skimmia species and cultivars (semishade)
Vaccinium ovata (light)
Vaccinium vitis-idaea and varieties (semishade)
Viburnum x burkwoodii (light)
Viburnum davidii (semishade)
Viburnum japonicum (semishade)
Viburnum odoratissimum (light)
Viburnum rhytidophyllum (light)
Viburnum suspensum (semishade)
Viburnum tinus and cultivars (full)

Deciduous Shrubs

Abeliophyllum distichum (light)
Acanthopanax sieboldianus (full)
Aesculus parviflora (semishade)
Aralia species and cultivars (light)
Aronia species, cultivars, and varieties (light)
Berberis species and cultivars (light)
Calycanthus floridus (light)
Chaenomeles species and cultivars (light)
Chionanthus species (light)
Clethra alnifolia and cultivars (semishade)
Cornus species and cultivars (light)
Cotoneaster species and cultivars (light)
Daphne species and cultivars (light)
Deutzia species and cultivars (light)
Enkianthus species (light)
Euonymus species and cultivars (light)
Forsythia species and cultivars (light)
Fothergilla species (light)
Hamamelis species and cultivars (light)
Hydrangea species and cultivars (light)
Hypericum species (light)

Ilex species and cultivars (light)
Jasminum nudiflorum (light)
Kerria japonica and cultivars (semishade to full)
Kolkwitzia amabilis (light)
Ligustrum species and cultivars (light to semishade)
Lonicera species and cultivars (light to semishade)
Paeonia suffruticosa and cultivars (light)
Philadelphus species and cultivars (light)
Potentilla parvifolia and cultivars (light)
Potentilla selections (light)
Rhamnus frangula cultivars (light)
Rhododendron species and cultivars (light to semishade)
Spiraea japonica and cultivars (semishade)
Stewartia species (light)
Symphoricarpos species and cultivars (light)
Syringa meyeri cv. 'Palibin' (light)
Viburnum acerifolium (full)
Viburnum carlesii (light)
Viburnum dentatum (semishade)
Viburnum dilatatum and cultivars (light)
Viburnum x juddii (light)
Viburnum lentago (light)
Viburnum macrocephalum (light)
Viburnum opulus and cultivars (semishade)
Viburnum plicatum and cultivars (light)
Viburnum prunifolium (semishade)
Viburnum setigerum and cultivars (light)
Viburnum sieboldii (light)
Viburnum trilobum (semishade)
Viburnum wrightii and cultivars (light)
Weigela species and cultivars (light)

SHRUBS FAVORING OR ADAPTABLE TO CONSISTENTLY MOIST OR WET SITES

Needle Evergreens

Chamaecyparis species and cultivars (moist)
Juniperus virginiana cultivars (moist to wet)
Picea abies cultivars (moist)
Thuja occidentalis cultivars (moist)
Tsuga canadensis cultivars (moist)

Broadleaf Evergreens

Daphne species and cultivars (moist)

Ilex glabra and cultivars (moist to wet)
Ixora coccinea and cultivars (moist)
Leucothoe species and cultivars (moist)
Mahonia lomariifolia (moist)
Myrica species (moist to wet)
Viburnum suspensum (moist)

Deciduous Shrubs

Aesculus parviflora (moist)
Aronia species and cultivars (moist)

Clethra alnifolia and cultivars (moist)
Cornus alba and cultivars (moist)
Cornus mas and cultivars (moist to wet)
Cornus sericea and cultivars (moist to wet)
Deutzia species and cultivars (moist)
Hamamelis vernalis (moist to wet)
Hibiscus syriacus cultivars (moist)
Hippophae rhamnoides (moist)
Ilex verticillata and cultivars (moist to wet)

Prunus glandulosa and cultivars (moist)
Rhododendron arborescens (moist)
Rhododendron vaseyi (moist)
Rhododendron viscosum (moist to wet)
Rosa blanda (moist)
Salix caprea (moist to wet)
Symphoricarpos orbiculatus (moist to wet)
Viburnum dentatum (moist)
Viburnum opulus and cultivars (moist to wet)
Viburnum trilobum (moist to wet)

SHRUBS WITH DROUGHT RESISTANCE

Needle Evergreens

Abies concolor cultivars
Juniper species and cultivars
Picea pungens cultivars
Platycladus orientalis cultivars

Broadleaf Evergreens

Abelia x grandiflora and cultivars
Aucuba japonica and cultivars
Berberis x mentorensis
Callistemon citrinus
Calluna vulgaris cultivars
Carissa grandiflora and cultivars
Cotoneaster species and cultivars

Erica species and cultivars
Euonymus japonica cultivars
Hypericum calycinum
Myrica species
Myrtus communis and cultivars
Nerium oleander cultivars
Pittosporum species and cultivars
Prunus ilicifolia

Deciduous Shrubs

Acanthopanax sieboldianus
Aronia melanocarpa and varieties
Berberis thunbergii and cultivars
Buddleia alternifolia

Caragana arborescens and cultivars
Chaenomeles species and cultivars
Cornus racemosa
Cotinus coggygria and cultivars
Cotoneaster species and cultivars
Cytisus species and cultivars
Elaeagnus species and varieties
Fothergilla major
Hippophae rhamnoides
Hypericum prolificum
Kolkwitzia amabilis and cultivars
Ligustrum species and cultivars
Lonicera maackii cultivars and varieties
Lonicera morrowii and cultivars

Myrica pensylvanica
Potentilla species and cultivars
Prunus maritima
Punica granatum and cultivars
Rhamnus frangula and cultivars
Rhododendron periclymenoides
Rosa carolina
Rosa rugosa and cultivars
Rosa spinosissima cultivars and varieties
Rosa virginiana
Rosa wichuriana
Symphoricarpos albus
Viburnum opulus and cultivars
Vitex agnus-castus and cultivars

SHRUBS WELL ADAPTED TO URBAN CONDITIONS

Needle Evergreens

Chamaecyparis pisifera cultivars
Juniperus chinensis cv. 'Pfitzeriana'
Juniperus chinensis cv. 'Pfitzeriana Glauca'
Picea pungens cultivars
Pinus sylvestris cultivars
Taxus cuspidata and cultivars

Broadleaf Evergreens

Aucuba japonica and cultivars
Euonymus fortunei cultivars
Euonymus japonica cultivars
Fatsia japonica and cultivars
Ilex crenata and cultivars
Ilex glabra and cultivars
Ligustrum species and cultivars

Mahonia aquifolium and cultivars
Myrica species
Nerium oleander cultivars
Pieris species and cultivars
Pittosporum tobira and cultivars
Pyracantha species and cultivars
Rhododendron carolinianum cv. 'PJM'
Rhododendron obtusum cultivars

Deciduous Shrubs

Acanthopanax sieboldianus
Aralia species and cultivars
Berberis thunbergii and cultivars
Caragana arborescens and cultivars
Chaenomeles species and cultivars
Chionanthus virginicus

Cornus alba and cultivars
Cornus mas and cultivars
Cornus sericea and cultivars
Deutzia scabra and cultivars
Elaeagnus species
Euonymus species and cultivars
Forsythia species and cultivars
Hamamelis species and cultivars
Hibiscus syriacus cultivars
Hydrangea species and cultivars
Kerria japonica and cultivars
Lagerstroemia indica and cultivars
Ligustrum species and cultivars
Lonicera species and cultivars
Philadelphus coronarius and cultivars
Potentilla species and cultivars
Rhamnus frangula and cultivars

Rhododendron periclymenoides
Rosa rugosa and cultivars
Rosa wichuriana
Spiraea bumalda and cultivars
Spiraea nipponica and cultivars
Spiraea x vanhouttei
Symphoricarpos species and cultivars
Syringa x prestoniae and cultivars
Syringa vulgaris and cultivars
Viburnum x carlecephalum
Viburnum dentatum
Viburnum x juddii
Viburnum lentago
Viburnum macrocephalum
Viburnum opulus and cultivars
Viburnum plicatum and cultivars

SHRUBS WITH RAPID GROWTH HABITS

Needle Evergreens

Cephalotaxus harringtonia
Juniperus chinensis cv. 'Hetzii'
Juniperus chinensis cv. 'Mint Julep'
Juniperus chinensis cv. 'Pfitzeriana'

Juniperus chinensis cv. 'Pfitzeriana Glauca'
Juniperus chinensis procumbens cv. 'Nana'
Juniperus communis cv. 'Repanda'
Juniperus communis depressa
Juniperus conferta

Juniperus conferta cv. 'Emerald Sea'
Juniperus horizontalis cv. 'Bar Harbor'
Juniperus horizontalis cv. 'Douglasii Morton Arboretum'
Juniperus horizontalis cv. 'Douglasii Wiltonii'

Juniperus horizontalis cv. 'Plumosa'
Juniperus sabina cv. 'Arcadia'
Juniperus sabina cv. 'Hicksii'
Juniperus sabina cv. 'Tamariscifolia'
Juniperus virginiana cv. 'Silver Spreader'

Picea abies cv. 'Procumbens'
Picea abies cv. 'Remontii'
Taxus baccata cv. 'Cheshuntensis'
Taxus baccata cv. 'Overeynderi'
Taxus baccata cv. 'Washingtonii'
Taxus cuspidata
Taxus cuspidata cv. 'Capitata'
Taxus x media cv. 'Brownii'
Taxus x media cv. 'Hatfieldii'
Taxus x media cv. 'Hicksii'

Broadleaf Evergreens

Berberis x chenaultii
Camellia reticulata cv. 'Buddha'
Camellia reticulata cv. 'Robert
 Fortune'
Camellia reticulata cv. 'Shot Silk'
Cotoneaster dammeri
Cotoneaster dammeri cv.
 'Skogholm'
Cotoneaster microphyllus
Cotoneaster salicifolius rugosus
Daphne x hybrida
Elaeagnus pungens
Fatsia japonica cv. 'Moseri'
Gardenia jasminoides cv.
 'Mystery'
Hypericum calycinum
Hypericum cv. 'Hidcote'

Ilex cornuta cv. 'Burfordii'
Ilex cornuta cv. 'Shangri-La'
Ilex crenata cv. 'Hetzii'
Ilex crenata cv. 'Latifolia'
Jasminum mesnyi
Ligustrum lucidum
Nerium oleander cultivars
Osmanthus x fortunei
Photinia x fraseri and cultivars
Prunus laurocerasus and cultivars
Pyracantha atalantiodes
Pyracantha fortuneana cv.
 'Graberi'
Pyracantha koidzumii cv. 'Victory'
Rhododendron catawbiense cv.
 'Catawbiense Album'
Rhododendron fortunei cultivars
Rhododendron maximum
Rhododendron minus
Viburnum x burkwoodii
Viburnum japonicum
Viburnum odoratissimum
Viburnum rhytidophyllum
Viburnum tinus

Deciduous Shrubs

Aralia species
Aronia melanocarpa
Buddleia davidii cultivars

Chaenomeles x superba cultivars
Chionanthus virginicus
Cornus species
Cotoneaster dielsiana
Cotoneaster divaricatus
Cotoneaster lucidus
Cytisus x praecox
Daphne x burkwoodi
Daphne mezereum and cultivars
Deutzia scabra cv. 'Mirabilis'
Elaeagnus multiflora
Elaeagnus umbellata
Euonymus alata
Euonymus europaea and cultivars
Forsythia species
Hamamelis species and cultivars
Hibiscus syriacus cultivars
Hydrangea paniculata cv.
 'Grandiflora'
Ilex verticillata cv. 'Polycarpa'
Jasminum nudiflorum
Kerria japonica and cultivars
Ligustrum species and cultivars
Lonicera species and cultivars
Philadelphus species and cultivars
Prunus x cistena
Rhamnus frangula and cultivars
Rosa californica
Rosa hugonis

Rosa rugosa and cultivars
Rosa spinosissima
Rosa spinosissima altaica
Rosa virginiana
Rosa wichuriana
Salix caprea
Spiraea x arguta
Spiraea x bumalda cv. 'Froebelii'
Spiraea nipponica and cultivars
Spiraea x vanhouttei
Symphoricarpos x chenaultii cv.
 'Hancock'
Symphoricarpos orbiculatus
Syringa x prestoniae and cultivars
Syringa vulgaris and cultivars
Viburnum acerifolium
Viburnum x carlecephalum
Viburnum dentatum
Viburnum lentago
Viburnum opulus and cultivars
Viburnum plicatum tomentosum
 cv. 'Lanarth'
Viburnum setigerum
Viburnum sieboldii
Viburnum trilobum
Vitex species and cultivars
Weigela species and cultivars

SHRUBS LOW, RAPID, AND DENSE FOR GROUNDCOVER USES

Needle Evergreens

Juniperus chinensis cv. 'Gold
 Coast'
Juniperus chinensis cv. 'Mint
 Julep'
Juniperus chinensis cv. 'San Jose'
Juniperus chinensis procumbens
 and cultivars
Juniperus chinensis sargentii
Juniperus chinensis sargentii cv.
 'Compacta'
Juniperus chinensis sargentii cv.
 'Viridis'
Juniperus communis and cultivars
Juniperus conferta and cultivars
Juniperus horizontalis and
 cultivars
Juniperus sabina and cultivars

Juniperus virginiana cv. 'Kosteri'
Pinus mugo pumilo

Broadleaf Evergreens

Abelia x grandiflora cv. 'Prostrata'
Calluna vulgaris and cultivars
Carissa grandiflora cv.
 'Horizontalis'
Carissa grandiflora cv. 'Prostrata'
Carissa grandiflora cv. 'Tuttlei'
Cotoneaster dammeri and
 cultivars
Cotoneaster microphyllus
Cotoneaster salicifolius repens
Erica carnea and cultivars
Erica vagrans
Euonymus fortunei cv. 'Emerald
 Gaiety'

Euonymus fortunei cv. 'Emerald
 'N Gold'
Gardenia jasminoides cv. 'Prostrata'
Hypericum calycinum
Hypericum moseranum
Mahonia repens
Prunus laurocerasus cv. 'Zabeliana'
Pyracantha koidzumii cv. 'Santa
 Cruz'
Vaccinium vitis-idaea
Viburnum davidii

Deciduous Shrubs

Aronia melanocarpa
Chaenomeles japonica and cultivars
Chaenomeles speciosa cv. 'Simonii'
Chaenomeles speciosa cv.
 'Umbilicata Nana'

Chaenomeles x superba cv.
 'Cameo'
Cotoneaster apiculatus
Cytisus albus
Cytisus x kewensis
Cytisus purpureus
Forsythia x intermedia cv. 'Arnold
 Dwarf'
Jasminum nudiflorum
Potentilla parvifolia cv. 'Pumila'
Potentilla selections cv. 'Longacre'
Rosa rugosa cv. 'Max Graf'
Rosa wichuriana
Spiraea japonica cv. 'Alpina'
Symphoricarpos x chenaultii
Symphoricarpos x chenaultii cv.
 'Hancock'

SHRUBS WITH COLUMNAR OR NARROWLY UPRIGHT HABITS

Needle Evergreens

Cephalotaxus harringtonia cv.
 'Fastigiata'
Platycladus orientalis cv.
 'Elegantissima'
Taxus baccata cv. 'Cheshuntensis'
Taxus baccata cv. 'Erecta'
Taxus baccata cv. 'Fastigiata'
Taxus baccata cv. 'Fastigiata
 Aurea'
Taxus baccata cv. 'Semperaurea'

Taxus baccata cv. 'Standishii'
Taxus x media cv. 'Viridis'

Broadleaf Evergreens

Buxus sempervirens cv.
 'Columnaris'
Buxus sempervirens cv. 'Fastigiata'
Euonymus japonica cv. 'Fastigiata'
Euonymus japonica cv.
 'Grandifolia'

Euonymus japonica cv.
 'Pyramidata'
Ilex crenata cv. 'Excelsa'
Ligustrum lucidum cv. 'Gracile'
Ligustrum lucidum cv. 'Nobile'
Ligustrum lucidum cv.
 'Pyramidale'
Osmanthus x fortunei cv. 'San
 Jose'
Photinia x fraseri
Viburnum tinus cv. 'Strictum'

Deciduous Shrubs

Berberis thunbergii cv. 'Erecta'
Ligustrum vulgare cv.
 'Pyramidale'
Rhamnus frangula cv. 'Tallhedge'
Syringa potaninii
Syringa vulgaris alba

SHRUBS DIFFICULT TO TRANSPLANT UNLESS YOUNG OR CONTAINERIZED

Needle Evergreens

Thuja occidentalis cv.
'Umbraculifera'

Broadleaf Evergreens

Berberis species, cultivars, or
varieties
Callistemon citrinus and cultivars

Calluna vulgaris cultivars
Daphne species and cultivars
Mahonia aquifolium and cultivars
Pyracantha species and cultivars

Deciduous Shrubs

Aralia species and cultivars
Berberis species and cultivars

Buddleia davidii and cultivars
Chaenomeles species, cultivars,
and varieties
Cotoneaster adpressus
Cytisus species, cultivars, and
varieties
Daphne species and cultivars
Hibiscus syriacus and cultivars
Hippophae rhamnoides

Paeonia suffruticosa cultivars
Vitex species, cultivars, and
varieties

Bloom, Adrian. *Conifers for Your Garden*. France: Sachets Floraiise. 1972.

Conner, E. Wesley. *The Back Pocket Guide to Ornamental Plants*. San Luis Obispo, Calif.: California Polytechnic State University Foundation. 1976.

Crockett, James Underwood. *Evergreens*. New York: Time-Life Books. 1971.

————. *Flowering Shrubs*. New York: Time-Life Books. 1972.

Courtwright, Gordon. *Trees and Shrubs for Western Gardens*. Forest Grove, Oregon: Timber Press. 1979.

Dengler, Harry William. *Handbook of Hollies*. Washington: American Horticultural Society. 1957, vol. 36.

den Ouden, P., and Boom, B. K. *Manual of Cultivated Evergreens*. The Hague: Martinus Nijhof. 1965.

Dirr, Michael A. *Photographic Manual of Woody Landscape Plants*. Champaign, Ill.: Stipes Publishing Company, 1978.

Everett, Thomas H. *The New York Botanic Garden Illustrated Encyclopedia of Horticulture*. New York: Garland Publishing, Inc. 1980.

Gault, S. Millar. *The Color Dictionary of Shrubs*. New York: Crown Publishers, Inc. 1976.

Grimm, William C. *Recognizing Native Shrubs*. Harrisburg, Pa.: The Stackpole Company. 1966.

Harrison, Charles R. *Ornamental Conifers*. New York: Hafner Press. 1975.

Hillier, H. C. *Hillier's Manual of Trees & Shrubs*. New York: A. S. Barnes and Company. 1973.

Hortorium, Liberty Hyde Bailey, Cornell University. *Hortus Third*. New York: The Macmillan Company. 1976.

McKelvey, Susan D. *The Lilac: A Monograph*. Baltimore: A. Hoen & Company. 1928.

Pizzetti, Ippolito, and Cocker, Henry. *Flowers: A Guide for Your Garden*. 2 volumes. New York: Harry N. Abrams, Inc. 1968.

Pokorny, Jaromin. *A Color Guide to Familiar Flowering Shrubs*. London: Octopus Books. 1975.

Rehder, Alfred. *Manual of Cultivated Trees and Shrubs*. New York: The Macmillan Company. 1940, rev. ed.

Sherk, Lawrence C., and Buckley, Arthur R. *Ornamental Shrubs for Canada*. Ottawa: Canada Department of Agriculture. 1968.

Southern Living Magazine Staff. *Trees & Shrubs, Ground Covers, Vines*. Birmingham, Ala.: Oxmoor House, Inc. 1980.

Taylor, Norman. *The Guide to Garden Shrubs and Trees*. Boston: Houghton Mifflin Company. 1965.

The Reader's Digest Association. *Reader's Digest Encyclopaedia of Garden Plants and Flowers*. London: The Reader's Digest Association, Ltd. 1973, rev. ed.

Viertel, Arthur T. *Trees, Shrubs and Vines*. Syracuse, N.Y.: Syracuse University Press. 1970.

Watkins, John V., and Sheehan, Thomas J. *Florida Landscape Plants*. Gainesville, Fla.: The University Presses of Florida. 1969.

Welch, Humphrey J. *Manual of Dwarf Conifers*. New York: Theophrastus Publishers and Garland STPM Press. 1979.

Wyman, Donald. *Shrubs & Vines for American Gardens*. New York: The Macmillan Company. 1969, rev. ed.

Appendix

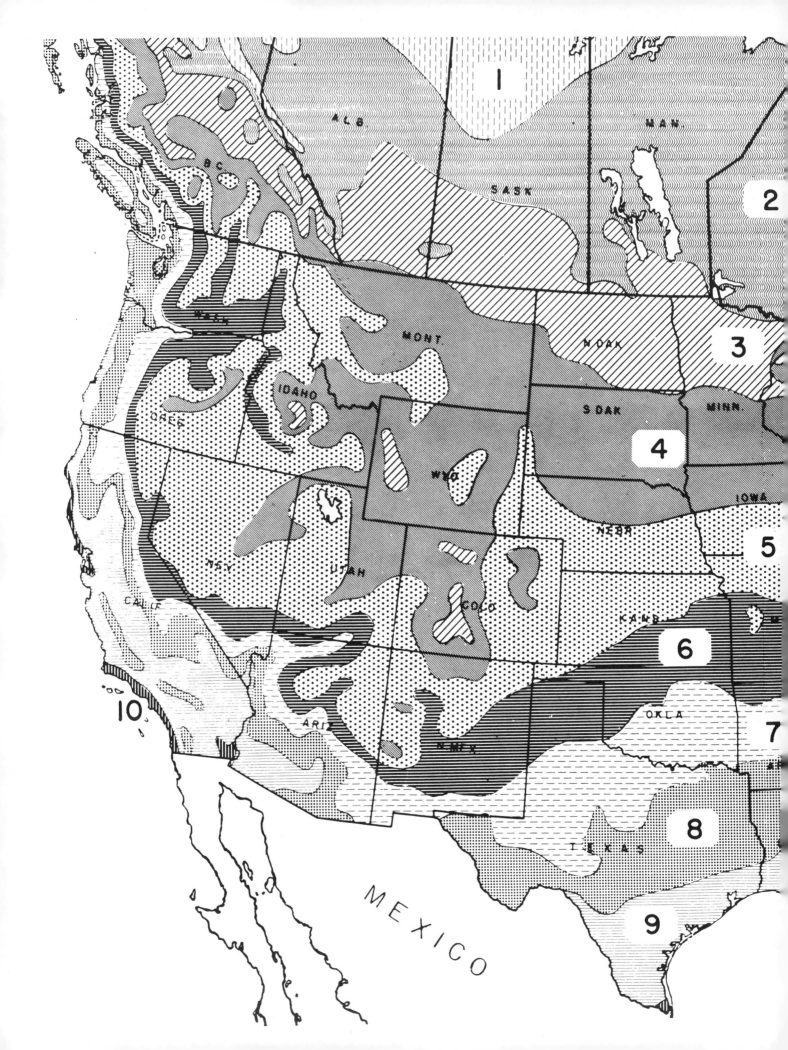

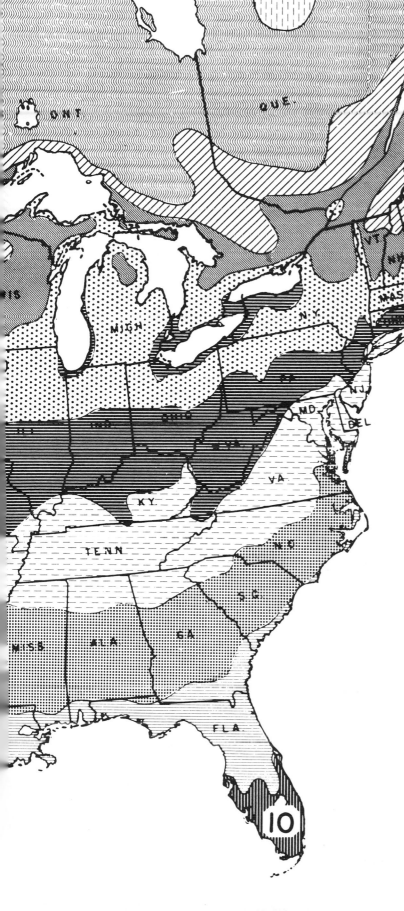

APPROXIMATE RANGE OF
AVERAGE ANNUAL MINIMUM
TEMPERATURES FOR EACH ZONE

ZONE 1   BELOW -50° F

ZONE 2   -50° TO -40°

ZONE 3   -40° TO -30°

ZONE 4   -30° TO -20°

ZONE 5   -20° TO -10°

ZONE 6   -10° TO   0°

ZONE 7   0° TO 10°

ZONE 8   10° TO 20°

ZONE 9   20° TO 30°

ZONE 10   30° TO 40°

Index

About the Author

Joseph Hudak is a nationally recognized landscape architect who was singled out in 1980 by *Town & Country* as one of this country's leading practitioners. His feature articles about landscape design and plant materials have appeared in publications such as *The New York Times, Horticulture, American Nurseryman, Flower & Garden,* and *House Beautiful.* His popular earlier book, TREES FOR EVERY PURPOSE (McGraw-Hill, 1980), was a selection of the American Home & Garden Book Club (Literary Guild).

Professor Hudak recently retired after a 20-year career teaching in the Department of Landscape Architecture at Harvard's Graduate School of Design. He was also affiliated for more than 25 years with the nation's oldest landscape firm, Olmsted Associates of Brookline, Massachusetts. Today, as a practicing landscape architect and public speaker, Professor Hudak is much in demand throughout the United States and abroad.